# Community Arts Education

# Artwork Scholarship: International Perspectives in Education

**Series editors: Anita Sinner and Rita L. Irwin**

The aim of the Artwork Scholarship series is to invite debate on, and provide an essential resource for, transnational scholars engaged in creative research involving visual, literary and performative arts. Approaches may include arts-based, practice-based, a/r/tography, artistic, research creation and more, and explore pedagogical and experimental perspectives, reflective and evaluative assessments, methodological deliberations, and ethical issues and concerns in relation to a host of topic areas in education.

Published previously:

*Provoking the Field: International Perspectives on Visual Arts PhDs in Education*, edited by Anita Sinner, Rita L. Irwin and Jeff Adams (2019)

*Living Histories: Global Perspectives in Art Education*, edited by Dustin Garnet and Anita Sinner (2022)

*A/r/tography: Essential Readings and Conversations*, edited by Rita L. Irwin and Anita Sinner (2024)

# Community Arts Education

## Transversal Global Perspectives

Edited by

*Ching-Chiu Lin, Anita Sinner
and Rita L. Irwin*

Bristol, UK / Chicago, USA

First published in the UK in 2023 by
Intellect, The Mill, Parnall Road, Fishponds, Bristol, BS16 3JG, UK

First published in the USA in 2023 by
Intellect, The University of Chicago Press, 1427 E. 60th Street,
Chicago, IL 60637, USA

Copyright © 2023 Intellect Ltd
All rights reserved. No part of this publication may be reproduced, stored in a retrieval system, or transmitted, in any form or by any means, electronic, mechanical, photocopying, recording, or otherwise, without written permission.

A catalogue record for this book is available from the British Library.

Copy editor: MPS Limited
Cover designer: Liu Hsun
Cover image: Liu Hsun
Production manager: Debora Nicosia
Typesetter: MPS Limited

Hardback ISBN: 978-1-78938-734-6
Paperback 978-1-78938-746-9
ePDF ISBN 978-1-78938-735-3
ePUB ISBN 978-1-78938-736-0

Printed and bound by CMP

To find out about all our publications, please visit our website. There you can subscribe to our e-newsletter, browse or download our current catalogue and buy any titles that are in print.

www.intellectbooks.com

This is a peer-reviewed publication.

# Contents

| | |
|---|---|
| List of Figures | ix |
| Acknowledgements | xiii |
| Introduction: Community Arts Education: Transversal Global Perspectives<br>  *Ching-Chiu Lin* | 1 |

## PART 1: TRANSVERSAL CONNECTIONS     15

1. Twenty-First Century Winter Journey: Exploring Comics, Adaptation and Community Art Education   17
   *Julian Lawrence*
2. The University as an Institute of Permanent Creation: Developing "a gift for living" in Neoliberal Times   39
   *Raphael Vella*
3. Seeing What Unfolds: New Ways of Exploring Community Art Education in Formal Learning Spaces   49
   *Kathryn Coleman and Marnee Watkins*
4. "Making University": The Role of Corporeality, Matter and Physical Spaces to Create a Sense of Community   61
   *Sara Carrasco Segovia*
5. I Wish You a Good Life: Embedding Intergenerational Learning Into Pre-Service Education Through Art, Community and Environment   72
   *Geraldine Burke*
6. Community-Based Art Education: Promoting Revitalization and Eco-Cultural Resilience for Cultural Sustainability   86
   *Timo Jokela and Mirja Hiltunen*

## PART 2: TRANSVERSAL PRACTICES — 99

7. Making Meaning, Creating (in) Community: An International Dialogue on Community Art Education Within Early Childhood Contexts — 101
   *Geralyn (Gigi) Yu, Alex Halligey and Judith Browne*

8. Identifying Images as a Strategy for Emotional Interaction With the Environment: Neighbourhoods as Engraving Support — 112
   *Jessica Castillo Inostroza*

9. We Are Small, but We Have Loud Voices: Children Leading the Way to Support Community Connections Through Art — 118
   *Sue Girak*

10. Infernal Learning: Becoming Members of Academic Communities — 128
    *Anniina Suominen, Tiina Pusa, Minna Suoniemi, Eljas Suvanto and Elina Julin*

11. Seeds in the Wind! A/r/tography School and Teacher Formation — 139
    *Leísa Sasso and Mirian Celeste Martins*

12. Transversalities Through Transdisciplinary Pedagogies: A South African Perspective on Community-Engaged Art Education — 148
    *Merna Meyer*

13. Building Bridges in the Community Through Opening Minds Through Art: An Intergenerational Abstract Art Programme for People Living With Dementia — 159
    *Stephanie H. Danker, Elizabeth Lokon and Casey Pax*

## PART 3: TRANSVERSAL SPACES — 171

14. International Art Symposia as a Space of Knowledge Creation and Creative Engagement — 173
    *Maria Huhmarniemi and Katja Juhola*

15. Collaborative Thinking, Creating and Learning on a Remote Greek Island: Towards Community Art Education for Sustainability — 185
    *Sophia Chaita and Georgia Liarakou*

16. Finding Possibility in the Liminality of Socially Engaged Arts: Fostering Learning and Wellbeing With Refugee Youth ... 198
    *Kate Collins*
17. Conversations With Gardens: Artful Spaces in Community Art Education ... 210
    *Trish Osler*
18. Community Dance as an Approach to Reimagine Place in Aotearoa/New Zealand ... 221
    *Pauline Hiroti and Rose Martin*
19. Pedagogical Implications in *La Austral, S. A. de C. V.*: Collective Storytelling Performances by Pablo Helguera and DREAMers ... 231
    *Eunji J. Lee*
20. Community Arts Education: Experiencing and Creating Our World ... 242
    *Shelley Hannigan and Merinda Kelly*

## PART 4: TRANSVERSAL RELATIONS ... 253

21. Colors of Connection: Public Art Making as an Activating Force for Community Art Education ... 255
    *Lynn Sanders-Bustle, Christina Mallie and Laurie Reyman*
22. Residing in Pedagogical Spaces Through Community Cultural Production ... 266
    *Jing Li*
23. Intercultural Eye for Art: Becoming a Member of a Global Community Through Arts-Based Exchange ... 275
    *Kazuyo Nakamura, Hye-Seung (Theresa) Kang, Wataru Inoue, Leah H. Morgan, Hisae Aoyama, Hannah Shuler, Atsuo Nakashima, Cheryl J. Maxwell, Takunori Okamoto and Mari Sankyo*
24. The Creation of a Community Teaching Artist Certificate Programme: Professionalization in the Gig Economy ... 287
    *Dustin Garnet*

25. Creative for Life: Planning and Delivering Intergenerational Art — 298
   Programmes
   *Jodie Davidson and Miles Openshaw*
26. Croatian Naïve Art as an Incentive for Multimodal Research — 308
   With Children
   *Helena Burić and Nikolina Fišer Sedinić*
27. Visual Ecologies: Artistic Research Transversing Stable, Dynamic — 318
   and Interstitial Relations in an Australian Settler Colonial Context
   *Kim Snepvangers*

Notes on Contributors — 331

# Figures

| | | |
|---|---|---|
| 4.1 | Appropriation of physical spaces through murals. Assembly of images: elementary education building, wall of the soccer field, entrance hut, hall of the Fine Arts Department. Photo by Sara Carrasco (2017). | 66 |
| 4.2 | Appropriation of physical spaces through protests. Assembly of images: on-campus protests with hooded university students. Photo by Sara Carrasco (2017). | 68 |
| 5.1 | Exploring our domestic waste and how waste travels to local beaches. Photos by Geraldine Burke (2019). | 73 |
| 5.2 | Exploring upcycling possibilities with waste and throw-away materials. Photos by Melanie Attard (2019). | 76 |
| 5.3 | Participants' templates and amulets inspired by local waste/wildlife intersections. Photos by Melanie Attard (2019). | 82 |
| 6.1 | Long-term inter- and multidisciplinary ABAR collaboration in Utsjoki. Pupils playing with the Mythical Boat in the schoolyard. Photo by Mirja Hiltunen (2006). | 90 |
| 6.2 | Place-based community art with traditional crafting material and techniques. Photos by Timo Jokela (2008, 2009). | 91 |
| 6.3 | Winter art ABAR development project in multi-ethnic villages. Photos by Timo Jokela (2014, 2018). | 92 |
| 7.1 | Open Streets Auckland Park, 7 April 2019. Photo by Sims Phakisi (2019). | 105 |
| 7.2 | CEI studio experience. Photo by Gigi Yu (2019). | 108 |
| 8.1 | My silhouette stamped in the environment II. Photos by Jessica Castillo Inostroza (2020). | 113 |

| | | |
|---|---|---|
| 8.2 | Creative process in the classroom II. Photos by Jessica Castillo Inostroza (2020). | 114 |
| 8.3 | Stamping the matrices in the neighbourhood. Photos by Jessica Castillo Inostroza (2020). | 115 |
| 8.4 | Stamping the matrices in the neighbourhood II. Photos by Jessica Castillo Inostroza (2020). | 115 |
| 8.5 | The identity of the class scattered in the environment. Final results. Photos by Jessica Castillo Inostroza (2020). | 116 |
| 9.1 | *Global Meltdown*. With an environmental message about global warming, the ice-cream sculpture was displayed at CBPS's 2019 Open Night exhibition. Photo by Sue Girak (2019). | 125 |
| 11.1 | Girls' bathroom of São José's School. Photo by Leísa Sasso (2019). | 144 |
| 11.2 | Cover of the book *Telling and Singing Stories*, GDF (2019). Photo by Leísa Sasso (2019). | 145 |
| 12.1 | The (P)ART framework. Design by Merna Meyer (2020). | 156 |
| 13.1a | (left to right) Miami student Jennie Kleinknecht and OMA founder Elizabeth Lokon welcome Gerry Thacker to the OMA program. Photo by Scott Kissell (2019). | 166 |
| 13.1b | (left to right) Amy Lewin supports Bonnie Moore with monotype printmaking. Photo by Buffy Hanna (2010). | 166 |
| 14.1 | Maria Huhmarniemi, The *Huff, Puff and Blow* (2017) environmental art in Äkäslompolo. Photo series by Heli Vepsäläinen (2017). | 177 |
| 14.2 | Art education practices in a dairy farm and a meadow. Photo series by Fabio Cito (2019). | 178 |
| 14.3 | Circular Economy team, members of the Martha society and kindergarten children playing together and creating a network installation. Photo series by Fabio Cito (2019). | 179 |
| 15.1 | Three-level analysis of the CA combined with Liepins' (2017) community elements. | 190 |
| 15.2 | Sample of first-level analysis. Photo by Sophia Chaita (2021). | 191 |

# FIGURES

| | | |
|---|---|---|
| 15.3 | A photo of second-level analysis of *Remember. Live. Dream.* Photo by Sophia Chaita (2020). | 192 |
| 16.1 | Graduate and high-school students play Augusto Boal's theatre game, Columbian Hypnosis, in an early one-on-one partnering activity. Photo by Michael Bussell (2018). | 204 |
| 17.1 | Veil Garden, *Jardins de Métis*/Reford Gardens. Courtesy of *Les Amis des Jardins de Métis* Collection (2019). | 215 |
| 17.2 | *Jardins de Métis*/Reford Gardens. Photo credit: Louise Tanguay. Courtesy of *Les Amis des Jardins de Métis* Collection (2019). | 218 |
| 20.1 | Shelley Hannigan. Jane, copper thread and wire. Photo by Shelley Hannigan (2019). | 248 |
| 20.2 | Shelley Hannigan. Embodied interconnections, wool felt, knitted and stitched threads. Photo by Shelley Hannigan (2019). | 249 |
| 21.1 | Participants creating the mural, *The Female Artist*, in the commercial district of Mapendo in Colors of Connection's Tunaweza Portraits Project, Goma, DRC 2019. Photo by Bernadette Vivuya. | 255 |
| 23.1 | A photo of Meina Okubo's Hometown Landscape. Photo by Atsuo Nakashima (2020). Copyright © 2020 Meina Okubo. | 279 |
| 23.2 | Photo of Madison Porter's Painting. Photo by Cheryl J. Maxwell. Copyright © 2020 Madison Porter. | 281 |
| 23.3 | Photo of Maycee Taylor and Takuto Hatano's Collaborative Work. Photo by Hisae Aoyama. Copyright © 2021 Maycee Taylor, Copyright © 2021 Takuto Hatano. | 282 |
| 23.4 | Ratio of six viewpoints of children's awareness at each grade level. | 284 |
| 25.1 | Intergenerational visual storytelling during a creative session. Photo by Jodie Davidson (2019). | 303 |
| 26.1 | Children's art inspired by folk motifs. Photos by Nikolina Fišer Sedinić (2019). | 310 |
| 26.2 | Ivan Lacković Croata, Late Autumn, 1964. © HMNU/CMNA (left). Late Autumn/aesthetic transfer, combined technique (felt-tip pen, graph paper, watercolours). Lota, R., 5, 10 years (right). Photos by Nikolina Fišer Sedinić (2020). | 310 |

| 27.1 | Kim Snepvangers (2018). "A rather novel marriage" in *Stories of Belonging*. Brisbane Anywhere Festival performance. Lightboxes, digital print on coloured film. Photo by Kim Snepvangers (2018). | 323 |
| 27.2 | Kim Snepvangers (2018). "Welcome to Our Home" – A4 Ilford Gallery Print using Ultra Chrome Ink (21.0 × 29.7 cm). Photo by Kim Snepvangers (2018). | 324 |

# Acknowledgements

This anthology was a vast undertaking, one that would have been impossible without the scholarship, expertise and dedication of the 55 contributors around the world. We would like to thank all contributors for embarking on this long journey with us in the midst of the global pandemic. We also acknowledge the reviewers for offering their insights, thoughts and suggestions throughout the rigorous review process, which has significantly enhanced the quality of this collection.

Additionally, we want to thank our publisher, Intellect, for their support, as well as Jelena Stanovnik, Project Development Manager and Debora Nicosia, Production Editor, for nurturing this book through to publication. Our heartfelt thanks also go to Amanda Goldrick-Jones, PhD, who took on the critical role of editing and preparing the manuscript for submission with rich knowledge, endless patience and an eagle eye.

Last but not least, we gratefully acknowledge the financial support for this book project from Simon Fraser University and the Social Science and Humanities Research Council (SSHRC) of Canada.

# Introduction:
# Community Arts Education:
# Transversal Global Perspectives

*Ching-Chiu Lin*

### *Situating Community Arts Education*

*Community Arts Education: Transversal Global Perspectives* is an international collaboration among 55 community professionals, scholars, artists, educators and activists from sixteen countries, including but not limited to Australia, Canada, Croatia, Finland, Greece, Japan, South Africa, Spain, the United Kingdom and the United States. This collective endeavour is situated in a very particular timeframe that spans the pre-pandemic and the pandemic and continues today. Many authors and potential contributors of this book address how they navigate their lives while trying to make sense of how the pandemic may have changed community arts education. In this collection, we consider "transversality" as "an aspect inherent to the nature of learning itself" (Ryder, 2018, p. vi). Specifically, transversality signifies both the overarching theoretical framework and the methodological structure for reimaging the complexity of community arts education, enabling "a dimension of pragmatic action which develops reciprocally and diagonally between entities instead of reverting to relationships of similarity, analogy or sameness" (Beighton, 2018, p. 49). As well, to move this collective scholarship forward, we make a distinction in philosophy and practice when defining the term "community arts education." We purposely favour the term *community arts education* over community-based arts education while acknowledging that the contributors to this book define the term within their unique contexts. Community arts education implies the necessary equality of education (e.g. pedagogical implementations) and a variety of practices (e.g. programming, organizational strategies and instruments) in regard to advancing and solidifying relationships between education and community through access to the artistic fields (Sinner & Conrad, 2015; Vaughan et al., 2017). With "field" defined as "a network, or a configuration, or objective relations between positions" (Bourdieu & Wacquant,

1992, p. 97), we see community as not just a place to enact curriculum; it is the curriculum itself – a practice in which community life, learning and learning activities and educational aims intersect (Bruce, 2018; Lin & Bruce, 2013). Thus, according to Cohen (1985), community is also best understood as a community of meaning.

From this perspective, community plays a crucial symbolic role in our sense of belonging as "people construct community symbolically, making it a resource and repository of meaning, and a referent of their identity" (Cohen, 1985, p. 118). Community is more than just a space or place of learning. Instead, community acts as a public sphere, adapted from Hannah Arendt's (1958) notion of a specific site of public engagement, social change and scholarly production that situates communal thinking and action as inseparable from the entanglement of individuals and community. Many authors in this collection have taken up this view to broaden their thinking of community and ground their community inquiry through intergenerational, cross-cultural and international collaboration.

Therefore, knowledge produced through creative research, artistic experience and artful interventions in communities is not merely a static entity but as Sutherland and Acord (2007) describe, "an interactive, in situ encounter" (p. 126) in which a person's actions participate in the production of community. In illustrating links among knowledge, space and community arts education, this collection shifts our point of view towards the co-constitutive nature of space and knowledge and allows us to understand knowledge as not prescribed or passive, but as an active and arising component of social life. We can thus conceptualize community art education as *embracing* community – "an emergent form of collectivity that is always in the making" (Rousell & Hickey-Moody, 2020, p. 82) – rather than *based on* community. In other words, we consider community arts education as a distinctive practice emerging from the complex relationships that form community through artful engagement, collaboration, experimentation and conversation. Several studies and practical cases throughout the book demonstrate these complex interrelationships from varied geographical locations.

## *Challenges Ahead*

Mainstream advocacy arguments for the arts in education often portray the arts with a transformative power to influence individuals and communities (e.g. Romanski, 2019). The arts have been seen as a catalyst for urban renewal (e.g. Illeris, 2017; Sacco, 2019) and cultural sustainability (e.g. Härkönen et al., 2018), a means for service learning (e.g. Alexander & Murphy, 2020; Alexander, 2015) and a therapeutic medium for health improvement (e.g. Baumann et al., 2021; Biro-Hannah, 2021), just to name a few. While this advocacy agenda – art to promote social cohesion or stimulate economic growth – emerges from a perceived need to reassert art's value in society, this characterization of the impact of the arts may impair our ability to explore and mobilize alternative ways of understanding the complex ways in which artistic practices are situated in community settings.

Scholarship in this area (Belfiore, 2011; Biesta, 2019; Gallagher & Neelands, 2011; Merli, 2002) warns that an inability to move beyond this *art-is-good-for-you* rhetoric may result in two consequences. First, the scholarly advancement of community arts education is trapped by the constant demand to "justify its usefulness in relation to governmental priorities" (Belfiore & Bennett, 2010, p. 7). Second, the premise that the arts presumably have the power to bring in social change may be an empty promise if conventional views of learning through the arts are reinforced with a veneer of innovation (Carpenter & Tavin, 2010; Gaztambide-Fernandez, 2008). Scholars have criticized such problematic discourse about the impact of the arts from the standpoints of culture policy analysis (Belfiore, 2002; Belfiore & Bennett, 2010), philosophical inquiry (Gaztambide-Fernandez, 2013; Tusa, 2007) and intellectual history (Belfiore & Bennett, 2008). Several authors in this book evoke the need for complexity in community practice to ponder and challenge how we imagine the role of the arts. This active discussion suggests a need to rethink a critical framework for understanding community arts education that challenges traditional assumptions about the arts.

Furthermore, to move the arts-impact debate ahead, scholars and practitioners argue that community arts education has evolved from an object-making orientation to emergent forms of collective, participatory, experiential, material and/or relational practice (Carpenter, 2019; Finkelpearl, 2013; Harvey & Cooke, 2021; Lawton, 2019; Lin, 2021). This evolution calls for new thinking about community arts education that foregrounds the potential for networked institutional enactment and collective relationships, rather than predictable outcomes or predetermined roles of individuals. This new thinking, as demonstrated in several chapters here, urges us to re-envision community arts education even as it is challenged by globalizing phenomena such as the COVID-19 pandemic; ongoing efforts to achieve justice for Indigenous peoples; continuing movement of immigrants and refugees; growing recognition of issues related to equity, diversity and inclusion in the workplace; and the increasing impact of grass-root movements and organizations. Addressing such realities through community arts education research, pedagogy and practice is crucial at this historical intersection of complex and ever-changing local and global dynamics that are restructuring silos of education and community. This edited volume responds to a compelling need for reimaging the role of the arts in community inquiry – a role that is responsive to the vexed relations among individuals, communities and the arts – to cultivate more sophisticated understandings of future pathways for community arts education.

## *Thinking Transversally*

We turn to the concept of transversality put forward by Guattari to explore new approaches to understanding community arts education. Guattari (2015) writes that "[t]ransversality is a dimension that tries to overcome both the impasse of pure verticality and that of mere horizontality" (p. 113). Initially, Guattari's theocratization of transversality served as a tool for reconfiguring power relations between therapists and patients at the La Borde psychiatric clinic in France where Guattari worked. Over time the notion has shifted, taking on broader philosophical implications for de-territorializing power, hierarchy, barriers and boundaries within institutions (Genosko, 2002). Growing recognition of transversality's potential is considered part of the theoretical architecture of globalization studies in education (Cole & Bradley, 2018). Transversality is imbricated in cartographies of the new materialism discourse (Dolphijn & van der Tuin, 2012), forms a dimension of the holistic learning process in teacher education (Sauvé, 2020) and serves as an approach to reconceptualizing technology-enhanced learning in higher education (Carmichael & Litherland, 2012). Following this thread, we "think transversally" to seek an ecological, cartographical understanding of the entangled relations embedded in community arts education practice: relations and practices intertwined with global/local multi-faceted phenomena and increasingly characterized by diverse populations. Such thinking allows us to reimagine the purpose and practice of community arts education as well as to map the in-between spaces (Deleuze & Guattari, 1988) in our encounters with past and present economic, political, educational and socio-cultural circumstances.

To think transversally, we draw upon Pinar's theorization of intellectual advancement through disciplinarity, which he termed *verticality* and *horizontality* (Pinar, 2007). Visually speaking, transversality relates to dimensions of intersection: that is, horizontal flows of synergistic dialogue and collective action between local needs and global influences, and vertical modes of boundary crossings and discursive disruptions within cultural institutions. Thinking transversally has become critical in a time where the intersections of global impact and local contexts have significantly affected how we envision the future of community arts education. The contributors to this book envision examples of community arts education research, pedagogy and practice as distinctive hubs of localized convergence for forming transverse linkages. Such linkages create nodes of entanglement: bringing resources, innovative responses and renewal to educational spaces.

We intend for this book to traverse nodes of entanglement and be situated as a nexus of interrelatedness that brings strategic and innovative recommendations to the field of community arts education. The varied contemporary understandings of community arts education explored in these chapters speak to a transversal intersection of the complex dynamics of individual and community needs in a pluralistic democracy. In this collection, the notion of transversality also suggests a pedagogic enactment that attends to artful learning through collective action within the relational context of everyday lived experience, aligning with Paulo Freire's reflexive form of education: envisioning social space as educational (Freire, 1993). Along this line of thinking, we consider community arts education as "transversal sites of becoming" (Thompson, 2015, p. 139), enabling us to envision knowledge as not given, but as experienced and re-experienced through a process of becoming (Irwin, 2013; LeBlanc et al., 2015; Massey, 1999).

## Overview of the Book

*Community Arts Education: Transversal Global Perspectives* is mapped into four parts as thematic clusters. As we review the varied contributions to this collection, we conceptually determined four clusters – connections, practices, spaces and relations – across chapters to map the intersecting assemblages of transversality. They offer departure points to understanding the active discourse around forms, values and processes of international perspectives on community arts education. Although each part has a focus, by its nature such a large collection is interwoven with a variety of themes recurring throughout the book.

**Part 1: Transversal Connections** offers insights into the possibilities of community art education programmes and partnerships involving post-secondary institutions. Chapters in this section traverse established boundaries to unveil the multiplicities of community arts education in unique contexts. In the opening chapter, **Lawrence**'s compelling and sophisticated graphic novel takes us on a professional journey to complete a comic-based research project in the United Kingdom. This collaboration between a university cohort and a charity for homeless people advocates for comics as a form of knowledge production, a means of making connections in the community and beyond and a critical method for revisioning community arts education through arts-based research methods. Responding to the impact of neoliberalism on higher education, **Vella** presents a new, interdisciplinary graduate programme in Social Practice Arts and Critical Education on the Mediterranean Island of Malta. This unique programme recognizes and incorporates ways in which art practice, theatre, community engagement and adult education intersect with and enhance the educational setting. During an artful education exchange between a university and several Australian primary schools, **Coleman** and **Watkins** showcase creative pandemic-informed pedagogies that provoke new understandings of community arts education through a/r/tography as practice-pedagogical-research. In a study involving pre-service art teachers in Chile, **Segovia** shares insights into how human and non-human connections help create a sense of community through intra-actions of matter, and how community arts practice creates and reinforces social dynamics: facilitating new ways of thinking and doing through community relations.

In Australia, **Burke**'s community art project provides a new materialist lens for examining community knowledge evoked through diverse community members' artful participation and ecological wisdom. **Jokela** and **Hiltunen** conclude Part 1 with a critical overview of current trends in Arctic community-based art education practice (ACAE) at the University of Lapland, Finland. By articulating how ACAE preserves and revitalizes Indigenous, local and situated Northern knowledge and fosters eco-cultural resilience in the rapidly changing North and the Arctic, Jokela and Hiltunen invite us to ponder how community arts education can help us envision an equality of nature and humans sought by global post-humanistic sustainability discourse.

**Part 2: Transversal Practices** showcases artistic and pedagogic practices (including hybrid models) associated with community arts education. These chapters prompt us to acknowledge the multiplicity of being when working with and for the community, as well as to appreciate the experiential, vulnerable and embodied knowledge created through the transversal nature of educational and artistic praxis. **Yu**, **Halligey** and **Browne**'s chapter takes the form of an international dialogue among community artist-educators in the southwest United States; Johannesburg, South Africa; and Ontario, Canada. Situating themselves within the intersecting yet disparate disciplines of early childhood education and community arts education, the authors create pathways, pedagogical approaches and new ways of perceiving how young children, families, teachers and their communities have the right to imagine. From Spain, **Inostroza** describes the artful learning relationship between affect and the neighbourhood in which one lives. Through text and images, she reflects on emergent and relational spaces that allowed for unexpected collaborations during the pandemic.

As a primary teacher in Australia, **Girak** shares her practice of disrupting the clear divides between school and community art programmes through partnerships with families and community groups to achieve a mutual goal of community cohesion. Cohesion, however, may not be the sole outcome. On that note, **Suominen**,

# INTRODUCTION

**Pusa, Suoniemi, Suvanto** and **Julin** offer a frank reflection on their roles as artists, educators and researchers in academic communities in Finland. Creative tensions are apparent in the case of Brazilian scholars **Sasso** and **Martins** who, inspired by the a/r/tographical methodological approach, share their process of shaping their poetical, pedagogical vision of an a/r/tographic school that embraces a hybridism of social performance with various community members. From a South African context, **Meyer** reflects on her professional journey of creating educative spaces for transversal understanding between university and community. And in the United States, **Danker, Lokon** and **Pax**'s intergenerational project reveals the potential of art for elders living with dementia, bringing together families, artists, healthcare professionals and university students to show how art builds bridges that enable cross-cultural and cross-disciplinary exchanges.

**Part 3: Transversal Spaces** attends to creating and reflecting on educative and artful spaces that allow relations and engagements to take place, illuminating the role of the arts in making pragmatic action more reciprocal, conditional and responsive. These chapters allow us to see community as an emergent and relational space for new ways of being, thinking and acting. Using the art-based action research method, **Huhmarniemi** and **Juhola** present three Finnish case studies that situate socially engaged art symposia as spaces of knowledge creation and creative engagement for addressing environmental crises across the globe. Also offering ways of rethinking community arts education as education towards sustainability, **Chaitas** and **Liarakou** describe an intergenerational collaboration between school children and islanders on the remote Greek island of Lipsi. On a related theme of intergenerational dialogues as socially engaged art practice, **Collins**' chapter demonstrates how attending to the liminal space where refugee youth search for their sense of belonging offers insights on ways of creating multi-layered intellectual exchanges in Baltimore, Maryland in the United States.

Multiple layering can also be viewed as a transversal shift in the ways art education engages community space. Focusing on *Les Jardins de Métis*/Reford Gardens in Quebec, Canada, **Osler** discusses space-time-mattering: a form of intra-active entanglement that shifts visitors' experience through a multi-sensory digital intervention. Through a community dance project in Aotearoa/New Zealand, **Hiroti** and **Martin** interweave themes of arts education, place-based pedagogy and Indigenous Māori philosophies to explore how bodily encounters and experiences can help young people question colonization, marginalization, belonging, place and identity. Also highlighting how participatory modes of art making can enable community as a space of knowledge creation and identity development, **Lee** shares her study on *La Austral, S.A. de C.V.*: a performative storytelling project by American artist Pablo Helguera and a group of young people impacted by Deferred

Action on Childhood Arrivals (DACA) and Development, Relief and Education for Alien Minors (DREAM). From Australia, **Hannigan** and **Kelly** share how their community art practice asserts the values of artistic co-creation, knowledge exchange and collaboration as legitimate ways of engaging authentically, critically and creatively with the community.

**Part 4: Transversal Relations** explores community arts education in terms of relations – and their entanglements – among peoples, places and disciplines. Describing networks of transversal relations, these chapters show that action and change in communities transpire when capacities merge, trust develops, social hierarchy is disrupted and connections form. **Sanders-Bustle, Mallie** and **Reyman** open this section with an overview of the 2019 Tunaweza Portraits Project's pedagogical strategies and programme in the Democratic Republic of Congo (DRC): a project highlighting the intertwining of relationships and social practice in response to community needs. Drawing on the notion of cultural production as political participation and civic engagement, **Li** provides a glimpse into a four-year ethnographic study of a community festival in the Downtown Eastside (DTES) neighbourhood in Vancouver, Canada. The participation of residents and artists shows the potential to stimulate intercultural exchange, intergenerational collaboration and community building. How relationships are forged through an international cultural exchange is the emphasis of **Nakamura, Kang, Inoue, Morgan, Aoyama, Shuler, Nakashima, Maxwell, Okamoto** and **Sankyo**'s chapter on the Indiana-Hiroshima Intercultural Eye for Art Project. Involving children in sixteen American and Japanese schools, this collaboration portrays the transversal intersections of global/local community engagement for cultivating children's intercultural sensitivity and friendships.

An ongoing teaching-artist professional development programme at California State University in Los Angeles (CSULA) focuses **Garnet**'s discussion on the professionalization of teaching artists from historical, political and philosophical perspectives. **Davidson** and **Openshaw** discuss how relationships traverse generations during an intergenerational art project in a residential care home setting in Perth, Australia. In this case, quality programming and learning are realized through a shared commitment and collective thinking among partners. At the other end of the age spectrum, **Burić** and **Sedinić** focus on Croatian kindergarten children's holistic development and artful community engagement through art as a social and relational practice lens, using Croatian folk and naïve art as a mode of inquiry. In the closing chapter for this collection, **Snepvangers** poses the question: How does a person "belong" in contemporary Australia within diverse identities and available community transversalities? This question evokes deliberations on disrupting social hierarchies and re-examining hidden histories for a transversal rethinking of micronarratives of discovery and progress in creative contexts.

INTRODUCTION

Snepvangers' artistic research offers an ecological perspective that invites artists, scholars and educational practitioners to consider the complex relations embedded in inquiries of, and for, community through artistic intervention, provocation, experimentation, dialogue and engagement.

## *Paths Forward*

This collection is situated in an unusual time when many of the projects have been conducted and written before the pandemic started, and the pandemic may not be over when this book is published. While some chapters reflect on the COVID-19 pandemic before it may be fully realized, this edited volume demonstrates the resilience coming from authors who map the challenges and opportunities of community arts education in this unique time. This collection represents a rich cartography of community arts education through diversification of socially engaged art, public pedagogy, community engagement, Arctic ACAE practice, artistic research, a/r/tography and hybridized practices. These chapters also reflect the growing impact of critical post-humanism, new materialism and world-centred education for conceptualizing community spaces and international educative borders. For these writers, thinking transversally means creating multi-layered intellectual exchanges and intersecting dialogue about how social institutions can engage innovative models of teaching and learning, as well as new artistic interventions in the international education landscape. The myriad perspectives in this collection make a unique contribution to "glocal" education by exploring – on an international scale – how and why creating artful spaces helps generate publicly accessible pedagogy through diverse and differentiated methods of teaching and learning. Together, international scholars and practitioners are revisiting community as a space of knowledge creation and the integral role of the arts in realizing pedagogical possibilities. In particular, they suggest new models and methods of community arts research and practice and potentially stimulating sustainable social change and innovation.

Across all chapters, these authors think transversally. They consider and embrace the blurred boundaries among the arts, cultural practice and educational discourse as well as the intersecting roles of artists, community professionals, educators, learners and members of the public. Such collective inquiry aims to develop a methodological and conceptual framework for new approaches to understanding community arts education. Perhaps most importantly, this book reflects Biesta's (2012) aspiration of *becoming public*: "about the achievement of a form of human togetherness" (p. 693). As a move towards "becoming public" through community arts education, we invite readers to think transversally with us: to open up possibilities and explore new synergies and methodologies for understanding how community art education research and practices can facilitate and create new relationships emerging from collaboration, experimentation and conversation across institutions and communities.

## REFERENCES

Alexander, A. (2015). Engaging a developmentally disabled community through arts-based service-learning. *Journal of Higher Education Outreach and Engagement, 19*(4), 183–206.

Alexander, A. & Murphy, E. (2020). "It started with this project:" A mixed methods examination of a service-learning project for pre-service art educators. *Studies in Art Education, 61*(4), 312–329.

Arendt, H. (1958). *The human condition*. University of Chicago Press.

Baumann, S., Merante, M., Sylvain-Holmgren, M., & Burke, J. (2021). Exploring community art and its role in promoting health, social cohesion, and community resilience in the aftermath of the 2015 Nepal earthquake. *Health Promotion Practice, 22*(1_suppl), 111S–121S. https://doi.org/10.1177/1524839921996083

Beighton, C. (2018). A transversal university? Criticality, creativity and catatonia in the globalised pursuit of higher education excellence. In D. Cole & J. Bradley (Eds.), *Principles of transversality in globalization and education* (pp. 47–64). Springer. https://doi.org/10.1007/978-981-13-0583-2_4.

Belfiore, E. (2002). Art as a means of alleviating social exclusion: Does it really work? A critique of instrumental cultural policies and social impact studies in the UK. *International Journal of Cultural Policy, 8*(1), 91–106. https://doi.org/10.1080/102866302900324658

Belfiore, E. (2011). The "transformative power" of the arts: History of an idea. In J. Sefton-Green, P. Thomson, L. Bresler, & K. Jones, (Eds.), *The Routledge international handbook of creative learning* (pp. 27–35). Routledge. https://doi.org/10.4324/9780203817568-10

Belfiore, E. & Bennett, O. (2008). *The social impact of the arts: An intellectual history*. Palgrave Macmillan.

Belfiore, E., & Bennett, O. (2010). Beyond the "toolkit approach": Arts impact evaluation research and the realities of cultural policy-making. *Journal for Cultural Research, 14*(2), 121–142. https://doi.org/10.1080/14797580903481280.

Biesta, G. (2012). Becoming public: Public pedagogy, citizenship and the public sphere. *Social & Cultural Geography, 13*(7), 683–697. https://doi.org/10.1080/14649365.2012.723736

Biesta, G. (2019). What if? Art education beyond expression and creativity. In R. Hickman, J. Baldacchino, K. Freedman, E. Hall, & N. Meager (Eds.), *The international encyclopedia of art and design education* (pp. 1–10). Wiley. https://doi.org/10.1002/9781118978061.ead058

INTRODUCTION

Biro-Hannah, E. (2021). Community adult mental health: Mitigating the impact of Covid-19 through online art therapy. *International Journal of Art Therapy*, 26(3), 96–103. https://doi.org/10.1080/17454832.2021.1894192

Bourdieu, P., & Wacquant, L. (1992). *An invitation to reflexive sociology*. The University of Chicago Press.

Bruce, B. (2018). Community as curriculum: Nurturing the ecosystem of education. *Schools*, 15(1), 122–139. https://doi.org/10.1086/697097

Carmichael, P., & Litherland, K. (2012). Transversality and innovation: Prospects for technologies-enhanced learning in times of crisis. In D. Cole (Ed.), *Surviving economic crises through education* (pp. 95–14). Peter Lang.

Carpenter, B. (2019). Community art curriculum. In R. Hickman, J. Baldacchino, K. Freedman, E. Hall, & N. Meager (Eds.), *The international encyclopedia of art and design education* (pp. 1–12). Wiley. https://doi.org/10.1002/9781118978061.ead087

Carpenter, S., & Tavin, K. (2010). Art education beyond reconceptualization: Enacting curriculum through/with/by/for/in/beyond/as visual culture, community, and public pedagogy. In E. Malewski (Ed.), *Curriculum studies handbook: The "next" moment* (pp. 244–258). Routledge.

Cohen, A. (1985). *The symbolic construction of community*. Tavistock.

Cole, D., & Bradley, J. (2018). *Principles of transversality in globalization and education*. Springer. https://doi.org/10.1007/978-981-13-0583-2

Deleuze, G., & Guattari, F. (1988). *A thousand plateaus: Capitalism & schizophrenia II* (B. Massumi, Trans.). The Athlone Press.

Dolphijn, T., & Tuin, I. (2012). *New materialism: Interviews and cartographies*. Open Humanities Press Imprint.

Finkelpearl, T. (2013). *What we made: Conversations on art and social cooperation*. Duke University Press.

Freire, P. (1993). *Pedagogy of the oppressed*. Continuum.

Gallagher, K., & Neelands, J. (2011). Drama and theatre in urban contexts. *Research in Drama Education*, 16(2), 151–156. https://doi.org/10.1080/13569783.2011.566986

Gaztambide-Fernandez, R. (2013). Why the arts don't do anything: Toward a new vision for cultural production in education. *Harvard Educational Review*, 83(1), 211–236.

Gaztambide-Fernández, R. A. (2008). The artist in society: Understandings, expectations, and curriculum implications. *Curriculum Inquiry*, 38(3), 233–265. https://doi.org/10.1111/j.1467-873X.2008.00408.x

Genosko, G. (2002). *Felix Guattari: An aberrant introduction*. Continuum.

Guattari, F. (2015). *Psychoanalysis and transversality: Texts and interviews 1955–1971* (A. Hodges, Trans.). Semiotext(e).

Härkönen, E., Huhmarniemi, M., & Jokela, T. (2018). Crafting sustainability: Handcraft in contemporary art and cultural sustainability in the Finnish Lapland. *Sustainability*, 10(6), 1–14. https://doi.org/10.3390/su10061907

Harvey, L., & Cooke, P. (2021). Reimagining voice for transrational peace education through participatory arts with South African youth. *Journal of Peace Education*, *18*(1), 1–26. https://doi.org/10.1080/17400201.2020.1819217

Illeris, H. (2017). Subjectivation, togetherness, environment: Potentials of participatory art for art education for sustainable development (AESD). *Nordic Journal of Art and Research*, *6*(1), 1–16. https://doi.org/10.7577/information.v6i1.2166

Irwin, R. L. (2013). Becoming a/r/tography. *Studies in Art Education*, *54*(3), 198–215. https://doi.org/10.1080/00393541.2013.11518894

Lawton, P. (2019). At the crossroads of intersecting ideologies: Community-based art education, community engagement, and social practice art. *Studies in Art Education*, *60*(3), 203–218. https://doi.org/10.1080/00393541.2019.1639486

LeBlanc, N., Davidson, S., Ryu, J., & Irwin, R. L. (2015). Becoming through a/r/tography, autobiography and stories in motion. *International Journal of Education Through Art*, *11*(3), 355–374. https://doi.org/10.1386/eta.11.3.355_1

Lin, C. (2021). Materiality and the meaning of aging. *Visual Methodologies*, *8*(1), 37–45. https://doi.org/10.7331/vm.v8i1.131

Lin, C., & Bruce, B. (2013). Engaging youth in underserved communities through digital-mediated art learning experiences for community inquiry. *Studies in Art Education*, *54*(4), 335–348. https://doi.org/10.1080/00393541.2013.11518907

Massey, D. (1999). Philosophy and politics of spatiality: Some considerations. In D. Massey (Ed.), *Power-geometries and the politics of space-time* (pp. 27–42). Hettner-Lecture, Vol. 2. Department of Geography, Heidelberg University.

Merli, P. (2002). Evaluating the social impact of participation in arts activities. *International Journal of Cultural Policy*, *8*(1), 107–118. https://doi.org/10.1080/10286630290032477

Pinar, William F. (2007). *Intellectual advancement through disciplinarity: Verticality and horizontality in curriculum studies*. Sense Publishers.

Romanski, N. (2019). Reigniting the transformative power of puppets through narrative pedagogy, contemporary art, and transdisciplinary approaches in art education. *Art Education*, *72*(4), 36–42. https://doi.org/10.1080/00043125.2019.1602496

Rousell, D., & Hickey-Moody, A. (2020). Speculative and symbolic forms of expression: New practices in community arts education. In N. Addison & L. Burgess (Eds.), *Debates in art and design education* (2nd ed., pp. 82–104). Routledge. https://doi.org/10.4324/9780429201714

Ryder, A. (2018). Foreword: The challenge for transversality in education today. In D. Cole & J. Bradley (Eds.), *Principles of transversality in globalization and education* (pp. v–viii). Springer.

Sacco, P., Ghirardi, S., Tartari, M., & Trimarchi, M. (2019). Two versions of heterotopia: The role of art practices in participative urban renewal processes. *Cities*, *89*, 199–208. https://doi.org/10.1016/j.cities.2019.02.013

Sauvé, L. (2020). Transversality, diversity, criticality, and activism: Enhancing E(S)E in teacher education. In D. Karrow & M. DiGiuseppe (Eds.), *Environmental and sustainability education in teacher education* (pp. 49–61). Springer International Publishing. https://doi.org/10.1007/978-3-030-25016-4_4

Sinner, A., & Conrad, D. (Eds.) (2015). *Creating together: Participatory, community-based, and collaborative arts practices and scholarship across Canada.* Wilfrid Laurier University Press.

Thompson, N. (2015). *Seeing power: Art and activism in the 21st century.* Melville House.

Tusa, J. (2007). *Engaged with the arts: Writings from the frontline.* I. B. Tauris.

Vaughan, K., Lévesque, M., Szabad-Smyth, L., Garnet, D., Fitch, S., & Sinner, A. (2017). A history of community art education at Concordia University: Educating the artist-teacher through practice and collaboration. *Studies in Art Education, 58*(1), 28–38. https://doi.org/10.1080/00393541.2016.1258530

# PART 1

## TRANSVERSAL CONNECTIONS

# 1

# Twenty-First Century Winter Journey: Exploring Comics, Adaptation and Community Art Education

*Julian Lawrence*

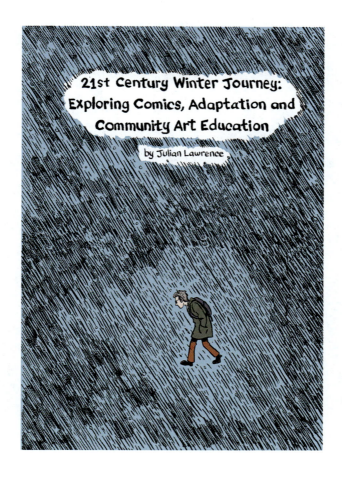

COMMUNITY ARTS EDUCATION

### Introduction

This chapter describes a collaborative comics-based research (CBR) project between a homeless charity and a cohort of Year Two university students.

*21st Century Winter Journey* is a visual essay exploring the status of Community Art Education (CAE) in Middlesbrough UK and the ways in which making comics impacts communities locally and internationally.

I have been teaching comics for seventeen years to students across Canada, the US and the UK. Forms of comics such as comic strips, comic books and graphic novels are recognized worldwide.

Arguably, artistic practices of making comics and cartooning are transferrable to schools, studios and universities everywhere.

As such, comics function as a transversal language and a form of participatory culture that links people and communities.

What follows is an analysis of the 21st Century Winter Journey project in the form of a visual essay/comic. I hope to widen conversations in CAE through theories of Research Informed Teaching (RIT), Just-In-Time Teaching (JITT) and Freire's (1996) "conscientização" (awareness).

These theories triangulate and locate learning in a community's relational and public spaces. In applying these theories to cartooning practices, a powerful pedagogical tool emerges.

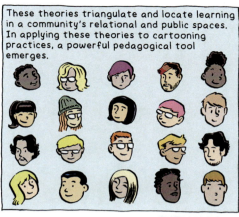

When students become researchers and make comics, they negotiate their understandings of community, their identities and their futures.

These understandings are evident in the reflections students wrote at the conclusion of the project.

RIT, JITT, awareness and cartooning guide the flow of artistic practice through shared group experiences within community spaces.

Tragically, the global pandemic hit as we were developing the comic, and all teaching migrated online. Thus, the value of the lifeworld community and the sharing of space became even more precious.

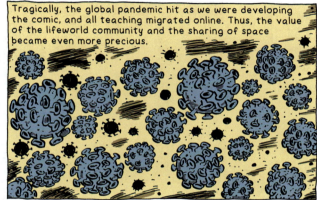

By making comics with a local charity, students developed an awareness of the roles they could play in their community and the relational spaces they shared with others.

Students also expanded their space of learning from the private, symbolic individual to group collaborations that flow into the world.

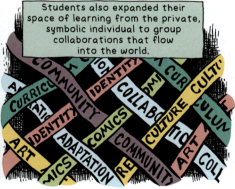

# COMMUNITY ARTS EDUCATION

The *21st Century Winter Journey* project challenged the Year Two students to make comics, do research beyond the classroom boundaries and explore the surrounding local community.

We partnered with staff and homeless members of Streetwise Opera (SWO) who were staging a performance of Schubert's opera *Winterreise*. SWO provides resources for homeless people across the UK to support community building.

Our task as a class was to collaboratively develop the opera's narrative with SWO and adapt the libretto into a graphic novel.

60-PAGE FULL COLOUR COMIC BOOK!

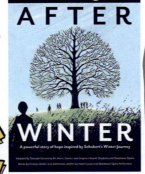

I randomly divided the class of twenty into five groups of four, with each group responsible for adapting five songs into comics.

Traditional comics-making methods informed the foundation of the project's artistic practice:

- ☑ Rough sketches and thumbnails based on research;
- ☑ Cleaner pencil drawings and lettering;
- ☑ Rendering inks and colours;
- ☑ Final, camera-ready artwork.

Following each iteration, SWO and I (as tutor) gave students feedback and revisions.

Keywords:
Comics; cartooning; Community Art Education; adaptation; collaboration

# TWENTY-FIRST CENTURY WINTER JOURNEY

# COMMUNITY ARTS EDUCATION

I'll answer that question shortly. Meanwhile, I complete the lesson plan for the upcoming Advanced Storytelling module I'm teaching.

As a Comics-Based Researcher (CBR) and educator, I integrate Research Informed Teaching (RIT) and professional practices of collective comics-making into my teaching (Brew, 2012; Cordingley, 2008; Kuttner et al., 2020; Uidhir, 2012).

The lesson plan for this Year Two university course includes twelve weekly lessons that apply professional and artistic practices of making comics as well as collaboration, research and adaptation (Abel & Madden, 2012; Brunetti, 2011; Lainé & Delzant, 2007; McCloud, 2006).

## ADVANCED STORYTELLING LESSON PLAN

- Week 1: Introduction to Streetwise Opera
- Week 2: Story Essentials/Create Small Groups
- Week 3: Character Development
- Week 4: Mapping Plot and Character
- Week 5: The Character Journey
- Week 6: Collaborative Authorship/Thumbnails
- Week 7: Streetwise Opera Preview
- Week 8: Pencilling
- Week 9: Revising
- Week 10: Clean Ups and Lettering
- Week 11: Inking and Colouring
- Week 12: Putting it all Together

With this project, I link collaboration with Streetwise Opera, a charity that supports people affected by homelessness. I want to observe the ways "people learn from each other in diverse contexts" (Thornton, 2013, p. 37) across relational spaces of learning through the transversal, transmedial and international language of comics (Groensteen, 2007; Jenkins, 2010; Lawrence et al., 2019).

# COMMUNITY ARTS EDUCATION

# TWENTY-FIRST CENTURY WINTER JOURNEY

Additionally, the comics medium performs as a participatory culture that links communities internationally (Delwiche & Henderson, 2012; Tilley, 2014). Thus, the opportunity to collaborate with a national UK charity on a comic book project is very exciting.

From the outset, I wanted the research design to include ways for students to develop a new awareness of their creative identities and discover opportunities to express their voices to a community.

"Conscientizaçao (or *awareness*) refers to learning to perceive social, political, and economic contradictions, and take action against the oppressive elements of reality."

(Freire, 1996, p. 17)

This first-time collaboration between Teesside University and SWO will work best with the Year Two students. They already have completed the foundational knowledge of making comics. The First Years lack experience, and the Third Years are too busy with final projects.

I am looking "to the potential and possibilities of education as a medium and practice of art making" whereby students' creative voices are supported by an awareness of their ability to move an audience (Irwin & O'Donoghue, 2012, p. 222).

CAE expands the space of learning from the private individual to group classroom collaboration that flows into the community.

"Sociologists and urban designers have long observed the importance of public spaces in the cityscape where people could congregate for sociability."

"Social interaction and cooperation reside at the nexus of social practice art, community art and community-based art education."

(Butsch, 2019, p. 28)

(Lawton, 2019, p. 207).

25

# COMMUNITY ARTS EDUCATION

# COMMUNITY ARTS EDUCATION

# COMMUNITY ARTS EDUCATION

"Just in time" teaching (Sinner et al., 2017) links to Bobby's sketch of the chorus, which answers our earlier question: 'How do we depict community in the comic?'

The students collaboratively detail the Traveller's journey, a metaphor of their own explorations into community and culture.

Here are just six of the fifty pages of comic art the students created:

COMMUNITY ARTS EDUCATION

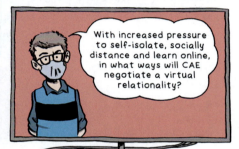

# REFERENCES

Abel, J., & Madden, M. (2012). *Mastering comics: Drawing words and writing pictures continued: A definitive course in comics narrative*. First Second.

Bostridge, I. (2015). *Schubert's winter journey: Anatomy of an obsession*. Knopf.

Brew, A. (2012). Teaching and research: New relationships and their implications for inquiry-based teaching and learning. *Higher Education Research and Development*, 31(1), 101–114. https://doi.org/10.1080/07294360320000565 71

Butsch, R. (2019). *Screen culture: A global history*. Polity Press.

Chomsky, N. (2012). *How the world works*. Penguin.

Cordingley, P. (2008). Teachers using evidence: Using what we know about teaching and learning to reconceptualize evidence-based practice. In G. Thomas & R. Pring (Eds.), *Evidence-based practice in education* (pp. 77–87). Open University Press.

Delwiche, A., & Henderson, J. J. (2012). *The participatory cultures handbook*. Routledge.

Fei, V. L. (2007). The visual semantics stratum: Making meaning in sequential images. In T. D. Royce & W. L. Bowcher (Eds.), *New directions in the analysis of multimodal discourse* (pp. 195–213). Routledge.

Finkelpearl, T. (2013). *What we made: Conversations on art and social cooperation*. Duke University Press.

Freire, F. (1996). *Pedagogy of the oppressed*. Penguin Books.

Groensteen, T. (2007). *The system of comics* (B. Beaty & N. Nguyen, Trans.). University Press of Mississippi. (Original work published 1999)

Hoad, L., Erlandson, T. A., & Mulyani, V. (2018). Mars: Design for the red planet. *Interiors*, 9(1), 30–41. https://doi.org/10.1080/20419112.2018.1485382

Irwin, R. L. (2013). Becoming a/r/tography. *Studies in Art Education*, 54(3), 198–215. https://doi.org/10.1080/00393541.2013.11518894

Irwin, R. L., & O'Donoghue, D. (2012). Encountering pedagogy through relational art practices. *International Journal of Art & Design Education*, 31(3), 221–236. https://doi.org/10.1111/j.1476-8070.2012.01760.x

Jenkins, H. (2010). Transmedia storytelling and entertainment: An annotated syllabus. *Continuum: Entertainment Industries*, 24(6), 943–958. https://doi.org/10.1080/10304312.2010.510599

Jones, D. S. (2020). History in a crisis—Lessons for Covid-19. *New England Journal of Medicine*, 382(18), 1681–1683.

Jones, S., & Woglom, J. F. (2013). Graphica: Comics arts-based educational research. *Harvard Educational Review*, 83(1), 168–189.

Karr, V. L. (2013). "Silver Scorpion" communal comics and disability identities between the United States and Syria. *International Journal of Education Through Art*, 9(2), 173–187. https://doi.org/10.1386/eta.9.2.173_1

Kuttner, P. J., Weaver-Hightower, M. B., & Sousanis, N. (2020). Comics-based research: The affordances of comics for research across disciplines. *Qualitative Research*, 2, 195–214. https://doi.org/10.1177/1468794120918845

Lainé, J. M., & Delzant, S. (2007). La realisation du storyboard. [Creating storyboards]. *Eyerolles*.

Langton, J., & Morris, R. J. (1987). *Atlas of industrializing Britain, 1780–1914*. Routledge.

Lave, J., & Wenger, E. (1991). *Situated learning: Legitimate peripheral participation*. Cambridge University Press.

Lawrence, J. (2017a). *Secret identities in the classroom: Negotiating conceptions of identity with comics and bilingual grade four students* [Master's thesis, University of British Columbia]. https://doi.org/10.14288/1.0343566

Lawrence, J. (2017b). The ninth art versus the tenth art: Visualizing conflicting worldviews between comics and screens. *Journal of Cultural Research in Art Education, 34*, 99–115. http://www.jcrae.org/journal/index.php/jcrae/article/view/78

Lawrence, J. (Ed.) (2020). *After winter*. Teesside University.

Lawrence, J., Lin, C.-C., & Can, I. (2019). Relational connections through the space of learning: Exploring youths' experiences of filmmaking with comics. *International Journal of Education Through Art, 15*(3), 297–308. https://doi.org/10.1386/eta_00004_3

Lawton, P. (2019). At the crossroads of intersecting ideologies: Community based art education, community engagement, and social practice art. *Studies in Art Education: A Journal of Issues and Research, 60*(3), 203–218. https://doi.org/10.1080/00393541.2019.1639486

LeBlanc, N., & Irwin, R. L. (2018). Teachers storying themselves into teaching: Comics as an emergent and relational form of research. *LEARNing Landscapes, 11*(2), 223–239.

McCloud, S. (2006). *Making comics: Storytelling secrets of comics, manga and graphic novels*. Harper.

Merleau-Ponty, M. (2004). *The world of perception*. Routledge. https://doi.org/10.4324/9780203491829

Middlesbrough. (2020). *Mayors launch £250m digital city development*. Middlesbrough.gov.uk. https://www.middlesbrough.gov.uk/news/mayors-launch-%C2%A3250m-digital-city-development

Musk, E. (2017). Making humans a multi-planetary species. *New Space, 5*(2), 46–61.

Office for Standards in Education, Children's Services and Skills. (2020). *Middlesbrough borough council inspection of children's social care services*. https://files.ofsted.gov.uk/v1/file/50143726

Sepper, D. L. (2013). *Understanding imagination*. Springer.

Sigoma. (2019). *SIGOMA response to the local government finance and the 2019 spending review inquiry*. https://www.sigoma.gov.uk/__documents/public/Inquiry-Local-Government-Finance-Final.pdf

Sinner, A., Wicks, J., & Zantingh, P. (2017). You have to judge on the spot: Just-in-time community art education. *Journal of Curriculum and Pedagogy 14*(1), 56–68. https://doi.org/10.1080/15505170.2016.1234984

Streetwise Opera (2020a). *About us*. Streetwiseopera.org. https://www.streetwiseopera.org/about/

Streetwise Opera (2020b). *At Streetwise Opera, everyone is a star*. Streetwiseopera.org. https://www.streetwiseopera.org/at-streetwise-opera-everyone-is-a-star/

Thomas, G. (2008). Introduction: Evidence and practice. In G. Thomas & R. Pring (Eds.), *Evidence-based practice in education* (pp. 1–18). Open University Press.

Thornton, A. (2013). *Artist researcher teacher: A study of professional identity in art and education*. Intellect.

Tilley, C. L. (2014). Comics: A once-missed opportunity. *The Journal of Research on Libraries and Young Adults*, 4(1). http://www.yalsa.ala.org/jrlya/2014/05/comics-a-once-missed-opportunity/

Uidhir, C. M. (2012). Comics and collective authorship. In A. Meskin & R. T. Cook (Eds.), *The art of comics: A philosophical approach* (pp. 47–67). John Wiley & Sons.

Vaughan, K., Lévesque, M., Szabad-Smyth, L., Garnet, D., Fitch, S., & Sinner, A. (2019). A history of community art education at Concordia University: Educating the artist-teacher through practice and collaboration. *Studies in Art Education: A Journal of Issues and Research*, 58(1), 23–28. https://doi.org/10.1080/00393541.2016.128530

---

Thank you to Delza Hoeberg-Lawrence for assistance with colouring.

For more comics and stories related to this project, visit:

https://streetwiseopera.org/after-winter-graphic-novel/

https://www.tees.ac.uk/schools/scedt/news_story.cfm?story_id=7552&this_issue_title=February%202021&this_issue=333

# 2

# The University as an Institute of Permanent Creation: Developing "a gift for living" in Neoliberal Times

*Raphael Vella*

*as the time will come*

*when all you're allowed to say is YESSIR*

*and it will last one hundred thousand and one years*

(Filliou, 1970, p. 218)

### Higher Education and Community Transmission

Faced by the COVID-19 crisis in 2020, scholarship was challenged to redefine itself in terms of current relevance and responsibility, reinterpreting past events and values through the lens of the present. As I read artist and poet Robert Filliou's *Teaching and Learning as Performing Arts* (1970) in the context of a global pandemic, extracts that might have sounded dated only a few months earlier, acquired a new meaning. In the closing pages of the book, Filliou refers briefly to using new technologies in education and wonders whether "we may very well use these devices to enslave man [sic], rather than to free him, to teach children to conform, rather than be themselves" (Filliou, 1970, p. 214).

At a defining moment characterized by online learning, the artist's technological concerns suddenly sounded very topical. While universities were quickly mobilized to cater for new realities triggered by the pandemic, students and academics in many countries reflected on cyber-surveillance, loss of autonomy and the further marginalization of learners from vulnerable backgrounds.

Closing higher education institutions for risk mitigation led many educators to ask what meaning words like "community" and "dialogue" might still have when public health authorities were busy warning people about "community transmission" and prescribing "social distancing." As Giroux (2020) argues, how can we now challenge the indifference of "a central pedagogical principle of neoliberalism that individual responsibility is the only way to address social problems" (para. 3)? How could pandemic-induced online pedagogies avoid the enslavement and social conformity that Filliou warns of? Could we dream, along with Žižek (2020), of a more positive "virus" that gives birth to an alternative world characterized by global solidarity rather than conspiracy theories, rampant racism, the survival of the fittest and a fear of others' bodies?

This chapter will argue that educators can engage with communities and avoid reproducing social and other inequalities only if they envision learning as a site that questions accepted notions of expertise and knowledge hierarchies. They can take inspiration from Filliou's vision for a radically different university that becomes a site for "permanent creation" (1970, p. 42), which he understood as a practice that is deeply entangled in daily life. Like other artists associated with the Fluxus avant-garde movement, Filliou believed in a non-elitist relationship between artists and audiences that would not be framed by notions of talent and expertise. Filliou saw permanent creation as the possibility of combining work and leisure through a continuous process of self-transformation, realized through multiple, co-creative interactions that encouraged a sense of experimentation and play. Fluxus artists like Filliou, Allan Kaprow, Alison Knowles and Robert Watts proposed "curricula" and pedagogies that revolved around collaborative strategies, the celebration of social connections and an avoidance of specialization (Miles & Springgay, 2019). For Filliou, artists' creative use of leisure can inform educators and learners about ways of transposing the act of creation onto life itself, presenting "an art of living" that is "always on the move, never arriving" (1970, p. 24).

While this participatory aspect bridges community art practices and other open-ended strategies of social engagement, dialogue between experimental artistic modes and communities depends on specific historical and cultural situations that may enable or inhibit such dialogues. For instance, analysing a social turn in art and education in a relatively marginal, post-colonial context would need to account for local perceptions about the arts (what is understood as "art" in the local context?), the value of experimentation (do artists have a right to experiment with local traditions?) and collective identity (who decides who we are and how we can be represented?).

To contextualize such situations, this chapter first gauges recent artistic and pedagogical practices on the Mediterranean island of Malta, briefly describing modernist developments on the island and recent community art practices. Next follows an overview of a new, interdisciplinary MA in Social Practice Arts and Critical Education introduced at the University of Malta in 2019. Reference is made to overlap in this programme among art practice, theatre, community engagement and adult education, and their possible significance in an island environment like Malta. I then discuss Filliou's participatory strategies and distrust of academic specialization, linking some of his key ideas and concepts to more recent examples of social practice in art and socially engaged approaches to art education. Finally, I ask how radical ideas – with roots in the 1960s and 1970s – can be reconceptualized in a twenty-first-century milieu dominated by a neoliberal ethos that is influencing debates on creativity and art education.

## *Art and Social Practice in Malta*

Malta's imbrication of art and community is rather peculiar. A brief personal and historical sketch will illustrate this point. My own training as a young artist in Malta in the 1980s and early 1990s was characterized by modernist European and North American aesthetic principles. Art was a rigorous exercise in reduction and rejection, distinct from popular or Baroque forms of art that surrounded us. Beginning around twenty years before the island's independence from British colonial power in 1964, modernism in Maltese art was understood as a hard-won style that needed to be defended from both traditionalism and insularism (Vella, 2007). On one hand, modernism represented a kind of counter-hegemonic struggle against a local, bourgeois culture dominated by ecclesiastical and other conventional artistic models. On the other hand, most modernist artists in Malta had received their training in Italy, England and France. Paradoxically, these connections with imported aesthetic criteria and pedagogies meant that modernism also sought to establish international ideals about progress and freedom: ideas that might have been interpreted as providing some sort of intellectual legitimacy to a colonial influence that was then in political decline.

Neither situation explains the whole story. The works these modernist artists produced at the time reveal a persistent sense of negotiation and loose stylistic boundaries and are largely not a case of straightforward mimicry. This negotiation gives rise to a contact zone composed of varying understandings of political agency and relations with local communities and patronage. Here, local visual artists provide entry into a more global cultural sphere by exploiting their international training. Therefore, a simple dichotomy of modernity or freedom on one side and nostalgic or "uneducated" taste on the other would not do justice to more complex layers of cultural processes and local dispositions.

One example of a very localized cultural practice was the involvement of a handful of artists in Malta like Gabriel Caruana and Antoine Camilleri in popular Carnival festivities between the 1950s and 1970s. They designed large floats, grotesque masks, costumes and posters, sometimes involving their students. This is how one of the oldest forms of theatrical expression in Malta (Cremona, 1995) provided a participatory backdrop for experimental art at the time. Since these designs were initiated by artists who considered themselves at the forefront of avant-garde practices in local art, these initiatives were somewhat different from other popular cultural traditions such as band clubs, whose members are generally amateurs participating in activities such as village feasts and teaching music to young people in the community.

However, the history of recent Maltese art in the public realm (e.g. Vella, 2008) shows that visual artists' engagement with participatory and community practices was not common in the 1980s and 1990s. Experimental events in alternative spaces by groups of artists started appearing in the first decade of the twenty-first century, while community-related projects in the arts picked up around 2012, soon after Valletta was declared European Capital of Culture for 2018. In the following years, artistic projects engaging different social groups – including migrants – were organized by artists, NGOs and others. However, problems related to accessibility, gentrification, commercialization and long-term liveability for residents in the city were also reported (Deguara et al., 2018; Zammit & Aldeiri, 2018).

Despite this increasing emphasis on communities' needs and engagement in the arts, available undergraduate and postgraduate degrees related to the visual arts in Malta were still restricted to fine arts, digital arts, art education and art history. Then in 2019, the Department of Arts, Open Communities and Adult Education at the University of Malta added a new, socially oriented degree to this list to strengthen the field's local research base. As coordinator of this two-year, interdisciplinary Master of Arts in Social Practice Arts and Critical Education, I aim to encourage students to contextualize their creative work in community settings: linking theatre, visual arts and education with theoretical and practice-based research. Students are expected to position themselves as engaged artists and educators and develop critical attitudes towards power relations. In study units on community engagement, social theatre and fieldwork, students discuss the challenges of co-creation with a special focus on the local context. The juxtaposition of theatre and visual art is intentionally directed towards understanding the arts in education as reflective processes or "performances" that transform current realities co-creatively. While this combination of areas is quite unique, comparable programmes elsewhere in Europe include the MA in Applied Arts and

Social Practice at Queen Margaret University in Edinburgh and the international Master Artist Educator programme at ArtEZ in the Netherlands.

In March 2020, when students in Malta were confronted by the pandemic, face-to-face sessions were called off and online sessions became a new, uncertain reality. Students in our master's programme faced the additional challenge of satisfying the requirement of social intervention within a strange climate allowing no close contact with others. This was a time for soul-searching questions. Amongst the many we asked (and couldn't answer adequately): What can social practice possibly mean in the context of social distancing? How could trust be built around practices of co-creation in a climate characterized by insecurity?

However, when the students helped to organize a series of online sessions with participants from an integration programme for migrants in Malta (one of the requirements for migrants' long-term residence status), COVID-19 turned into a subject of debate rather than a limitation. The impossibility of in-person contact reflected the migrants' powerlessness in a political environment in which vulnerable foreigners were often perceived as virus carriers. Nevertheless, the migrant participants and postgraduate students collectively engaged in an online debate about issues related to identity and worked on spontaneous, creative games and projects that they shared amongst themselves. For example, in one of these projects, participants produced individual narrative flipbooks that they shared on screen in a process of self-discovery and disclosure. Conversations about integration and belonging were cordial, but there were moments of discomfort as everyone gauged the limits of "participation." We all cautiously acknowledged that this was hardly an ideal dialogic situation, but the online sessions did present us with a rather peculiar and unforgettable social experience.

## *Permanent Creation*

This ambivalent experience instigated me to reflect on Filliou's fear, referenced earlier in this chapter, that educational technologies would one day be used to instil conformity in the young. While he created poetic proposals to liberate others from social and political alienation, fellow artist Allan Kaprow wrote that the role of schools should be to change human values, fostering play and "long-term experimentation" as the basis of society (Kaprow, 1993, p. 124). Sometimes hailed as a precursor of relational aesthetics and a cult figure amongst other experimental artists (Patrick, 2010), Filliou broadly shared ideas about art and education associated with other Fluxus artists, such as the importance of process over end result and an opposition "to artistic professionalism and art as a commercial object or means to a personal income" (Williams & Noël, 1998, p. 41).

Filliou's and artist George Brecht's maxim – "Whatever you do, do something else" – invited artists to invent and "disinvent" objects, hence learning and unlearning whatever turns art into a complacent acceptance of the known (Frederickson, 2019, p. 34). Filliou and Brecht dreamt of an Eternal Network: an inclusive, non-competitive and boundless network showing that life is more important than art. The Eternal Network "connects all that has been, all that is, and all that might be" (Frederickson, 2019, p. 34); artists in such a network could rid the art world of its obsessive competitiveness by agreeing "to advertise other artists' performances together with our own" (Filliou, 1970, p. 204). This spirit of exchange was also evident in Brecht and Filliou's plan to set into motion a "non-school," which would invite "Alfred the bricklayer, Antoine the fisherman, Fernand the plumber" (p. 200) and others to share knowledge of their trades and experiences with other people.

Between 1967 and 1970, Filliou worked on ideas that developed into *Teaching and Learning as Performing Arts* (1970). This period coincided with the uprisings of May 1968 in France, and Filliou empathized with the sense of alienation felt by young people: "The students' unrest was already mine, their revolution my revolution" (1970, p. 12). Presenting an experimental model of education, his artist's book is perhaps a reflection of these restless times. The book leaves roughly one-third of its space to readers to add whatever they wish, hence becoming co-producers rather than passive observers (Léger, 2012, p. 71). In it, he develops the notion of Permanent Creation, which he also refers to as "art" or "artmaking" (Patrick, 2010, p. 52). By applying "participation techniques developed by artists" (1970, p. 12) to the problems of teaching and learning, Filliou believes that universities can develop a non-hierarchical Institute of Permanent Creation in which guest artists communicate "a way of life, an art of living" (1970, p. 69), rather than specialized skills or the laws of the marketplace. By avoiding the economic circuits of art, his hypothetical Institute of Permanent Creation aimed to advance a revolutionary standard of value built around innocence, imagination, freedom and integrity (1970, p. 45) rather than competition and self-advertising. Teachers and learners would engage in dialogues that establish a pedagogical model that is not "handed down from above" (1970, p. 114) but reflects the belief that "[e]verybody is a potential artist" (1970, p. 82). Education is an interdisciplinary process through which people learn to live like artists, without a pre-established curriculum: "developing a gift for living" (1970, p. 42). These beliefs extend Filliou's notion of Permanent Creation, which underlined the possibilities of establishing decentralized relationships that transcend geographical, social and other boundaries. Filliou believed that intellectuals who are "isolated from the community" are analogous to artists who are "bound up with an isolated professionalism" rather than "a social milieu" (1970, p. 127). Like composer John Cage, whose ideas and teaching formed the intellectual basis of much Fluxus thought, Filliou argued against the compartmentalization of education.

This concern with the social milieu and the use of creative powers to transform society is comparable to Joseph Beuys' well-known notion of social sculpture. Arguing incessantly against a "niche existence" for art (Beuys, 2010, p. 15), Beuys believed that society could avoid the "dead end of private capitalism" (p. 16) only by focusing on human creativity. In Beuys' view, a revolution through art is possible by putting together the fractured segments of human knowledge and developing an expanded concept of art around creativity: a concept in which "every human action is declared a piece of Art" (as cited in Filliou, 1970, p. 169). Similarly, for Filliou, Permanent Creation is a collective task that cuts across every day and encapsulates the features and ideals of childhood.

Akin to the aims of participatory art, Filliou's pedagogical goals render the role of educational "expert" obsolete; instead, "the teacher becomes a guide, helping students find information and determine how it might be adapted to their particular needs" (Higgins, 2002, p. 203). This aspect of Filliou's thought can also be compared to more recent, socially engaged pedagogical practices in art and design (e.g. Helguera, 2011; Sholette et al., 2018; Spencer, 2019). Yet, to some who work in higher education today, these possibilities might seem too distant in a system dominated by a so-called "market model." Indeed, how can an educational system led by corporate agendas sustain alternative forms of knowledge? Following Filliou, we might ask ourselves this: can we, as educators, "try to see if innocence and imagination [...] can be the base upon which to build a new theory of value" (1970, p. 78)?

## *Education, Creativity and Risk*

> *I think, first of all, we need a situation in which nothing is being transmitted: no one is learning anything that was known before. They must be learning things that were, until this situation arose, so to speak, unknown or unknowable: that it was due to the fact of the person coming together with other people [...] that this new knowledge which had not been known before could become known.*
> (John Cage, interviewed by Filliou, 1970, p. 114)

The German art educator Wolfgang Zacharias has described post-1968 art education as a non-instrumentalist broadening of aesthetics that moves away "from a hierarchical and dominant high culture while striving to learn the art of living" (as cited in Keuchel, 2015, p. 102). But in today's volatile political and economic climate, it might sound naïve to champion Permanent Creation as an alternative to a market regime. It might sound unrealistic to think of creativity as a principle that blurs distinctions between a successful person and a "failure" (Filliou, 1970, p. 74) when individualism and creativity are now touted as pillars of a neoliberal ideology. We are surrounded by signals indicating that individual agency is crucial in matters related to creativity and success, and that the ultimate goal of creative work – especially flexible labour carried out remotely – is to catalyze the competitive economy we already know (Mould, 2018). Universities are arguably abandoning their role as providers of a public service and resorting to a "bare pedagogy" that supports standardization, privatization and an "economic neo-Darwinism" (Giroux, 2010, p. 185). If creative work serves mainly to strengthen the expansion of the known, Filliou's hope for an education based on the unpredictability of Permanent Creation seems to have little if any significance today.

Because artists increasingly define themselves in business-friendly terms (entrepreneurs and innovators, for example), creativity in education is often co-opted by an ideology that sees educational goals as career-driven (Kalin, 2018). In particular, Kalin critiques the US Partnership for 21st Century Skills (P21) for placing learners' management of their own learning at the centre of the educational process. Kalin also warns about depoliticized collaborative practices in art education that avoid or discourage dissent because they simply echo neoliberal goals like productivity and efficiency. In attempting a more radical understanding of creativity in education, Kalin borrows from philosopher Giorgio Agamben the term "decreation." For Agamben (2004), decreation is a potentiality, a thinking through of what could have been otherwise. It is not destruction but an acknowledgement of the possibility of having acted differently since every creative act is defined "by its capacity to de-create the real" (2004, p. 318). Transferred to art education, decreation for Kalin (2018) resists the instrumentalization of creativity. Art education can reconceptualize creativity as a process of thinking through the potentiality of the not-yet-known. Creativity in higher education can therefore be conceived in ways that highlight the unfamiliar.

This reconceptualization is how Permanent Creation can remain *permanent*: by rejecting prescriptive and delimiting competencies and administrative measures. Putting this differently, and following Biesta (2013), we need to unlearn the certainties of current educational discourse (focused on accountability, outcomes and hard evidence) and embrace the weakness, risks and creative dimensions of education. As Biesta asserts,

> I am interested in education as itself a creative "act" or, to be more precise, in education as an act of creation, that is, as an act of bringing something new into the world, something that did not exist before.
>
> (2013, p. 11)

Without taking these creative risks, "education itself disappears and social reproduction, insertion into existing orders of being, doing, and thinking, takes over" (Biesta, 2013, p. 40). If we accept the idea that education is fundamentally a dialogical process to which different participants bring something new, we also acknowledge Filliou's concern about conformity in education: except the situation is potentially worse now because we know, more than ever, about the detrimental links between market-driven educational policies and social justice.

## *Imagining Alternatives*

Positive openings exist outside academia: for instance, not-for-profit "ecoversities" and alternative educational spaces influenced by Freire, Illich and others (Blewitt, 2013). In environments of this sort, it is still possible to imagine education and art in the community as sites of interruption and Permanent Creation. It is also crucial to conceive alternative futures for art, education and activation of a "gift for living" (Filliou, 1970, p. 42) *within* academia. The MA programme referenced earlier is an attempt to replace colonizing attitudes and economy-based discourse with hospitality and solidarity while retaining a space for unpredictable, de-familiarizing situations involving community participants. Through this programme, we hope to develop a vision of creativity that transverses boundaries between art education and the wider community, fulfilling Filliou's vision of a place "where we will create, and by creating, make claims upon this part of the world" (Filliou, 1970, p. 116).

## REFERENCES

Agamben, G. (2004). Difference and repetition: On Guy Debord's films. In T. McDonough (Ed.), *Guy Debord and the situationist international: Texts and documents* (pp. 313–319). The MIT Press.

Beuys, J. (2010). *What is money? A discussion*. Clairview Books.

Biesta, G. J. J. (2013). *The beautiful risk of education*. Paradigm.

Blewitt, J. (2013). EfS: Contesting the market model of higher education. In S. Sterling, L. Maxey, & H. Luna (Eds.), *The sustainable university: Progress and prospects* (pp. 51–64). Routledge.

Cremona, V.-A. (1995). Carnival in Gozo: Waning traditions and thriving celebrations. *Journal of Mediterranean Studies*, 5(1), 68–95. https://muse.jhu.edu/article/670101

Deguara, M., Pace Bonello, M., & Magri, R. (2018). *Community inclusion and accessibility in Valletta 2018*. Valletta 2018 Foundation. https://valletta2018.org/wp-content/uploads/2017/03/Theme-3-2015-Community-Inclusion-Space-Cover_v4.pdf

Filliou, R. (1970). *Teaching and learning as performing arts*. Verlag Gebr. König.

Fredrickson, L. J. (2019). Life as art, or art as life: Robert Filliou and the eternal network. *Theory, Culture & Society, 36*(3), 27–55.

Giroux, H. (2010). Bare pedagogy and the scourge of neoliberalism: Rethinking higher education as a democratic public sphere. *The Educational Forum, 74*(3), 184–196.

Giroux, H. (2020). The COVID-19 pandemic is exposing the plague of neoliberalism. *Truthout*. https://truthout.org/articles/the-covid-19-pandemic-is-exposing-the-plague-of-neoliberalism/?utm_campaign=Truthout+Share+Buttons&fbclid=IwAR2GaXnUs-iafLeO8QlPLifXsd-8jyU8IqL94gTBp4PSDLDI1vuA5KqM_rCA

Helguera, P. (2011). *Education for socially engaged art: A materials and techniques handbook*. Jorge Pinto Books.

Higgins, H. (2002). *Fluxus experience*. University of California Press.

Kalin, N. (2018). *The neoliberalization of creativity education: Democratizing, destructing and decreating*. Palgrave Macmillan.

Kaprow, A. (1993). Education of the un-artist, Part II. In J. Kelley (Ed.), *Essays on the blurring of art and life/Allan Kaprow* (pp. 110–126). University of California Press.

Keuchel, S. (2015). Arts education in the age of cultural diversity: A basis to gain cultural identity in a risk society. In B. van Heusden & P. Gielen (Eds.), *Arts education beyond art: Teaching art in times of change* (pp. 93–111). Valiz.

Léger, M. J. (2012). A Filliou for the game: From political economy to poetical economy and Fluxus. *RACAR: Revue d'art canadienne/Canadian Art Review, 37*(1), 64–74.

Miles, J., & Springgay, S. (2019). The indeterminate influence of Fluxus on contemporary curriculum and pedagogy. *International Journal of Qualitative Studies in Education, 33*(10), 1007–1021. https://doi.org/10.1080/09518398.2019.1697469

Mould, O. (2018). *Against creativity*. Verso.

Patrick, M. (2010). Unfinished Filliou: On the Fluxus ethos and the origins of relational aesthetics. *Art Journal, 69*(1–2), 44–61.

Sholette, G., Bass, C., & Social Practice Queens (2018). *Art as social action: An introduction to the principles and practices of teaching social practice art*. Allworth.

Spencer, A. M. (2019). Informal education: A new lens on socially engaged design practices. *The International Journal of Art and Design Education, 38*(4), 785–797.

Vella, R. (2007). Provision and privation: Art education in Malta. In R. Vella (Ed.), *On art and art education in Malta* (pp. 7–25). Allied Publications.

Vella, R. (Ed.). (2008). *Cross-currents: Critical essays on art and culture in Malta*. Allied Publications.

Williams, E., & Noël, A. (1998). *Mr. Fluxus: A collective portrait of George Maciunas 1931–1978*. Thames and Hudson.

Zammit, A., & Aldeiri, T. (2018). *Assessing the relationship between community inclusion and space through Valletta 2018 cultural infrastructural projects. Summary report 2018: 2018 Research*. Valletta 2018 Foundation. https://www.um.edu.mt/library/oar/handle/123456789/42820

Žižek, S. (2020). *Pandemic! COVID-19 shakes the world*. OR Books.

# 3

# Seeing What Unfolds: New Ways of Exploring Community Art Education in Formal Learning Spaces

*Kathryn Coleman and Marnee Watkins*

Innovating within formal standardized art education/s can be risky. The risk, however, outweighs the urgency to see art education as a site of and for affect that enables and opens provocation, interruption and contestation between artist and art forms, and sites and places of being and knowing. This chapter shares a significant story of emerging creative pandemic-informed pedagogies that are generative and digital, trusting and agentic, and that seek to shift understandings of community art education through a/r/tography as practice-pedagogical research. Our work is underpinned by the following questions: How can an initial art teacher education class and a primary school create the space and time for a community art education project? How can we create space and time for informal learning within a formal learning environment? We write as a site of data analysis, a process of "rite-ing" (Healy et al., 2022) the work of studio-based pedagogical practice (Sawyer, 2015) as a ritual to propose an art-school-modelled initial teacher education curriculum (Morris & Coleman, 2019) within the fold of a/r/tography (Irwin, 2008). As Bickel (2004) posits,

> ritual creates the container or third space for the alchemy of a/r/tographical inquiry to unfold within. The breadth and depth of a/r/tography as ritual when engaged with openness and commitment can greatly expand the learning imaginary of students, educators, artists and lifelong learners.
> 
> (p. 111)

This chapter is designed around the effect of the fold, the unfold and refold as both a metaphor for openings, opportunities and *becomings* in-between. In this chapter, we use the metaphor of the folding process of making paper aeroplanes. This action and practice of folding is iterative when the paper is folded, unfolded and refolded symmetrically. To take this metaphor out of the paper and into our method-pedagogy, we unfold our a/r/tography as community art education and fold and refold our processes iteratively to explore how through making and writing in relational dialogue. With/in this method-pedagogy, we have been afforded space to create, communicate and collaborate as intergeneration agents of change in the "Child+Adult Art Response Project" (Watkins & Coleman, 2019).

The project involves child artists in a small number of primary schools in metropolitan and regional Victoria, Australia, practising with adult artists in the Master of Teaching (Visual Arts and Design) at the Melbourne Graduate School of Education (MGSE) in an artful education exchange. This exchange between artists of different generations is community-based art education. While both groups of artists participate in art education communities of practice, this exchange is an a/r/tographic practice of relatedness (Bickel et al., 2011) outside of the formal. Within this project, the artists receive an invitation to participate and visually and textually respond to INSIDE|OUTSIDE as a conceptual, pedagogical and material provocation. The provocation, which can be responded to in any form, mode or medium, has been a constant within the project fold since the first year of encounters in 2016 (Watkins et al., 2019). We define a provocation as an encounter within creative pedagogy (Aleinikov, 2013) through relational art practices (Irwin & O'Donoghue, 2012). The provocation is an artful event, inquiry-driven and open-ended encounter. We use the provocation in this space between formal and informal art education/s.

With/in this artful project, each artist is offered equal time to generate a creative response to the provocation of INSIDE|OUTSIDE, with the artwork then being shared as a new art encounter through "gifting" the works to each other across the generations – from adult to child and child to adult. Within this project, practice can be defined as a recurring, situated action informed by shared meanings (Schatzki et al., 2001) and adheres to the premise that *practice* is critical because practitioners develop *knowing through doing*. Practice is the common thread that holds the multiple dimensions of this art education community together. Knowing within this speculative a/r/tography (Coleman & MacDonald, 2020) is understood as "an ongoing social accomplishment, constituted and reconstituted in everyday practices" (Orlikowski, 2002, p. 252). Within the community art education context, we believe practices are shared experiences that create new ways of knowing in relation to the other as artists within a creative ecology that informs and lives across formal and informal art education/s. The pedagogic *affect* (Healy & Mulcahy, 2020) of the interactions among art practice, materialities, communities, creativities, participations and provocations are all in relation to each other depending on the site of the encounter.

## Folding In-Between

Each year, the project invites artists through their "formal" art educators to participate in INSIDE|OUTSIDE. Here, folding is a pedagogical act, similar to teaching someone how to fold a paper plane. The art educator invites through a provocation – the invitation – and the fold is never quite the same, cannot be repeated and is always presented by an iterative process of folding and refolding, unfolding and refolding. This folding is an act of disruption as the invitation is not opened in class as with many other "formal" art education/s; rather, it is left to each participant (child and adult artist) to respond to as they choose, in whatever medium, form or material practice as they prepare for their intergenerational gifting while becoming art educators with/in the community method-pedagogy encounter. We locate this folding in-between as an important third space pedagogy (Gupta, 2015) for community art education. We begin by folding you as reader into our in-between to explore the new sites we are sighting and open our new ways of cit[e]ing new theories and methods of learning that seek to challenge the "imagined geography" of art education. Leander et al. (2010) present three metaphors of learning – learning-in-place, learning trajectories and learning networks – to challenge this perceived as well as real geography in teacher education. Hopfinger (2015), while focusing on devised performance rather than visual arts, discusses relevant aspects of intergenerational artmaking: the role of "entangled listening" (responding to human and non-human elements), the creative agency of non-professional children and adults and interactions between humans and non-human materials. Thinking within the fold has allowed us to see how the project might create new conditions for exploring community art education in new creative ecologies. Our creative process and product (as a lived event within INSIDE|OUTSIDE) of performance is an ecological shift. This framing re-positions agency as embedded in creative practice rather than belonging to individual people or places: agency is an enactment with/in community.

Within intergenerational projects that "enable powerful learning opportunities" (Cutcher & Boyd, 2018) for participants, community is established and created as a form of connection. Intergenerational projects take on many forms against varying pedagogic canvases, and the literature of intergenerational projects evidences a strong philosophy of community building through intergenerational exchange programmes, specifically between the elderly and young people: for example, young children singing for residents in aged care (MacCallum et al., 2010). Community is central to what constitutes best practice in intergenerational projects like this, including the impact on individuals and communities and how they can inform policies and practices about working with young people and maintaining the wellbeing of our older population in care. Within the intergenerational scholarship, there is co-making, such as collaboration with professional and non-professional child and adult performers, or families engaged in co-making in community arts-based installations at galleries and museums (Hopfinger, 2015). There is making art with children as an enterprise seen through a different intergenerational learning lens, specifically collaborative processes where adult and child complete a joint artwork as equal partners (Kouvou, 2016). In these contexts, the child teaches and learns from the adult, and the adult teaches and learns from the child. Our scholarly encounters have also allowed us to explore pre-service teachers or experienced teacher studies, finding these are often inspired by Reggio Emilia pedagogies that position young children as agentic creative artists who "thrive when making art with teachers who share their experience" and who, through a Vygotskian approach, acknowledge and extend what they do (Cutcher & Cook, 2016).

Through Kouvou (2016), we uncovered that "the adult's presence and endorsement of non-school thematology appeared to release a latent need in children to express themselves about and indeed to share themes, ideas and images probably forbidden or not encouraged in the classroom" (p. 288). Kouvou, who worked with pre-service early childhood teachers and children aged 5 to 6 years, engaged in collaborative drawing projects over a school term. Their project resulted in valuable learning about pedagogy for the pre-service teachers, shaping their view of how children can express themselves through drawing and the role that drawings they can play in facilitating such expression. Here we found an ally who had discovered that when you shift the agency of the practice from responder to artist as storyteller, place and sense maker, a comm*unity* can be formed.

If we bring you back into the fold of our guiding questions, we are troubled by how new ecologies are formed through our a/r/tography as practice-pedagogical research. This generative project within formal art education in schools and in initial teacher education can be the agent of change to create new ways of knowing how socially engaged community art education practices are *affective as* third spaces. Gupta (2015) suggests that third space pedagogy "requires us to move away from adopting a stance of 'one right way' and becoming more accepting of thinking and working within grey areas replete with ambiguities" (p. 268). Intergenerational a/r/tographical work is rendered through practices provoked by socio-cultural-material engagement and pedagogical change across sites. As such, this project extends from the university/formal school to community through its relational "pedagogical hybridity" into communities, homes, studios, backyards and bedrooms as sites of learning (Gupta, 2015, p. 269). The project as hybrid pedagogy is community art education, newly formed and co-created each year as a new cohort of beginning teachers and new upper primary students are folded into and with the project. This folding is substantially different from both artists' usual sites of "school-based art education" as it is not delivered, sited or taught. It is participatory: intergenerational artists come together to learn from and with each other about things that matter to them through a creative a/r/t exchange. In this affective and relational community art education project, renderings are performed within the event outside of formal learning sites by all artists who participate; they are exhibited and curated for and with comm*unity* to provide knowledge-sharing through material, digital, aesthetic, performed and textual concepts. As an event assemblage, the project's a/r/t-data or da(r)ta (Coleman, 2021) is entangled and intertwined between the sites (human, non-human and more-than-human) and sights (schools, community, homes, scholarly work).

At this time, we live within a new fold, a fold that has been unknown to many of us until recently. This fold is both local and global and has had a huge effect on artists and art educators, as an economic crisis that began with a health crisis continues to affect the precarity of this community. Because of the resilience that Australian artists and art educators in the pandemic of 2020 (Coleman & Selkrig, 2020) have continued to show us, this project uses the fold, the unfold and refold as a signifier of flight and change with times of crisis.

The fold is also a metaphor for our a/r/tographic pandemic shifts. COVID-19 closed any opportunity for school-based research in 2020, so we unfolded and refolded the paper while we rethought the project design. Our creative pandemic pedagogies that forced us to reimagine the Child + Adult Artist Response Project resulted in a meaningful pause to reflect upon our communities and then see how the project could be a catalyst for connection during a time of disconnect in lockdown. As a result, the project exchange during COVID-19 afforded us new folds, new pandemic-informed pedagogies that offered a renewed understanding of affect through the project as a site of community art education. It provided new art encounters in this transversal space and created new cites, sites and sights of and for practice (Konrad-East & Coleman, 2020). During quarantine and teaching from home, the pivot online (MacDonald & Coleman, 2020) required a break from data collection. The ethical responsibilities to our artists meant that we felt the need to offer the project as an artful inquiry, a community building, community art education site to consider how learning at home, how isolation and anxiety, could be a place to ponder and channel emotion through the creative process. We were able to see why "community arts and cultural development is distinct from other arts practice as it is the creative processes and relationships developed with community to make the art that defines it, not the art form or genre" (Australia Council, 2020). Within this truly artful exchange, participants became community artists, and each in that role became community art educators. This shift or turn is not possible within formal art education, where the roles of participants (artists, researchers or teachers) as active agents of change are hindered by hierarchies and systemic structures both ontological and epistemic.

INSIDE|OUTSIDE is a new opportunity every year, as these two words that sit side-by-side are filled with new ideas and concepts as political, social and cultural slippages occur. Do INSIDE|OUTSIDE reflect each other, like opposite walls or objects sitting close by? With 2020 unfolding as it was, we began new conversations with INSIDE|OUTSIDE, our communities of practice, ideas of a/r/t and each other about what INSIDE|OUTSIDE could be. We continued the dialogue of the artful encounter that was so rich in all senses, but as a/r/tists rather than as co-researchers or participants in a study. INSIDE|OUTSIDE now had new relevance as we all went home and inside. Stripping away the research and data collection left us a different kind of knowing: a digital, yet analogue, collaboratory studio community of practitioners. Collaboratory is a term often used in the sciences, a third space for co-design, co-creation and sci-curiosity (Ward Davies et al., 2020). As Wulf (1989) suggested, a collaboratory is a "center without walls, in which the nation's researchers can perform their research without regard to physical location, interacting with colleagues, accessing instrumentation, sharing data and computational resources, [and] accessing information in digital libraries" (p. 19). The pandemic and COVID-19 have shifted our sites of knowing and practice well beyond the sites of our schools, opening the walls of our learning spaces out into individual artists' homes and studios. We watched as the group collaboration unfolded and the dynamics/constellation of the group shifted.

In Victoria, Australia we had one of the longest and strictest lockdowns during 2020: 122 days in one stage-4 lockdown period. Our students across sectors learned at home, while educators created and designed remote emergency art education online and in take-home packs. As a result of this at-home but at-school affect, INSIDE|OUTSIDE created new conditions for the third space to be creative and new. This third space creates connections and comm*unity* between unknown artists, shifting the dynamics of exchange between the adult and child artists and the art educators involved who participated for the first time. Folding this chapter into flight and "rite-ing" the data as we have written has enabled us time to look back at this shift: to stop and reflect on how the project has always played a significant role in the unity of artists who have participated annually since 2016 in this conceptual, hybrid pedagogical and material provocation. With each shared artwork, we share how it has enacted a new encounter through a creative turn, into an act of community art education. Now, folds hold new stories.

## *Unfolding Art Making as Research*

The creative processes and relationships developed within the community that make the art define how our art making as research will unfold. Secondary visual art and design teachers in Victoria use a continuum curriculum: an F-10 iterative pedagogy that builds and scaffolds practice outcomes over time through teaching and learning as *artist and audience* through making and responding (Victorian Curriculum and Assessment Authority, 2017). This continuum of formal art education begins in the early years of schooling (F) and ends in year 10, at ages 15 to 16. This conceptual framing is developed through the *affect of being* within the project being asked to listen, act, respond, ideate, inquire and practise as an artist and audience member, enacting the curriculum from within before developing the capabilities to be on the outside and perform the curriculum as an artist–teacher. We could read the curriculum, embody the scholarship and develop informed evidence-based units of work and lessons that demonstrate what learning and teaching needs are in visual arts and design education. Alternatively, we can sit within the culture and community of the curriculum, critically engaged through the intersection, the entanglement of being *with* practice and becoming within a living inquiry as intercultural practitioners through encountering pedagogies. With/in the fold is a school-based artist-teacher who could read the curriculum, embody the scholarship and develop informed evidence-based units of work and lessons for children, demonstrating what learning and teaching needs are in visual arts and design. However, our teaching practices are founded in the Victorian Curriculum where we teach that our "students are both artist and audience in the Arts" (VCAA, 2017). As a/r/tographers we develop a deeper schema of how to teach and learn as artists and audience, as makers and responders through active participation with/in space, pedagogies, artistry, community dynamics and environments (Wright & Coleman, 2019).

## *Refolding*

An intergenerational a/r/tographical approach allows meanings to be co-created, shared and interpreted by participatory, interaction and engagement of the children and adults as individuals. In 2020, we have felt the *affect* (we use a multiplicitous series of contextual affects) with/in the creative turn (Harris, 2014) as all the roles shifted. We have folded deeper within INSIDE|OUTSIDE as these words took on greater meaning and significance in our lives and the roles of researchers, participants and artists blurred further while at home – a great equalizer in terms of the artist role felt during COVID. Through creative pandemic pedagogies, INSIDE|OUTSIDE shifted from a/r/tful provocation with intergeneration agents of change to new encounters in other third spaces, creating rich community energies that supported all participants to stay invested in the project.

The 2020 collection of a/r/tful responses and dialogue (https://doi.org/10.26188/13298579) exemplifies this folding and unfolding, refolding and folding of the plane as a metaphor. Within the project, there are no strict boundaries, structures or predetermined outcomes for a research project. We work within a flat ontology where renderings are performed, exhibited and curated with (comm)unity to cultivate knowledge-sharing between sites and sights. Our project is designed for encounters to reflect, encourage and not restrict the *becoming* creative agency of teachers or children. A project such as this, integrated within an initial teacher education programme, creates a space for the embodied and embedded (Braidotti, 2019) to emerge outside the fold. Our project with artist adults in a graduate school of education, who are *becoming* art teachers, with children *as* artists is rendered through practices provoked by socio-cultural-material engagement and pedagogical change. The teachers are accomplished artists and designers, with many representing galleries and active clients. During 2020, the folds (pedagogical, practice-based and led, playful, artful, educational and da(r)ta driven) were more intimate and responsive to each other. The artists knew they had to hold space for each other since limited access was available for generative making and knowing as artists. We witnessed new visual and textual folds emerge as artists wrote to each other and gifted works that afforded new community art education through *becoming with*: through shared experiences, an ethic of care and response-ability (Haraway, 2016) and reciprocity.

This act of making work as a *becoming* teacher is as new as it is for the child artists, imagining and thinking about the concept of INSIDE|OUTSIDE in a similar but very different space. Together, child and adult artists arrive within the project as an event assemblage where da(r)ta is entangled and intertwined between the sites and sights. Da(r)ta is time and place-based; these art-data sources are processes and products, artist statements and the a/r/tful community exchanges that through practice we see develop across the community. Placing a community art education project within the initial teaching education curriculum (in the second semester of the master's program) reifies the professional identity shift as the artist begins to fold researcher and teacher into their selves. We identify as a community of a/r/tist practitioners rather than individuals. Together we respond. Together we look at all of the works children produce, and we interpret, read, investigate, explore and share our thinking about the ideas that emerge from the children's artful experiences and interpretations of INSIDE|OUTSIDE. We look for the criticality, for the creative, and for the fun; we read for affect and that is often overwhelming. Every year, we are surprised because we are not looking at the art as teachers or researchers; we are looking *as* artists in relation, interacting in-relations that are always *becomings* (Hickey-Moody, 2013). Here in this site, the *becoming* teacher-fold reveals new teaching discussions and new ideas for how we design hybrid pedagogies that invite and initiate making and responding with young people as community.

## What We Found in the Folds

The project allows *becoming* teachers to see the intellectual capacity of young children to think and respond as artists, something that the usual hierarchical relations between teacher and child learner far too often overlook. The teachers and students, child and adult partners appear "to enter a liminal, transitional space where 'hierarchical orderings of values and social status' (Turner, 1981, p. 162) do not impinge on learning, but serve to catalyse critical, creative and artful thinking as practice" (Watkins et al., 2019).

As a speculative practice, we have found new ways of exploring community arts education in formal learning spaces within creative pandemic pedagogies to see the folds, refolds and unfolds creating change, as each year of da(r)ta is generated, responded to, collected, curated and refolded. Our da(r)ta and our practice with/in tells us we are seeing global and local concepts emerge, socio-cultural influences and political ideologies presented by both child and adult artists. Even this binary identifier of child and adult, inside and outside is a troubling one for us to encounter in the community and will continue to be post-COVID-19. Age, experience and credentials do not make an a/r/tist; rather, an artist knows how to see, look, feel and respond through a creative and critical lens. A/r/tists have a creative practice that enables a way of being and knowing that is artful, playful, curious, imaginative and critical: unbound by formal learning but driven by the affect of *being*. A/r/tists in this project can theorize and relationally position their work in discourse and dialogue. With further technical skills and life experience, this ability to *be* shifts.

## REFERENCES

Aleinikov, A. G. (2013). Creative pedagogy. In E. G. Carayannis (Ed.), *Encyclopedia of creativity, invention, innovation and entrepreneurship*. Springer. https://doi.org/10.1007/978-1-4614-3858-8_13

Australia Council for the Arts. (2020). *Community arts and cultural development*. https://www.australiacouncil.gov.au/artforms/community-arts-and-cultural-development/

Bickel, B. (2004). *From artist to a/r/tographer: An autoethnographic ritual inquiry into writing on the body* [Master's thesis]. The University of British Columbia, Vancouver, Canada. https://dx.doi.org/10.14288/1.0055045

Bickel, B., Springgay, S., Beer, R., Irwin, R. L., Grauer, K., & Xiong, G. (2011). A/r/tographic collaboration as radical relationality. *International Journal of Qualitative Methods*, 10(1), 86–102. https://doi.org/10.1177/160940691101000107

Braidotti, R. (2019). *Posthuman knowledge*. Polity Press.

Coleman, K. (2021). Doing digital and visual autoethnography. In T. E. Adams, S. H. Jones, & C. Ellis (Eds.), *Handbook of autoethnography* (2nd ed.). Routledge. https://doi.org/10.4324/9780429431760

Coleman, K., & MacDonald, A. (2020). What are artists and art educators teaching us about how we can conceive and deliver teacher professional learning into the future? In R. Ferdig, E. Baumgartner, R. Hartshorne, R. Kaplan-Rakowski, & C. Mouza (Eds.), *Teaching, technology, and teacher education during the COVID-19 pandemic: Stories from the field* (pp. 13–16). AACE – Association for the Advancement of Computing in Education. https://www.learntechlib.org/p/216903/

Coleman, K., & Selkrig, M. (2020, May 11). When the going gets tough, artists and arts educators get going. *EduResearchMatters Blog*, Australian Association and Research in Education. https://www.aare.edu.au/blog/?p=5463

Cutcher, A., & Boyd, W. (2018). Preschool children, painting and palimpsest: Collaboration as pedagogy, practice and learning. *International Journal of Art & Design*, 37(1), 53–64. https://doi.org/10.1111/jade.12113

Cutcher, A., & Cook, P. (2016). One must also be an artist: Online delivery of teacher education. *International Journal of Education & the Arts*, 17(13), 1–18. http://www.ijea.org/v17n13/

Gupta, A. (2015). Pedagogy of third space: A multidimensional early childhood curriculum. *Policy Futures in Education*, 13(2), 260–272. https://doi.org/10.1177/1478210315579540

Haraway, D. J. (2016). *Staying with the trouble: Making kin in the Chthulucene*. Duke University Press.

Harris, A. M. (2014). *The creative turn: Toward a new aesthetic imaginary*. Sense. http://dx.doi.org/10.1007/978-94-6209-551-9

Healy, S., Coleman, K., Johnson Sallis, R., & Belton, A. (2022). Encountering a pedagogy of the world in a university setting. In S. Riddle, A. Heffernan, & D. Bright (Eds.), *New perspectives on education for democracy creative responses to local and global challenges*. Routledge.

Healy, S., & Mulcahy, D. (2020). Pedagogic affect: Assembling an affirming ethics. *Pedagogy, Culture & Society*, 29(4), 555–572. https://doi.org/10.1080/14681366.2020.1768581

Hickey-Moody, A. (2013). *Youth, arts, and education: Reassembling subjectivity through affect*. Routledge. https://doi.org/10.4324/9780203855829

Hopfinger, S. (2015). Wilding performance. *Performing Ethos: International Journal of Ethics in Theatre & Performance*, 5(1–2), 137–144. https://doi.org/10.1386/peet.5.1-2.137_1

Irwin, R. L. (2008). A/r/tography. In L. M. Given (Ed.), *The SAGE encyclopedia of qualitative research methods*. Sage. https://dx.doi.org/10.4135/9781412963909

Irwin, R. L., & O'Donoghue, D. (2012). Encountering pedagogy through relational art practices. *International Journal of Art and Design Education, 31*(3), 221–236. https://doi.org/10.1111/j.1476-8070.2012.01760.x

Konrad-East, E., & Coleman, K. (2020). *C+AARP INSIDE|OUTSIDE Response 1, 2020*. University of Melbourne. https://doi.org/10.26188/13298579

Kouvou, O. (2016). Drawing with children: An experiment in assisted creativity. *International Journal of Art & Design Education, 35*(2), 275–290. https://doi.org/10.1111/jade.12056

Leander, K. M., Phillips, N. C., & Taylor, K. H. (2010). The changing social spaces of learning: Mapping new mobilities. *Review of Research in Education, 34*(1), 329–394. https://doi.org/10.3102/0091732X09358129

MacCallum, J., Palmer, D., Wright, P., Cumming-Potvin, W., Northcote, J., Brooker, M., & Tero, C. (2010). Australian perspectives: Community building through intergenerational exchange programs. *Journal of Intergenerational Relationships, 8*(2), 113–127. https://doi.org/10.1080/15350771003741899

MacDonald, A., & Coleman, K. (2020). Art education: Using new resources and skills. In *Teacher*. Australian Council for Educational Research. https://www.teachermagazine.com.au/articles/art-education-using-new-resources-and-skills

Morris, J., & Coleman, K. S. (2019). Fluid identities in multiple cultural practices: How practice changes becoming teachers' perceptions of themselves. *Journal of Artistic & Creative Education, 13*(1), 1–14. https://jace.online/index.php/jace/article/view/196

Orlikowski, W. J. (2002). Knowing in practice: Enacting a collective capability in distributed organizing. *Organization Science, 13*(3), 249–273. https://doi.org/10.1287/orsc.13.3.249.2776h

Sawyer, R. K. (2015). A call to action: The challenges of creative teaching and learning. *Teachers College Record, 117*, 1–34.

Schatzki, T. R., Knorr-Cetina, K., & von Savigny, E. (Eds.). (2001). *The practice turn in contemporary theory*. Routledge. https://doi.org/10.4324/9780203977453

Turner, V. (1981). Social dramas and stories about them. In W. J. T. Mitchell (Ed.), *On narrative* (pp. 137–164). University of Chicago Press.

Victorian Curriculum and Assessment Authority. (2017). *Victorian curriculum: The arts*. https://victoriancurriculum.vcaa.vic.edu.au/the-arts/introduction/about-the-arts

Ward Davies, A., Godic, B., Healy, S., Coleman, K., Nguyen-Robertson, C., Wouters, N., Urlini, J., & Shubsmith, J. (2020). Post studio methods: Being scicurious as a site for research. *Journal of Artistic and Creative Education, 14*(2). https://jace.online/index.php/jace/article/view/486

Watkins, M., & Coleman, K. S. (2019). An artful experiment: The Child+Adult Art Response Project. In *InSEA World Congress Proceedings* (pp. 792–798). University of British Columbia. https://www.insea.org/docs/inseapublications/proceedings/vancouver/PROCEEDINGS-small.pdf

Watkins, M., Grant, R., Coleman, K., & Meager, N. (2019). Entering the liminal through the side door: A "Child+Adult Art Response Project" as portal for student voice and deep thinking. *International society for education through art*. (InSEA) EPublications. https://doi.org/10.24981/978-LTA2018

Wright, S., & Coleman, K. (2019). studioFive–A site for teaching, research and engagement in Australian arts education. In C. H. Lum, & E. Wagner (Eds.), *Arts education and cultural diversity: Policies, research, practices and critical perspectives* (pp. 115–133). Springer. https://doi.org/10.1007/978-981-13-8004-4

Wulf, W. A. (1989). The national collaboratory – A white paper. In J. Lederberg, & K. Uncaphar (Eds.), *Towards a national collaboratory: Report of an invitational workshop at the Rockefeller University*, March 17–18 (Appendix A). National Science Foundation, Directorate for Computer and Information Science Engineering.

# 4

# "Making University": The Role of Corporeality, Matter and Physical Spaces to Create a Sense of Community

*Sara Carrasco Segovia*

This chapter focuses on the role of the body in initial teacher education and emerges from research conducted with a group of students pursuing their arts education degrees (five women and three men between 20 and 27 years old) in a Chilean public university. From participants' stories, it was possible to realize how human and non-human connections (students, matter, architecture and physical spaces) help create another kind of knowledge related to the notion of community and "making university." Such knowledge engenders a public and subversive pedagogy that deals with art, education, community, affects and corporeality. In addition, these participants' stories highlight that the practice of community arts creates and reinforces social dynamics and facilitates other ways of thinking and doing by means of community relations.

The expression "community art," which emerged in the 1970s mainly in the United States and the United Kingdom, described artistic practices involving public collaboration and participation in the artwork or performance that attempt to achieve social improvement through art (Palacios, 2009). In this research, the notion of community art education transgresses the initial boundaries demarcated by the importance of the artwork's social context and the implications for the audience to connect it with a broad notion of pedagogy, art and research. According to Fernando Hernández (2019), "the notion of art has been expanded" (p. 65); thus, artistic practices can blur the notion of authorship and territory and provide meaningful strategies for arts-based research (ABR). Pedagogy is understood as the production of identities, the ways in which we learn to understand ourselves in conjunction with the world. In this sense, any artistic activity is pedagogical because it produces identities (Hernández, 2012). Therefore, pedagogy is understood both from a schooling perspective as formal or institutional education as well as from a community art perspective, which connects education with everyday life.

As an art teacher and a researcher, I find community art education helps me develop onto-epistemic-methodological and ethical perspectives: engaging students in learning experiences based on the exploration and solution of real problems in their daily environments, and in turn politicizing memory by sharing stories (St. Georges, 2018). Due to the relevance of stories and sharing experience, for this study, I opted to employ fragments of what the participants said with ideas and theoretical resonances emerging about body and the notion of community based on the stories. The participants for this study included eight students in their third year of art teacher education. Specifically, in this chapter, I argue some topics with the ideas of four participants – Rafael, Camila, Carla and Patricio – who provide other perspectives and counterarguments.

During the investigation, it was possible to observe how the body concept expands to different territories of the educational experience beyond the classroom, traditional academic knowledge and cognitive understanding of the learning process. The study also revealed different connections among bodies, physical spaces and materiality that constitute teacher education. Thus, the body is constituted as an entanglement of human and non-human forces with its own agency. A performative notion of the body breaks into and moves within several spheres of the educational spectrum, at both personal and community levels and beyond formal, institutional and/or academic settings. In this investigation, the body is understood beyond its symbolic, socio-cultural and biological sense where only human forces are working. I use Grosz's concept of "corporeality" (Grosz, 1987, 1994, 2004) to describe this point of view of the body as a process that exists in its own constitution, as a performative action that displays zones of proximity to the world.

In this context, the notion of "community" embodies feelings of "belonging" with respect to matter and physical spaces of the university (gardens, walls, murals, buildings, etc.). At the same time, this investigation involved different methods of appropriating the university and multiple ways that bodies can inhabit the institutions, generating "ways of thinking about human experience as intra-acting with aspects of the world that we classify as non-human" (Hickey-Moody & Willcox, 2019, p. 2). In this vein, art not only acts as a powerful motivator for citizen participation and social change to face inequalities and challenges (especially low-income students in this case) but also as an example of how to be in harmony with the agency of all matter. An inadvertent effect is that students may also consider how "pedagogy can be constituted as material, affective and in rhythm" (Springgay & Zaliwska, 2019, p. 37).

In line with the connections among corporeality, spaces, matter, community and belonging, I wondered: Do students connect with matter that is part of their educational process? How do bodies that make up "the student body" inhabit institutional spaces? How does the body engage with "otherness" and spaces? Do the students create a sense of community that goes beyond academic experience? What roles do a strong sense of community and belonging play in the knowledge construction and learning process of these students? These questions, in relation to the students' goal of becoming teachers of art, open lines of thought about the notion of body and corporeality, reflecting the intra-actions and revealing how students are situated within university settings.

The practice of community arts creates and reinforces social dynamics and facilitates other ways of thinking and doing. From the feminist new materialist theories, making reference to Grosz's concept of "corporeality," "diffraction" (Barad, 2007; Haraway, 1997; Sehgal, 2014), "intra-action" (Barad, 2012), "entanglement" (Lather & St. Pierre, 2013) and the importance of the "matter" (Barad, 2007, 2012), I propose an essential question: How do these theories help us to think in a broader way about the body and art education, and why we should focus on fostering a strong sense of community within the world of higher education?

I present this chapter as an open space to rethink and reimagine artistic practices and the community spaces created by our corporeality, considering a pedagogy that remains in harmony with different forces.

## *Corporality and Matter: Subversive Actions and Ways to Appropriate Spaces*

Bodies are activated within institutional community spaces using different subversive actions and ways of appropriating those spaces where students often feel so alienated. In addition, bodies reveal social, cultural and political impacts, and it is possible to identify the position of students inside the institution as well as their ways of finding their own place in the university. As Planella (2006) states, "bodies begin to take on an architectural and projective dimension from the physical spaces that constitute it" (p. 231, translation by the author). Likewise, the roles of experience, affects/emotions and corporeality become fundamental because learning and knowledge go beyond the classroom. As Rafael comments, "Spaces stiffen our bodies so much. They are training us how to operate inside a cubicle. It is not an innocent action" (second round of interviews, 2014).

Rafael talks about traces that traditional education leaves on bodies: for example, by the furniture used to control different educational spaces to school the body. In this statement, the forces involved respond to the different influences that formal education has on the construction of corporeality. These influences affect the body and are part of the learning process. As Rafael suggests, personal stories reveal enlightening questions about the body and the territories it occupies within teacher education, where physical spaces and materiality play an important role.

In this network of interactions, students not only appropriate the institutional spaces but also create a sense of community and belonging to find their place in the university, which does not always respond to their needs and/or current world demands. Hickey-Moody and Willcox (2019) present community-focused, intra-active, ABR strategies for interrogating and understanding expressions of community and belonging, proposing that "each community not only diffracts their differences through art, but intra-acts with the other through an on-going time space that is concerned with the ethics of understanding and ultimately with becoming enmeshed as a community" (p. 18). In this process, a feeling of belonging is engendered when students embrace institutional spaces they do not always feel are their own through creative and artistic expressions.

Even though several examples about co-habiting locations and producing artistic expressions emerged from this research, in this chapter, I focus on three ways in which bodies are put into action and inhabit the university environment through subversive activities to appropriate institutional space: (1) the use of gardens and outdoor areas as a powerful force in the corporeal constitution and process of becoming teachers; (2) the use of public/private spaces through social and political murals and paintings and (3) the action of the body on campus through subversive acts of resistance and student protests.

To visualize Barad's notion of intra-action involved in this student community, I created collages, an assembly of images as knowledge creation, to present physical spaces of the university and unveil how participants placed themselves in these spaces. Also, I explore audio/visual evidence and participants' stories to create new data from the fieldwork. As Hickey-Moody and Willcox (2019) note, "indeed, creation is the object of the research process, rather than discovering something that is 'there' to be known [...]. This comes to show that data generated and collected through fieldwork is co-created by the fieldwork assemblage" (p. 5).

## First Way to Appropriate Spaces:
## Gardens and Outdoor Areas of the University

The constitution of my corporeality has been influenced by university environment and the feeling of community raised by sharing in the outdoor areas of the university, as the wide gardens [...] the relationships that I established with my classmates due to the spaces was more significant than academic knowledge.

(Carla, second round of interviews, 2014)

In Carla's statement, it is possible to observe the relationship of the body, matter and physical spaces: namely, the importance of the body's proximity to the world (Rogowska-Stangret, 2017) in the process of becoming an art teacher. The roles of experience, affective relationships and sense of community are fundamental to educational processes. As Atkinson (2012) notes, knowledge and education are understood beyond the classroom, and pedagogy needs to act against the state and open ways towards corporeal and affective learning which go beyond the cognitive dimension.

Carla's statement reveals that university gardens are more than simple spaces of transition. They act as essential elements in social relations and the sense of community that students build as part of their training as future art teachers. Community spaces where interests and other kinds of learning take place expand students' understanding of what constitutes knowledge. Therefore, the sense of community is related to the empowering of a body that resists and cannot be controlled; the feeling of community has to do with new ways of encountering social relations that enable delocalized or deterritorialized communities (Freire, 1993). Here, performances like the circus and music take possession of the institutional space; art is the way to be in harmony with the agency of all matter (Springgay & Zaliwska, 2019).

## Second Way to Appropriate Spaces:
## Social and Political Murals and Paintings

The participants noted diverse ways of inhabiting institutional spaces: for instance, appropriating them and connecting with matter through wall paintings and murals of a socio-political nature. Figure 4.1 indicates elements and symbols marking the political and social positioning of the students: the hammer and sickle representing the union of workers and normally the communist movement, the red star with five points alluding to the proletarian class and workers, as well as allusions to Indigenous people of South America, the Chilean flag and more. Note a slogan that says: *De la sala de clase a la lucha de clases* or in translation, "from the classroom to the class fight."

Since 2006, Chile has been internationally known for massive mobilizations of primary, secondary and higher education students (with the support of teachers). The purpose is to make visible the deep inequalities reproduced by the social and educational system and to highlight the role played by the state in this matter.

FIGURE 4.1: Appropriation of physical spaces through murals. Assembly of images: elementary education building, wall of the soccer field, entrance hut, hall of the Fine Arts Department. Photo by Sara Carrasco (2017).

Therefore, murals as art practices open a path for new materiality as a way of highlighting inequalities and making a social difference.

This university is known for the progressive ideas of both students and faculty and for resisting traditional and conservative ideas. As Patricio points out:

> Here we are united by a feeling of politic disconformity and revolutionary ideas […]. We are a great community linked by these ideas even if we are from different degrees. The different buildings are connected through the gardens. Since the campus is huge, it is also in the gardens and outdoor spaces where people meet and connect through community actions, such as eating, selling different things, playing music, dancing, or painting murals, among others.
>
> (First round of interviews, 2014)

In Patricio's statement (also see Figure 4.2), it is possible to see the strong positions that students take in relation to the university, as well as the actions they take to appropriate these spaces and find their place in the university. Political forces, social struggle and educational demands are very present in their imagination as teachers; hence, the intra-action of these forces alludes to social commitment, political actions, agency and the body as a space of resistance. This intra-action shows an intention to fight and work for a common good and find a balance in ways of doing, being and living as future teachers. Such action arises mainly from students' and teachers' discontent about the socio-economic and educational conditions they experience daily. Quality education in Chile is still a privilege, not a human right.

Planella (2006) explains that territories and scenography help to implement corporeal pedagogies because it is in the physical space where pedagogy configures the presence of bodies and sets the body's subjectivities and objectivities. Hence, community art education connects with pedagogy, art and research as a producer of identities related to how we inhabit the world. In this sense, community art education not only connects education with everyday life but also produces intra-actions with non-human forces as physical spaces and matter. This study presents strategies to interrogate and understand expressions of community and students' feeling of belonging by forefronting the vital importance of the body as central in learning processes, as well as identifying those creative methods as ways of co-habiting institutional spaces and creating communities.

## Third Way to Appropriate Spaces: Subversive Actions of Resistance and Students' Protests

The wide outdoor spaces and the configuration of the buildings in this university, combined with the political and social context that has historically marked this institution, have helped to determine the possibilities, the bodily dispositions and the different kinds of appropriation that students exercise in these spaces through specific practices such as student protests and subversive actions.

The opinions offered by some of the participants argue about the strength of the students to rebel, confront and subvert everything that confronts their political and social ideologies. These acts are simultaneously connected to teachers' work, understood from the point of view of commitment and social struggle. It is precisely through the student's protests and subversive actions, as well as the use and appropriation of spaces by inhabiting them, that students can find deinstitutionalized practices to defend what may be described as their besieged territory (Bauman, 1999, p. 71). Likewise, these actions seek a desire for a new order, producing fractures with the everyday and, especially, renewing and restoring social bonds.

In Figure 4.2, it is possible to see a collage of different images about several attempts of subversion and understanding of the resistant body beyond the normative and the available systems of meanings, to build a new language that resets its own limits within the prevailing hegemonic culture (McLaren, 1997). At once, these visual narratives embody the diffractive body, where education and matter are part of community-making. The dialogue with community

COMMUNITY ARTS EDUCATION

FIGURE 4.2: Appropriation of physical spaces through protests. Assembly of images: on-campus protests with hooded university students. Photo by Sara Carrasco (2017).

members, physical spaces and non-human forces have shaped these students' lives. The reciprocity achieved through such dialogue is in line with all the constituent elements of the learning process and educational spectrum.

## "Making University": The Sense of Community and Belonging

This campus includes large and extensive gardens, natural areas, typical flora and fauna of the space, vast open areas and large built structures. It has soccer fields, music rooms, several event rooms, kindergartens for the children of students and staff, libraries, dining room, bars and more. Its wide expanse frames the sensation of a place where it is possible to "make (create) university": that is to say, a space open to the diversity of artistic and cultural activities, making it possible to share beyond the classroom and the traditional institutional architectures in a more holistic way with the university community. The students who participated in my study share feelings of "community" and "belonging" as products of human and non-human interactions. At the same time, it is possible to notice "how some community art practices make way for a new materiality of communities" (Hickey-Moody & Willcox, 2019, p. 2). Accordingly, creative methods are a way of being entangled with communities.

Barad (2012) refers to an entangled state of agencies that goes beyond how we traditionally conceive of agency, subjectivity and individualism. For Barad, this entanglement requires an analysis that allows us to theorize relations between social and natural worlds as a continuum: that is to say, how people interact with matter and how one is transformed by the other, understanding that "the forces at work in the materialization of bodies are not only social and the bodies produced are not all humans" (Barad, 2007, p. 225). Barad's theories suggest that we exist only in relation to our environments; more than this, they allow us to see our research as open-ended ways of changing environments and changing people. However, it is relevant to remember that the feeling of community not only develops in a physical and delimited place but within the new forms of social and virtual relationships, where the possibility of delocalized communities has appeared.

In the Chilean system, education is a commodity, and the student is a consumer (Piussi, 2010). It is marked by a segregationist nature, reducing the right of citizens to access public, secular, quality education. Therefore, as art teachers and researchers, we must recognize and socially validate the importance of areas that constitute educational systems in a broader way. We need to think how indispensable universities are for community life, understood as a network of connections where community art practices play a key role.

Community art education is a professional sector in which the arts are used as methods for engagement and empowerment, especially within marginalized communities and vulnerable sectors of society. In this research, the arts provide a personal space for students to explore their creativity and authentic self-expression as resistance practices while at the same time highlighting social inequalities. In this way, we seek to address social and cultural issues relevant to students and provide an avenue for them to improve their well-being while creating a sense of community within a formal educational institution. Community art education is continually expanding because it promotes an onto-epistemic-methodological and ethical perspective: connecting education with life by engaging students in learning experiences based on personal and local experiences. By means of artistic expressions, students remain connected with the world, finding answers to real problems in their daily environments by politicizing memory and sharing stories (St. Georges, 2018).

## REFERENCES

Atkinson, D. (2012). Contemporary art and art education: The new, emancipation and truth. *International Journal of Art and Design Education, 31*(2), 5–19.

Barad, K. (2007). *Meeting the universe halfway: Quantum physics and the entanglement of matter and meaning*. Duke University Press.

Barad, K. (2012). Thinking with intra-action. In A. Y. Jackson & L. A. Mazzei (Eds.), *Thinking with theory in qualitative research: Viewing data across multiple perspectives* (1st ed., pp. 118–136). Routledge.

Bauman, Z. (1999). *In search of politics*. University Press.

Freire, P. (1993). *Pedagogía de la esperanza: un reencuentro con la pedagogía del oprimido* [Pedagogy of hope: Encountering with the oppressed pedagogy]. Siglo XXI.

Grosz, E. (1987). Notes toward a corporeal feminism. *Australian Feminist Studies, 5*(1), 1–15.

Grosz, E. (1994). *Volatile bodies: Toward a corporeal feminism*. Indiana University Press.

Grosz, E. (2004). *The nick of time: Politics, evolution, and the untimely*. Duke University Press.

Haraway, D. (1997). *Modest_Witness@Second_Millennium.FemaleMan_Meets_OncoMouse: Feminism and Technoscience*. Routledge.

Hernández, F. (2012, April 20). *Pedagogías de la cultura visual: expandir el saber a partir de crear relaciones* [Pedagogies of visual culture: Expanding knowledge by creating relationships] [Conference session]. Casa Nacional del Bicentenario, Buenos Aires. https://casadelbicentenario.cultura.gob.ar/

Hernández, F. (2019). Researching the unknown through arts-based research to promote pedagogical imagination. In A. Sinner, R. L. Irwin, & J. Adams (Eds.), *Provoking the field: International perspectives on visual arts PhDs* (pp. 57–68). Intellect.

Hickey-Moody, A., & Willcox, M. (2019). Entanglements of difference as community togetherness: Faith, art, and feminism. *Social Sciences, 8*(264), 1–21. https://doi.org/10.3390/socsci8090264

Lather, P., & St. Pierre, E. (2013). Post-qualitative research. *International Journal of Qualitative Studies in Education, 26*(6), 629–633. https://doi.org/10.1080/09518398.2013.788752

McLaren, P. (1997). *Pedagogía critica y cultura depredadora. Políticas de oposición en la era posmoderna* [Critical pedagogy and predatory culture. Politics of opposition in the postmodern era]. Paidós Ibérica.

Palacios, A. (2009). El arte comunitario: origen y evolución de las prácticas artísticas colaborativas. Arteterapia [Community art: Origin and evolution of collaborative art practices]. *Papeles de arteterapia y educación artística para la inclusión social, 4*, 197–211.

Piussi, A. (2010). Universidad: hacer de la crisis una oportunidad [University: Transforming the crisis to an opportunity]. *Rizoma freireano, 7*, 1–8.

Planella, J. (2006). *Cuerpo y Educación* [Body and education]. Desclée de Brouwer.

Rogowska-Stangret, M. (2017). Corpor(e)al cartographies of new materialism: Meeting the elsewhere halfway. *The Minnesota Review, 2017*(88), 59–68.

Sehgal, M. (2014). Diffractive propositions: Reading Alfred North Whitehead with Donna Haraway and Karen Barad. *Parallax*, *20*(3), 188–201. https://doi.org/10.1080/13534645.2014.927625

Springgay, S., & Zaliwska, Z. (2019). Learning to be affected: Matters of pedagogy in the artists' soup kitchen. In J. Ringrose, K. Warfield, & S. Zarabadi (Eds.), *Feminist posthumanisms, new materialisms and education* (pp. 34–46). Routledge.

St. Georges, D. (2018). Reflections of the tide: The adventure of the woman and the sea. In A. Sinner, R. L. Irwin, & T. Jokela (Eds.), *Visually provoking: Dissertations in art education* (pp. 201–215). Lapland University Press.

# 5

# I Wish You a Good Life: Embedding Intergenerational Learning Into Pre-Service Education Through Art, Community and Environment

*Geraldine Burke*

"Our Waste, Our Place, Our Actions" brought pre-service teachers, University of the Third Age (U3A) (seniors) and primary school children together across institutional, generational and formal/informal educational divides. This project was part of an Art-Reach experience embedded in a pre-service teacher education unit at Monash University, Melbourne, entitled "Art, Community and Environment": a unit prompting pre-service teachers to explore changing notions of art, community and environment through the porosity of time and place (Barad, 2017; Malone, 2017). The pre-service teachers investigate colonial, Indigenous and contemporary vantage points, simultaneously moving from objective, subjective and intersubjective ways of knowing through art.

From the outset, the seniors were keen to participate in our project – a friendly event where generations hosted each other at various institutions while connecting through art. They explored the ways plastic, everyday waste, wildlife, land and sea intersect as environmental concerns in our region (see Figure 5.1), and how creative action builds awareness and provokes further action through art. This place-making project shared intergenerational "waste wisdom" as we – the participants and the author (an immersed arts-based researcher and university lecturer) – investigated throw-away materials sourced from everyday life and their potential to affect our local wildlife/environment. Simultaneously, participants created individual and shared artworks that prompted creative waste possibilities and opened conversations about waste proliferation, recycling versus refusal and lifecycle thinking. A primary connecting belief for all participants was that

FIGURE 5.1: Exploring our domestic waste and how waste travels to local beaches. Photos by Geraldine Burke (2019).

wildlife in our coastal region (Mornington Peninsula, Victoria, Australia) has the right to waste-free life and that our waste behaviours can help realize this potential or not. One child participant summed up this sentiment when she titled her artwork of local wildlife "I wish you a good life."

In making art and sharing stories and experiences, the 120 participants combined reflections and questions arising from artworks and ponderings about waste to inform a series of group e-posters (https://bit.ly/2L0QLk9). These resources spread the news of our project's learning across institutions and online as our micro-actions rippled into larger actions and change. For example, the seniors reported more favourable views of local school children on account of the project and marvelled at the children's creative capacities. The children were moved to write to their local shopping centre requesting reusable plastic packaging in stores while suggesting waste reduction strategies. Meanwhile, pre-service teachers developed practical know-how in planning, teaching and reviewing intergenerational teaching strategies that could translate into future teaching opportunities.

The posters live on as resources for future students, while the project was a finalist in the Sustainable Communities: Victorian Tidy Town (2020) competition. Through regional sharing sessions, the project was showcased to the larger community so that other towns and communities could become aware of each other's work. These ripples indicate how the project affected immediate participants and how its enduring resources continue to inform a broader community. Future pre-service teachers, school children, seniors and community groups can learn about the project through posters and video, and pre-service teachers can call on their experience to run future intergenerational community art projects.

## *Learning in an Art, Community and Environment Unit*

Foundational to the art, environment and community unit undertaken by the pre-service teachers is an exploration of how art reveals attitudes to community and place. For instance, they explore how colonial artists illustrated the Australian landscape at a remove, while Indigenous approaches to place and "Country" are represented as a way of "being" and "caring" (Bird-Rose, 2017, p. 38) through kinship, where "living (is) a part of networks of relationships" (p. 43). As Bird-Rose (2017) suggests:

> Country [...] is multi-dimensional: it consists of people, animals, plants, Dreamings, the dead and the yet to be born, underground, earth, soils, minerals and waters, surface water and air. There is a sea Country and land Country; sky Country too. Country has origins and a future; it exists both in and through time. [...] Country has its own story, its people and everything else are part of it, and from generation to generation, the story is not over.
>
> (pp. 37–38)

Through this juxtapositional learning, pre-service teachers rethink their position on art/community/environment as intersecting concepts. Post-ecological views of art education are informed by "ecological, holistic, and place-responsive perspectives toward learning" (Sameshima & Greenwood, 2015, p. 166). This view sits within a growing awareness of our implication in the Anthropocene (Crutzen, 2006). Importantly, this sense of deep and felt non-human connection to place/time/people is reiterated each teaching session as we increase our respect for the local environment, our understanding of Country and the entanglements that Country holds with our art, community, culture and heritage.

For this project, the aim was to flip dominant views of the community by embracing human/non-human intersections (our waste, our place and our actions). Instead of thinking of community as just a social unit with shared interests and locale, we considered our community to include humans, local wildlife and our waste. In this conception, community is imagined as intra-acting with and being in common with the social and ecological, and in so doing, positions the human as being in relation with the non-human.

## Upcycling, Waste Possibilities and Community Action

Li et al. (2016) suggest that plastic waste "commonly found in water bodies and beach sediment [...] originates from two major sources, land-based and ocean-based, with domestic, industrial and fishing activities being the most important contributors" (section 7). Our project asked participants to reconsider everyday waste from their domestic environments for creative repurposing while also prompting intergenerational conversations about waste options. We asked what creative repurposing we could undertake to explore upcycled potentials for waste and rethink waste as a valued resource for art making, rather than as a land and sea hazard. This led to curious, playful engagement with plastic and waste as a material that has expressive and functional attributes. Participants also sourced and explored safe ways to work with domestic waste and industrial offcuts so materials were clean, sanitized in environmentally appropriate ways and considered for possible allergies. Meanwhile, washed-up, broken-down detritus from local beaches was displayed after being sanitized; participants could touch these objects wearing gloves but did not use these pieces. Single-use plastic bottles, cardboard packaging, old CDs, plastic cutlery, unwanted coat-hangers, waste cardboard, old t-shirts and wooden offcuts were assembled into a range of artworks. Such projects prompt valuable inquiries into the meaning and purpose of art as well as our responsibility for ethical and future-orientated use of materials.

## Sharing Our Waste

While making art together, we shared what kind of upcycling actions (or otherwise) took place across our everyday lives, our different generations, institutions and communities. We considered what waste products could be revalued (or not) through creative upcycling and how we could reduce community waste by refusing excess, by not using or acquiring items in our daily lives that could become waste. Through making and sharing intergenerational insights, we reflected upon waste and its impacts from multiple perspectives. We discussed the merits and problems of upcycling versus recycling, and shared ideas and practices about preventing, refusing, reducing, reusing, remaking, repairing, repurposing, restoring, recycling, redesigning, respecting, remembering, upcycling and life cycle thinking. Our approach positioned waste as a vital material (Bennett, 2010) that we called back into our creative repertoire to problem-pose and problem-solve (Harris & de Bruin, 2017, p. 66) potentialities and affordances of plastic and waste for a creative possibility (see Figure 5.2). Instead of waste being out-of-sight and out-of-mind,

FIGURE 5.2: Exploring upcycling possibilities with waste and throw-away materials. Photos by Melanie Attard (2019).

we rediscovered the properties of waste through material thinking (Bolt, 2013) and playful immersion (Burke, 2016).

Our hope for this and future arts-based research projects is that art making agitates boundaries between teaching/learning/environment/community/formal/informal contexts. Thus, the requirements of each intra-act articulate in mutually revealing ways. Art making is critical to this approach because it represents a boundary-crossing event (Akkerman & Bakker, 2011). The liveliness of its affect activates the potential for shifts towards pedagogies with allodial properties named by MaRhea (2018, p. 1) and the potential for greater ecological awareness and group wisdoms (Sternberg, 2019, pp. v–vi).

## Community Envisioned in Our Place-Based Intergenerational Art Project

Our project sought to develop an understanding of community through the porosity (Barad, 2017; Malone, 2017) of art making with broad-based, regional, local knowledge: by understanding how humans are implicated in other animals, plants and entities like waste that materially course through us (Neimanis, 2017). Through art and shared narratives, participants considered their community's impact on the environment, how local wildlife can be adversely affected by a community's waste and how, in turn, wildlife can be considered part of the community in which we live. In this way, we positioned the notion of "community" as a social/ecological unit of living entities (human/wildlife) that share commonality through place and the norms and challenges that waste brings.

We considered our sense of shared community and place in terms of human/wildlife/waste intersections, an approach "[i]n line with post humanist research practices [that] offer a new ethics of engagement for education by including the nonhuman in questions about who matters and what counts" (Taylor, 2016, p. 9). When we question "the constitutive role played by humanist dominant paradigms, methodologies and methods in working as actualizers of normative procedures" (p. 9), we are more able to think through the dolphin who swallows the plastic bag and the life of the plastic bag that connects community with dolphins. We are able to think of ourselves-dolphin-plastic bag as a series of intra-active nodes forming our sense of place and wellbeing of non-humans within it.

## Emerging Insights and Research Provocations

### A/r/tographic

From an a/r/tographic viewpoint, the plethora of intra-actions (LeBlanc & Irwin, 2019, p. 5) enabled fertile inquiry through rich material thinking with and about living and non-living things. Of interest and inspiration for us regarding a/r/tography is positioning art making as an energizing force for transforming thinking and actions. From the outset, the anticipation of art making was a source of connectivity, pleasure, empathy, goodwill and aesthetic engagement with daily life. The art making was an abundant and central experience which deliberately positioned all participants as artists/researchers/teachers, no matter their age/status. Whether through shared vulnerability, similarities, interests or differences, our art making together "with" waste enabled "cultivated, patient, sensory attentiveness to nonhuman forces" (Bennett, 2010, p. xiv) to gesture towards "thing power"

(p. 6) and reimagine our waste as an actant that moves beyond a status as an object to "aliveness, constituting the outside of our own experience" (p. xiv). Latour (2005) helps us see the importance of actants (like waste) as part of networks of shifting elements interconnecting to affect the system. Our waste as actant incited us to explore non-living inter-relationships while providing all-too-available material for abundant art making. In turn, our art making generated goodwill among participants through mutually supportive non-judgemental assisting and appraising. For the pre-service teachers, an expansive and life-affirming appraisal of children's art making as relational was a priority, in conjunction with the success criteria of our local curriculum requirements (Victorian Curriculum and Assessment Authority, 2019).

Seniors, children and pre-service teachers engaged in the process, production and event of art making. Their rich art making and storying were captured through art/text combinations. Participants also moved beyond this stage as their lived, processed, produced, (re)processed and (re)produced experiences provoked questions and prompted action. Through making 35 digital posters, participants engaged in creative analysis (Burke, 2018, p. 124) that enabled reflexive and shared (re)communication. In this way, participants curated and shared the essence and message of their learning while experiencing a/r/tographically inspired art/text communications. As an immersed arts-based researcher and facilitator of the project, I also curated a further set of posters to share project processes with this community and others as ongoing resources for future waste/place/action/learning. This sharing of resources was integral to the project's pedagogical strategies and provoked new understandings of suitable methods for community art practice.

## Waste and Materiality

Garber (2019) called attention to transformative potential in the way makers and learners live when "thickened experiences" and "first-hand sensitivities to making" (p. 7) help them find underlying "causal structures" (Barad, 2007, p. 140). This was true of our project: exploring how waste is entwined in our places and actions created space for shifts in thinking that rippled into further action. The making events, instructions and experiences were designed to develop attentiveness to waste and its properties/potentials/ubiquity while building participants' creative, environmental and material knowledge through art.

One of the most important qualities of our intergenerational, community-based pedagogy is to nurture: to enable relational learning across generations that foster and stimulate shifts. The shifts occur through new materialist sensibilities that provoke "negotiations with meaning, materials, and cognitive and affective experience" (Garber, 2019, p. 17). Our bringing waste back into our art-making space, to learn with it and with each other, relates to what Jørgenson et al. (2018) call the "socio-material" trajectories of "waste practices" (p. 814). Providing richly layered social-eco-material contexts for attending to these trajectories prompted a re-evaluating and reimagining of our waste consumption across generations. Helguera's (2011) view of transpedagogy is useful here, as it suggests a "collective construction of an art milieu, with our artworks and ideas" that work with a "collective construction of knowledge" and the belief that art "is a tool for understanding the world" (p. 80). Our project did not fully embrace transpedagogy as explored by Truman and Springgay (2015), where "the pedagogical process becomes the artwork" (p. 151), but our project does reveal the power of a pedagogical event that calls participants to be artists/researchers/teachers together (Springgay et al., 2008): in this case, a means to shift thinking about waste/wildlife/human/non-human as explored through a collaborative art event.

## Working With Wisdoms

To encourage deeper thinking and longer-term reflection, we prompted participants with discussion points such as: What waste wisdoms can we share? What waste questions do we still want to ask? What further possibilities can we do with our waste? What insights did I learn from other generations? As Miriam, a U3A participant, wondered during one of the upcycling events: "This is a good idea to upcycle waste, but where will this art end up in 10 years' time? Will it go to landfill or be taken apart and used for art again?" Another wondering emerged as apprehension and shyness subsided through the art-focused intra-activity. Some U3A members reported a sense of joyous wonder about children's capacities and abilities in the project with comments such as, "It's just that I was so heartfelt happy to see how engaged they are with all that stuff." As a participant researcher and facilitator, I also observed shifts in the way the children, pre-service teachers and seniors moved from wariness to wonder – their willingness to listen, help, share and respond. This makes me wonder about art making in relation to wonder and wondering, the porosity of wonder, the relational exchange of what we do and do not know and how all of it relates to wisdom (Sternberg et al., 2019).

Our project encouraged sharing of generational wisdom and actively posed what Sternberg et al. (2019) refer to as "wisdom-based problems" that explore "real problems we face in life that involve competing interests [that go beyond] clearly defined single correct answers [and that in turn require] 'ethical decision making'" (pp. v–vi). For Sternberg et al., "wisdom recognizes […] uncertainty and ambiguity [as] intrinsic to many of the greatest challenges facing us" (p. vi). In exploring wisdom-based problems, participants called on their collective wisdoms.

These wisdoms were shared through generational and waste wisdom for the common good by considering each other's viewpoints:

- A senior couple gave children an interactive performance with recycled puppets made from their everyday waste.
- A senior opted to show her bokashi bucket to explain how regenerating food waste in her apartment led to sharing the healthy compost with others.
- A senior shared her know-how on upcycling scrap fabric into rag-made jewellery.
- The most senior participant, aged 89, took to the microphone sharing stories from when she was a child – when lunches were wrapped in cloth (there was no plastic packaging for food). Children listened with silent amazement as they imagined a time (in the past and future) without daily plastic encounters.

In turn, seniors listened with awe as children showed plastic bricks they made from plastic bottles filled with spent sweet wrappers as part of their school's garden wall initiative. The participants brought their waste/life wisdom to the event, and the project experience encouraged them to share it with others. This sharing opened space for transversality; through intra-actions and exchanges, shifts occurred in participants' viewpoints and understandings about our waste, our place and our actions towards sustainability.

## *"Our Waste, Our Place, Our Actions" and Community Art Education*

> To me, the art provided the medium which gave people opportunities to discuss common issues where nobody was right or wrong […] it generated thought about waste and preventing waste […] it actually gave the kids equal opportunity to input […]. I think the actual intergenerational connections […], especially for the children who don't have older people in their lives, gave the opportunity to interact on a level playing field with older people. They're a part of our community […] to walk down the street and recognise a senior, and say "G' day", it's developing a sense of community, and what is a community after all?
>
> (Senior participant)

As with many intergenerational projects, connecting our institutions and participants to community and broader social networks through art "provided improved access to information, resources and services" (Morgan & Aleman-Diaz, 2016, p. 2). In keeping with Dustin et al. (2019), joining these social networks in community plays a vital role in reforming art education within pre-service education.

Academic outreach to community contexts ensures that academe stays relevant to real-world issues while simultaneously building community capacity. The participants' comments during/after the art-making events suggest that attentive intra-action created opportunities for practical, meaningful ways to be respectful and respected. Participants' discovery of the affordance of materials created space, without overt push and pull, for an engaged and respectful mutuality that was more tangible than esoteric.

Almost every aspect of our project has an amplifying effect: not least the questions to carry further regarding the persistence of age/life stage, siloed institutional learning versus hybrid community, formal/informal and intergenerational learning, the relevance and affordances of community art education for the real world and the ways we are implicated in human/waste/wildlife/environment complexities (see Figure 5.3). These are complex issues.

Our project prompted learning through an allodial sense of place of human/non-human, and intergenerational learning by exploring self/others through contemporary waste issues. Motivated participants explored the potential of waste as they upcycled everyday waste through art making. Pre-service teachers developed the capacity to work in intergenerational contexts and learned to harness moments of shift as an innate aspect of transformative pedagogy. Children developed agency to talk with, learn from and teach the seniors. They shared their pro-active waste actions with seniors; they helped teach the seniors how to use iPads to create project posters and they enjoyed sharing local wildlife experiences with the seniors. In turn, the children were fascinated by the waste behaviours and solutions afforded by seniors.

Like many contemporary artists, we saw the detritus of our lives as a challenge. In the process we learned to pose and solve problems, creatively reimagining hybrid art/craft/designer/maker processes. At the same time, we learned about the changing material practices of artists and designers who have creatively repurposed food waste into bio-plastic designs, worked with polluted water to make paintings, created sculptures from waste and reimagined architecture and jewellery through upcycling. Such material challenges are an important addition to art education in twenty-first-century contexts so that we can together reimagine new ways to work with materials that prompt upcycle and life cycle thinking. According to Harris Lawton et al. (2019) community-based art education "encourages stakeholders to be transgressive: to question and break down barriers, to be self-expressive and self-empowered, and to shift paradigms through collaborative creative endeavour" (p. 30). This transgression is made stronger through repeated projects and encounters. As such, we continue ongoing relationships with participating institutions, enabling further community-informed projects with new groups of children, pre-service teachers and seniors to emerge. Our approach to community

FIGURE 5.3: Participants' templates and amulets inspired by local waste/wildlife intersections. Photos by Melanie Attard (2019).

art education enabled knowledge creation about creative waste possibilities. Our project prompted social change as participants worked in common to explore the implications of living with wildlife and with waste, as explored through creative engagement for and with community. And yet our project felt like the beginning: joyous and generative, prompting the desire for ongoing relational projects. With enthusiasm for discovering further possibilities, we now ask:

- What role can social networks and communities play in educational and social change within pre-service education?

- What could be different about pre-service units if intergenerational community members were included in ongoing experiences?
- How could we redesign units as continuous projects with community and industry partners developed successively year on year?
- Can we teach for the shift that shared wisdom brings?
- Can we adapt or share projects across international contexts so that communities can share each other's approaches to important global issues?

## ACKNOWLEDGEMENTS

Mornington Peninsula Shire, Place-making grant; Partners: Mornington U3A (thanks to Libby Wilson) and Monash University; with Mornington Park Primary School (thanks to Kathleen Lord) Artwork: Intergenerational participants (with permission).

## REFERENCES

Akkerman, S., & Bakker, A. (2011). Boundary crossing and boundary objects. *Review of Educational Research*, 81(2), 132–169. http://doi.org/10.3102/0034654311404435

Barad, K. M. (2007). *Meeting the universe halfway: Quantum physics and the entanglement of matter and meaning*. Duke University Press.

Barad, K. M. (2017). Troubling time/s and ecologies of nothingness: Re-turning, re-membering, and facing the incalculable. *New Formations*, 92(31), 56–86. https://doi.org/10.3898/NEWF:92.05.2017

Bennett, J. (2010). *Vibrant matter: A political ecology of things*. Duke University Press.

Bird Rose, D. (2017). Country and the gift. In J. Adamson & M. Davis (Eds.), *Humanities for the environment: Integrating knowledge, forging new constellations of practice* (pp. 33–45). Routledge. https://doi.org/10.4324/9781315642659

Bolt, B. (2013). Towards a "new materialism" through the arts. In E. Barrett & B. Bolt (Eds.), *Carnal knowledge: Towards a "new materialism" through the arts* (pp. 1–15). I. B. Tauris.

Burke, G. (2016). Finding creative agency through playful immersion. In V. Loy & K. B. Lim (Eds.), *Serious play: Perspectives on art education* (pp. 72–79). Singapore Teachers' Academy for the aRts (STAR).

Burke, G. (2018). Revealing the photo book as an arts-based educational research tool. In A. Sinner, R. L. Irwin, & T. Jokela (Eds.), *Visually provoking: Dissertations in art education* (2nd ed., pp. 118–128). Lapland University Press. https://research.monash.edu/en/publications/revealing-the-photo-book-as-an-arts-based-educational-research-to

Burke, G. (2019). *Our waste, our place, our actions: An intergenerational place-making project (Version 1)*. Monash University. https://doi.org/10.26180/5e0162cf17429

Crutzen, P. J. (2006). The "Anthropocene." In E. Ehlers & T. Krafft (Eds.), *Earth system science in the Anthropocene* (pp. 13–18). Springer Berlin Heidelberg. https://doi.org/10.1007/3-540-26590-2_3

Garber, E. (2019). Objects and new materialisms: A journey across making and living with objects. *Studies in Art Education*, 60(1), 7–21. https://doi.org/10.1080/00393541.2018.1557454

Harris, A., & de Bruin, L. (2017). Steam education: Fostering creativity in and beyond secondary schools. *Australian Art Education*, 38(1), 54–75.

Harris Lawton, P., Walker, M. A., & Green, M. (2019). *Community-based art education across the lifespan: Finding common ground*. Teachers College Press.

Helguerra, P. (2011). *Education for socially engaged art: A materials and techniques handbook*. Jorge Pinto Books.

Jørgenson, N. J., Madsen, K. D., & Læssøe, J. (2018). Waste in education: The potential of materiality and practice. *Environmental Education Research*, 24(6), 807–817. https://doi.org/10.1080/13504622.2017.1357801

Latour, B. (2005). *Reassembling the social: An introduction to actor-network theory*. Oxford University Press.

LeBlanc, N., & Irwin, R. L. (2019). A/r/tography: Curriculum and pedagogy, research and assessment methods, educational theories and philosophies. In N. LeBlanc & R. L. Irwin (Eds.), *Oxford research encyclopedias: Education*. Oxford University Press. https://doi.org/10.1093/acrefore/9780190264093.013.393

Li, W. C., Tse, H. F., & Fok, L. (2016). Plastic waste in the marine environment: A review of sources, occurrence and effects. *Science of the Total Environment*, 566–567, 333–349. https://doi.org/10.1016/j.scitotenv.2016.05.084

Ma Rhea, Z. (2018). *Land and water education and the allodial principle: Rethinking ecological education in the postcolonial age*. Springer. https://doi.org/10.1007/978-981-10-7600-8

Malone, K. (2017). *Children in the Anthropocene: Rethinking sustainability and child friendliness in cities*. Palgrave Macmillan. https://doi.org/10.1057/978-1-137-43091-5_7

Morgan, A., & Aleman-Diaz, A. (2016). Measuring what matters for young people's health and wellbeing: An asset approach. *Learning for Well-being Magazine*, 1, 1–9. https://www.l4wb-magazine.org/mag01-art02-morgan-alemandiaz

Neimanis, A. (2017). *Bodies of water: Posthuman feminist phenomenology*. Bloomsbury Publishing Plc.

Sameshima, P., & Greenwood, D. A. (2015). Visioning the centre for place and sustainability studies through an embodied aesthetic wholeness. *Cultural Studies of Science Education*, 10(1), 163–176. https://doi.org/10.1007/s11422-014-9615-y

Springgay, S., Irwin, R. L., & Kind, S. (2008). A/r/tographers and living inquiry. In J. G. Knowles & A. L. Cole (Eds.), *Handbook of the arts in qualitative research: Methodologies, examples and issues* (pp. 83–92). Sage Publications.

Sternberg, R. J. (2019). Where have all the flowers of wisdom gone? An analysis of teaching for wisdom over the years. In R. Sternberg, H. Nusbaum, & J. Glück (Eds.), *Applying wisdom to contemporary world problems* (pp. 1–19). Palgrave Macmillan. https://doi.org/10.1007/978-3-030-20287-3_1

Sternberg, R. J., Nusbaum, H., & Glück, J. (2019). Preface. In R. Sternberg, H. Nusbaum, & J. Glück (Eds.), *Applying wisdom to contemporary world problems* (pp. v–vi). Palgrave Macmillan. https://doi.org/10.1007/978-3-030-20287-3_1

Sustainable Communities: Tidy Towns Awards (2020). Education Finalists. https://www.kvb.org.au/library/tidy_towns2020_finalists_education/

Taylor, C. A. (2016). Edu-crafting a cacophonous ecology: Posthumanist research practices for education. In C. A. Taylor & C. Hughes (Eds.), *Posthuman research practices in education* (pp. 5–24). Palgrave Macmillan. https://doi.org/10.1057/9781137453082_2

Truman, S. E., & Springgay, S. (2015). The primacy of movement in research-creation: New materialist approaches to art research and pedagogy. In T. Lewis & M. Laverty (Eds.), *Art's teachings, teaching's art. Contemporary philosophies and theories in education* (Vol. 8, pp. 151–162). Springer. https://doi.org/10.1007/978-94-017-7191-7_11

Victorian Curriculum and Assessment Authority. (2019). *Victorian curriculum, the arts, visual arts: Structure.* https://victoriancurriculum.vcaa.vic.edu.au/the-arts/visual-arts/introduction/structure

# 6

# Community-Based Art Education: Promoting Revitalization and Eco-Cultural Resilience for Cultural Sustainability

*Timo Jokela and Mirja Hiltunen*

This chapter presents a critical overview of current trends in community-based art education practice at the University of Lapland (UoL). We are aware that education systems, in their different forms, have been carriers and promoters of colonialism in the Arctic. In addition, life in the Arctic has been affected socially and economically by climate change, utilization of natural resources, urbanization and an ageing population in rural regions (Nordic Council of Ministers, 2011; Stephen, 2018). Because education systems are also potentially significant in countering such changes and discourses, community-based art education should also launch awareness-raising activities to break down stereotypes and traditional roles of art education itself in the Arctic.

These current environmental and eco-social changes call for a new sense of interconnectivity among our visual art education programmes at the university, including programmes in or outside of schools as well as our projects focusing on lifelong learning. Making progress towards a more sustainable world requires education programmes that foster informed, empowered and just societies with opportunities for lifelong learning. When building the capacity of art educators, artists and facilitators to support more innovative and participatory approaches to community-based art education, we are aiming to make a significant contribution to a more sustainable practice concerning the rapid changes we are facing in the Arctic.

In the first section of this chapter, we introduce the main principles of community-based art education at the UoL, its connections to international discussions on community art education and the art-based action research (ABAR) strategy developed at the UoL that has guided our activities (Jokela, 2019). In the second section, we connect community-based art education to the current discussion on Arctic art (Huhmarniemi & Jokela, 2020). Our concept of Arctic community-based art education (ACAE) refers to participatory activities focusing on the potential to support living and wellbeing in rapidly changing, multi-ethnic communities in the North and the Arctic. In the third section, we illustrate three ACAE projects whose activities have brought together different age groups and participants to develop their artistic learning and working culture while expanding the domain of art education into different sectors of society. In subsequent sections, we illustrate and discuss the ACAE projects using the following key theoretical concepts: Indigenous knowledge, Indigenous education, Northern knowledge, decolonization, place-based approaches, cultural revitalization and eco-cultural resilience. These theoretical frames of reference underpin the concept of ACAE. We conclude by reflecting on the ACAE activities involving education for cultural sustainability, new materialism and post-humanism. We are interested in determining how ACAE can provide the agency to hold onto and revitalize Indigenous, local and situated Northern knowledge as well as foster eco-cultural resilience in the rapidly changing North and the Arctic.

## *Community-Based Art Education and the ABAR Strategy*

Developments in community art education are closely linked to a general move to democratize arts and culture socially and politically, with everyone given the chance to participate. Europe in the 1990s saw a renewed interest in ideas such as "art as a source for life" and "art and culture for identity." Critically and socially engaged educational practices of art education emphasize the importance of understanding context. At the centre of learning is the aim of raising possible forms of injustice and oppression that influence the participants' own communities. For achieving this goal, social aspects themselves can be considered materials of artistic work (Dewhurst, 2014; Matarasso, 2019; Williams, 2003).

At UoL, we define community-based art education as practices through which a community can use art to introduce and distribute themes that are meaningful and topical for the community and its surroundings. Community-based art education has been developed and explored from the very beginning in our interdisciplinary northern science and art community, accomplished through interactions with multi-field projects since the late 1990s (Hiltunen, 2009). The goal has been to develop a context-sensitive, interdisciplinary and situated art-based research culture. We have collaborated intensively with scholars in educational science, social science, social work and Sami research, and with researchers at the University of Lapland's Arctic Centre. The need for community-based activities and sustainable art education research and practices was also identified in multidisciplinary collaboration with the University of the Arctic's[1] thematic network, Arctic Sustainable Arts and Design (ASAD, 2020; Jokela & Coutts, 2018).

Joint knowledge creation through contemporary art in multi- and transdisciplinary ventures in Northern sparsely populated areas has indicated that a community can also be enabled to remember and notice marginal or unrecognized circumstances and groups. By community, we refer to a group of people whose identity as a group lies in their interaction and sharing, shared emotional connection, feeling of belonging or sharing a sense of personal relatedness. Artistic activity observes a community's sociocultural environment and traditions, which can undergo transformations in artistic processes and affect the future (Hiltunen, 2009). As part of their training to become art teachers, art education students work with practitioners in different fields when participating in multi-field projects in both the general school system and informal art education, covering the areas of social services, health care and tourism.

The common ground for community-based art education can be found not only in the embodiment of performativity, critical reflection and social change within art learning but also in critical pedagogy that describes contemporary art and art education as engaged with ecological issues. The consequences of neglecting local human and natural communities include degraded habitat, loss of wilderness, alienation, rootlessness and lack of connection to communities (Tilbury & Wortman, 2008). Critical community- and place-based pedagogy provides a framework for the theory and practice of art education that is concerned with both community and ecological issues (Hiltunen, 2010; Jokela, 2018; Martusewicz et al., 2015).

The methodological choice for most of the activities and studies has been ABAR. More a research strategy than a complete methodology, ABAR has been developed at the UoL to combine artistic practices with regional development and community empowerment (Jokela, 2019; Jokela et al., 2015). ABAR aims to develop the professional methods and working approaches of the artist–teacher–researcher and the artist–researcher. The strategy shares some common features with international arts-based research, a/r/tography, artistic research and action research. In all these research approaches, practical and theoretical research are conducted simultaneously; research topics are situated in the middle ground of art and other fields of research such as social sciences, studies on education and regional development. The objectives of ABAR are to identify and distinguish problems at the local level and to create solutions through artistic work that often involves various means of collaboration with community members, artists and research peers. ABAR is especially rooted in process-oriented dialogical and place-specific forms of world of art: for example, environmental and community art and pedagogical settings and practices of community-based art education (Härkönen et al., 2018; Hiltunen, 2009; Jokela, 2018).

## *Arctic Art as a Tool for Rethinking Community-Based Art Education*

The concept of Arctic art was introduced within the ASAD network to refer to contemporary art, design and media productions that address Arctic themes and the sustainability of the Arctic region (ASAD, 2020; Jokela & Coutts, 2018). The concept of Arctic art is concerned with the need to re-examine and change the viewpoint of Western art and culture to champion ethical principles as well as the cultural and social sustainability of activities in the North and the Arctic.

Arctic art has been used mainly for activities that reflect and renew Arctic cultural heritage or create new artistic forms of expression based on nature, culture and current debates. Arctic art includes the art of Indigenous peoples and other peoples in the region, as well as their art parallelism and overlap. The concept is politically and pedagogically charged as it is used to highlight the specificities of Arctic art and culture – from the local level to international cultural policy – and to promote sustainability and diversity. Arctic art is renewing the understanding of the North and the Arctic, creating a connection between the past, present and future of the Northern Hemisphere (Huhmarniemi & Jokela, 2020; Jokela et al., 2019).

Arctic art also refers to an alternative way, familiar to Indigenous cultures, of seeing art, design and craft as an intertwined whole integrated into everyday life – unlike in the dualistic Western culture where art, design and crafts are separated into separate fields and types of education (Guttorm, 2015; Jokela, 2017). In this chapter, concepts of Arctic art and community-based art education are merged and described as ACAE.

## *ACAE Project Examples*

Utsjoki is the most northern municipality in Finland. Of its approximately 600 residents, the majority are Sámi. In the Fire Fox project (2004–06), we explored the Northern Lights, astronomy and the cosmos, legends of the polar night and water in its different modes through multidisciplinary workshops and snow and ice sculpting (Figure 6.1). Throughout the years, several different kinds of art and science workshops have been held with the local school and community members. The magnificent rivers are vital elements in Utsjoki; in addition to reindeer herding (the main source of livelihood), fishing is an important livelihood. On 20 March 2015, the community celebrated the 92 per cent solar eclipse with *The Ohcejoga URSA* (Upper Lapland's Astronomical Association) by doing ice fishing and winter art together. Art has become a space for cultural encounters where individual and cultural pre-occupations and prejudices are challenged. Artistic practices have acted as a catalyst to trigger events or changes within a community. Every participant is a learner of Indigenous and Northern knowledge, where intergenerational sharing is characteristic.

Wooden public artworks in northern environments (Figure 6.2), created as life-long learning projects with communities, are often based on traditional construction techniques and local folklore where Indigenous and non-Indigenous storytelling merge. Local people's participation in the design process is an essential part of community-based environmental art. Combining handcraft-based contemporary art practices with place-specific, intergenerational and intercultural approaches creates an open space for dialogue where the values and the perceptions of cultural heritage can be negotiated.

FIGURE 6.1: Long-term inter- and multidisciplinary ABAR collaboration in Utsjoki. Pupils playing with the Mythical Boat in the schoolyard. Photo by Mirja Hiltunen (2006).

FIGURE 6.2: Place-based community art with traditional crafting material and techniques. Photos by Timo Jokela (2008, 2009).

For improving winter art education in schools, villages and tourism communities, it has been crucial to have a pedagogic dialogue between contemporary art and Sámi Indigenous practices. For that reason, UoL development projects were arranged with both art education and Sámi craftwork (*duodji*) education at the Sámi University of Applied Sciences in Kautokeino, Norway (Figure 6.3). At the joint workshops, ways of working were created such that contemporary art and traditional principles of Sámi craft were conjoined and integrated. The aim of the education project was to develop working practices of contemporary art that respected the values of the Sámi culture in a sustainable way, including aims of decolonization and revitalization, and offered an open space for multi-ethnic dialogue as well. As a consequence of community-based winter art education, several communities have developed their own ways of implementing and using contemporary art strategies in different educational settings, such as local schools, as well as promoting new livelihoods like "experience tourism."

FIGURE 6.3: Winter art ABAR development project in multi-ethnic villages. Photos by Timo Jokela (2014, 2018).

## *Decolonization and Northern Knowledge*

We are aware that across the Arctic and around the world, the voices of Indigenous Peoples are increasingly being listened to (Drugge, 2016; Kuokkanen, 2020; Smith, 1999; Valkonen & Valkonen, 2019). Calling for the decolonization of methods of Indigenous research, they question Western ways of "knowing" and research. Kuokkanen (2000) suggests the idea of an "Indigenous paradigm" that would refocus or "re-centre" research on concerns, worldviews and cultural practices from Indigenous perspectives. In the area of education, Keskitalo (2010) has stressed the need for fundamental change in Sámi schools. She sees decolonization as a long-term process that requires dismantling the power of administrative, cultural, linguistic and psychological colonialism. Many scholars have argued that Indigenous knowledge systems have much to offer as a basis for Indigenous research, particularly in the areas of art, design and culture (Guttorm, 2015). Alongside contemporary art, the study of Indigenous cultures provides valuable guidelines for the wider development of ACAE. Among other things, the knowledge created by Sámi educational and cultural research is valuable in developing ACAE pedagogy.

This clearly has significance beyond Indigenous cultures, as many non-Indigenous peoples in the North have similar histories, situations and challenges.

However, there is a limitation in seeing ACAE as only an Indigenous practice. In ACAE, we have followed Chartier's (2018) notion of the Arctic as a multi-ethnic, multi-cultural and multi-lingual place. Indigenous and non-Indigenous cultures impact each other and are bound to nature in the same locations, to the extent that it may be difficult to determine just how local Indigenous and non-Indigenous knowledge of nature differ from each other.

Knowledge arising from a connection to nature can be addressed from the perspectives of traditional knowledge, traditional ecological knowledge, Indigenous knowledge, tacit knowledge and/or local knowledge (see Helander-Renvall & Markkula, 2017; Porsanger & Guttorm, 2011; Valkonen & Valkonen, 2019). In ACAE, the term "Northern knowledge" has been used to distinguish that from Indigenous knowledge systems (Huhmarniemi & Jokela, 2020). The Northern way of knowing combines cultural heritage related to nature and ecosystems, as well as tacit material knowledge, with the making and use of art and the visual symbols of cultures. Our ACAE examples show how Northern knowledge enables reflection and action and acknowledges that non-Indigenous cultures also have traditions tied to nature and know-how worthy of maintenance and revitalization. This knowledge is not ethnically inherited and owned but can be learned, researched and developed by means of ACAE.

## *Place-Based Approaches and Situated Learning*

In ACAE, our aim has been to work sensitively with multi-ethnic communities to strengthen vitality and regional development through art, culture and art education. In a Northern knowledge system, places are essential. Place-based strategies have been the foundations upon which much of our research and development work for ACAE has been built.

ACAE activities in Northern places and communities can also be understood as economic development strategies, especially in collaboration with sustainable tourism (Huhmarniemi & Jokela, 2019). In lifelong learning, it is often the practice to use places and a community's capacity to make economic progress. Building on existing strengths, this approach focuses on culture and the unique features of particular places to boost existing businesses or create new ones. According to Daniels et al. (2015), a place-based strategy is a reaction to conventional top-down, single-sector, national-stage development projects. Connecting ACAE with EU-funded regional development projects has led to new collaborations among schools, public and business sectors in remote places. In

ACAE projects, sustainability also lies in community-based thinking where place and local eco-culture (Dessein et al., 2015; Soini & Birkeland, 2014) represent both problem and possibility, form and process. We promote social learning by using local eco-culture and place-conscious and place-responsive teaching to aim for sustainable ways of living.

## *Revitalization*

To restore and renew the values and traditions of eco-culture and Northern knowledge systems in a contemporary socio-cultural context, revitalization has become a key process in ACAE. The concept of "revitalization" exists at the intersection of tradition and innovation. In ACAE, this often means merging methods of contemporary, traditional and sustainable ways of making art. Auclair and Fairclough (2015) have described revitalization as a practice that renews and remakes cultural traditions that are part of social construction. In ACAE projects, revitalization does not mean returning to a historical culture and identity that would be authentic or unmixed. Revitalization is always based on an interpretation of history that changes according to our sources of historical knowledge as well as personal and communal perceptions, judgements and values. Revitalization conducted by means of ACAE does not refer only to educational and cultural practices but also to places, villages and whole regions based on their local, regional identity and potential vitality.

Revitalization, as it is understood in ACAE, is an approach for achieving cultural sustainability; it is often intergenerational and intercultural with the aim of transmitting traditional knowledge, artistry and cultural practices to new generations and new community members. Forgotten symbols, rituals and crafts are often studied, and new meanings are created for them as the traditional and the modern are constantly reformed in contemporary art.

## *Eco-Cultural Resilience*

Residents of the Arctic face a challenging situation as the base of their cultural identity is being shaken by ongoing changes (Stephen, 2018). Resilience is demanded in order to face rapid environmental changes in the wake of social and cultural shifts. Resilience thinking has attained prominence in a number of research disciplines as well as in policy making for sustainable development. It is also closely linked with education, knowledge and human capacity building. For example, working with winter art has increased young men's trust that knowledge from their own eco-culture with its specific natural conditions has a future – even during the transformation of livelihoods. Winter art has offered new opportunities for men who can no longer find work in their traditional livelihoods (Jokela, 2019).

When analysing ACAE projects, we agree with Jules Pretty (2011), a professor of environment and society, who has explained that eco-cultures need to regain their connections with the environment to improve their own resilience. Pretty has underscored the need for ways to connect knowledge with action to produce optimal outcomes for both nature and culture, especially in times of change, and has suggested that eco-cultural systems can be redesigned by emphasizing the incorporation of local and traditional knowledge. The action of ACAE projects supports eco-cultural resilience by fostering the capacity of individuals, communities and natural entities to cope with changes, adapt to them and even transform them into new possibilities.

Professor of rural development Arora-Jonsson (2016) has argued that to promote eco-cultural resilience, we need to produce situated knowledge and demand recognition of the value of place-based knowledge and different ways of knowing. Using the Northern knowledge as a base for ACAE projects, we acknowledge situated knowing with nature as discussed in new materialistic (Gamble & Hanan, 2019) and post-humanistic research paradigms (Ulmer, 2017). The interactive and spiritual eco-cultural relationship of Arctic communities with nature and its ecosystems is an important element of ACAE.

## *Conclusion*

In this chapter, we have discussed how ACAE can provide the agency to hold onto and revitalize Indigenous, local and situated Northern knowledge as well as foster eco-cultural resilience in the rapidly changing North and the Arctic. ACAE projects at UoL, connected to local eco-cultures and respecting Northern knowledge, have been realized using place-based methods for contemporary art. In ACAE, Northern knowledge can be shared not only with locals but with newcomers and even guests. These projects, developed and evaluated using ABAR methodologies, were shown to support decolonization and revitalization in rural communities and thus also promote eco-cultural resilience.

Eco-cultural resilience is enhanced by cultural empowerment and strong regional identity. This resilience supports communities facing rapid changes in the Arctic by helping them transform their traditions into a contemporary culture and in response to existing needs. By means of ACAE, art educators and artists can help communities share traditions and pass on the material and spiritual culture of the Arctic to new generations, even those outside the northern region.

Finally, this long-term art-based action research has provided insights into the benefits of art education and artistic training in the Arctic. From our research, we conclude that ACAE as a means of promoting decolonization, revitalization and situated Northern knowledge is critically important for art education and artistic training in the Arctic. In addition, ACAE methods and ABAR strategies have the potential to play a role in promoting global post-humanistic sustainability thought, through reconsidering our connection with nature and the relationship between nature and humans.

## NOTE

1. The University of the Arctic (UArctic) is a network of universities, colleges, research institutes and other organizations concerned with education and research in and about the North. UArctic builds and strengthens collective resources and infrastructures that enable member institutions to better serve their constituents and their regions (University of the Arctic, 2021, https://www.uarctic.org/).

## REFERENCES

Arora-Jonsson, S. (2016). Does resilience have a culture? Ecocultures and the politics of knowledge production. *Ecological Economics, 121*, 98–107. https://doi.org/10.1016/j.ecolecon.2015.11.020

Arctic Sustainable Arts and Design. (2020). *The Arctic Sustainable Arts and Design (ASAD) thematic network*. https://www.asadnetwork.org/

Auclair, E., & Fairclough, G. (2015). Living between past and future: An introduction to heritage and cultural sustainability. In E. Auclair & G. Fairclough (Eds.), *Theory and practice in heritage and sustainability: Between past and future* (pp. 1–22). Routledge.

Chartier, D. (2018). *What is the "Imagined North"?* Presses de l'Université du Québec.

Daniels, J., Baldacchino, G., & Vodden, R. (2015). Matters of place: The making of place and identity. In K. Vodden, R. Gibson, & G. Baldacchino (Eds.), *Place peripheral: Place-based development in rural, island, and remote regions* (pp. 23–40). ISER Books.

Dessein, J., Soini, K., Fairclough, G., & Horlings, L. (Eds.). (2015). *Culture in, for and as sustainable development: Conclusions from the COST Action IS1007 Investigating Cultural Sustainability*. University of Jyväskylä.

Dewhurst, M. (2014). *Social justice art: A framework for activist art pedagogy*. Harvard Education Press.

Drugge, A.-L. (2016). How can we do it right? Ethical uncertainty in Swedish Sami research. *Journal of Academic Ethics, 14*, 263–279. https://doi.org/10.1007/s10805-016-9265-7

Gamble, C. N., & Hanan, J. N. (2019). What is new materialism? *Journal of the Theoretical Humanities, 24*(6), 111–134. https://doi.org/10.1080/0969725X.2019.1684704

Guttorm, G. (2015). Contemporary Duodji: A personal experience in understanding traditions. In T. Jokela & G. Coutts (Eds.), *Relate North: Art, heritage & identity* (pp. 60–76). Lapland University Press.

Härkönen, E., Huhmarniemi, M., & Jokela, T. (2018). Crafting sustainability: Handcraft in contemporary art and cultural sustainability in the Finnish Lapland. *Sustainability*, *10*(6), 1907. https://doi.org/10.3390/su10061907

Helander-Renvall, E., & Markkula, I. (2017). On transfer of Sámi traditional knowledge: Scientification, traditionalization, secrecy, and equality. In A. Xanthaki, S. Valkonen, S. L. Heinämäki, & P. Nuorgam (Eds.), *Indigenous peoples' cultural heritage: Rights, debates, challenges* (pp. 104–129). Brill.

Hiltunen, M. (2009). *Yhteisöllinen taidekasvatus: Performatiivisesti pohjoisen sosiokulttuurisissa ympäristöissä* [Community-based art education: Through performativity in the northern socio-cultural environments] [Doctoral dissertation], The University of Lapland, Rovaniemi. http://urn.fi/URN:NBN:fi:ula-20111141039

Hiltunen, M. (2010). Slow activism: Art in progress in the North. In A. Linjakumpu & S. Wallenius-Korkalo (Eds.), *Progress or perish: Northern perspectives on social change* (pp. 119–138). Ashgate.

Huhmarniemi, M., & Jokela, T. (2019). Environmental art for tourism in the Arctic: From handicraft to integrated art and reform on artists' skills. *Synnyt/Origins*, *1/2019*, 63–80. https://wiki.aalto.fi/pages/viewpage.action?pageId=151504259

Huhmarniemi, M., & Jokela, T. (2020). Arctic arts with pride: Discourses on Arctic arts, culture and sustainability. *Sustainability*, *12*(2), 604. https://doi.org/10.3390/su12020604

Jokela, T. (2017). Art, design, and craft interwoven with the North and the Arctic. In M. Huhmarniemi, A. Jónsdóttir, G. Guttorm, & H. Hauen (Eds.), *Interwoven* (pp. 4–11). University of Lapland.

Jokela, T. (2018). Culture sensitive participatory art as visual ethnography in the North. *Visual Ethnography*, *6*(2), 89–112.

Jokela, T. (2019). Arts-based action research in the North. In G. W. Noblit (Ed.), *Oxford research encyclopedia of education*. Oxford University Press. https://doi.org/10.1093/acrefore/9780190264093.013.522

Jokela, T., & Coutts, G. (2018). The North and the Arctic: A laboratory of art and design education for sustainability. In T. Jokela & G. Coutts (Eds.), *Relate North: Art and design education for sustainability* (pp. 98–117). Lapland University Press.

Jokela, T., Hiltunen, M., & Härkönen, E. (2015). Art-based action research: Participatory art for the North. *International Journal of Education Through Art*, *11*(3), 433–448.

Jokela, T., Huhmarniemi, M., & Hautala-Hirvioja, T. (2019). Preface. [Special issue]. *Synnyt 1/2019*, 6–12. https://wiki.aalto.fi/pages/viewpage.action?pageId=151504259

Keskitalo, P. (2010). *Saamelaiskoulun kulttuurisensitiivisyyttä etsimässä kasvatusantropologian keinoin* [Searching for cultural sensitivity in Sámi school through educational anthropology]. Dieđut. Sámi allaskuvla.

Kuokkanen, R. (2000). Towards an Indigenous paradigm from a Sami perspective. *The Canadian Journal of Native Studies, 20*(2), 411–436.

Kuokkanen, R. (2020). Reconciliation as a threat or structural change? The truth and reconciliation process and settler colonial policy making in Finland. *Human Rights Review, 21*(3), 293–312.

Martusewicz, R., Edmundson, J., & Lupinacci, J. (2015). *EcoJustice education*. Routledge.

Matarasso, F. (2019). *A restless art: How participation won and why it matters*. Calouste Gulbenkian Foundation.

Nordic Council of Ministers. (2011). *Megatrends. TemaNord 2011:527*. https://nordregio.org/publications/megatrends/

Porsanger, J., & Guttorm, G. (2011). Building up the field study and research on Sámi traditional knowledge (Arbediehtu). In J. Porsanger & G. Guttorm (Eds.), *Working with traditional knowledge: Communities, institutions, information systems, law and ethics* (pp. 98–125). Diedut.

Pretty, J. (2011). Interdisciplinary progress in approaches to address social-ecological and ecocultural systems. *Environmental Conservation, 38*(2), 127–139. https://doi.org/10.1017/S0376892910000937

Smith, L. T. (1999). *Decolonizing methodologies: Research and Indigenous peoples*. Zed Books.

Soini, K., & Birkeland, I. (2014). Exploring the scientific discourse on cultural sustainability [Special Issue]. *Geoforum, 51*, 213–223. https://doi.org/10.1016/j.geoforum.2013.12.001

Stephen, K. (2018). Societal impacts of a rapidly changing Arctic. *Current Climate Change Reports, 4*(3), 223–237. https://doi.org/10.1007/s40641-018-0106-1

Tilbury, D., & Wortman, D. (2008). How is community education contributing to sustainability in practice? *Applied Environmental Education & Communication, 7*(3), 83–93. https://doi.org/10.1080/15330150802502171

Ulmer, J. (2017). Posthumanism as research methodology: Inquiry in the Anthropocene. *International Journal of Qualitative Studies in Education, 30*(9), 832–848. https://doi.org/10.1080/09518398.2017.1336806

Valkonen, J., & Valkonen, S. (2019). On local knowledge. In T. H. Eriksen, S. Valkonen, & J. Valkonen (Eds.), *Knowing from the Indigenous North. Sámi approaches to history, politics and belonging* (pp. 12–25). Routledge.

Williams, J. (2003). Where the arts, education and society intersect. *Lifelong Learning in Europe, 8*(2), 32–38.

# PART 2

## TRANSVERSAL PRACTICES

# 7

# Making Meaning, Creating (in) Community: An International Dialogue on Community Art Education Within Early Childhood Contexts

*Geralyn (Gigi) Yu, Alex Halligey and Judith Browne*

*Children have the right to imagine. We need to give them full rights of citizenship in life and society.*

(Malaguzzi, 1994, p. 5)

*Pulling at the Threads*

This chapter is the culmination of a dialogue that occurred over several months among authors Gigi Yu (southwest United States), Judith Browne and Alex Halligey (Johannesburg, South Africa) and from interviews with Karyn Callaghan, Kathy Cope and Jason Avery (Ontario, Canada). We are all connected through an international network of Reggio Emilia-inspired educators. The Reggio Emilia approach, named after the Italian city, was formed after the Second World War. Distinctive features of this approach to early childhood education include the democratic participation of children, parents, educators and citizens; the transversality of disciplines; the use of pedagogical documentation; the theory of the hundred languages (Moss, 2018) and the pivotal role of artists.

Loris Malaguzzi, founder of the Reggio Emilia approach, embraced the idea of ensuring children's and adults' rights to engage actively in the expressive languages of art making as integral to the knowledge-building process and brought artists into the educational project in the role of *atelierista* (Cagliari et al., 2016). Malaguzzi's view of the role of art and artists in facilitating communal, curious engagement in discovering and making social worlds is at the heart of our considerations in this chapter.

As artists/educators/researchers, we reflected on three Reggio-inspired projects as case studies:

- *The Collaborative Educators Institute* (CEI) is a community of diverse early childhood educators organized by Christie Colunga at the Paradise Valley Community College located in the southwest United States. From 2016 to 2021, Gigi facilitated encounters with artistic thinking and artistic spaces as alternative pathways for reimagining teaching practices. Both educators' and children's artistic investigations are documented for ongoing collaborative reflection, planning and sharing with the broader education community.
- *Open Streets Auckland Park* in Johannesburg, South Africa was a school-centred, arts-based enquiry expressing itself in a neighbourhood event, research report and wider invitation to research and reimagine city streets with children. The project was initiated within Mimosa School in late 2018. Judith was involved in her capacity as Mimosa's *atelierista* – a connector-of-dots, holding and interweaving the threads this initiative entailed. Alex was involved as a researcher and artist who works with understanding placemaking in city contexts. She was brought on board to help design research tools for documenting the Open Streets neighbourhood event and to coordinate the compilation of a report on the project's process (2019).
- *Artists at the Centre* (A@C), a fifteen-year-long project, introduced artists as consistent disrupters into childcare and family resource centres in Hamilton, Ontario. The project brought artists into childcare programmes where children and families encountered materials and each other – described by founding member Karyn Callaghan as "spaces for children to express their thinking" (personal communication, 17 April 2020). Early childhood educators and artists met for a study group eight times a year. The project process was documented and presented in annual public exhibitions.

We pulled at the threads of these three examples and looked for patterns connecting our work and differentiating it. What follows reflects key themes of our dialogue and the metaphors – the ways of "carrying across" or transversalities – we found for articulating them. As Greene (1997) offers, "[a] metaphor not only involves a reorientation of consciousness, it also enables us to cross divides, to make connections between ourselves and others, and to look through other eyes" (p. 391). Similarly, our conversations took shape through metaphors that held shared meaning for us. Although located in distant contexts, we were able to create a space of listening, respect and presence for our dialogue, a place where we could attend to self, each other, our connections and differences. We all returned to this notion of respect and careful attention – in the United States, Canada and South Africa – as the foundation for the work we champion in this nexus of community arts, early childhood engagement and public pedagogy. Each section is framed as a dialogue, articulating the threads of our thinking while tying in our three case studies. We start with considering how we define community across our contexts, then move on to the centrality of working with the notion of community in each of our projects, the role of imagination and art making, and finally the usefulness of documentation processes.

### *Community and Context*

In our early discussions, Karyn Callaghan asked: How do we as individual artist-educators define community? Looking back over the threads of our conversations spread over time and space, our definition of community as artist-educators as informed by the Reggio Emilia approach is not bound by identity markers or geography, but by the *quality* and *texture* of relationships among people, places and materials. We did not seek to become artists as "illuminated visionaries" but instead situated ourselves in collaboration with our communities (Cohen-Cruz, 2005; Helguera, 2013). The Reggio Emilia approach positions the hundreds of languages of both children and adults as the connecting force for participation in community:

> Participation gives value to and makes use of the hundred languages of children and of human beings, viewed as plurality of points of view and of cultures; it requires and fosters forms of cultural mediation and develops in a multiplicity of occasions and initiatives for constructing dialogue and the sense of belonging to a community.
>
> (Reggio Children, 2010, p. 11)

As Kathy Cope reminded us, the word *context* in Italian translates to weaving together. The more we shared our work, the more the particular weave of our own contexts became apparent. Our definition of community evolved as we spoke through our experiences with children, teachers, families, materials and context. Key to this process was an openness and a quality of listening – a willingness to be "changed" by being "in" exchange with each other's thinking and ideas.

**ALEX:** *South Africa bears a weighty history of racial oppression through colonization from 1652, to state institutionalized racial segregation in the form of Apartheid from 1948, which was only incrementally dismantled over the course of 1990 to the first democratic election in 1994. Talking about "community" in South Africa is contentious because it can come to mean pockets of "poor" people, people of a particular racial group, people still ghettoized geographically. There has not been enough repair work across economic, geographic, housing and social divides for the term "community" to sufficiently encompass a whole city or region whilst still containing difference. These inequalities run deep in South Africa's schools. In the context of systemic racism and inequality, where the dream of a free and fair post-1994 society is at best deferred, Freire's [2002] vision of education as an act of liberation is all the more urgent.*

**JUDITH:** *What I find most compelling about the Reggio Emilia approach is its humanity, respect for children and its commitment to an everyday democracy. And while Mimosa exists in the same fractured context as any other South African school, there is also something that sets it apart. Something I hesitantly want to call a commitment to participatory democracy and diversity, to being together in a way that honours our differences but also makes space for connection. It would be too easy to call it a happy family, but that is not it at all. Sometimes being in a relationship is hard, uncomfortable even restless. It is a place of tension and friction, a place where you are seeking to become better than you currently are. What holds us together through those uncomfortable times? I think a generosity and respect for who we are now, and a hopefulness for who (and how) we can still be.*

**ALEX:** *The Reggio Emilia approach reminds us in a South African context that community is about relationships: how we understand and negotiate our material world together. The Open Streets Auckland Park project drew attention to how communities need not be defined by geography, economic brackets, race or institutional affiliations. Through Open Streets the "community" Mimosa School keys into was revealed to connect children, family, friends of all ages, Auckland Park residents, pedestrians, street vendors, formal and informal waste collectors, artists and environmentalists, all coming from a wide variety of Johannesburg areas [see Figure 7.1].*

FIGURE 7.1: Open Streets Auckland Park, 7 April 2019. Photo by Sims Phakisi (2019).

**GIGI:** *The southwest United States is known for its scenic beauty, rich artistic traditions and multicultural history. Despite its allure, it consistently ranks at the bottom in child wellbeing and education. Often, early childhood educators are required to use pre-packaged curricula developed by large textbook companies to address the education deficits. Curriculum decisions are generally made by those in "leadership" positions, detached from the community and life of classrooms. The image of the child and educator are seen as limited, linear and non-distinct [Moss, 2018]. The Reggio Emilia approach principles inspire the CEI to reimagine education together, placing creativity, imagination, and aesthetics at the heart of teaching and learning while simultaneously challenging dominant, prescribed ways of knowing.*

**ARTISTS AT THE CENTRE PROJECT:** In articulating how A@C worked within the context of Hamilton, Ontario, Karyn reflected on how both artists and children generally occupy marginal spaces. Bringing the two together over a fifteen-year-long project served as generational work in creating new kinds of community: from the margins, between children, parents, broader family and friend circles, educators, artists, people in different economic brackets, people from different parts of the city or even the province.

## Seeing With New Eyes

In our dialogue, we recognized that flipping the deficit lens for children and early childhood educators is about taking up Malaguzzi's (1994) challenge to look within ourselves to realize our image of children. Children become guides to a more considered enactment of community as we start to pay closer attention to their strengths, strategies, creativity and curiosity. As artists/educators, we begin to reconsider how children are perceived and received within our communities and their power to shift our communal engagements for the better.

> **GIGI:** *In our conversation about A@C, Kathy described being with children as opening up the possibility of seeing herself as an artist with new eyes and freshness to create. Being open to exchanging ideas with children and seeing them as competent communicators and contributors changes our work as a result. Karyn concurred, describing how artists would go back to their studios bursting with ideas after working with children. The potential emerges for a mutual reciprocity in meaning-making for the child, adults and wider community.*

> **JUDITH:** *As your image of children changes, so your own work as an artist or educator changes. That is the "shared gaze" children and artists (and teachers, parents, neighbourhoods, communities) offer each other in the exchange of really seeing each other, really being seen. We are held, and we grow, in that gaze.*

> **ALEX:** *Working with Mimosa school children and teachers on the Open Streets project made me mourn the limited child image-ing I was at the receiving end of as a child. At the time, Judith expressed that working with children offers the opportunity to go back and unlearn our childhood education and to relearn how to "be" in a more expansive way. Hearing Karyn, Jason and Kathy talk about their work through A@C brought up all these same feelings of sadness, longing and gratitude at what is possible when working with children. Working as collaborators with children opens up the potential for fuller living for the children at the same time as it restores much of what was missed for us as artists/teachers/guardians/friends of children/co-researchers in our own growing up. Malaguzzi's desire for a focus on children to engage, enrich, heal the whole community is borne out.*

## *The* Atelier *as Transversal Subversion*

Along with the introduction of artists within Reggio Emilia schools, Malaguzzi insisted on the presence of the *atelier* (studio) as a "subversive force" (Vecchi, 2010, p. 58). A laboratory where children, teachers and artists research the world *together, with* materials, the *atelier* is not just a space but also a way of seeing and being that disrupts tired ways of "doing school." The culture of the *atelier* opens up new possibilities for considering art making within and with communities. Art making becomes less about final products and more a focus on the process itself – the meaning that is socially constructed through the art of welcoming in and weaving together people, materials and possibilities (Helguera, 2013). A striking contrast to forms of education that separate by subject area and expertise, the *atelier* is intentionally transversal. Similarly, A@C considered how art materials could be used thoughtfully and respectfully, not with the sole intention of creating art products. For example, learning to draw was thought of as drawing to learn. Children were invited to think through what Reggio Emilia educators refer to as the hundred languages – drawing, painting, moulding, moving, talking and building. These languages disrupted and subverted more conventional ways of engaging children and created dialogue among artists, educators and children in a context of careful, respectful listening.

> **GIGI:** *During CEI gatherings, we attempt to create an* atelier/studio *atmosphere [Figure 7.2] where the educators are given time and space for open-ended, hands-on research with materials, rather than through step-by-step "prescribed" instruction, subverting what many are accustomed to in their formal classroom situations. Through researching and discovering with each other and the materials, they construct their own intentionality and relationship with materials. Reggio educator Marina Mori (2019) describes educators' formative encounters with art materials: "[I]f we [educators] didn't participate in this language, we would not be able to hear the children and their language." Working communally with art materials, the educators become the transversal connector for transformative dialogue and meaning making with each other, the material and the children.*

> **JUDITH:** *The practice of the* atelier *in South Africa is incredibly new. Part of being employed as an* atelierista *is determining what this means within our unique context. For me, the subversive role of the* atelier *is in making new paths where there are no paths [Malaguzzi, 1994]. Seeing a thought that connects, the thread of something salient that might not have been visible or seemed possible before – and following it. It is a flexibility of mind, a "what if" posture, a curiosity to step into the unknown – feeling the pull of what*

FIGURE 7.2: CEI studio experience. Photo by Gigi Yu (2019).

*might be possible. It demands incredible courage on the part of teachers and schools who welcome it in. A willingness to be changed.*

**ALEX:** *The role of the* atelier *in the Reggio Emilia approach heartens me greatly. To put time and space aside for the subversive, for disrupting to make new, transversal paths is both a radical and an essential act for living with more consideration in the world and with a greater attentiveness to our individual agency to build community through relationality, joyfully and inclusively. Open Streets Auckland Park was a project to expand the* atelier *out into the networks of Mimosa School. I am struck that A@C was a similar project but extended over fifteen years and stands as testament to the power of a Reggio Emilia-inspired* atelier. *Karyn, Jason and Kathy describe the positive impact on children and families as they re-encounter participants in the project years after an initial engagement. The project contributed to a transformation of early years pedagogy throughout Ontario. And in policy-tangible form, in 2015 Hamilton created a Charter of Rights for Children and Youth with input from over 1,500 children in the form of drawings and words, which laid the foundation for consulting children on future decisions regarding neighbourhoods* [Callaghan et al., 2017].

## *Intertwining Imagination and Reality*

Greene (1995) draws attention to imagination as a way to confront our current realities: "the capacity to invent visions of what should be and what might be in our deficit society, in the streets where we live and our schools" (p. 5). Our conversations centred much on the intertwining of imagination and reality as the channel for nurturing and expanding our communities.

**JUDITH:** *During our conversation, Jason spoke so beautifully of imagining as a process of hypothesising what is true and what is possible. Imagining helps us navigate, explore and make meaning of the world. Vecchi [2010] writes that "only by dreaming does each person grow" [p. 27]. Open Streets was in some sense a dreaming-into-being. Could we take the vision of Mimosa as a place of belonging, dancing, drumming and gift it to our neighbourhood? Could we, in the process, dream up new possibilities for our street, ourselves and each other? Each day we walked the street with children, they showed us beauty in the most unexpected places. They brought us into close encounters with what we would rather overlook or bypass or forget – a crack in the wall, a sewer cover or dustbin. Children were able to dream of the possible – a home for spiders, a window to an underground world, a bin for dinosaur bones. In a way, their research continues to dream us into being. They give us new eyes on what it is we do together every day.*

**GIGI:** *"Dreaming up new possibilities" reminds me why A@C took so readily to the Reggio Emilia approach. The artists were open to approaching each day with the children like a "blank canvas," prepared with points of departure yet open to the wonder that comes from the unexpectedness in art making. This way of being contrasted with that of teachers who were more accustomed to having daily plans with goals and objectives. I recall one of the CEI sessions when participants joined together at a college campus raku pottery studio. Raku pottery is a process filled with unanticipated moments, mystery and drama, as one is never certain of the outcomes. In this experience, teachers made a connection between the unpredictable – the imagination – and hypothesizing within the raku pottery process and the realities of their classrooms. By letting go of expectations, wonder-filled surprises emerged and new realities imagined. As discussed in our conversation with A@C, the role of the educator is to hold all the threads together. Both imagination and reality are interwoven within the life of the classroom.*

**ALEX:** *Imagination is how we journey into alternative perspectives of the world and ourselves. As Judith and Gigi so evocatively express, the exquisite paradox is that our full attentiveness to the real material (clay, sewer covers) draws out our imagination, and conversely the play of our imagination facilitates a greater attentiveness to the materially real.*

## *Documentation: Weaving the Threads Back Together*

All three projects valued documenting, reflecting on and sharing experiences as a way of creating meaning. For A@C, publications and public events were a way to honour the processes and work of children, artists and the families. During the Open Streets event, children's research into their neighbourhood was shared and converged with academic forms of research, culminating in a report launched at a local university. In the process, teachers and children at Mimosa started to take the work they did together more seriously – embracing and embodying the title of researchers. The art material encounters with both the CEI participants and the children in their classrooms were documented and periodically shared through virtual small-group reflection meetings as an opportunity to collaboratively make sense of the ongoing work. A final exhibit was curated by CEI participants; documentation of the children's art-making processes was displayed alongside the educators' documentation. The exhibit was shared at an "Educators' Exchange Day" for the broader education community.

Within each of our communities, documentation marks the praxis: how we move theories into practice, how practice makes theories for us to live by, provisionally and emergently. In documentation, we return to a central thread and are able to weave ourselves and the meaning we are making into wider and wider circles. The emphasis on curating documentation for public display with an attentiveness to aesthetic experiences also critically serves to give visibility to community arts education within early childhood. The deep work of praxis we describe here is brought into public view and is a means for shifting children, artists and educators away from the periphery into the centre of reimagining and transforming the realities of how we all live in community. Through documenting, as we do in a sense with this chapter, we pull at the threads so they can be seen individually and weave them back together for a new perspective on the nature of community.

## *Conclusion*

In developing this chapter, we worked to understand what transverses our three international projects. Each context nurtured transversalities: weaving together the arts, notions of community and early childhood education. Our shared ideological alignment is as singular as our contexts are diverse. We are all invested primarily in understanding community as formed through relationships and the importance of nourishing creative connections. All our projects use the arts as a caring, respectful – but also subversive and disruptive – facilitating medium for (re)imagining, (re)thinking and (re)making community together. Our conversations simultaneously highlighted the distinct differences of our contexts and the efficacy of our shared, Reggio Emilia-inspired approach in mobilizing creative, dynamic, positive social change within the particular weaves of our individual situations. We hope that our philosophical alignment inspires others working in early childhood community arts settings across the globe.

## REFERENCES

Cagliari, P., Castagnetti, M., Giudici, C., Rinaldi, C., Vecchi, V., & Moss, P. (Eds.). (2016). *Loris Malaguzzi and the schools of Reggio Emilia: A selection of his writings and speeches, 1945–1993*. Routledge.

Callaghan, K., Long-Wincza, V., & Velenosi, C. (2017). "Of Not For": The evolving recognition of children's rights in a community. *Journal of Childhood Studies, 42*(4), 17–36.

Cohen-Cruz, J. (2005). *Local acts: Community-based performance in the United States*. Rutgers University Press.

Freire, P. (2002). *Pedagogy of the oppressed*. Seabury. (Original work published 1970)

Greene, M. (1995). *Releasing the imagination: Essays on education, the arts, and social change*. Jossey-Bass.

Greene, M. (1997). Metaphors and multiples: Representation, the arts, and history. *Phi Delta Kappan, 28*(5), 387–394.

Helguera, P. (2013). *Education for socially engaged art: A materials and techniques handbook*. Jorge Pinto Books.

Malaguzzi, L. (1994). Your image of the child: Where teaching begins. *Child Care Information Exchange, 3*, 52–56.

Mori, M. (2019, June 29). Atelier *preparation meetings for the 15th NAREA Summer Conference*. [Audiovisual recording]. NAREA Archives.

Moss, P. (2018). *Alternative narratives in early childhood: An introduction for students and practitioners*. Routledge.

Reggio Children. (2010). *Indications: Preschools and infant-toddler centres of the municipality of Reggio Emilia* (L. Morrow, Trans.). Istituzione of the Municipality of Reggio Emilia. https://www.reggiochildren.it/en/publishing/indications/

Vecchi, V. (2010). *Art and creativity in Reggio Emilia: Exploring the role and potential of ateliers in early childhood education*. Routledge.

# 8

# Identifying Images as a Strategy for Emotional Interaction With the Environment: Neighbourhoods as Engraving Support

*Jessica Castillo Inostroza*

This visual essay shares an artistic experience developed in primary education using an a/r/tographic perspective composed by different artists. Fundamentally, it graphically reflects on the interaction with the place in which one lives. Its aim is to generate a relationship between affection and neighbourhoods, proposing the latter as an artistic space capable of receiving and collecting the figures of its inhabitants to become an engraving and human print support. The worldwide health crisis beginning in 2020 redirected the initial plan, opening new solutions based on the interpretation and assessment of each process.

*Previous History*

As a professor, engraving artist and researcher, I have designed an experience based on various previous reflections in order to achieve an emotional interaction amongst primary education students and their neighbourhood. The fundamental language used is that of engraving because it is also my own language, and it is my motivation to investigate distinct ways to non-traditionally incorporate engraving into the classroom (in other words, through more uncommon impression processes and conditions) as an exercise of technical transgression that allows for the generation of new content. Another principal motivation is the assessment of everyday spaces as constructors of identity which our daily lives naturally influence, providing context to each experience. This appreciation leads to two engraving

# IDENTIFYING IMAGES AS A STRATEGY

FIGURE 8.1: My silhouette stamped in the environment II. Photos by Jessica Castillo Inostroza (2020).

conclusions: we can understand the neighbourhood as a large matrix from which images are extracted, and at the same time, the neighbourhood becomes a support for receiving them. A/r/tography (Irwin, 2013) is the main methodology of visual investigation and proposed pedagogy employed because it utilizes my own tools as an investigator, engraving artist and professor. These tools include my artistic processes and practices as devices that are subsequently extrapolated to the classroom to generate artistic experiences with the students.

I suggest a personal piece that asks students about the relationships between people and places and how, together, they allow for the creation of an artistic space in the act of engraving the image itself onto different everyday surfaces: *Prints on the skin of the neighbourhood*. The piece comprehends the neighbourhood as a place of knowledge and containment that offers its own properties (textures, colours and shapes) to embrace the print, becoming both the support and stage for creation. Furthermore, it has the intention of leaving an emotional mark when the image itself is "submitted," enriching the neighbourhood's attributes and making the person-place link evident (see Figure 8.1).

## *Experience With the Students*

I was accepted at Miguel Hernández primary school in Granada, Spain for one year to do workshops in artistic education with the objective of delving into the creation of engraving in the fifth and sixth years of primary. The last experience revolved around the piece *Prints on the skin of the neighbourhood*. Its intention was to provoke a direct interaction with the neighbourhood, assessing the experience of walking through it and living in it, to be conscious of the fact that this relationship leaves a print on each person as well as on the place. The experience considers one's emotional response to be an acceptable cultural process, implicitly containing the senses of belonging, affection, attachment and feeling because the understanding of everyday environments begins with the assessment of one's own life (Gómez & Fenoy, 2016).

The creative process with the students was developed in the following way. To begin, students were asked what sensations invaded them when they walked through the neighbourhood on the way to school: identifying movements, smells, sounds and other important impressions. We imagine ourselves on this path. How can we interpret these sensations? We project ourselves into the neighbourhood and arrive at a self-portrait which personifies us as inhabitants.

Each student chose a part of their body to be drawn and posed in front of a piece of transparent acetate that another student held, who outlined the first with a marker. The silhouette from this exercise represented each student's unique essence and is the protagonist of the following actions. The silhouette was translated to ethylene-vinyl acetate (EVA) foam, glued to cardboard and perforated with pencil (see Figure 8.2). The intention of the matrix was to look for a place in the neighbourhood in which to stay, a creative action that connects the emotional interaction between someone and the environment as well as their overwhelming perceptions when walking and the elements that link them. In a prior experience, the students had used clay to extract images and shapes of the neighbourhood, creating matrices to "emotionally appropriate" it. This time would be the opposite: they would leave their mark on the neighbourhood.

When we were about to go out into the neighbourhood to walk around and leave our print/self-portrait on it, the state of alarm due to COVID-19 occurred. The schools were closed, and it was impossible to collectively intervene in the neighbourhood with the matrix as originally planned. A curriculum is flexible and considered to be emergent (Herrera & Didriksson, 1999); thus, as a teacher, I decided to close the experience through the interpretation of the students' work based on my knowledge of each student. The final solution was to personify each student with the help of my son

FIGURE 8.2: Creative process in the classroom II. Photos by Jessica Castillo Inostroza (2020).

(a member of the group), interpreting each portrait and looking for a place for each: a gesture in which affection and empirical assessment of each person is present.

With the matrices in hand, we took small outings to discover distinct areas capable of adapting and receiving each image. The procedure included the staining of each matrix in the place and its direct impression onto the chosen surfaces through corporal pressure (hand and foot). This process generated an important change in the place, and each self-portrait became an "event" on the landscape, shaping a bridge between a person and context (see Figures 8.3 and 8.4).

FIGURE 8.3: Stamping the matrices in the neighbourhood. Photos by Jessica Castillo Inostroza (2020).

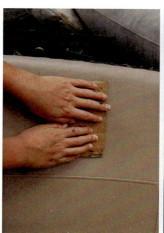

FIGURE 8.4: Stamping the matrices in the neighbourhood II. Photos by Jessica Castillo Inostroza (2020).

FIGURE 8.5: The identity of the class scattered in the environment. Final results. Photos by Jessica Castillo Inostroza (2020).

Each self-portrait finally found its place and with it, the neighbourhood received and contained the identifying image as a symbol of life within it. New symbolic images were created, transforming the neighbourhood into an artistic space and structuring a scaffolding as an interaction with the medium (see Figure 8.5).

In conclusion, I believe that engraving possesses extensive creative possibilities beyond its traditional use. Coupled with a/r/tography, teaching-learning is strengthened because when the creative process is genuinely shared, artistic and pedagogic practices improve. An emotional focus and assessment create a close personal link to the neighbourhood since people construct their referential universe through their surroundings. Finally, opening the project up to previously unplanned artistic solutions does not diminish the possible results, but instead enriches them.

ACKNOWLEDGEMENTS

*Special Thanks*: The writer is grateful for the financial backing of the National Commission of Scientific and Technological Investigation, ANID PFCHA/DOCTORADOBECAS CHILE/2016-72170041.

REFERENCES

Gómez, C., & Fenoy, B. (2016). La sensorialidad como estrategia para la educación patrimonial en el aula de educación infantil [Sensoriality as a strategy for heritage education in the pre-school classroom]. *EARI. Educación Artística Revista de Investigación, 7*, 54–68. http://dx.doi.org/10.7203/eari.7.8010

Herrera, A., & Didriksson, A. (1999). La construcción curricular: innovación, flexibilidad y competencias [The construction of the curriculum: Innovation, flexibility and skills]. *Revista Educación Superior y Sociedad (ESS), 10*(2), 29–52. https://www.iesalc.unesco.org/ess/index.php/ess3/article/view/146

Irwin, R. L. (2013). Becoming a/r/tography. *Studies in Art Education, 54*(3), 198–215. https://doi.org/10.1080/00393541.2013.11518894

# 9

# We Are Small, but We Have Loud Voices: Children Leading the Way to Support Community Connections Through Art

*Sue Girak*

*We are small, but we have loud voices.*

(Sophie, aged 11, personal communication, 5 December 2018)

A school community can be the foundation and driver for community-based art education (CBAE) that can strengthen ties within a school, and the following example can be used as a model for other schools and communities. This chapter describes how City Beach Primary School's (CBPS) visual arts programme reflects the school's vision of building strong relationships with its families and cultivating external partnerships to encourage ties with the local community: embodying the school's motto *Achieving Together with Pride*. CBPS is a small suburban school in Perth, Western Australia. The parents embrace the "country-school" feel reminiscent of small rural schools and whole-heartedly support and advocate for opportunities to invite families into the school, supporting their children through art exhibitions, performances or sporting events, all of which have become the school's nucleus. In this chapter, I propose a concentric construct by which children's art can bring the community together, and the school can be a hub for social cohesion.

Primary schools are dynamic places. Working as an a/r/tographer in this context, I conduct informal classroom-based inquiries through a/r/tographic action research, a model I developed during my post-graduate study. Through this method of inquiry, I design student-centred programmes to support community connections. The examples discussed in this chapter demonstrate that CBAE initiated in a school is a context-driven process rather than a template.

*Sculptures @ City Beach* (S@CB), which began as a lunchtime activity, has grown into a major exhibition where adults are no longer passive observers of children's achievements; instead, they are participants who collaborate with their children. The *Footprint Project* was conceived to teach a mathematical concept through art, but quickly took on a life of its own and transformed into an investigation of plastic pollution, which inspired children and community groups in Beijing, China and Mandurah in Western Australia to do the same. The final example of a student-centred programme is an ongoing partnership with the local Rotary Club, which began as a chance encounter during a school tour and has resulted in a revamp of the Year 6 art programme to accommodate volunteers' expertise. By listening to children rather than approaching projects with predetermined assumptions, I encourage them to make art with personal and social relevance and welcome the community to join in.

## *Educational Context*

According to McClure et al. (2017), quality arts education is determined by a set of principles that offer children an eclectic mix of media and techniques within a dynamic programme that supports aesthetic expression. The art teacher's role is to listen and respond to students' diverse interests and abilities to support their diverse way of making meaning through art making. This inquiry-based approach to art education applies to various contexts, including school-based community art education where there is provision for collaborations between the school and community groups. In CBPS's case, the school is the hub of a community that generates outside interests through civically engaged art education. Shields et al. (2020) argue that "civic engagement is not just concerned with identifying societal and political structures. It is also concerned with how young people understand themselves as civic agents capable of starting and sustaining change" (p. 123): an objective included in these programmes.

Shields et al. (2020) assert that teachers play a significant role in creating openings for students to become critical thinkers and makers through civically engaged art education. Their approach aligns with that of Austin (2008), who describes community arts to engage and support active participation regardless of perceived talent or skills "to foster change and achieve empowerment" (p. 176). Through CBAE, students can make connections with their local community by actively pursuing partnerships with schools, artists and arts organizations (Austin, 2008; Luo & Lau, 2020; Ulbricht, 2005). While these methods empower children to make their voices heard, the premise of this chapter is more in line with Blatt-Gross' (2017) position that "the process of making art might play a constructive role in establishing a sense of community cohesion" and that "collective artmaking offers a vehicle through which joint endeavours can facilitate connections and commonalities" (p. 52). In Western Australia, the Visual Arts Curriculum's *Response* substrand "sharing the arts through performance, presentation or display for an audience" (School Curriculum and Standards Authority, n.d., p. 2) opens the way to use a/r/tography as a method to plan for and deliver student-centred programmes that support community connections.

A/r/tography is a well-established methodology supporting the multidimensional identity of creative practitioners as they work within the realm of artist/researcher/teacher (Irwin & Springgay, 2008). It is a context-driven, practice-based methodology, ever-evolving and unfolding (Irwin et al., 2017). My current teaching emerged from my post-graduate study and my motivation to bring a symbiosis of art making, research and pedagogy into the art room. Primary schools are dynamic places, and as one project ends, another begins. As such, I engage in informal research through a/r/tographic action research, a model I developed during my PhD studies. The model incorporates dual-action research spirals that reflect the symbiotic nature of my a/r/tographic practice to help me identify the critical moments that connect and complement my teaching and creative practices. A/r/tographic action research provides a context allowing me to examine critical or "ah ha" moments to theorize about my praxis (Girak, 2015). Yet the rhizomatic nature of a/r/tography (Coleman, 2018) often sends me off on tangents. While an exhilarating experience in the studio, it is a disruptive habit in a primary school because children have time constraints dictated by a curriculum, so I have learned to harness the tangents through a/r/tographic action research. In this chapter, I discuss three critical moments that demonstrate how CBAE can be embedded into a school's regular art programme through genuine partnerships with families and community groups, achieving a mutual goal of community cohesion.

## *Sculptures @ City Beach*

*[My daughter and I] went up to the school late at night to lay the shells together as part of her sculpture. [She] found it exciting and exhilarating, and we both loved the time together and the challenge.*
(Parent, personal communication, 20 July 2020)

The CBPS art programme includes the S@CB annual exhibition, a tradition that started in 2008. S@CB is timed to coincide with *Sculpture by the Sea*, an internationally acclaimed exhibition. Every March, the school makes its annual pilgrimage to Cottesloe Beach to view sculptures in situ. Since its inception, participation in S@CB has been voluntary. Children create sculptures from salvaged materials at home and exhibit them at school. In 2016, my first year at the school, I was expected to continue the tradition. My first exhibition was a baptism by fire as my predecessor relied on her tacit knowledge to organize and host the event. With little paperwork to rely on, the only option was to put faith in the principal's reassurance that everyone knows what to do, and it "just happens." No matter whom I asked, the response was the same. The school had a custom of inviting exhibiting artists to judge the children's sculptures. I had no contacts in the art world, so I began volunteering at *Sculpture by the Sea* to recruit judges. Through these new connections, I found four artists to judge the school exhibition; as well, a CBPS student was invited to present the *Sculpture by the Sea* Kids Choice Award, and the school was gifted an ephemeral sculpture to lengthen the artwork's life a little longer.

After the smooth transition of my first year, the principal told me that S@CB should evolve the exhibition to reflect my teaching style. However, in the following year came a change in administration, and I was offered an exit strategy: having fulfilled my initial obligation, I could have dropped the exhibition altogether. Yet I decided to continue with the tradition to strengthen the close-knit school community as families value the long-lasting friendships they make through the school. Therefore, as the first event in the school calendar, the exhibition is an opportunity to welcome new families to the community.

Nevertheless, I needed to modify the format to address covert parental involvement in their children's artwork. In my first year, I observed that instead of taking a passive role viewing their children's sculptures, parents enthusiastically supported their children's creative endeavours – so much so that sculptures with obvious adult help were passed off as individual submissions. There were several awkward conversations with parents as they tried to convince me how their young children could spot-weld or single-handedly use power tools to create larger-than-life-sized sculptures. To reduce covert parental involvement, my choices were to take complete control and have the children make their sculptures in class, or to embrace the idea of families working together to make art. Knowing that a classroom programme could not deliver the quality of thought and effort that I saw coming from home, I included a category for family collaborations. There are no more uncomfortable conversations as parents and grandparents openly celebrate how much they love working with their children. While some adults take a back seat and are there to lend a helping hand when needed, others enjoy being able to bring their whole family together to work on a project.

In 2020, the parent exhibition *Sculpture by the Sea* was in a precarious position, struggling to maintain long-term sponsorship. I flagged to parents that a sculpture exhibition without the backup of *Sculpture by the Sea* might not be sustainable. However, buoyed by their children's enthusiasm for the event, the parents rejected my concerns outright and suggested alternatives such as an Open Night sculpture exhibition or artist-in-residence sculpture programme to safeguard S@CB. Since the first exhibition, parental commitment has meant that its success no longer relies on a motivated teacher working alone. The school community contributes to the event's sustainability. As families move on to high school, they recruit new volunteers because S@CB has become a tradition they are unwilling to abandon.

## *Footprint Project*

An idea originating at CBPS and moving into the wider community was the *Footprint Project*. The first iteration, *Walking Together with Pride*, was introduced to give students a practical example of the mathematical concept of scale and proportion and soon became a set of large-scale footprints to convey the scale of global plastic pollution. CBPS is in a beachside suburb with ocean views of Perth's pristine white-sand beaches; for that reason, it is very easy for students to underestimate the environmental degradation caused by single-use plastic pollution.

During one lesson, I wondered out loud what it would be like to make a large-scale artwork that could be photographed by a drone. I did not expect to see children bursting with ideas as their hands shot up straight into the air. Their overwhelming enthusiasm had caught me off guard. At this early stage, I did not know where the idea would take us, so I turned to the class and asked them what they thought. At that moment, I was reminded that children want to make their opinions known and that if permitted, they could instigate community art initiatives.

*Walking Together with Pride* was the first of three collaborative *Footprint Projects*, embodying the school's motto of *Achieving Together with Pride* and its values of respect, responsibility and resilience. Since the planning process was to be collaborative, the students and I decided to make a site-specific installation to show the school physical evidence of their single-use plastic consumption. We asked families to collect and count the plastic bags they brought home from the supermarket and to use them to make artwork based on the school community's environmental footprint. Since this would not be a permanent artwork, a drone's aerial camera would record the event. As a collective, we agreed on most things; however, the students rejected my idea of making 160 footprints to represent every student. Instead, they favoured eight "giant" footprints to represent each year's group. We placed the footprints on the school oval, to look as if they were "walking" towards the ocean.

During the production phase, being surrounded by thousands of plastic bags may have looked like mayhem and a mess, but the students were personifying the school's motto and values from a pedagogical perspective. They collaborated in small groups by negotiating and allocating tasks, demonstrated resilience by overcoming frustrations as they learned to work together in teams, taught their friends new skills and took pride in the finished product as they reworked areas they deemed as below standard. Respect and responsibility for the environment increased as Year 1s spent their lunchtimes protecting birds by busily collecting plastic rubbish in the playground. These essential life skills were being learned and practised in an authentic arts-led context.

The children seemed genuinely shocked by the number of shopping bags they collected. One child concluded, "From the amount of plastic bags we collected, City Beach parents must go shopping all the time." They suggested ways to reduce waste by either reusing plastic bags they already had or adopting reusable bags. Many children said that using discarded materials in art increased their awareness of the effect plastic pollution had on animals, the ocean and the ecosystem. Others began to see the potential in other salvageable materials, reflected in their S@CB sculptures the following year.

Later that year, I announced to my classes that I would be presenting the *Footprint Project* at conferences in Hangzhou, China and Daegu, South Korea. The children were proud that an international audience would see their artwork. After the Hangzhou presentation, the Director of the Arts and Physical Education programme from the Beijing New Talent Academy (BNTA) approached me to investigate ways to introduce creative reuse into an arts-led education for sustainability programme in her school. Together we spent eighteen months exploring strategies, including practical advice from my students on maintaining student engagement. In May 2018, I was invited to the school to see the outcomes of their creative reuse programme. From various recyclable materials, primary students made ten large-scale footprints leading visitors to the school's entrance. Creative reuse was a new concept for many of the teachers at the school; the vice-principal told me he was sceptical until he received numerous phone calls from parents telling him their children had not grasped the concept of sustainability and the ramifications that pollution had on the environment until they started making art from discarded materials. The children's response became the catalyst to embed creative reuse into BNTA's art visual arts programme.

Closer to home, eleven schools and community groups from Mandurah, Western Australia adapted the *Footprint Project* for the Stretch Festival in May 2018. In response to *Walking Together with Pride*, the Mandurah community participated in *Put a Lid on It!* They exhibited 33 footprints at the Mandurah Estuary, including the footprints loaned from CBPS. By 2018, the Western Australian government had banned single-use plastic bags, so the community used non-recyclable plastic bottle tops to make their footprints. While measuring the impact of the site-specific installation on passers-by was not practical, I listened to people's reactions as they viewed the work or by talking to them directly. They told me that the footprints initiated conversations in families about waste and the lack of recycling facilities in Western Australia. When speaking to families about their involvement in the project, I found that like the CBPS and BNTA families, they were shocked to see how much plastic was used in packaging and were motivated to find alternative ways to reduce waste.

## Rotary Volunteer Programme

*Your three Rotarians LOVE your art classes. So lots of benefits for all concerned – especially in the mental health department of the old boys.*
    (Spouse of a Rotary volunteer, personal communication, 15 October 2020)

In 2018, the Rotary Club of Cambridge, Western Australia met with CBPS's newly appointed principal to investigate how they could fulfil their mission to provide service to others at the school. On a tour of the school, a Rotarian and his spouse visited the art room. If they had come any other day, I doubt our ongoing relationship would have commenced; however, by chance the Year 1 class was learning about Paul Cummins' 2014 Tower of London *Blood Swept Lands and Seas of Red*, an installation that marked the centenary of the outbreak of the First World War. Not wanting to disturb the children, the visitors stood at the door, but the distraction was too much for the children, so I invited them in. During a discussion, one child who would only have been three years old in 2014 recalled seeing the exhibition in London. He shared vivid memories of his experience, and the visitors followed suit enthusiastically by sharing their memories. Then as suddenly as they appeared, they left and I thought nothing more of the interruption. Afterwards, the Rotarian told me how he was so moved by the visit that he was eager to volunteer in the art room. This proposition aligned with the school's policy of making connections with the broader community and the Rotary Club's mission of service to others. Grateful for the additional help, I was also interested in the principles of intergenerational pedagogy based on the premise of reciprocal relationships and the respectful sharing of knowledge and skills (Cartmel et al., 2018). So, Jeremy and Max started volunteering in the Year 5/6 class once a fortnight. I thought they would be most helpful working with the older students, who at the time were working in small groups to design and construct large-scale papier mâché ice-cream sculptures for an up-and-coming exhibition (see Figure 9.1).

FIGURE 9.1: *Global Meltdown*. With an environmental message about global warming, the ice-cream sculpture was displayed at CBPS's 2019 Open Night exhibition. Photo by Sue Girak (2019).

Until the Rotarians and I began to understand each other, working with the volunteers had its logistical challenges. Fortnightly visits meant that the ice-cream project was structured to fit around the Rotarians' availability. Soon the visits became weekly when Jeremy recruited another Rotarian, David, to volunteer. For the volunteers, working with me also posed challenges. My flexible approach in an inquiry-based art room would have been a far cry from the structured arts and crafts lessons they would have had as children. The Rotarians had high expectations of what the children could achieve and were surprised that they did not know how to use hand tools. Rather than allowing the volunteers to simply give students the answers, I had to persuade them to accept an inquiry-led method.

When the initial project ended, the Rotarians immediately asked, "What's next?" While there was no next project, no one wanted to see the partnership end. As such, the Rotarians' enthusiasm became a turning point for my upper-school art programme; that marked the moment I chose to make the art room the centre of a community partnership with the local Rotary Club. To maintain ties with the Club, CBPS has worked behind the scenes to make keep the partnership viable. The school administration ensures that my timetable fits in with the volunteers' availability, and I have modified the Year 6 programme significantly to provide opportunities for volunteers with non-arts backgrounds to act as mentors. The Rotarians are reliable volunteers, so their ongoing support has been instrumental to the sculpture programme's success and the addition of a lino printmaking programme.

## *Conclusion*

Using three examples, this chapter has described a bespoke approach to CBAE in a suburban primary school. These examples show that even within one school, an art teacher can employ a mix of strategies to promote community cohesion through school-based art programmes. Whether it is to organize activities that embrace family collaborations, explore themes of environmental degradation through art making, or enjoy the benefits of a volunteer scheme, the school's motto *Achieving Together with Pride* grounds the art programme. It takes more than a single event to establish genuine relationships; as well, in each case the collaborations are student-centred, and the school art programme has become a community hub. Therefore, to maintain community spirit for the long term, teachers need to surrender control, listen to what their students and families want and explore ways to facilitate the process of strengthening the school community through art education.

## REFERENCES

Austin, J. (2008). Training community artists in Scotland. In G. Coutts & T. Jokela (Eds.), *Art, community and environment: Educational perspectives* (pp. 175–192). Intellect Books. https://doi.org/10.1111/j.1476-8070.2009.01616.x

Blatt-Gross, C. (2017). Creating community from the inside out: A concentric perspective on collective artmaking. *Arts Education Policy Review, 118*(1), 51–59. https://dx.doi.org/10.1080/10632913.2016.1244781

Cartmel, J., Radford, K., Dawson, C., Fitzgerald, A., & Vecchio, N. (2018). Developing an evidenced based intergenerational pedagogy in Australia. *Journal of Intergenerational Relationships, 16*(1–2), 64–85. https://doi.org/10.1080/15350770.2018.1404412

Coleman, K. S. (2018). Through the looking glass: Reflecting on an embodied understanding of creativity and praxis as an a/r/tographer. In A. Sinner, R. L. Irwin, & T. Jokela (Eds.), *Visually provoking dissertations in art education* (pp. 50–59). Lapland University Press.

Girak, S. (2015). *Forget me not: An exhibition – and – Creative Reuse: How rescued materials transformed my a/r/tographic practice: An exegesis* [Unpublished doctoral dissertation]. Edith Cowan University, Joondalup. https://ro.ecu.edu.au/theses/1618/

Irwin, R. L., Agra Pardiñas, M. J., Barney, D. T., Chen, J. C. H., Dias, B., Golparian, S., & MacDonald, A. (2017) A/r/tography around the world. In G. Barton & M. Baguley (Eds.), *The Palgrave handbook of global arts education* (pp. 475–496). Palgrave Macmillan. https://doi.org/10.1057/978-1-137-55585-4_29

Irwin, R. L., & Springgay, S. (2008). A/r/tography as practice-based research. In M. Cahnmann-Taylor & R. Siegesmund (Eds.), *Arts-based research in education: Foundations for practice* (pp. 103–124). Routledge.

Luo, N., & Lau, C. Y. (2020). Community-based art education in China: Practices, issues and challenges. *International Journal of Art & Design Education, 39*(2), 445–460. https://doi.org/10.1111/jade.12287

McClure, M., Tarr, P., Thompson, C. M., & Eckhoff, A. (2017). Defining quality in visual art education for young children: Building on the position statement of the early childhood art educators. *Arts Education Policy Review, 118*(3), 154–163. https://doi.org/10.1080/10632913.2016.1245167

School Curriculum and Standards Authority. (n.d.). *The arts – Scope and sequence – P-6*. Government of Western Australia. https://k10outline.scsa.wa.edu.au/

Shields, S. S., Fendler, R., & Henn, D. (2020). A vision of civically engaged art education: Teens as arts-based researchers. *Studies in Art Education, 61*(2), 123–141. https://doi.org10.1080/00393541.2020.1740146

Ulbricht, J. (2005). What is community-based art education? *Art Education, 58*(2), 6–12. https://doi.org/10.1080/00043125.2005.11651529

# 10

# Infernal Learning: Becoming Members of Academic Communities

*Anniina Suominen, Tiina Pusa, Minna Suoniemi, Eljas Suvanto and Elina Julin*

> *Countless times, I have been told that I cannot behave, I don't fit. Apparently, I don't speak or create art like a real artist and I cannot behave like an academic (woman). My relationship with things and my ways of being have been remarked as too animistic, my themes too personal, and my speech reminiscent of a child's speech. I then began to speak with a lowered voice and with more conviction as I became more comfortable with the academic rhetoric.*
>
> (From shared research materials: reflective writing by a research group member)

Metanarratives on academic communities of knowledge and practice are learned at all educational levels, internalized to some extent and, in turn, performed repeatedly throughout one's artistic and academic careers. In a way, such narratives elaborate a sense of oneness, a semi-fictional story of a Finnish nation constituted on the ideals of equality and democracy. In our research project, we critically explore this grand narrative. We argue that many aspects of social and cultural inequality are silenced and marginalized in the creation of a system that does indeed provide opportunities for all aspiring academics to succeed but fails to recognize and take into consideration many socio-economic, cultural and linguistic backgrounds. We approach this grand narrative critically and by intentionally assuming simultaneously centralized and fringe perspectives. Although our project is bound to and framed by Finnish society and educational institutions, our research is less about specific locations and more about belonging to somewhat abstract academic and higher education communities that, regardless of their seemingly permeable boundaries, exercise power and exclusivity.

Through our collective work, we attempt to articulate some of the often hidden and silenced struggles of persons from non-academic and/or less economically advanced backgrounds as they enter into an academic community. These communities, while generally perceived as progressive and liberal, are often rather exclusive and instituted on academic norms of talent and intelligence founded on cultural capital, which young people with less privileged backgrounds have not had equal opportunities to acquire. However, rather than dismissing the crucial work and knowledge production generated by an academic community, we argue for more inclusive communities of academics and arts professionals founded on a commons: a sense of sharing, knowledge generation, belonging and participation. Trained in the highest-ranking academic and art schools in Finland, we feel it is partially our responsibility to participate in exposing the commonly silenced experiences of bias, discrimination and inaccessibility existing within academic institutions and traditions.

In this chapter, we explain the context of our project and our orientations. Next, we discuss feminism and class as concepts and theories that have significantly influenced our research process. The third section discusses our method and introduces the research materials. We then elaborate on the thematic, collective research process and discuss two of our themes through examples from the narratives used as research material. Finally, we evaluate the process of this research thus far and articulate some of our strategies for further inquiry and action.

## *Context, Orientations and Positionalities*

When we refer to academic communities and contexts, we frame our experiences through art and art education institutes that are by and large located in the capital region of Helsinki. All five of us are part of these communities through our roles as academics, professionals and students. Thus, in one way or another we are all associated with the leading universities in Finland. It is also our shared concern how (seemingly) homogenous is the group of people working or studying in these contexts compared to the larger population of the country.

As artists, educators and researchers, we present our research work to illustrate systemic, subtle oppression. We are fully aware of how the Finnish welfare and educational system has made it possible for us to acquire the education and professional privileges we currently possess. By sharing our partially conflicting and contradictory academic growth stories, which are much more porous and inconsistent than the typical success stories presented in academic contexts, we reveal some of the previously unspoken narratives that speak of insecurities, uncertainty, shame and guilt. We also articulate the tremendous strength required to succeed when struggling financially, or when finding out that one's ways of being are perceived as culturally unfit within academic discourse. We come from different family backgrounds from a variety of areas of the country, and we are also diverse in gender and sexual orientations.

One standpoint (Harding, 2007) we share is that we do not come from established academic families with significant economic wealth. While there is little to no research about families' cultural or economic wealth in Finland, the country is small enough to see how certain family privileges are passed down through the generations. The same applies to the visual art world, film and literary arts. Through our collective work, we initiate broader debate and discussion concerning the experiences of children and young people who desire academic and artistic careers, but come from economically disadvantaged or otherwise unstable backgrounds, or whose families for various reasons do not participate in the cultural events and dialogues valued by academia. By sharing our collective research process, we present a counternarrative to the dominant view of academia as a community of independent intellectuals engaged in critical inquiry.

## *Feminism and Class*

We draw from and respect intersectional feminist concepts of artistic, embodied and non-linguistic/linear modes of knowing. Our project leans on feminist intersectionality (Cho et al., 2013) to address educational accessibility, with particular attention to normative notions of societal and cultural class. These notions of class, regardless of their common use in discourse and as a reference point, are hushed and silenced in the context of the arts and art education. Intersectional feminist theory and research recognize class as one of the aspects generating and maintaining structures of injustice and inequality (Suoranta & Ryynänen, 2014).

Through our research, writing and artistic process, we formed a central theoretical dialogue with Beverly Skeggs' (1997, 2004) scholarship on class and gender, which in turn draws from Foucault (1970, 1977) and Bourdieu (1979). For Skeggs, class is not a permanent category but a performative process undergoing constant making and remaking. Skeggs builds upon Judith Butler's (1990) gender theory by claiming that social and cultural class is not something people are born into and in which they remain but is formed through actions and discursive negotiations. Skeggs (1997) introduced the concept of respect and argued that "respectability is one of the most ubiquitous signifiers of class" (p. 1). In academic circles, respect and respectability are often established through rather complicated rhetoric and a knowledge base most familiar to those who have had opportunities to obtain and further this knowledge, which in turn initiates access and secures respectability. Many of the narratives included in the research materials generated by our research group speak of language, respect and respectability, or the sensed lack of these.

Notions of class are closely related to notions of democracy (Alhanen & Perhoniemi, 2017). A linkage between education and democracy is evident through John Dewey's influence on Finnish critical education theorists and art educators (see also Goldblatt, 2006). To Dewey, democracy is not simply a political system but an evolving experience of living together and sharing (Dewey, 1916; Suoranta, 2003; Tomperi & Piattoeva, 2005). Alhanen and Perhoniemi (2017) have proposed that education, for Dewey, was a platform for sharing and learning from one another, enabling mutual interclass understandings to emerge. Indeed, traditionally Finnish society has not been perceived as class-based and hierarchical. However, this notion appears to be another blind spot in the metanarrative (Anttila, 2016; Erola, 2012; Järvinen & Kolbe, 2007) rather than the actual felt and experienced reality of many. This is the case despite the founding of the free public schooling structures, and later by the establishment of financial aid in the 1970s available for those who needed it, obtaining academic training and careers has been accessible for everyone regardless of socio-economic background.

According to Skeggs' (2004), class is a dynamic process in which conflicts and struggles are acutely present. As Bourdieu's notions of class emerged in relation to the French culture and context and Skeggs' in relation to British cultural and socio-political movements, we use their theoretical reflections to mirror our experiences in the Finnish context (Anttila, 2016; Erola, 2012).

## *Method and Materials*

As we discussed our research themes and artistic processes, our collective process began to take shape. Each of us wrote vignettes and reflections focused on experiences and memories related to art, art education and art museums: framed by family cultures and influenced by experiences of class. We also wrote about how the arts and education in the arts played a role in shaping and changing our status and access to cultural circles in society. We wrote these stories in relation to artworks we had created over the years, and we also began new artistic processes that allowed us to further inquire into our emerging understandings. Our main research material consists of narratives and artwork that are analysed in dialogue and through informal modes of sharing, paying attention to bodily and emotional affect, showing empathy and looking for resonance and relatability. In a way, we adapted a version of narrative analysis (Riessman, 2008). Reading each other's stories, explaining our own and discussing both shared particularities and differing aspects of our stories made us sensitive to the highly emotional nature of this process.

Through this collaboration and our writing process, we wanted to question the often-perceived binary division between academic and non-academic categories by identifying and bringing to the discussion more diversified notions of academics and art (education) professionals working in the field. In this way, we hope to contribute towards building a more diverse community of learning and knowing. Our aim is to articulate how normative and historical notions of class are still partially maintained in academic institutions, as notions of "educated" or "talented" persons still influence student-selection criteria and colour academic conversations.

Our stories depict glimpses into our journeys of becoming and conquest. These are stories of claiming, questioning, naming and renaming. They are also stories of loss and denial: gaining access to something highly desirable has meant distancing oneself from ways of being, speaking, believing and thinking that do not fit if one desires to be part of academia and the art world. Our stories speak of liminal learning between and in the shadows of educational and welfare institutions. We have no desire to dismantle the Finnish educational system but rather to defend its integrity by initiating more meaningful discussions concerning access, equality, equity and fairness. We characterize our internalized "becoming" stories as infernal for the emotional burden that is carried in silence and for the behaviours that are considered disruptive and challenge academic norms. We nicknamed this whole process *infernal learning*, as sharing and consequently beginning to understand ourselves and our peers was frequently coloured by some sort of pain and turmoil. Our aim is to share journeys of becoming, initiation and acceptance within the academic community – a community made possible by the Finnish social and legal justice system that supports a fair and democratic educational system. We recognize our privilege and know we would not be holding our current positions, or perhaps would not have achieved our academic degrees, had it not been for the equalizing policies in our institutional systems. Still, these journeys have not been painless, requiring adaptation to values and speech often previously strange to us. This in turn mandated hiding aspects of ourselves and our families and asked us to become different people.

Amongst our research group, we feel comfortable and safe when sharing our personal stories. Still, we feel uncertain and concerned about voicing our infernal learning narratives as personalized, singular experiences. In this text, rather than identifying persons, we speak with a common "we" voice and write from the perspective of resonance and relatability. Some could see this decision as contradictory to our philosophy of, and aims for, creating a more equitable learning and knowledge commons, which entails valuing and respecting diverse contributions based on the interests, needs and abilities of community members. However, we see our approach as epistemologically essential. The "we" is rather flexible, like a common body of water: sometimes it includes all of us, and sometimes it speaks for one. Our inquiry consists of stories written by all authors of this chapter.

## *The Thematic Process: Establishing a Sense of Sharing*

In this chapter, we discuss two of the themes we use to frame our experiences in relation to theory and research carried out by others: (1) our tendencies for overachievement, and (2) shame, pain and emotional disingenuity.

In contemporary Finnish society, conflicts and differences between and across classes may not be obvious as the distinctions of class are also fluid and flexible. These conflicts and further divisions into not/belonging are not divisions between the elite and working class, but rather refined indications and distinctions through manners, habits and performativity – evident through the use of time, relationships and shared through social media. This point is important as we define our orientation to this discussion through academic and non-academic divisions, which we see as clear classifications. For us, this is a perspective or a position, a way of looking and a certain way of question-posing as Skeggs (2004) might express these class themes. The specificity of one's orientation brings to the forefront experiences, feelings and situations that prompt emotional and embodied reactions.

### Overachievement and the Habits That Created Passages

What became evident through our shared texts was the urge to overachieve and constantly prove our worth. This sense of urgency to prove our value and capabilities – combined with the simultaneous, constant sense of insufficiency – shaped our experiences and made us "fighters" in various ways. We each did well in school, managed our studies, kept on progressing despite some rather significant instabilities and insecurities in our (family) lives. In many ways, the pressures of succeeding were partly because of our gratitude for the system that enabled us to succeed. Unfortunately, this drive to improve and perform easily blurs the lines between reasonable and unreasonable expectations; thus, many of our shared stories also deal with disproportionate expectations for endurance and tolerance.

I have developed ways of being super-fast and efficient with the task when I have the time and space for concentration. There have been numerous incidents in my life that in my mind have confirmed this self-perception of laziness and being an ill-fit in the academy. The earliest I recall took place when my teacher in elementary school told me that she would never give me the small monetary scholarship at the end of each school year if she wasn't obliged to do so based on my high grades. I respected her so much and my school world evolved around performing well so that she would approve of me. I wanted and I needed the money, but her clear dislike of me made earning it dirty.

I have high expectations for myself, and that easily transfers into high expectations for my students. From the perspective of class-identifiers, I am a doer and a practitioner, a body in action. Not an instructor or a supervisor giving instructions to guide practice, the work carried out by others.

This constant self-driven obsession to improve, to do better and to serve others is perhaps one of the more heart-wrenching aspects of our stories. Each of us has had to contemplate the truer desires and motivations driving us towards constant advancement. We have asked – are we driven by ambition, gratitude or obsession? Many psychologists and researchers have studied self-efficacy and motivations. We also sense this urgency with our students.

### Shame and Pain, Emotional Disingenuity

To familiarize oneself with and become accustomed to previously unknown worlds and experiences requires a transition from one to another – a movement either towards or away. Skeggs (2004) writes about mobility and people's access to spaces and ability to move between them. In our case, these are conceptual, social and physical spaces. Skeggs also explores how movement and mobility carry pain, both emotional and physical. Living on the fringes or within the liminal spaces is tasking. Sensitive, fragile and essential learning happens within these spaces, but the constant balancing act, like walking a tightrope, is accompanied by a nagging awareness of no safety net underneath. Besides physical moves, transitioning into high school and then progressing through advanced studies, we were also students at a meta-level, learning how to be, how to belong and how to either become noticed or avoid unnecessary attention.

Shame was also strongly associated with and present in our short stories and vignettes. We confessed how we had been ashamed of our family backgrounds and the sense of disability and lack of fluency this caused. Then again, we were also ashamed of our insufficient gratitude for the genuine cultural opportunities and experiences provided for us. We realized how transitions into the academic and art worlds colonized us to perceive our original orientations and perspectives as something of less value and less dignity.

> I feel a sort of guilt: I have been fortunate to have a loving, wonderful family, so why do I critique them in this manner? How come I am not more appreciative of how well things have played out and how fortunate I have truly been? I am ungrateful.
> On the other hand, it feels good to write about this.

Occasionally, we caught ourselves in emotional disingenuity:

> Following a conference abroad, I spent a weekend at an art teacher friend's expat home. Old friends from the time they attended Sibelius high school were also visiting. We hung out on the couch and watched Finnish news. The film crew interviewed a homeless person who shared how they survived freezing cold nights sleeping in paper recycling bins. They shared poems they had written. The young cultural elite sharing the couch with me, mockingly mimicked the homeless person and laughed uncontrollably. "No-one in Finland can be homeless! They get money from social services. It's their own fault." I got up and sneaked past the grand piano, pretending to go to the bathroom. I escaped to the room designated as my bedroom in this huge house. I was tearing up. I was angry. I shook. Why didn't I confront their behaviour? Why didn't I ask them to stop laughing at people? Why didn't I say, the person featured on TV was my gang friend from teenage years? You don't know anything about him. You don't know about their addict parents, about the years spent in institutions, the abuse and incest. You know nothing. I was hurting for all homeless people, for my friend, for myself, because I said nothing. What a coward shit I had become!? I was Peter and the rooster crowed.

We both inherit and socially construct and reconstruct our sensibilities for forming meanings and associations with things (e.g. Skeggs, 1997). As art educators, we are influenced by backgrounds tied up in notions and experiences of class. These experiences have developed our empathetic sensibilities for people with diverse backgrounds and life experiences. For some of us in the research group, addictions and mental health issues were part of our childhood and youth years. On the flip side of the empathic abilities we developed, we also developed high ethical and performance expectations, ruthlessness and lack of mercy for ourselves, in some ways reflected in our relationships with others. We have experienced "unbelonging," which has often resulted in practices in art and arts education that offer opportunities for others, rather than for us, to attach and relate.

I have often felt like an outsider. Partially because I actively seek for new places and opportunities, but often against my choice. I believe that this sense of exclusion I have faced, aids me in my teaching. I can relate to situations that are new and strange to the students. I have been an outsider in my own country and abroad. I have tried to find my place and perhaps this process is still ongoing?

I have spoken about museums and elitism, but I don't find my words resonating with others. I feel misunderstood. A colleague once stated: "Museums are not elitist, they offer 'all kinds of programming'."

Rarely – if ever – do we speak about such practices and policies that relate to class. Class is something subtle and invisible, so "it" cannot be solved by adjusting lights or changing the font size. How could we work to dissolve these biases and discriminatory practices without further alienation and othering? The disability movement "nothing about us, without us" slogan could be a guiding principle in this work.

Through our narratives and research processes, we voice our experiences; in this way, they have an opportunity to grow, to become part of the wider and broader agenda of changing inequality and unjust norms. Through our further analysis of our materials, we aim to generate solutions on how to create learning communities and safer learning spaces that may ease these pressures and support a culture that is more generous and forgiving. Our scholarship, art and practice actively seek to not only address normative notions of class and inaccessibility but also generate possible solutions and opportunities to belong and to form a union or community.

## *Concluding Thoughts*

In this chapter, we have shared the beginning stages of our infernal learning through stories of becoming members of academic communities, and we are articulating strategies for the subsequent stages of this research. In building more inclusive arts and arts education communities within higher education, we aim to deconstruct oppressive structures. We believe that the first step is to make the prevalent issues visible. The second step is to share our experiences and, in this way, show that our experiences are much more varied, porous and inconsistent than is often perceived. Then we can begin to dismantle the unjust and discriminatory cultures, structures and processes currently in place. We believe it is possible to create less oppressive cultures that are sensible, sensitive and appreciative of broad notions of diversity.

Academic hegemony and colonization operate by the same principles as other forms of colonization: convincing us to admire and adhere to hegemonic cultures and artistic phenomena and (in)directly demanding that we grow out of the values and ideals that formed our earlier understandings of ontology, epistemology and aesthetic sensibilities. Academic traditions have set themselves apart and above other cultures of knowing, being and doing: maintaining hierarchies through rhetorical and institutionalized structures. These structures have prevented the development of a commons and of radical democracy and prevented intersectional knowing from gaining ground. By and large, like royalty, academe has surrounded itself with a culture of inaccessibility and exclusiveness to maintain devotion and admiration. In this way, academic and in many instances arts communities maintain class hierarchies, separating persons who have knowledge and access to advancements from those who need to be informed, educated and civilized.

For us, to build and establish an academic and arts commons demands systematic and conscious dismantling of subtle, normative and discriminatory class structures so that spaces and cultures of accessibility and availability can be built. To establish a knowledge and artistic commons entails a commitment to gentle and radical activism of thought and practice. We can begin the work from within by recognizing our diverse paths and experience and by reckoning our diverse, critical and sensuous ways of being and understanding (Gershon, 2019; Kumashiro, 2000; Suominen, 2019; Suominen et al., 2019). We must support establishing processes that encourage all people to perceive participation in the arts, culture and academic conversations as their inherent right. The United Nations Declaration of Human Rights outlined this right decades ago, but we seem to have forgotten that it applies across our institutions of learning. We should continue to advocate for high-quality education in the arts for children and young people regardless of their geographic location and/or the socio-economic make-up of their neighbourhood. We can support the building of diverse arts and culture opportunities that are accessible and meaningful to all. We need to collectively establish cultures and practices that encourage all interested applicants to envision themselves as artists and academics. Finally, we need to actively and urgently dismantle exclusive structures and work towards building safer learning environments and honour broader social diversity.

## REFERENCES

Alhanen, K. & Perhoniemi, T. (2017). *Demokraattinen perintömme* [Our democratic heritage]. Vastapaino.

Anttila, A.-H. (Ed.) (2016). *Luokan ääni ja hiljaisuus: Yhteiskunnallinen luokkajärjestys 2000-luvun alun Suomess a*. Vastapaino.

Bourdieu, P. (1979). *La distinction: Critique sociale du jugement* [Distinction: A social critique of the judgement of taste]. Routledge.

Butler, J. (1990). *Gender Trouble: Feminism and the subversion of identity*. Routledge.

Cho, S., Williams Crenshaw, K., & McCall, L. (2013). Toward a field of intersectionality studies: Theory, applications, and praxis. *Intersectionality: Theorizing Power, Empowering Theory, 38*(4), 785–810.

Dewey, J. (1916). *Democracy and education*. The Free Press.

Erola, J. (Ed.). (2012). *Luokaton Suomi? Yhteiskuntaluokat 2000-luvun Suomessa*. Gaudeamus.

Foucault, M. (1970). *Les mots et les choses – une archéologie des sciences humaines* [The order of things: An archaeology of the human sciences]. Routledge. (Original work published 1966)

Foucault, M. (1977). *Surveiller et punir. Naissance de la prison* [Discipline and punish: The birth of the prison]. Pantheon Books. (Original work published 1975)

Gershon, W. (Ed.). (2019). *Sensuous curriculum: Politics and the senses in education*. Information Age Publishing.

Goldblatt, P. (2006). How John Dewey's theories underpin art and art education. *Education and Culture, 22*(1), 17–34.

Harding, S. (2007). Feminist standpoints. In S. N. Hesse-Biber (Ed.), *Handbook of feminist research: Theory and praxis* (pp. 45–69). Sage.

Järvinen, K., & Kolbe, L. (2007). *Luokkaretkellä hyvinvointiyhteiskunnassa. Nykysukupolven kokemuksia tasa-arvosta*. Kirjapaja.

Kumashiro, K. (2000). Toward a theory of anti-oppressive education. *Review of Educational Research, 70*(1), 25–53.

Riessman, C. K. (2008). *Narrative methods for the human sciences*. Sage.

Skeggs, B. (1997). *Formations of class and gender: Becoming respectable*. Sage.

Skeggs, B. (2004). *Class, self, culture*. Routledge.

Suominen, A. (2019). Sensuous and artistic curriculum towards the disruption of the normative. In W. Gershon (Ed.), *Sensuous curriculum: Politics and the senses in education* (pp. 175–194). Information Age Publishing; Landscapes of education.

Suominen, A., Pusa, T., Raudaskoski, A., & Haggrén, L. (2019). Centralizing queer in Finnish art education. *Policy Futures in Education, 18*(3), 358–374. https://doi.org/10.1177/1478210319837836

Suoranta, J. (2003). *Kasvatus mediakulttuurissa*. Vastapaino.

Suoranta, J., & Ryynänen, S. (2014). *Taisteleva tutkimus*. Into Kustannus Oy.

Tomperi, T., & Piattoeva, N. (2005). Demokraattisten juurten kasvattaminen. In T. Killakoski, T. Tomperi, & M. Vuorikoski (Eds.), *Kenen kasvatus? Kriittinen pedagogiikka ja toisinkasvatuksen mahdollisuus* (pp. 247–286). Vastapaino.

# 11

## Seeds in the Wind! A/r/tography School and Teacher Formation

*Leísa Sasso and Mirian Celeste Martins*

*In finding the ground, the origins of the flight were also discovered.*

(Barros, 2017b, p. 17)

Manoel de Barros (1916–2014) is a Brazilian poet who "carried water in a sieve" and taught us "to sow" butterflies (Barros, 2017a, p. 6). He invites us to find poetical pedagogical practices in the schoolyard. A school based on initial and continued formation draws out artistic and pedagogical practices that promote dialogue among theory, practice and poetics. Reinventing the curriculum through art and the intrusion of poetics into the classroom finds power in the concept of a/r/tography, not as a norm but as a diffusion of ideas, where the seeds waiting for light and water on the soil are stirred by the restlessness of contemporary times.

A/r/tography is a research methodology (Sinner et al., 2013) that can be transposed to basic education as a philosophy, as it integrates artistic actions with theory in pedagogical practices that become poetic. A/r/tography affects us as teachers and learners, and it has the potential for community transformation. We believe that it is easier to articulate transversal themes for curricular proposals if we can work playfully and pleasantly, in dialogues, in narratives and with (re)creations and (re)meanings of everyday life. We want the (re)construction of education as we know it: a move away from an education where students are passive and lined up, an education that horrified Paulo Freire in the 1960s and that still remains today in many schools as a rock-wall impasse. In this sense, what are we trying to do is nothing more than an old proposal for work in education, where art is added on.

For decades, Paulo Freire (1989)[1] had been talking about this need for a new school, an experimental school, a school for the application of dialogical theories with pedagogical practices. In 1989, when he was secretary for the Department of Education of the City of São Paulo, Freire spoke to an audience of children and young people:

> Have you started to miss your life, the beauty of life? Because there is also an ugliness in life, anger. Anger can also be beautiful. There is not one thing that can be just beautiful or ugly. Sometimes there is a cuteness in anger, which pushes us to change the world, to fix life. But I think that the fundamental, at least the fundamental for me, since I was your age, until today when I am already reaching a little old age, I always looked for the cute. This beauty of the school has to do with the joy of studying, the joy of fulfilling the duty, of respecting the limit that the teacher gives, that the principal gives. It has to do with the beauty of going to the director and saying: Director, I didn't agree with today's limit. It's beautiful to say that! It's the beauty of being people! Well, the school has to become a space of beauty. So, Art has a huge role not only in school life, but in people's lives. And let you know that what we are doing together, here and now is part of a beautiful quest, too, the quest to change the school.
> 
> (Freire, 1989, authors' translation)

After more than 30 years, the beauty is still missing in education. As teachers, we still seek beauty in simple things, in a clean and well-maintained school or the floral arrangement on the teacher's table. We demonstrate care with the environment where we live and work with clean, unvandalized walls and with the music that replaces the siren announcing the beginning of classes. We want generosity and kindness everywhere. Freire recognized that poetics is necessary in people's lives. We argue that as school is an essential part of life, art and poetics are essential in education.

Fruitful dialogues have been brought together to promote a/r/t/ography as a philosophy of education that goes beyond a research methodology. In Brasilia and São Paulo, distant in space and close in affectionate exchanges, we sow art. We seek to train teachers embedded in this new philosophy of education based on art. In this context, we focus on what Leisa called the Artographic School, reinforcing the art and writing of the artist/creator, researcher and teacher, improving the education profession, emphasizing the hybridism of social performance with the mother/father of the family, the community leader, the politician: in other words, the hybridism of social performance. Thus, in this chapter, Leísa narrates this construction process of a new and different school showing poetic actions in dialogue with the Brazilian Basic Education curriculum. This process materializes in collaborative and interdisciplinary actions that seek ways to articulate practices in schools with the poetics of students' daily lives and the scientific knowledge of the teachers.

## The Artographic School

This work expanded at the end of 2018 when Leísa finished a doctorate in art at the University of Brasília and returned to work as a teacher in public education. She was then invited to coordinate schools' pedagogical practices in São Sebastião, a suburb of Brasília and a city of 180,000 inhabitants. São Sebastião has 1,270 teachers who serve 22,457 students of all ages. In a framework of collaboration between the University of Brasília and the Mackenzie University of São Paulo, and with the involvement of the research group in which we both participate, we work with the managers, supervisors and teachers under the direction of the Brasília Department of Education in the implementation of governmental public policies. In this immense structure – comprising 700 schools in fourteen cities involving about 500,000 people, 400,000 students and 62,000 educators – Leísa led the São Sebastião Pedagogical Unit, which we named the *Artographic School*, with twenty dedicated teachers on staff. In this project, she is responsible for guiding and monitoring pedagogical activities in basic education in 30 schools with 1,270 teachers serving 22,457 students of all ages. There are three high schools, seven schools for the final years of elementary school, fourteen schools for the early years of elementary education, twelve schools for early childhood education and three day-care centres, with some schools serving different stages of education.

We think it is important to highlight that this is a community. But to demonstrate the challenges that arise, we have adopted a concept of community from Maffesoli (1996) in dialogue with Michel Gaillot in the French magazine *Bloc Notes of Contemporary Art and Culture*. This definition corresponds to the meaning of community defined by the feeling of belonging:

> What I call the ideal of community is a way of adopting the opposite view of the perspective linked to democracy. I mean, community meetings, this is how it works, where you have to take action. […] the trend is the community defined by the feelings of belonging. He has an experience here and now with others on a given space, with the values I agree, which are community characteristics. […] it is when there can be a creation that is not a production. Just as I make a distinction between work and creation, I would make a distinction between creation and production. I cannot act accordingly, but in fact there is something that can be a work of art in the same way in the act of the community; registering in moments.
> (Maffesoli, 1996, pp. 71–72, author's translation)

This reference to the Maffesoli community's act is one of the central ideas of the Artographic School. We want to be part of poetic and pedagogical actions that affect schools and transform them into more sensitive learning communities. The artistic and pedagogical events are intended to disseminate works that consider, articulate and create dialogues between curricular themes and concepts. For example, narratives involve stories of peace, art, kindness, gratitude, adventures, poetic creations, affections, homes, colours, lightness, beauty, travel, wisdom, loyalty, knowledge, joy, friendships, freedom, optimism, growth and sociability. We believe that these are desirable concepts of meaning and reframing for strengthening community and for community use.

One of the actions carried out within the scope of this initiative was the promotion of events called "Artistic and Pedagogical Turns." Topics such as bio-economics, socio-emotional competences, methodologies and active learning were addressed, and successful experiences were shared with teachers. The idea is to encourage reflections by educators who try to shift the focus from education to teaching to learning, in an attempt to reverse poor results of our students in assessments like the *Programme for International Student Assessment*, or PISA. Some examples of this work of continuing education for teachers encourage us to persist in the work of the Artographic School. In some cases, we have already managed to promote sensitive attitudes among educators, always attentive to each other, in addition to provocative approaches that seek solutions that have not yet been explored.

A small example of this new way of thinking and doing education was the intervention that teachers did in the bathrooms of one of the schools we coordinate. To attempt to end bathroom vandalism, the teachers created a space for the students to have a voice and free expression on a wall of sticky notes. This unusual voice space practically ended the problem and had even more significant outcomes. For example, a student used this space to call for help as she was thinking about committing suicide. She was supported by a student network, thanks to the appeals she made on sticky notes in the bathroom: something she might not have had the courage to do in other circumstances.

In fact, artistic interventions, however simple, have an enormous effect on the school environment. Many stories can be told or sung with the same sensitivity. Expanding from the concept of the Artographic School, the researcher–artists integrate pedagogy with drawing, which offers another conceptual architecture both in continuing and in initial education courses.

Offering teachers and future teachers subjective tools for enabling poetics within pragmatic and objective school environments is an essential task. Some examples encourage us to share, but these initiatives are, in fact, seeds thrown in the wind. We can never impose on teachers a philosophy that they do not recognize and accept as valid. As teachers, researchers and artists, we have no alternative but to plant ideas that may or may not flourish. We will never know if the field is fertile, but we are sure that neither flowers nor fruits are possible without seeds.

We understand that a/r/tographic work with teachers is urgent and cannot be postponed. Therefore, in all meetings with managers, teachers, educational advisors and coordinators in Brasília, we insist on convenience, opportunity and the need to give art the leading role in changing education. Metaphorically implanting the word "utopia" next to the metallic seal describing the Department of Education's heritage (placed on all furniture) is an appeal for everything to improve and for the ideas and wishes of a good school to materialize.

## *I Belong to the School and the School Belongs to Me*

The actions of the Artographic School, and the activities carried out at the Presbyterian University Mackenzie with Mirian Celeste, give a glimpse into a proposed pedagogical time–space, but in ways that punctuate here and there. This proposal, innovative in its concepts and approaches, materializes in poetic and pedagogical events that bring affection, knowledge and new experiences to bear on teaching and learning. We are researching learning concepts based on the idea of belonging, the challenge and the desire to know more, to elaborate on and solve problems in ways that are relevant to our students and the wider community.

The transformation of the school from a space of passage to a space of belonging can be achieved. The example of the school that intervened in the bathrooms ultimately generated belonging and a change in the students' behaviour. It is necessary to explain that the bathrooms in many schools in Brazil are poorly maintained. The bathroom wall before this intervention was always covered with obscene words, denoting a total lack of connection between the students and the school (Figure 11.1). About this initiative, the Educational Advisor stated:

> I realized that the bathrooms are a place of refuge for many. I believe that tidying up the bathroom, in a simple way, showed that beauty can also be simple. For our students from the periphery where the people live in poverty, the simple is part of their reality. They saw that it is possible to transform reality. Also, they take great care of that space. We saw no more gibberish, swearing, no vandalism. Both girls and boys started to care as if it were part of their home. Taking care of the bathroom helped them to take care of the rest of the school. We also had a significant reduction in cases of self-harm at school because they used the bathroom for these practices.
> (Moura, S. G., personal communication, 7 June 2020)

FIGURE 11.1: Girls' bathroom of São José's School. Photo by Leísa Sasso (2019).

This initiative was shared with the other schools in São Sebastião in an event or "happening" that brought together all teachers for the final years of elementary and secondary education. We regularly seek to disseminate the artistic and pedagogical practices of teachers who are not necessarily art educators, not necessarily artographers, but collectively embrace that which brings poetics to the school space. To paraphrase Allan Kaprow (1996), we like to see life confused with art:

> Happenings are events that things just happen. [...] In contrast to the arts of the past, they have no structured beginning, no middle, no end. Its form is open as to its end, and it is fluid, nothing clear is sought, however, nothing is acquired, except the certainty of a certain number of facts to which we are attentive beyond the normal. They exist for a simple bet, only for a small number, and they always happen on the occasion of new bets. These events are essentially plays, more unconventional. The singular fact, its primitive energy, and the fact that derive from American Action Painting rites.
> (Kaprow, 1996, p. 48, author's translation)

With this definition of "happening" in mind, another artistic and pedagogical event was conceived in 2019. We wanted schools to present their works to their administrations: including theatrical presentations and exhibitions during a book

## SEEDS IN THE WIND! A/R/TOGRAPHY SCHOOL AND TEACHER FORMATION

fair that involves all public schools in São Sebastião. Such an event is significant, given the deficiencies that students have in literacy. Every year we gather the best poetry creations from students of all ages in one book and present them at this event, along with other productions. Many of our students have illiterate parents. Encouraging students to read and write is one of our biggest challenges, and all schools in São Sebastião have this goal in common. Challenging students to tell their stories, experiences and feelings is also a way of involving them in pedagogical and artistic practices. Telling stories for the youngest children is a necessity because the school is, for many students, the only space where they live with books (Figure 11.2).

During the "Happening" of 2019, called "Telling and singing stories of São Sebastião," we were surprised by what was presented by the schools. One featured a large collectively created "Action Painting" panel inspired by Jackson Pollock.

FIGURE 11.2: Cover of the book *Telling and Singing Stories*, GDF (2019). Photo by Leísa Sasso (2019).

Two teachers, one of art and the other of Portuguese, promoted this mighty interdisciplinary work in one of our schools. The large panel was used to express students' emotions in the face of words that referred to concrete situations. Faced with words like fear, faith, laziness, betrayal, jealousy, death, love, friendship, the students wrote poems. These words were then gathered, associated with colours and placed on a mural, creating a pictorial effect.

This event – "Telling and singing stories of São Sebastião" – was brought together in a small 160-page book of students' poetry and illustrations. The event was the culmination of the work of coordinators and teachers who are encouraged to establish dialogues among students' daily lives, poetics and curricular pedagogical practices. A student from the second year of primary class produced this:

> My name is Laura. One day my grandma had died. The other day I went back to Grandpa's. I thought my grandma was there but she wasn't and I was sad. And I told my mom that and she told me: Laura, when people die they never come back.
> (Sasso, 2019, p. 110)

Unfortunately, it is inevitable that teachers will be confronted with reports of violence and crimes by students. São Sebastião is a city with high crime rates, and it is quite common that our students have experienced or witnessed crimes, including at home. It is not possible to know precisely the extent to which the violence of these students' daily lives penetrates schools and how professionals are coping with this reality. The fact is that students and teachers are experimenting with pedagogical alternatives, some of which help us heal ourselves while others help generate affection.

## *To Continue Sowing ...*

As long as we do not recognize the educational importance of art, we cannot modify Brazilian education. It is not enough to change curricular content, modify assessment methods and encourage the use of technologies. It is also necessary to insert art, sensitivity, creativity and pleasure for education to be genuinely transformative. The Artographic School's proposal seeks poetry that disrupts education to touch souls.

In Greece centuries ago, Plato expelled the poets from the temple in his idealized "Republic." Now it is the school's turn to open its doors to poets and artists and their productions, and associate these with pedagogical practices and curricula to significantly transform education. The discipline of art has a fundamental role because it provides the necessary techniques to work in a creative, affectionate, playful way, and – it must be said – a more efficient and effective way.

Forging relationships among art, science and philosophy enables a better understanding of this multifaceted world in which we live, a planet integrated within infinite connections. We can no longer understand the world from specific disciplines but from an interdependent and interdisciplinary approach, a method in which art has a role to play. And when art at school works to generate empathy and criticism, ethics and aesthetics meet. Seemingly banal actions such as creating a colourful mural in the bathroom stimulate creativity, reason and sensitivity to solve problems and conflicts.

For schools as centres of art and culture in poor communities, where knowledge creation links to the need for social change, a/r/tographic pedagogy encourages critical thinking, engaging each student in building a better world. It is evident to all those who study and work to improve education that these ideas still have a long way to go. Therefore, we do not assert that a/r/tography is a kind of educational utopia, but we emphasize exceptional gains for education in the process of reaching it. As Paulo Freire taught us, we must do everything possible today to reach the impossible tomorrow. That is why we continue to sow.

## NOTE

1. This video, originally located at http://saosebastiao.se.df.gov.br/escolaartografica/?cat=23, was no longer available by the time this book went to print.

## REFERENCES

Barros, M. (2017a). *The water keeper*. Alfaguara.
Barros, M. (2017b). *Exercise of being a child*. Editora Salamandra.
Kaprow, A. (1996). The happenings on the New York scene – 1961. In J. Kelley (Ed.), *Kaprow: Art and life combined* (pp. 46–56). Editions du Centre Georges Pompidou.
Maffesoli, M. (1996, September/October). Festive effervescence: Michel Maffesoli interview with Michel Gaillot. *Blocnotes, contemporary art & culture, 13*, 65–74.
Sasso, L. (2019). *Telling and singing stories*. State Department of Education GDF.
Sinner, A., Leggo, C., Irwin, R. L., Gouzouasis, P., & Grauer, K. (2013). Analyzing the practices of new academics: Theses that use research methodologies in education based on art. In B. Dias & R. Irwin (Eds.), *Art-based educational research: A/r/tography* (pp. 99–124). Editora da UFSM.

# 12

# Transversalities Through Transdisciplinary Pedagogies: A South African Perspective on Community-Engaged Art Education

*Merna Meyer*

In African folklore, a Swahili tale depicts the relationship between a monkey and a shark, a story about the needs of two creatures living in two worlds. The shark needs the heart of the monkey to save his ill king and invites the monkey on a journey with the aim of killing him to ensure that his king will live. The adventurous monkey agrees to go on a journey to learn and experience new things. But on the trip, the monkey finds out about the shark's plans and tricks him into thinking that he left his heart behind and that they need to return to terra firma to fetch it. As soon as the monkey sets foot on dry land, he escapes from the shark, thus abruptly ending their journey and brief relationship. Neither of them gains what they really wanted from the experience, and both end up with negative memories of each other (Lang, 1910).

In this fable, the clandestine motives of one character resulted in both parties feeling alienated, their ways separated, leaving negative memories of their brief encounter. The discouraging experience increased their distrust of each other; both resented the fact that they had not benefitted from the relationship, missing an opportunity to establish social cohesion between two parties from different communities.

As a lecturer in art education, my initial experience of community-engaged art education resonates with the story of the monkey and the shark: my first attempt to conduct engaged research in communities resulted in similar outcomes. It was a harsh learning experience that highlighted my initial lack of understanding of translating transdisciplinary pedagogies into diverse contexts. I did not realize then that genuine collaboration could be reached only when needs, goals and a vision are shared between two parties.

Defining community art education is tricky as we move among intersecting concepts such as community-based art education, community engagement and social practice art (Lawton, 2019). These three concepts have a common motive: engage in democratic concepts of civic responsibility, social justice and meaningful human interactions to build social cohesion in society. In accord with these concepts, my motive in this chapter is to demonstrate how I guided student art teachers to become socially engaged professionals during a service-learning (SL) art curriculum programme involving the community, with the aim to answer this question: *How can I equip student art teachers with the necessary skills that will guide them to become participatory and socially engaged leaders and citizens?* To that end, I describe my professional journey towards creating spaces for transversal understanding between university (campus) and community through art education. First, I illustrate my initial (mis)conception of community art education using a vignette, then discuss South African higher education – defining policies on community engagement and arguing why SL should be regarded as a vital academic strand of community art education. I follow this with an explanation of how I changed my methodology to guide student teachers more effectively in becoming socially engaged professionals within their communities. The chapter concludes with recommendations for further developments in community art education. My story unfolds against the historically burdened backdrop of the South African context.

**Vignette:** Disillusionment

About a decade ago, I was approached by a corporate funder from one of the mines who wanted to re-invest in the surrounding community as part of their social responsibility programme. They wanted students to decorate an outside mural for a newly erected pre-school building in Letsopa, just outside Ottosdal, North-West Province, South Africa. I involved a group of ten junior primary school Art Education students with this outreach project. My initial "othering" approach was evident in the following italicized words: *I wanted to reach out towards the community, improve* their *place (the school in the township area), utilizing* our *creative output, giving* our *expert knowledge as a token of* our *care for* their *living environment* (Meyer, 2015). Painting the walls was a daunting task; 100 m² had to be completed in two days with limited prior knowledge of the task, design layout or mural painting techniques. The students and I engaged in pre-consultation with the mine group but not with the community, as it was not required then. Consequently, we had no real understanding of the township culture and context or the children's preferences and did not consider involving them or the teachers in the decision-making process. We proceeded in our one-sided, singular way, painting the walls with colourful animal scenes decorated with playful monkeys swinging from the branches.

(Meyer & Wood, 2016)

The student art teachers' positive feedback on the experience reinforced my sense of accomplishment with the project. But at the end of the weekend, we saw onlooking children literally hiding behind the bigger children's backs. We were not prepared for their reactions – they were too scared to get closer. We heard later that they were afraid of the monkeys. We were unaware of their cultural sensitivities and learned that in some rural areas, monkeys are used by parents to discipline children by threatening them when they misbehave, e.g. "The monkeys will come and fetch you if you are naughty." The monkeys are also a reminder of a mythical figure called the *tokoloshe*, a short three-legged creature that threatens people's lives at night. That explains why some older generations have their beds on bricks, like stilts, raised off the floor to avoid the creature (Meyer, 2015).

In my view, our community art project was successful – I received positive feedback from the students, corporate sponsors, teachers and the university. But it was the children's frightened expressions and their reluctance to set foot on their new playground that left visual imprints on my mind. To me, this was a turning point: when *our* acts of goodwill to improve *their* livelihood evoked alienation. Like the monkey/shark fable, our ways separated, turning this potential long-term community-engaged art project into another ad hoc venture. Since then, my perceptions of community art education have changed towards seeing community art as *with* and *by* the community for social change and mutual understanding. I, therefore, started to investigate new ways of teaching community art education in engaged ways to obtain lasting memories and sustainable partnerships.

## *Service-Learning as Transdisciplinary Pedagogy in Art Education*

South Africa's education policy framework, including the Higher Education Act (No. 101 of 1997) and White Paper 3, requires the transformation of higher education through community service programmes to develop students' social responsibility and awareness of how they can contribute to nation-building and the development of a more just and humane society (South African, 1997). The Higher Education Quality Committee also requires academically based community engagement, with reference to SL as an integrated, qualitative and accredited teaching and learning practice (Osman & Petersen, 2013). Thus, SL as a form of public pedagogy requires graduates to be skilled communicators, analytically competent and able to deal with change and diversity. SL within art education is regarded as a transformative and socially reconstructive practice that extends the purposes of art education: to educate and provide service opportunities that transform and give meaning to our lives (Taylor, 2002). This out-of-school type of learning in community settings can provide an environment for art teachers to experiment with new types of learning relations, social structures and cultural contexts (Westraadt, 2018). With SL pedagogy, the parameters of linear, discipline-orientated education are extended towards a broader transdisciplinary context (Wilson, 2013) – grounded in transformational critical, social humanist theories with a socially engaged art approach (Helguera, 2011) using experiential (Kolb, 2014) and reflective practices (Schön, 1983). However, developing community-based participatory action learning and action research methodologies (Wood, 2019; Zuber-Skerritt, 2015) can give a greater voice to communities if they are engaged from the start of the project.

At the North-West University (NWU) and specifically in the Creative Arts department, we started off with some informal services to the community. As with the monkey/shark story, these were well-intended, volunteered, community outreach programmes providing a service to the community to promote "feel-good, positive social values" (Helguera, 2011, p. 10), but they lacked substantive mutual engagement and meaningful art-based practices. SL was introduced to the final-year art education students to encourage community-based learning. Currently, our SL projects last for a semester (four months) and conclude with a professional development framework for art education graduates that could steer them towards socially engaged leadership. This art pedagogy is different from an established lifelong community art education partnership, whereby community art teachers help foster artistic skills and outputs within the community. Instead, the SL programme is designed to assist novice art teachers with pedagogical strategies to work in participatory ways with communities through art-based activities to become compassionate, visionary and self-directed leaders in their careers. In the following case studies, I explain how I conduct campus-community engagements through cyclic interactions with each other.

## Case Study One: Building Visions

One year after the kindergarten outreach, another project was initiated by the urban planning faculty of the NWU to upgrade an undeveloped municipal area in a nearby township (Wood & Meyer, 2016). The ashes of apartheid were still evident in dilapidated houses surrounded by bare ground. Three third-year primary school art students and four community participants enrolled on the project to aesthetically enhance a corner yard in the area. English was adopted as the lingua franca for better understanding. To protect their identities, as some community youths were younger than eighteen, I used codes to name them: C 1–4 for the community youths and S 1–3 for the student participants. This was the first time I introduced a participatory form of action research (Zuber-Skerrit, 2015) to the groups to improve my previous one-sided approach. With action research, participants look, think, act and reflect together on the following learning cycles: (i) relationship-building, (ii) planning, (iii) skills application and (iv) reflecting (Wood & Meyer, 2016).

The students and community youths engaged in several relational activities to build trust and gain insight into the community youths' living context. During the relationship-building cycle, the walk-and-talk open-air activity (McKinney, 2011) orientated the two groups to the site and amplified the community's need for a playground area. The youths experienced a sense of ownership as they showed the students around, looked at the surroundings and visualized the changes they wanted to see in the park. One student (S3) remarked: "I am committed to the project. I would like to see something that will give them joy." To further stimulate ideas and improve their visions for the park, students gathered reference material from the urban planning faculty and exposed the youths to samples of landscape planning. The students also showed the youths some maquettes of previous playground structures they completed. Vision-building and project planning became a pertinent design activity they conducted together. The youths learned that "If you are going to make a park, you must make sure that you've got nice plans, that tomorrow that people look[ing] at that park can feel joy" (C2). This joy was evident when the park became a public amenity on Mandela Day, 18 July 2013. The youths became equal "owners" of their communal space.

## Findings and Discussion

From the cyclic interactions and reflective student notes, three themes emerged: (i) both groups gained mutual insights and dismantled stereotypical assumptions about each other; (ii) the (P)ART process shifted power relations; (iii) all participants experienced personal and professional development through transversal art activities (Wood & Meyer, 2016). Both groups initially "othered": for instance, students wanted to learn *about* the community youth, rather than *with* or *from* them. However, power relations shifted as the youths' initial quietness as "passive acceptors of domination" (Freire, 1985, p. 81) changed to an interactive engagement of life-sharing experiences and visions for the park. The community youths gave voice to their expectations of the park, recognized the needs and challenges involved and started to make suggestions on how it should be developed. Through planning and design, art-based methods helped to mediate meaningful conversations (Helguera, 2011). For the students, understanding the experiences and perspectives of those from different backgrounds became a vital lifeskill, especially for prospective teachers who wield inherent power over the cognitive and value formations of learners (Wood & Meyer, 2016).

## Case Study Two: Transdisciplinary Making/Upcycling

Two years later, a transdisciplinary elephant project was proposed on campus to create a new historic symbol that stands as a metaphor for transformation and decolonization (Meyer & Balfour, 2020). Initially, at the management level, careful curriculum and logistical planning was needed to accommodate the many intersections of engagement – academics, students, school children, community members and an industry expert in recycled craft-making projects. Our intention was not only to engage in a decolonized discourse about traditional symbols but also to equalize privilege and power by working with two communities outside campus: the Sebone Women's Craft group and school learners from a nearby children's home. The art education students consisted of 24 final-year primary school teachers, 15 high-school teachers and 7 technology education students. The Sebone Women's Craft Group consisted of nine women (aged 25–45) and eight school children (aged 12–15). English was used to communicate along with Afrikaans, Sotho and Tswana. Project management principles (Meyer & Balfour, 2020) governed assigning of roles and transdisciplinary engagement. We adopted a participatory form of action research similar to the case study above and adjusted the cyclic actions to fit in with all the stakeholders' tasks. These included (1) conceptualization and consultation; (2) designing and construction; (3) coordinating, making and implementing; and (4) reflecting and celebrating the completion of the project.

This project consisted of four phases. In Phase 1, staff and students reconceptualized the elephant from an education perspective in which found objects and waste materials (glass, plastics, paper, tin etc.) could be upcycled to create artistic forms. From art students' drawings, an elephant was chosen with a raised trunk, symbolizing hope. The technology education students and their lecturers drew up the structure and material specifications of the elephant. Art education students met with orphaned children and steered the monochromatic concepts towards eclectic designs, which were embedded into the final artwork. In Phase 2, the structure was completed, involving various community groups in the construction process. In Phase 3, two workshops were organized with more hands-on engagement between campus and community members. The community women started to apply their craft-based skills, using the available resources to complete a mosaic-type platform for the elephant. From these women, the students learned hands-on, art-based skills such as weaving and beading. They also saw how the women cleaned up and maintained an orderly working platform. In Phase 4, the unveiling of the Elephant was publicly celebrated on International Teachers' Day, together with invited schools, participants, children, district office officials, local teachers and campus management.

*Findings and Discussion*

Several socially engaged themes emerged from this project, including (i) the participants' recognition of one another's roles and responsibilities during the process, (ii) the value of the creative process to shift perceptions and enable professional development and (iii) deeper trans-disciplinary insight about diversity and intersectional learning practices (Meyer & Balfour, 2020). Utilizing SL as an engaged and participatory pedagogy – where students, academics, children and community women learned skills together – enabled an exchange of roles and communication and the development of critical and creative skills. Art became a meaningful tool to mediate transversalities in a large *bricolage* project where students make do with what is at hand and recombine them to create something new (Lévi Strauss, 1966). The value of the creative process as a mediating tool is evident in students' remarks about the value of individual artistry and recognition of how art can mobilize people from different backgrounds. Their appreciation for each other's contributions and intersectional practices in diverse contexts became amplified, showing that the impossible can be achieved. In one student's words, "Everyone came to realize each other's value: We learned not to keep everything just for [sic] ourselves but see the value in sharing something with others [...] to work in a group together to reach a bigger goal."

This project led to an appreciation of community as part of teacher education even alongside the many challenges encountered, such as the interconnected roles and different responsibilities of the various stakeholders and organizers, the short timeframe (three months), language barriers between the different groups and the diverse circumstances of the children and women coming from various contexts. In my view, we moved towards a more inclusive curriculum: transforming symbols into new and meaningful metaphors and using social *bricolage* and participatory methodologies amongst diverse groups. But to sustain campus-community engagement in higher education, students need a more innate leadership framework to guide them with socially engaged art projects.

## Case Study Three: Celebrate and Create Own Communities

Here, I propose how the (P)ART model framed students' roles as *p*articipatory *a*rtists, *r*esearchers and *t*eachers, and enacted social responsibility. For the most recent community engaged project, I developed the theme of "Living my Leadership in a Diverse and Healthy Environment" with the pedagogical intention of connecting students' learning experiences of leadership to a broader discourse on social responsibility and environmental issues (Meyer & Wood, 2019). The project involved 26 final-year art education students engaging with fifteen children of diverse cultural backgrounds from a nearby children's home/orphanage. During the first semester, they met with each other on campus in the afternoons for five weeks. The groups were exposed to out-of-class learning sites to address "green" issues through various art-forms and to raise awareness about global environmental conditions (Gore, 2017). I used the (P)ART model with seven platforms to guide students through socially engaged art processes, towards leadership. Students first developed their professional identity (indicated in the middle), and then through a process of orientation, relationship-building, vision-building and celebration they obtained socially engaged and participatory leadership skills (Meyer & Wood, 2019) (see Figure 12.1).

## Findings and Discussion

The following themes were drawn from students' reflections on their learning during each cycle: (i) learning relational skills and teaching with sensitivity, (ii) developing socially engaged art practices and (iii) realizing the importance of collaborative practices (Meyer & Wood, 2019). When applying the previously discussed cycles in their professional framework, students found that teaching out of class could be, in the words of S12, "a truly free and creative exercise as opposed to classroom teaching methods." Both groups developed socially engaged art-based skills as they jointly started "planning their projects, figure [sic] out what to do and how we are going to do it" (S5). They brainstormed and identified environmental issues they wanted to address. One particular group of learners who called themselves "envi-tists" (environmental activists, according to S21) caught my attention. They actively started to run their own environmental club at a school under the guidance of a student during her teaching practice. They produced functional recycled vertical planters and ran all sorts of awareness campaigns. Addressing the third theme, the importance of collaborative practices, the university group concluded with an exhibition event at the children's home. They connected their teaching to the children's contexts publicly: "We celebrated because we achieved our goals, the learners reached their learning objectives and we overcame our obstacles" (S1). They gained enough confidence to exhibit their work together and applied gallery-walk strategies to explain the social significance thereof.

FIGURE 12.1: The (P)ART framework. Design by Merna Meyer (2020).

These students affirmed my belief that art education helps to overcome barriers when it becomes accessible to all: "[E]very single learner, regardless whether they have the subject art, can do art" (S6). Providing opportunities for artistic development by the students, the children became more skillful in making, cutting and colouring their own artworks. At the exhibition, the children's home manager concluded that the students gave the children blankets of hope by upskilling their abilities. The (P)ART framework enabled students to take leadership into their own hands, opening transversal art-based spaces to engage with communities in their own ways.

## *Conclusion*

I have narrated and reflected on how my initial community art education practices evolved over the past ten years: from one-sided to a more reciprocal, inclusive and transdisciplinary approach. I explained how I utilized SL as an art pedagogy with the students through a cyclic process of action research to frame students' professional development and to promote relational, visionary, applied and public display skills amongst campus-community groups. The (P)ART professional development framework guided students to mediate their leadership roles in transdisciplinary and diverse contexts. Despite the challenges of working in unfamiliar terrain, with language barriers and unusual timeframes, the campus-community participants – unlike the monkey and the shark – did form trusting relationships and cultural awareness of the "other" and established mutual transversal, learning opportunities through art-based methods. Both groups benefitted from the process. But, in my view, community art education could become sustainable, only if the emphasis is placed on *community–campus* partnerships instead of focusing on *campus-community engagements*. Who needs to take social responsibility over whom is a binary that still needs to be critiqued to ensure a sound and just citizenship for future community art education programmes.

## REFERENCES

Freire P. (1985). *The politics of education: Culture, power and liberation*. Bergin & Garvey.

Gore, A. (2017). *An inconvenient sequel: Truth to power: Your action handbook to learn the science, find your voice, and help solve the climate crisis*. Rodale Books.

Helguera, P. (2011). *Education for socially engaged art: A materials and techniques handbook*. Jorge Pinto Books.

Kolb, D. A. (2014). *Experiential learning* (2nd ed.). Pearson Education.

Lang, A. (1910). *The Lilac fairy book*. Courier Dover Publications.

Lawton, P. (2019). At the crossroads of intersecting ideologies: Community-based art education, community engagement, and social practice art. *Studies in Art Education, 60*(3), 203–218. https://doi.org/10.1080/00393541.2019.1639486

Lévi Strauss, C. (1966). *The savage mind*. University of Chicago Press.

McKinney, B. L. (2011). *Therapist's perceptions of walk and talk therapy: A grounded study* [Unpublished doctoral dissertation]. University of New Orleans.

Meyer, G. M. (2015). *Exploring community partnerships for service-learning in creative arts education through participatory action research* [Unpublished master's dissertation]. North-West University.

Meyer, M. (2020). Guiding student art teachers towards engaged professionalism in a South African context. In G. Coutts & T. Eça (Eds.), *Learning through art: International perspectives* (pp. 407–429). InSEA Publications. https://www.insea.org/wp-content/uploads/2021/12/LTA2.pdf

Meyer, M., & Balfour, R. (2020). Old symbols for new journeys: Re-imagining transdisciplinary collaboration for learning and transformative practice in education. *Africa Education Review, 17*(1), 141–158. https://doi.org/10.1080/18146627.2018.1486686

Meyer, M., & Wood, L. (2019). Rethinking the roles of the art educator as participatory artist, researcher and teacher (P)ART: A South African perspective. *International Journal of Education Through Art, 15*(3), 265–280. https://doi.org/10.1386/eta_00002_1

Osman, R., & Petersen, N. (Eds.). (2013). *Service learning in South Africa*. Southern Africa: Oxford University Press.

Schön, D. A. (1983). *The reflective practitioner: How professionals think in action*. Temple Smith.

South African Government. (1997). *Programme for the transformation on higher education: White paper 3*. https://www.gov.za/documents/programme-transformation-higher-education-education-white-paper-3-0

Taylor, P. G. (2002). Service-learning as postmodern art and pedagogy. *Studies in Art Education, 43*(2), 124–140. https://doi.org/10.2307/1321000

Westraadt, G. (2018). Service-learning through art education. *South African Journal of Childhood Education, 8*(1), 1–8. https://doi.org/10.4102/sajce.v8i1.511

Wilson, L. (2013). *A framework for effective practice in community engagement in higher education in a postgraduate programme at North-West University* [Unpublished doctoral dissertation]. Stellenbosch University.

Wood, L. (2019). *Participatory action learning and action research: Theory, practice and process*. Routledge.

Wood, L., & Meyer, M. (2016). A participatory approach to service-learning in creative arts education: A win-win learning opportunity for campus and community? *Journal of Education, 65*, 31–54. http://hdl.handle.net/10394/24100

Zuber-Skerritt, O. (2015). Participatory action learning and action research (PALAR) for community engagement: A theoretical framework. *Educational Research for Social Change, 4*(1), 5–25.

# 13

# Building Bridges in the Community Through Opening Minds Through Art: An Intergenerational Abstract Art Programme for People Living With Dementia

*Stephanie H. Danker, Elizabeth Lokon and Casey Pax*

Learning experiences can be more effective when they involve the community and have impacts on life beyond school (Lawton, 2019). When learning experiences involve creative participation for older adults, there can be positive effects on the overall quality of life (Cohen, 2006). Opening Minds through Art (OMA) was founded in 2007 at Miami University, Oxford, OH, in the United States, as an intergenerational weekly abstract art programme. Facilitated as a group session, the programme includes one-on-one interactions between university students and people living with dementia. The programme is headquartered at the Scripps Gerontology Center, a centre of excellence at our university. Currently, over 200 sites across the United States and Canada facilitate OMA programmes in their local communities.

OMA promotes reciprocal relationships between university students and elders living with dementia, building bridges through art across age and cognitive barriers (Lokon et al., 2012). This chapter traces the structure and evolution of the programme as well as research conducted about the benefits of the programme for elders living with dementia and university student participants (see https://www.scrippsoma.org/research/). As Lawton and LaPorte (2013) note, "Transformative learning empowers individuals to explore and analyse themselves and engage with their community through both traditional and non-traditional visual art forms and experiences" (p. 318). One alumna of OMA, currently an art therapist working in a continuing care community, shares perspectives on the transformative properties of the OMA experience as an individual, professional and community member. We make multidisciplinary connections between the fields of art education and gerontology, and we explore implications and recommendations for how art educators can learn from a programme like OMA.

## *Theoretical Background*

Naming has power. There is significance in what people living with dementia are called by those who are caring for them; naming can set up power structures and indicate social values. When administering training and experiential learning for participants in an intergenerational art-making programme like OMA, empowering and sensitive language is an initial way to demonstrate care. Often, people living with dementia are known as patients, clients or residents rather than citizens; this assumes a loss of agency and perceived loss of self (Dupuis et al., 2016). Person-centred ethics (Kitwood, 1997) prioritizes the person over the condition they live with and is a hallmark of OMA. The arts can provide people living with dementia with a new social role as an artist, which can evoke a sense of control, confidence and self-esteem while conjuring feelings of aesthetic satisfaction (Lokon et al., 2012).

Also key to recognizing people living with dementia as active agents in shaping their own lives and experiences is a focus on citizenship (Dupuis et al., 2016). The relational nature of citizenship (Miller & Kontos, 2016) emphasizes the important role of building and sustaining interconnectedness. There is transformative potential in community, arts-based approaches for fostering a sense of belonging (Dupuis et al., 2016). Art making can be a democratizing tool, to "invigorate citizenship and individual and community capacity by facilitating personal expression and shared communal vision" (Basting, 2018, p. 746). It is possible to learn how to be better participatory members of a community by recognizing the importance of supporting the citizenship of others (Dupuis et al., 2016).

## *Structure and Outcomes of Programming*

The arts, cultural community development and dementia care can come together to provide a framework for a "Creative Community of Care" (Basting, 2018, 2020). Core elements of this framework include "open systems; all activities are accessible; the arts are immersed into the environment of care; projects build on existing assets and rituals; projects evolve over long periods of time; and projects have high cultural value/capital" (Basting, 2018, p. 744). OMA programming builds upon this framework. To build intergenerational relationships, the same pairs of students or community volunteers and older adults living with dementia meet weekly over the course of the entire semester. The art projects are designed to be accessible to people even in the later stages of the disease. OMA capitalizes on the older adults' remaining strengths such as the ability to state preferences for colours, textures and tools; create new compositions by combining collage pieces; feel satisfaction and pride from completing an art piece; and most importantly, reciprocate friendships with OMA students/volunteers. The weekly art-making sessions culminate in a community-wide art show displaying abstract artworks that are highly coveted by families and community members at large. Oftentimes, these art pieces are auctioned to generate funds to sustain the programme.

The success of the OMA programme depends on collaboration among the elders, staff at all levels, families and volunteers as equal partners. OMA's art projects are process-based with each step stated in clear and simple terms, allowing people of all abilities to succeed. Founded on a playful exploration of abstract art, OMA creates an environment that is "dementia normal – in which dementia did not in any way limit one's ability to make beauty and meaning" (Basting, 2018, p. 749). The long-term partnership between elders and volunteers, over one to two semesters or more, is critical in developing not only the friendship between each pair but also the elders' body of work. OMA culminates in an annual or semi-annual art exhibition and reception for the entire community, inside and outside the care home, to celebrate the creativity built through the programme. The vital role of such partnerships is also reflected in Windle et al.'s (2018) research, which identified and analysed the theoretical foundations and outcomes of visual art programmes for people experiencing dementia. Four main outcome areas were reported: (1) social connectedness; (2) wellbeing, including pleasure, enjoyment, and quality of life; (3) changes in public perceptions and attitudes; and (4) cognitive processes (subjective memory, verbal fluency) (Windle et al., 2018, p. 706).

OMA research shows that the one-on-one format built social connectedness and resulted in improved wellbeing (Sauer et al., 2016). Unpublished survey data of 388 OMA art show attendees, collected between 2008 and 2013 in Oxford, Ohio, indicates that these end-of-term exhibitions did change the public's perception of the creative capacity of people living with dementia. Before the OMA art show, attendees were asked whether it was possible for people with dementia to express themselves creatively. On a scale of 1–5 (where 1=don't think so and 5=do think so), the pre-attendance score averaged 3.6. However, after attending the OMA art show, the score averaged 4.9 (Lokon, 2013). As a result of attending OMA art shows, the general public came to appreciate the creative capacity of people living with dementia.

## *Transformative Possibilities*

Intergenerational arts programmes that engage participants in social interactions can lead to both personal and communal transformation (Lawton, 2004; Lawton & LaPorte, 2013). Further, the arts can "create transformative spaces to challenge dominant assumptions, foster critical reflection, and envision new possibilities for mutual support, caring and relating" (Dupuis et al., 2016, p. 358). At the same time, the arts can become an accessible communicative tool for people living with dementia to express themselves and participate as equals (Basting, 2018). As well, intergenerational relationships through art can be transformative for both parties (Lawton, 2004).

As shown above, OMA's art shows do challenge the public's dominant assumptions about the creative capacity of people living with dementia. The people with dementia also expressed increased confidence in their own creative capacity. They saw their abstract artwork transformed in their own eyes from a "mess" or "hodge podge" to something beautiful, worthy of gallery and museum display (Sauer et al., 2016). University students from various departments who volunteered in OMA were also transformed, according to critical reflections in 300 weekly journal entries written by 59 student volunteers. Thematic analyses of these entries show evidence of students' transformation (see Lokon et al., 2012). Students not only increased their knowledge about dementia but also improved their comfort level in engaging with people who live with dementia. They also increased their "liking" or allophilia of this often-marginalized group of older adults (George et al., 2021; Lokon et al., 2012, 2017, 2018, 2019; Yamashita et al., 2011).

## OMA Methods

Grounded in person-centred ethics (Kitwood, 1997, 1998; Post, 1995), OMA requires volunteers and facilitators to engage in training that covers characteristics of dementia as well as communication and facilitation skills. Weekly sessions take place at several local care communities. At Miami University, university students can earn service-learning and honours course credit or participate in an extracurricular club setting. Sessions culminate in a gallery exhibition at the end of each semester to celebrate the artists' accomplishments and to "educate the public about creative capacities of people with dementia" (Yamashita et al., 2011, p. 5). Over 2600 Miami University students have participated in OMA from 2008 to 2021.

OMA rents a studio space in the Oxford Community Arts Center (OCAC) where supplies are kept and managed, and where student leaders and volunteers come together to plan and practise the activities they will facilitate with OMA artists. The term "OMA artists" refers to people living with dementia who participate in the OMA programme. Student leaders and staff members who lead the programme are referred to as "OMA facilitators."

Before the COVID-19 pandemic, the OCAC would host vibrant, well-attended evening community events called "Second Friday Celebration of the Arts" on the second Friday of every month. OMA would open their studio to the public. Student and faculty leaders would interact with the public and invite them to try an OMA art activity. They would educate about initiatives, inform about upcoming OMA art exhibitions and invite people to browse OMA merchandise to support the programming.

In the midst of the COVID-19 global health crisis, planning and implementation of OMA look quite different, but there is no slowing down on the mission. Digital tablets enable online meetings every other week. Virtual OMA modules, two weeks long, include other art forms in addition to visual arts such as poetry, storytelling, music and art-viewing. At the end of the semester, the university students create a video, audio or printed final project capturing the entire semester's creative expression of their elder partners. These final projects are then presented to the elders as their parting gift that can be shared with the elders' families and friends.

---

*Personal and Professional Takeaways From OMA:*
*Casey Pax, Art Therapist*

OMA taught me about the power of art to connect people in a community. I still vividly remember the woman I volunteered with nine years ago now. I formed a relationship with someone I would have never met otherwise. In training high school volunteers for my own programme, I saw that art was the bridge that led to conversations and connections with people across age and cognitive differences. This solidified my desire to intertwine art in my career and to connect with others, especially older adults, who I feel do not get adequate recognition in our society.

I can honestly say without participating in OMA I would most likely not be an art therapist for older adults. As a result of witnessing the power art has to draw older adults with dementia and cognitive impairment out of their shells and connect, as well as the transformative power of relationships (volunteers and residents alike), I chose to become an art therapist. I currently work in a care community in Chicago, serving adults ranging from independent living to memory care, with a whole host of abilities and cognitive levels. I now have increased training to work under an "art as therapy" model, as well as a more clinical model as I work with older adults facing life transitions, changes in disability, loss, and grief. I also work with families, helping them navigate communications with their relatives with dementia and helping them process that experience. I hope to begin intergenerational work as part of my practice.

Art as therapy can be equally as important and successful as more clinical models of art therapy, in my opinion. OMA shows that individuals do not need previous art or clinical experience to make a connection; this helps to increase their self-esteem and self-worth through creating art in community. I saw with OMA the pride individuals would experience after seeing their artwork framed in a show. This process of becoming an artist was inherently therapeutic in making them feel productive. There is value in learning something new, especially if the medical world is telling you, and what you are feeling, is just a string of losses.

OMA can be beneficial for communities on multiple levels. If you are thinking of the community in the sense of the immediate nursing environment, OMA can change the way staff see a resident. They may only have one viewpoint of a resident, especially one with progressed memory loss (such as "combative," "late stage" or "anxious") and assume that a resident cannot learn new things or change their behaviour. OMA can show staff that residents have the capacity to learn and grow and create. Changing the perspective of nursing staff can lead to more person-centred care and a more just environment for older adults. Additionally, when the self-worth and self-esteem of residents changes and they feel more capable and engaged, they may be able to better advocate for themselves, or become more content and happier in their own environments, which greatly benefits the immediate community.

Furthermore, if we think about the community at large, meaning our towns, state and country, and beyond, [then] having young people learn about cognitive impairment and dementia especially, and take it a step further in allowing them the opportunity to build a relationship with an older adult, can greatly reduce stigma associated with ageing and cognitive differences. I have witnessed volunteers go from fear and apprehension to acceptance and even affection as they learn about their elder partner. This is an impact that will extend beyond involvement in the programme and will further ripple out in all different directions in our society. I have had volunteers from my programme go on to study in nursing, wanting to work with older adults, or pursue community health, wanting to affect the societal limitations holding older adults from the resources they need and deserve.

## Connections for Art Educators

Art educators can benefit from learning about programmes like OMA as a model for multi-disciplinary and intergenerational learning, for arts advocacy across institutions for social justice and for connecting reflective practice to assessment within a community setting.

### Opportunities for Experiential, Multi-disciplinary Learning

Art educators can seek out established programmes in their communities with the potential for reciprocal benefits. Finding such opportunities involves imagining a partnership between educational institutions and the larger community beyond the campus. How can students contribute to the mission of a community programme? How might community participants benefit from the relationship? In other words, an art educator should not only be concerned about the benefits to their students. While art therapists trained in clinical contexts aim to provide therapy, art educators can facilitate therapeutic art experiences for learning. Art educators can learn from gerontologists and healthcare professionals, who best know the people living with dementia in their care. As therapeutic art programmes like OMA exemplify, experiential learning can use art as a bridge to form the relationship at a conceptual and organizational level between partnering groups. More significantly, creating art together increases social connectedness between generations and becomes an avenue for relationship-building between individuals in the community. Our focus is not on the outcome of the artwork as much as the process and the experience together, striving to facilitate a social interaction through art making (see Figure 13.1a and b).

OMA demonstrates that when artwork is generated out of a process that respects autonomy and supports the existing strengths and capabilities of elderly learners, the artwork produced can be of high aesthetic quality. Additionally, relationships can be strengthened through recognizing multi-disciplinary connections; the expertise of leaders outside of the arts working in conjunction with art educators can deepen understanding and impact multiple stakeholders within a community.

### Documentation and Arts Advocacy Across Institutions for Social Justice

OMA trains volunteers using person-centred experiences designed with the flexibility to establish support structures that create failure-free experiences for their elder partners. The transformative capacity of relationships through intergenerational engagement with art can begin to "chip away" at one of the most ubiquitous yet invisible forms of social injustices: ageism, or discrimination based

FIGURE 13.1a: (left to right) Miami student Jennie Kleinknecht and OMA founder Elizabeth Lokon welcome Gerry Thacker to the OMA program. Photo by Scott Kissell (2019).

FIGURE 13.1b: (left to right) Amy Lewin supports Bonnie Moore with monotype printmaking. Photo by Buffy Hanna (2010).

on one's advanced age in our case. Having experienced first-hand a genuine friendship with an older person living with dementia and witnessing their creative capacity is bound to confront one's ageist values. Such experiences when combined with reflection enable students to appreciate the humanity of older adults marginalized by their age and dementia diagnosis. For their part, elderly learners who bridge age and cognitive divides through intergenerational art programming may be more inclined and able to bridge other divisions, such as race, gender, sexual orientation, class, abilities and other factors that separate communities.

In our experience, OMA exemplifies the potential for the arts to build bridges across differences and create a more inclusive community. Celebrating the artists' accomplishments in a public space embedded in the community can lead to more awareness and support for the programme. Public programming around an exhibition further engages audiences and advocates for social justice across institutions. Positive experiences with the arts can change public perception and attitudes. Caroline Lehman-Croswell, executive director of OCAC, summarized the significance of OMA to the community:

> Without organizations like OMA, and the individuals affiliated with OMA, the OCAC would not be able to fulfil its mission as effectively and expansively. OMA's mission to build bridges across age and cognitive barriers through art making aligns beautifully with OCAC's mission to enrich lives and build community. OMA brings in a variety of individuals who might otherwise not be here: people with memory issues, their caretakers and students. Working together, OMA and OCAC connect artists, students, retirement communities, visitors and arts organizations. The spirit of the OMA programme adds to the loving, generous, caring spirit that OCAC works to create.
> (C. Lehman-Croswell, personal communication, 27 July 2020)

## *Reflections and Assessment*

Dewey has suggested that "understanding, comprehension, means that the various parts of the information acquired are grasped in their relations to one another, a result that is attained only when acquisition is accompanied by constant reflection upon the meaning of what is studied" (1933, pp. 78–79). OMA's students write reflective journals as a way to process their new understandings of working with their partner through art in ways that coincide with best practices for art educators. Through reflective journaling, both leading up to a teaching experience and after its implementation, practitioners can assess their methods and effectiveness.

Student leaders for OMA often create their own visual representations of their reflections on experiential learning and relationship building. OMA students are encouraged to create something tangible, often a narrative, to share with the family of the elder they worked with at the end of their semester together. It is standard practice in OMA for students to write two letters at the end of the semester, one to their elder partner and one to their partner's family members. In these letters, they reflect on lessons learned and share highlights from the semester, along with expressions of gratitude for the opportunity to spend time together. In the virtual OMA, students record (with permission) their weekly virtual interactions. At the end of the semester, they edit these videos and add music, sound effects and other images to develop a storyline of their time together.

Reflective representations like these, through writing and art, can bring forth personal understandings afforded through a shared learning experience. Collecting and preserving these reflections can become a way to assess programming and capture the experiences of all stakeholders. OMA researchers have analysed student reflections and found that the "bridge built across age and cognitive barriers through art is the bidirectional enhancement of personhood in a caring relationship" (Lokon et al., 2012, p. 350). Learning and meaning making take time and thoughtful reflection, which can directly correlate to continuous assessment of programmatic goals.

## Conclusion

Building relationships is the main significance of OMA; art becomes the outcome of a relationship. OMA provides a unique co-constructed learning experience, structured by experts who understand the needs of the elder artists and delivered by university students engaged in experiential learning, with open minds and hearts. Centring the programme on training, facilitation of accessible art experiences and one-to-one sustained interactions provides university students with a greater appreciation of how visual art can be a method to build relationships, creative capacity and self-esteem: both in people with dementia and in themselves. OMA provides a visual way to represent how people can care for one another in community.

## REFERENCES

Basting, A. (2018). Building creative communities of care: Arts, dementia, and hope in the United States. *Dementia*, 17(6), 744–754.

Basting, A. (2020). *Creative care: A revolutionary approach to dementia and elder care.* HarperCollins.

Cohen, G. D. (2006). Research on creativity and aging: The positive impact of the arts on health and illness. *Generations*, *30*(1), 7–15.

Dupuis, S. L., Kontos, P., Mitchell, G., Jonas-Simpson, C., & Gray, J. (2016). Re-claiming citizenship through the arts. *Dementia*, *15*(3), 358–380.

George, D., Lokon, E., Li, Y., & Dellasega, C. (2021). "Opening minds through art": Participation in a nursing home-based expressive arts program to improve medical students' attitudes towards persons living with dementia. *Journal of the American Geriatrics Society*, *69*(8), E23–E26. https://doi.org/10.1111/jgs.17338

Kitwood, T. (1997). *Dementia reconsidered: The person comes first*. Open University Press.

Kitwood, T. (1998). Professional and moral development for care work: Some observations on the process. *Journal of Moral Education*, *27*(3), 401–411.

Lawton, P. H. (2019). At the crossroads of intersecting ideologies: Community-based art education, community engagement, and social practice art. *Studies in Art Education*, *60*(3), 203–218.

Lawton, P. H., & La Porte, A. M. (2013). Beyond traditional art education: Transformative lifelong learning in community-based settings with older adults. *Studies in Art Education*, *54*(4), 310–320. https://doi.org/10.1080/00393541.2013.11518905

Lokon, E., Kinney, J. M., & Kunkel, S. (2012). Building bridges across age and cognitive barriers through art: College students' reflections on an intergenerational program with elders who have dementia. *Journal of Intergenerational Relationships*, *10*(4), 337–354. https://doi.org/10.1080/15350770.2012.724318

Lokon, E., Li, Y., & Parajuli, J. (2017). Using art in an intergenerational programme to improve students' attitudes toward people with dementia. *Gerontology and Geriatrics Education*, *38*(4), 407–424. https://doi.org/10.1080/02701960.2017.1281804

Lokon, E., Sauer, P. E., & Li, Y. (2019). Activities in dementia care: A comparative assessment of activity types. *Dementia*, *18*(2), 471–489. https://doi.org/10.1177/1471301216680890

Post, S. G. (1995). Alzheimer disease and the "then" self. *Kennedy Institute of Ethics Journal*, *5*(4), 307–321.

Sauer, P., Fopma-Loy, J., Kinney, J., & Lokon, E. (2016). "It makes me feel like myself": Person-centered versus traditional visual arts activities for people with dementia. *Dementia: The International Journal of Social Research and Practice*, *15*(5), 895–912.

Windle, G., Gregory, S., Howson-Griffiths, T., Newman, A., O'Brien, D., & Goulding, A. (2018). Exploring the theoretical foundations of visual arts programs for people living with dementia. *Dementia*, *17*(6), 702–727.

Yamashita, T., Kinney, J. M., & Lokon, E. (2011). The impact of a gerontology course and a service learning program on college student's attitudes toward people with dementia. *Journal of Applied Gerontology*, *32*(2), 139–163. https://doi.org/10.1177/0733464811405198

# PART 3

## TRANSVERSAL SPACES

# 14

# International Art Symposia as a Space of Knowledge Creation and Creative Engagement

*Maria Huhmarniemi and Katja Juhola*

Art symposia that bring artists together to collaborate with each other and with locals are one way of initiating community art education (CAE). In this chapter, we discuss socially engaged art symposia that respond to ongoing environmental crises, eco-anxiety and the increased need for nature-connectedness. Environmental crises have challenged art and education and underscored the requirement to transcend anthropocentrism: to have empathy and respect towards non-human nature. Ecological crises call for activist art and art–science collaborations to bring critical and creative thinking together and to produce strategies that deepen humans' relationships with non-human nature. We ask how community artists and art educators can create transformative experiences in communities at international art symposia. Therefore, our research question is—How do art symposia complement educational encounters?

In this chapter, we aim to identify factors that support learning and cross-disciplinary, cross-artistic and cross-cultural confluences in art symposia. We present three case studies in which we follow the approach of art-based action research (ABAR) to develop art symposia as CAE. These events include opportunities for community participation, such as workshops and joint artistic productions, together with local schools, village associations and similar organizations. Both authors have had initiators' roles in these events in addition to serving as curators and artist-researchers.

## *Dialogical Contemporary Art in Village Communities*

Fear, restlessness, melancholy and stress caused by environmental crises have increased in the 2000s (Searle & Gow, 2010). In addition to climate change, local environmental conflicts and loss of biodiversity can cause anxiety, which is further worsened if community members do not know how to express their fears or make changes that impact their community. We consider how an art symposium can be an activist art intervention in which artists and locals together communicate their environmental concerns, foster agency to act towards environmentalism and create grass-root local actions and political statements.

In the twenty-first century, artists' concerns for the environment have been addressed through art–science collaborations, which have also had educational aims and methods (Ballengée, 2015; Da Costa, 2008). However, Finnish scholar Anniina Suominen (2019) points out that the current social and ecological problems are beyond art education. She, therefore, proposes a new kind of art education that brings together social justice campaigns and activism projects: an approach designed to form partnerships with multiple individuals and cases. In our consideration, the approach to art education should be broad and include informal education that targets ecological issues in a number of ways. We understand informal education to work through art and dialogue, enlarging experience, connectedness and cultivation of communities (Jeffs & Smith, 1999). We also favour art symposia that have an intended local and political impact and include artistic research and art and science collaborations.

New materialism and post-humanism have been noted as some of the most important emerging trends in the humanities and social sciences (Ferrando, 2013; Gamble & Hanan, 2019). New materialism can be seen as a cross-disciplinary effort to change assumptions about human and non-human; it seeks to focus on materiality. Post-humanism is understood in this chapter as a parallel philosophical paradigm that considers ethical and moral concerns beyond the human species. Both paradigms have directed aims and chosen methods for the art interventions discussed in this chapter.

CAE in the context of art symposia has its background in a wider dialogical and pedagogical turn in contemporary art (Bishop, 2006; Bourriaud et al., 2002; Helguera, 2011; Kester, 2004). Thus, we consider the art symposium as a way to facilitate creative sharing and collaborative art making that can enhance social inclusion, foster mutual understanding and empathy among community members, and support connectedness and joyful relation to nature. Learning to cooperate is an important ability for promoting sustainable development (Jónsdóttir, 2017); in our consideration, collaborative skills are practised in art symposia among artist peers and participants and, to some extent, with elements of non-human nature. CAE and community arts are seen in this chapter as one potential way to enhance a connection to nature and expand our sense of empathy and kinship.

## ABAR for Impacting Art Symposia

ABAR is a research strategy that guides the progress of research cycles: aim, setting, intervention and evaluations (Jokela, 2019). Reflection and conceptualization often occur along the whole process and intensify during the phase of writing research conclusions. Art is implemented as a catalyst for change: community empowerment, informal learning, co-design of local environments and transformation of values and habits. Art is simultaneously a target for development; in this case, the art symposia are intended to impact community arts. In our case, the previous research cycles have already been conducted. This research covers the curation of participatory art (Juhola, 2019), ethical principles in art symposia (Juhola et al., 2020), environmental education in an art symposium as a leverage point for sustainability (Raatikainen et al., 2020) and power relations in an art symposium (Juhola & Moldovan, 2020) as it relates to CAE.

ABAR has been implemented extensively in community-based art education in multi-cultural communities in Lapland (Hiltunen, 2010; Jokela, 2019; Jokela et al., 2019). Stakeholders and community members have been included in the research processes in many ways, to the extent the research was community-driven. In our case, the participating artists and scientists at the symposia were engaged as co-researchers; research aims and methods were discussed and agreed together with them. Community members, school teachers and pupils participated in artistic interventions and contributed to the research data through their artistic production, self-reflection and discussions. The data to be analysed consist of visual documentation of the process and the artworks created that illustrate experiences and symbolize value transformations. As is typical of arts-based research (Leavy, 2009), art serves non-verbal thinking and value creation as well as making those traits visible.

Art has the potential to influence people's thinking, values, worldviews and sense of empathy. Art can have some immediate impact, and long-term engagement in communities and cyclic interventions enhance long-term empowerment and social change.

## Artistic and Pedagogical Interventions in a Multi-level Dialogue

For this chapter, we have selected three cases for closer examination. First, we present a 2017 installation by Huhmarniemi at the Art Äkäslompolo event and workshops, produced to support community engagement. Second, we present two art projects conducted at the International Socially Engaged Art Symposium (ISEAS) 2019: *Meadows and Wood-Pastures*, carried out with a group of school students; and *Circular Economy*, a collaborative art intervention among artists, environmental experts, young children and elderly women from the Martha society.

Huhmarniemi's work in Äkäslompolo was created in several stages. The process started with a gathering of a group of artists and locals to consider needs and brainstorm themes for an art event. In the first gathering, the overall idea was to make environmental art within the liminal space between the national park and tourism sites to expand experiences of nature and present cultural values for tourists through place-specific art. Later, the community members communicated a need to oppose an iron-ore mining plan since a long-term plan was being promoted by the mining company. At the next stage of the workshop, Huhmarniemi invited village residents to participate in a willow-sculpting workshop in May 2017, in which participants learned the basics of willow weaving, got to know the artist and further discussed the theme for the forthcoming symposium, which Huhmarniemi was both curating with artist Satu Kalliokuusi and contributing to as an artist. Willow weaving itself did not represent resistance to the mining plan, but the crafting workshops attracted many community members to the gathering and enabled dialogue.

In the workshopping stage, the first elements for the environmental art installation were built. The installation, *Huff, Puff and Blow*, consisted of a series of wooden hut frames with materials from the pine forest such as cones, stones and pine saplings (see Figure 14.1). The title of the installation metaphorically associated the mining plan with the threatening big bad wolf described in the English folk tale. The installation raised the question: "What did the threatening wolf mean before, and what does it mean today, for the local community?" The dialogue did not cover wolf as animal but as a common symbol in tales, and Huhmarniemi considered art education as a way to enhance the cultural literacy of tales. The installation was finalized and published as part of an art symposium in which other Nordic artists also created artworks in nature: some in close collaboration with locals and some in an artist-led process open for interaction with locals.

In 2018, the symposium was arranged for a second time. Some artists based their work on stories told by locals; others offered short courses or arranged inclusive events. For the opening event, a children's workshop was conducted by Huhmarniemi and a music teacher, Teija Enroth. The workshop included a guided tour, applying environmental education methodologies in a created environmental art forest. The tour included a play, artistic activities and dialogue encouraging children to interpret the artworks. At the *Huff, Puff and Blow* installation, children were asked to ponder what could cause harm to the forest. "Thunder may strike" was one of the dangers they noted. Because the children were mainly 4- to 5-year-olds, they did not express worry about the mine project. However, art and

FIGURE 14.1: Maria Huhmarniemi, The *Huff, Puff and Blow* (2017) environmental art in Äkäslompolo. Photo series by Heli Vepsäläinen (2017).

environmental education can also create events in which environmental concerns may be expressed.

Huhmarniemi's artistic work was followed by a series of political postcards and an installation shown in art galleries. The postcards had a picture of the installation and an address typed on them to be sent to decision-makers in Finland and the municipality. Thus, the impact of the art intervention was targeted to a wider audience than just the locals.

The *Meadows and Wood-Pastures* project in ISEAS 2019 was curated by Juhola and carried out by Huhmarniemi, as well as by Finnish conservation biologist and landscape ecologist Kaisa Raatikainen and Chilean choreographer and dance educator Hugo Lagos. The team collaborated with a group of fifth-grade students (aged 10 and 11 years) and their teachers for a one-week process. A wide range of objectives included efforts to explore the art–science collaboration as an approach to familiarizing participants with agricultural nature, biodiversity conservation and the agency of non-human natural elements, such as animals and plants, and to guide participants into sensitive encounters with local nature (Raatikainen et al., 2020). The process encouraged conscious awareness and learning of one's own body language and fostered discussions on human connectedness to ecosystems.

During the *Meadows and Wood-Pastures* process, four outdoor working sessions were arranged, lasting from a few hours to a whole day. Art education practices enabled the pupils to deepen their relationship with nature (see Figure 14.2). The meadow as a working site offered a direct possibility to observe both biodiversity and the loss of it. The focus on arts and science-based teaching varied and was partly integrated. The agency of natural elements was targeted by observing different strategies that plants have for spreading their seeds. Sensitivity exercises guided pupils to move on a rock with bare hands and feet and with closed eyes. The last session of the intervention was arranged at the schoolyard as a performance of spreading meadow plant seeds to establish a school meadow. In the performance, participants wore self-made crowns decorated with stems of plants, symbolizing human power to act benevolently in and for nature.

The children who participated in the *Meadows and Wood-Pastures* intervention live in the countryside. Some of them have farmers as parents. During and after the symposia, we were concerned about the ethical and ecological problems in

FIGURE 14.2: Art education practices in a dairy farm and a meadow. Photo series by Fabio Cito (2019).

industrialized food production and pondered whether animal rights should have been discussed more when visiting a cow house (Raatikainen et al., 2020). On the other hand, the workshop focused on how small-scale sustainable agriculture could increase biodiversity through human and animal collaboration.

A circular economy is a concept used to define the aims of eliminating waste and using recycling resources. The 2019 project titled *Circular Economy* was a collaboration between two community artists, Fié Neo (Singapore) and Tuula Nikulainen (Finland), and two environmental experts: circular economy specialist Sini Ilmonen and sustainability specialist Ari Kivelä. They engaged with the community cross-generationally, including 3- to 6-year-old kindergarten children and the Martha society, which promotes wellbeing and quality of life in the home and carries out cultural and civic education in Finland. The aim was to teach children about the circular economy through art.

Over four days, the group carried out four interventions to deepen participants' understanding of a circular economy and its practical implementations. The first intervention was a net of threads made together by children and the Marthas, which illustrated how all things and beings are connected to each other (see Figure 14.3). For the second work, the group designed an outdoor game in which they tackled the impact of the forest industry in the context of the children's worldview: for example, how animals lose their homes if too much wood is used industrially. In the third intervention of the *Circular Economy* team, the children were asked to bring along both their favourite and least favourite toy. The children had to explain why they loved or disliked their toys. Then group members, together with the children, found ways to make the unfavourable toys more comfortable so that they could be appreciated again and children would learn sustainability thinking. The event ended with a group reflection in which all participants described their

FIGURE 14.3: Circular Economy team, members of the Martha society and kindergarten children playing together and creating a network installation. Photo series by Fabio Cito (2019).

experiences and included a story about a Singaporean artist and first experiences of nature, which was exciting for the children, and it also opened up Finnish participants' view of the Finns' close and effortless relationship with nature. Eventually, the children drew their reflections from the week on a large piece of paper, which was also on display in the gallery in addition to the woven web, photographs and video work. Later, the Martha society expressed the will to continue collaborating regularly with the kindergarten. As well, all the interventions in ISEAS 2019 were shared with the wider community in two exhibitions arranged at the end of the symposium.

The case studies presented in this chapter are some of many interventions created by artists in ISEAS with a variety of local communities since 2017. Sites, participants, working methods and themes have varied from year to year, but some structures, such as mentoring and daily reflection sessions among participating artists, have been successfully developed to support artists involved with CAE.

## Curators, Participating Artists and Community Members – All Learning

Dialogue, trust and openness are important tools in community art and CAE. For trust to be built, it is important that the community knows the curator and artist. In successful community art projects, artists have worked prominently and as part of a community for several years and have accumulated an in-depth understanding of participants (Helguera, 2011). In the cases discussed in this chapter, trust was created over a long period with several phases of meetings and creative collaboration. For ISEAS 2019, Juhola had gained participants' trust based on previous interactions, as well as having been a community member and socially engaged artist who had done several art projects with local school children. In Äkäslompolo, the collaboration began by identifying community leaders to collaborate and connect with, and several gatherings were arranged to familiarize the curator with the community.

There are many potential strategies for initiating CAE through art symposia. The artist can teach community members-specific methods for creating art and thus create a dialogical encounter, as happened in the willow-sculpting workshop. Alternatively, artists can lead artistic processes that aim to facilitate creative involvement and co-production of knowledge and transformative experiences, as we witnessed in the *Circular Economy* workshop with the kindergarten. In a community-driven process, invited artists and community members can make art together as a team from the initial design phase and throughout the whole process. Artists can also implement their own material expressions to communicate environmental values and the concerns of locals. Community members can be invited to the opening and closing events of the symposium. Pedagogically tuned discussions and exhibition tours can be arranged as part of the symposium; as well, exhibitions can share reflections from and documentation of the symposium with a wider audience to expand the impact, which can be furthered by video documentation and social media. Thus, pedagogical approaches can be applied to socially engaged art symposia. The goal, however, is not for outsiders to bring art and culture into communities, but rather for artists to interact with the community, listen to them, learn from them and share something in return.

Based on the analysis of our research data, three groups benefit from potential learning in a socially engaged art symposium: curators (in this case the curator–artist–teacher–researchers authoring this chapter), participating artists and the community members. We reflected on our own learning along with the ABAR cycles when evaluating the results of each symposium and setting aims for the next one. Our learning process was bolstered by co-authoring research articles, which involved knowledge sharing, dialogue and self-reflection. While the art took place in the community and at the working sites, the process of discussing the experience in research as well as in published ISEAS books and social media-sharing supported wider learning and the impact of the art.

While in Äkäslompolo, participating artists worked independently with the community; although supported by curators, the concept of ISEAS was based on cross-artistic and artist–scientist teams. Evidence from the team members' reflections in ISEAS showed that the process of the symposium has the potential to enhance intuition, sensitivity and growing openness to unplanned situations. The spirit of conversational art can be seen when initiating these kinds of unplanned directions (Bhabha, 1998). The reflection by artists was in line with the concept of "a third space," which critical theorist Homi Bhabha described as a space in which something new and hitherto unidentified can be created (Rutherford, 1990). We see learning opportunities in these kinds of experiences. In the Bhabhian sense, art symposia can become a third space that, as a hybrid, is larger than the compilation of the individual participants and where the artists empower themselves as well as learn.

The aim of CAE in art symposia is often to empower the community, support participation and empathy and strengthen agency; in our cases, we focused on environmentalism and the opposition of an industrial plan that threatened others' livelihoods and nature. CAE leans on the concept of reinforcing agency by supporting communities seeking to influence their own living environments (Hiltunen, 2010), as was evidenced in the children's meadow performance in support of biodiversity. Communal activities offer opportunities for participation and the associated experience of involvement, which has a potentially empowering effect (Hiltunen, 2010). If successful, the act of participating strengthens self-trust in personal skills and abilities to influence the wider community (Hiltunen, 2010). Both artists and members of the community are active creators of knowledge, works of art, events and, to some extent, their conceptualization.

## *Conclusion*

Art symposia are one way of initiating innovative approaches in CAE, fostering learning and creating transformative experiences that encourage deeper and more respectful interactions among community members and non-human nature. Three perspectives on learning converge in the art symposium: those of the curators, participating artists and community members. Practising art as a community in nature strengthens social dynamics, empowers participants in an age of eco-anxiety and nurtures connectedness to nature. Strategies for CAE in an art symposium include positioning artists as learning facilitators and co-artists with community members and non-human nature and providing a space for pedagogically tuned public events and exhibitions.

Our recommendations for stimulating the learning of curators are the ABAR approach, collaborations such as co-authoring, reflective research on processes and results of art symposia. Further, to foster learning and empowerment among participating artists, we recommend inviting heterogenous artists' groups with diverse cultural knowledge and life experiences as well as art–science collaborations, mentoring, daily reflection sessions and walking, and similar physical engagement in the surrounding natural environment. Art symposia have the potential for supporting cultural learning, networking and deepening of kinships. To achieve transformative experiences among community members, we suggest inviting locals to make art together with teams of international and local artists; to have several phases in the collaboration, such as pre-events and meetings to discuss the aims of the symposia; and to engage locals with planning the intervention. When artists work together with locals, communities have a powerful impact on artists and vice versa. We conclude that the process of making art together helps sustain and promote CAE and that art symposia have the potential for enhancing knowledge creation and creative engagement.

## REFERENCES

Ballengée, B. (2015). *Ecological understanding through transdisciplinary art and participatory biology*. Plymouth University. https://pearl.plymouth.ac.uk//handle/10026.1/3254

Bhabha, H. K. (1998). Conversational art. In M. J. Jacob & M. Brenson (Eds.), *Conversations at the Castle: Changing audiences and contemporary art* (pp. 38–47). MIT Press.

Bishop, C. (2006). *Participation*. MIT Press.

Bourriaud, N., Pleasance, S., & Woods, F. (2002). *Relational aesthetics*. Les presses du reél.

Da Costa, B. (2008). Reaching the limit. When art becomes science. In B. da Costa & P. Kavita (Eds.), *Tactical biopolitics: Art, activism, and technoscience* (pp. 365–386). The MIT Press.

Ferrando, F. (2013). Posthumanism, transhumanism, antihumanism, metahumanism, and new materialisms: Differences and relations. *Existenz: An International Journal in Philosophy, Religion, Politics, and the Arts, 8*(2), 26–32. https://www.existenz.us/volumes/Vol.8-2Ferrando.pdf

Gamble, C. N., & Hanan, J. N. (2019). What is new materialism? *Journal of the Theoretical Humanities, 24*(6), 111–134. https://doi.org/10.1080/0969725X.2019.1684704

Helguera, P. (2011). *Education for socially engaged art: A materials and techniques handbook*. Jorge Pinto Books.

Hiltunen, M. (2010). Slow activism: Art in progress in the North. In A. Linjakumpu & S. Wallenius-Korkalo (Eds.), *Progress or perish. Northern perspectives on social change* (pp. 119–138). Ashgate.

Jeffs, T., & Smith, M. (1999). *Informal education: Conversation, democracy and learning*. Education Now.

Jokela, T. (2019). Arts-based action research in the North. In *Oxford research encyclopedia of education*. Oxford University Press. https://doi.org/10.1093/acrefore/9780190264093.013.522

Jokela, T., Huhmarniemi, M., & Hiltunen, M. (2019). Art-based action research: Participatory art education research for the North. In A. Sinner, R. L. Irwin, & J. Adams (Eds.), *Provoking the field. International perspectives on visual arts PhDs in education* (pp. 45–56). Intellect.

Jónsdóttir, Á. B. (2017). *Artistic actions for sustainability: Potential of art in education for sustainability* [Unpublished doctoral dissertation]. University of Lapland, Rovaniemi. Acta electronica Universitatis Lapponiensis open access.

Juhola, K. (2019). Curating participatory art in the time of Anthropocene. *Design & Art Papers, 7*(1), 27–44.

Juhola, K., Huhmarniemi, M., & Raatikainen, K. (2020). Artistic research on socially and environmentally engaged art – Ethics of gathering. *Ruukku – Studies in Artistic Research, 14*. https://doi.org/10.22501/ruu.696352

Juhola, K., & Moldovan, S. (2020). International art symposium in focus on educational places and power relations. *Research in Art and Education, 2*, 23–46. https://doi.org/10.54916/rae.119293

Kester, G. (2004). *Conversation pieces: Community and communication in modern art*. University of California Press.

Leavy, P. (2009). *Method meets art. Arts-based research practice*. The Guilford Press.

Raatikainen, K. J., Juhola, K., Huhmarniemi, M., & Peña-Lagos, H. (2020). "Face the cow": Reconnecting to nature and increasing capacities for pro-environmental agency. *Ecosystems and People, 16*(1), 273–289. https://doi.org/10.1080/26395916.2020.1817151

Rutherford, J. (1990). The third space: Interview with Homi Bhabha. In J. Rutherford (Ed.), *Identity: Community, culture, difference* (pp. 207–221). Lawrence and Wishart.

Searle, K., & Gow, K. (2010). Do concerns about climate change lead to distress? *International Journal of Climate Change Strategies and Management, 2*(4), 362–379. https://doi.org/10.1108/17568691011089891

Suominen, A. (2019). Apptivism, farming, and EcoJustice art education. In R. Foster, J. Mäkelä, & R. A. Martusewicz (Eds.), *Art, ecojustice and education: Intersecting theories and practices* (pp. 141–152). Routledge.

# 15

# Collaborative Thinking, Creating and Learning on a Remote Greek Island: Towards Community Art Education for Sustainability

*Sophia Chaita and Georgia Liarakou*

How might collaborative art making as a form of community art education (CAE) enable learning for sustainability? On the small, remote Greek island of Lipsi, an intergenerational collaboration between school pupils and adult community stakeholders was initiated by the local high school artist–teacher–researcher as a form of sustainability research held at the school. The research aimed to re-envision the role of education and explore solutions for compressed and exaggerated community feelings termed as the "island effect" (Baldacchino, 2018, p. xxv): in this case disconnectedness, inertia and inability to design their island's future. Engaging the island community as part of this extracurricular voluntary participatory experience involves commitment, aimed at encouraging community sustainability. Thinking, creating and learning in a group affords possibilities often entirely overlooked or dismissed by individual island inhabitants. In this sense, the collaboration may be seen as an instance of collective pedagogy (Desai, 2020).

Our hypothesis is that island CAE may contribute towards the transformation of community limitation perceptions in the manner that Brinklow (2015) describes an island liberates an artist:

> within the very physical and limiting boundary of an island, artists feel a freedom they don't feel elsewhere: the island forces them to go deeper into themselves, allowing them to be more who they are, which in turn allows for endless possibility.
>
> (p. 170)

According to Petzold and Ratter (2019), islands reflect spatial relations and dependencies, power structures and connections which may have transferable meaning for other places facing sustainability challenges. Looking at CAE on this remote small island, we consider its potential value in the broader quest for community sustainability.

The term "community" is complex and resists a single definition; however, for the purpose of this article, we adopt Liepins' (2017) approach to community as a broad, fluid social phenomenon: that is, peoples' interaction with spaces and structures, meanings and practices constitute community. Both Liepins' approach and the theoretical context of cultural ecology (Dillon, 2015) support the notion that community is practised through interaction with the environment and is mutually constitutive. With this in mind, we discuss CAE on Lipsi using Dillon's cultural ecology framework, placing emphasis on the core of CAE: that is, making a community artwork (CA). Finally, using Liepins' community framework, we analyse CA making at three progressive levels to determine the possible contributions of CAE to sustainability.

## *The Community of Lipsi*

A small Greek island in the Aegean southeast of the mainland, Lipsi has a number of characteristics particular to remote islands. Distanced from central governance, the 16 km² area with a population of less than 800 has limited natural resources, yet is known for its natural and cultural environment. Tightly knit and tradition-bound while simultaneously diverse with a scope of flexibility, Lipsi is typical of remote island communities. Permanent residents share common connections regarding the origin and traditional culture, though meanings of identity, livelihood practices and community sustainability appear to differ. Lipsi faces local problems such as the Greek economic crisis and youth out-migration, in addition to worldwide demographic and socio-economic issues challenging remote community sustainability (Liarakou et al., 2014).

Sustainability is a regulative, ongoing process resisting a single definition. Education for sustainability is the process of identifying values and defining concepts to develop the skills and attitudes necessary to understand and appreciate inter-relatedness among inhabitants, their culture and natural surroundings (Liarakou & Flogaitis, 2007). Similarly, contemporary environmental art reflects the world as "a place of interaction and connection" (Gablik, 1992, p. 150). Focusing on the interrelationship between island inhabitants and their remote environment as an interconnected system, we suggest that experiencing the creation of a CA may help build knowledge around "the 'special' qualities of place embedded in everyday life" (Lippard, 1997, p. 37); in turn, this experience might offer participants the opportunity to start thinking about sustainability so as to counteract some of the "island effect" mentioned above. Being, thinking and creating together may heighten empathy and awareness of participants as knowledge bearers and creators.

## Context and Theoretical Framework

Our intergenerational-collaboration participants were eleven high-school students and two grandparents, two municipality councillors, a café-fishing store owner, a fisher, a hospitality person, an agricultural co-op representative, a travel agent, a homemaker, a primary school teacher and a high-school art teacher. Ages ranged from 14 to 75; pace of work and skill set varied too. The advantage was taken of generational diversity. That everyone's contribution was valued gave participants pleasure, which ensured continued participation in the CAE course.

This collaboration invested entirely in participants' experience, which lies at the heart of making the CA and of CA as learning. For example, participants were included in creating the title as well as applying ideas and local knowledge to designing and making the CA. Learning is an adaptive process where learners' conceptual schemes are progressively reconstructed by the perception of experiences and ideas (Dillon, 2015). The CA is a collaborative experience providing valuable lived experience, which may change the community's orientation towards sustainability. Created within a research context, the CA may be characterized as researcher-initiated; the researcher's control, however, was limited to encouraging participants to listen collectively and deeply to each other's memories, views, needs and dreams.

Preceding the CA making, the researcher–artist teacher facilitated and guided participants through a CAE course – offered at the school two afternoons a week over three months – designed to engage group collaboration and interaction with the environment. Since participants with little experience of art or intimidated by the idea of making art faced barriers to participation, "place" was chosen as a theme. This proved to be an accessible and significant entry point since "place is not just a thing in the world, but a way of understanding the world" (Cresswell, 2015, p. 18). Location, however, acquires meaning only when locale and a sense of place are combined with it (Cresswell, 2015).

Five sessions of the CAE course mentioned above enabled participants to sense Lipsi as a place of "meaning and experience" (Cresswell, 2015, p. 19). The first session was a guided visualization of the island fifteen years into the future – visions then expressed as drawings. The second was a mapping of Lipsi's cultural assets, from which emerged three traditional techniques – dry stonewalling, fishnet making and handicrafts – considered essential to island identity. The third session involved researching these techniques in the field: for example, discovering locations of stone varieties. For the fourth session, community participants taught each other, peer to peer and regardless of age, about transmitting the three traditional techniques to all. The fifth session focused on creating a collaborative, lived experience of imagination, thoughts and ideas, collective decisions and making strategies. During the CAE course, participants assumed artist/researcher/teacher roles (Irwin et al., 2006) as follows:

- As researchers on a quest for sustainability, they explored key traditional techniques, fundamental to island identity, needing preservation and adaptation.
- As teachers, they taught traditional techniques peer to peer and contextualized the school as a place where meaning and experience of the world transpires.
- As artists, they collaborated on making the CA.

## *Community as A/r/tographers From a Cultural Ecological Perspective*

Focusing on the artist's role, a CA was created with selected techniques and materials. Responding to the task of creating a CA to commemorate the school's thirtieth anniversary, community participants were encouraged to collaborate, express and share their ideas, applying knowledge gained from preceding CAE course sessions. Reassured their contributions would not be judged, participants' outlooks, aesthetic values, capabilities – differentiated by age, knowledge and skill, and interest in collaboration – were respected. The properties and functions of selected materials and techniques were then explored through interrelated "conceptual" and "perceptual" modes of engagement: that is, as "continuation" or "change," respectively (Dillon, 2015). For creating the CA, community participants in the conceptual mode, exhibiting relational engagement, drew on experience with selected materials associated with established routine activities and traditional knowledge: stones from dry stonewalling, net from fishing and crochet from handcraft. Simultaneously, in the perceptual mode of "living the moment," they perceived new possibilities and changed the routine. Using these routine materials in the unconventional school setting in an unconventional a/r/tographic way reflects co-constitutional engagement. In other words, by sharing the moment, participants, the school and materials simultaneously co-construct each other's being. In this sense, ways of engaging with CAE or ways of "being" in the school do not occur in isolation of each other. The "conceptual" and "perceptual" modes of engagement constantly re-form each other in ways that are themselves relational and co-constitutional. It follows that the CA created through these two modes may also be viewed and analysed through these modes.

## Three-Level Analysis of the CA Experience

The CA entitled *Remember. Live. Dream* is analysed first from coastal sustainability indicators (Schernewski et al., 2014), moving on to Kress and Van Leeuwen's (KvL) (2006) grammar of visual design and finally progressing to a/r/tographic renderings (Springgay et al., 2005). This order demonstrates the possible co-constitutional nature of CAE and likely its potential to contribute towards education for community sustainability. Following Irwin's (2013) argument that art making is pedagogy in movement from the known to the unknown, the three-level analysis traces how CAE shapes community as it searches for sustainability. Through interactive movement among levels, the Lipsi community is shaped. On the first level, coastal sustainability indicators served as a bridge between spaces and structures of Lipsi (known) and a quest for sustainability (unknown). These connections influence meaning on the next level, presented in KvL's terms as information value: moving from the known (left) to the unknown (right). At the third level, renderings reveal the community reshaping itself in its search for sustainability, moving between practices of continuity (known) and practices of change (unknown). Inextricably connected with the theoretical framework, each level adds credibility to the research process (Chaita et al., 2018).

An overview of the progression of this three-level analysis and its connection to Liepins' (2017) community framework is described through four numbered processes in Figure 15.1. Starting at the centre, participants come together as a group with the intention to create the CA. Spiralling outwards, spaces and structures [1] are significant through their connection to coastal sustainability indicators through selected materials and elements of the CA, enabling the materialization of meanings. KvL's (2006) grammar of visual design applied to the CA encourages systematic, consistent patterns of meanings [2]. The new awareness of these patterns validates the continuation and change of practices [3]. A/r/tographic renderings (Springgay et al., 2005) at the heart of the CA experience shape community continuity and change (Chaita et al., 2018).

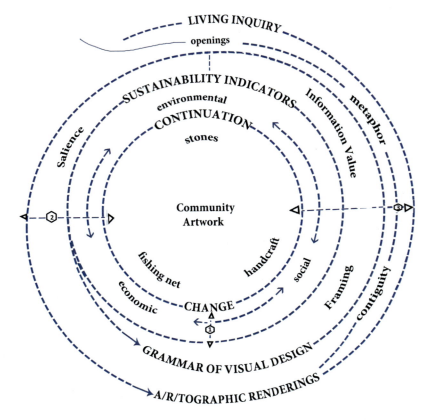

FIGURE 15.1: Three-level analysis of the CA combined with Liepins' (2017) community elements.

## Coastal Sustainability Indicators

Figure 15.2 illustrates a sample of first-level analysis. The first column shows the coastal sustainable development indicator (Schernewski et al., 2014) and its definition. The second shows a CA element that supports the specific definition connecting it to the indicator. The third substantiates how the element depicted in the image satisfies its connection to the particular indicator. The association of CA elements with coastal sustainability indices was based on evidence found in the elements of the CA and meanings generated by place. The connection was qualitatively based on researchers' perceptions that the meanings of elements satisfactorily comply with the proposed indices or definitions derived from the indicator-based sustainability assessment tool (Karnauskaitė et al., 2019).

| Environmental Quality Indices | CA Elements | Analysis for Substantiation |
|---|---|---|
| **Biodiversity and Nature Protection**<br><br>Definition: protection and support of natural habitats, their biodiversity and the quality of key natural sites. |  | Indigenous stones in the artwork refer to the dry stone terracing method. Optimizing valuable land, it is used to improve rainwater percolation, reduce soil erosion and encourage local biodiversity.<br><br>Fish communities are an important source of food and livelihood. Maintaining and protecting the rich, diverse fish communities supports overall biodiversity of other marine species too. |

| Economic Indices | CA Elements | Analysis for Substantiation |
|---|---|---|
| **Business involvement**<br><br>Definition: economic value derived from local natural resources or a human-made, cultural-heritage resource. | <br> | Traditional low impact productivity, for example fishing nets with large openings, support the economic sustainability indices where income is derived from the local natural resource: i.e. fish of the appropriate size/age ensuring continuation of species.<br><br>Reference made to the school co-op called *Technoleipsia* supports promotion of entrepreneur partnerships, local products and fair trade as well as the idea of school as a place for learning co-op partnership principles. |

| Social well-being identity and culture indices | CA Elements | Analysis for Substantiation |
|---|---|---|
| **Community partcipation**<br><br>Definition: encourages volunteer collaboration for community solidarity, cultural heritage and biodiversity conservation. |  | Handshake of opposites indicates trust and collaboration. Similarly capitalized words love, collaboration and solidarity possibly indicate social cohesion gained through community participation. |
| **Cultural identity and heritage**<br><br>Definition: protects, monitors and safeguards local natural, historical, archaeological, religious, spiritual and cultural heritage associated with identity. |  | Reference made to the starfish, which is the emblem of the island. As well, the local handcrafted crochet technique suggests support for the safeguarding of natural and cultural heritage. |

FIGURE 15.2: Sample of first-level analysis. Photo by Sophia Chaita (2021).

## The Grammar of Visual Design

Understanding the meaning being communicated by content may prove challenging without taking form into account. Progressing on to the second level of analysis – using KvL's (2006) concepts of framing, information value and salience – attempts to further analyse the creation of meaning.

Framing helps to distinguish relationships between elements. Elements belonging together are placed close to each other, aiding understanding. Figure 15.3 identifies three frames. In the central frame, crumpled paper, plastic water bottles, plastic bags and aluminium foil are grouped along three vertical lines. Relative proximity identifies them as belonging to the same information unit: that is, recyclable materials. Similarly, flanking this frame on each side are two additional

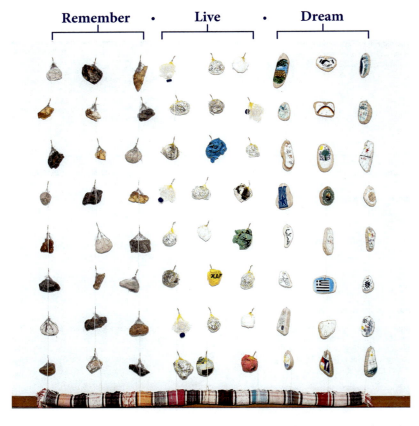

FIGURE 15.3: A photo of second-level analysis of *Remember. Live. Dream*. Photo by Sophia Chaita (2020).

information units. Grouped along three vertical lines, the left frame contains information referring to stone types found on the island, and the right frame contains handcrafted pebbles with information regarding future aspirations. The three information units form a cohesive triptych.

The triptych correlates with the title *Remember. Live. Dream* and three units of time: past, present and future, respectively. Looking at the frames' placement and their relation to KvL's (2006) information value appears to confirm this correlation. Information value designates meanings to specific elements in a visual composition according to their placement in relation to other elements. In terms of the horizontal (left–right) axis, stones aligned to the left of the centre represent given information shared as known, a space from which the message is directed. Conversely, pebbles aligned to the right represent new information that may be disputed, as no consensus has yet been reached regarding the meaning. In other words, stones are presented as known, self-evident information with which the community agrees. This corresponds with the first word in the title "remember" and comprises the point of message departure; the stones insinuate heritage known from the past. Conversely, pebbles allude to the final title word "dream" and indicate reference to the perhaps disagreed-upon new "contestable" information regarding the future, which is unknown.

Returning to the whole, the centre significantly displays salient recycled waste units as the nucleus of information and refers to the central word of the title "live" as symbolic of the present. The centre as presented "mediates" between a potentially polarized past and unknown futures.

## A/r/tographic Renderings

Renderings (Springgay et al., 2005) illustrate conceptual practices between continuity and change and how these create meanings from experiences in currently held spaces, structures of place and community, and what they might become. These also help identify and organize research findings in the CA.

## Living Inquiry

Focusing on the interrelation between abstract theoretical concepts and lived experience, knowledge creation is formed as a living inquiry (Irwin & de Cosson, 2004). Through this inquiry, the community creating the CA enacts small shifts towards sustainability. These shifts include an increase in capacity for learning, decision making and action. The group learns by observing facts, questioning and analysing meaning. They recognize cultural assets, question how traditional techniques may contribute to future island identity, and analyse how change affects community, improves relationships and increases community cohesion while altering future conceptions of place. Decision making and action are undertaken throughout the CA creation.

## Contiguity Between the CA and Community Aspirations

The title *Remember. Live. Dream* denotes community future aspirations. The community aspiration "remember" seeks continuing revitalization of past traditional techniques and heritage associated with identity, while "live" pertains to the quality of life as present "lived experience." The aspiration to "dream" refers to change. Community and heritage simultaneously co-construct each other's being; the former is empowered to positively envision the future, while the latter, diversified with new functions and roles, secures continuity of the technique.

## Understandings of Metaphor in the CA

Stone, symbolic of both the island and the environmental goal of sustainable development, is a metaphor for a sense of permanence and community continuity. Stone, a native material, is an integral element of the island, rich in associations for Lipsians. Touched in some way by human activity, stones take on other dimensions, such as dry-stone terracing, that bring about environmental change. On the other hand, asymmetrical sea-worn pebbles are literally nature-changed stones that symbolize natural continuation and change. Similarly, the handcrafted smoothly rubbed pebbles symbolize the continuation of traditional techniques; however, material and technique shift their utility and meaning as they become an art. Both become a celebration of identity, symbols of community optimism and a metaphor for social wellbeing.

Making fishing nets, the final traditional technique to be preserved, runs through the whole artwork. This serves as a metaphor for the economic aspect of sustainable development as it alludes to fishing as a major source of livelihood. While continuing to reference livelihood, in the artwork the fishing net becomes a network connecting past, present and future: referring to the connection between generations, between community and place as well as between place and the world.

Finally, the nucleus of the artwork, recyclable waste, alludes to how local living has a global impact. Creatively reusing discarded recyclable materials in the central frame also suggests that this is also the way forward for traditional techniques. Adapted like the recyclables into something new, local techniques may become art to spark sustainability awareness in Lipsi and other places as well.

## Conclusion

The three-level analysis of Lipsi's community art experience verifies notions of mutual constitution of community and environment as held by both Liepins (2017) and Dillon (2015). In this sense, CAE has much to offer island community sustainability. Understanding how predominant and underlying factors of CAE influence the co-constitution of community and environment on this remote island may have important implications for sustainability worldwide, given that social fragmentation, habitat loss and out-migration are issues that jeopardize communities globally.

By focusing on Lipsi, this chapter offers only a glimpse of CAE and education towards sustainability. A partial research perspective cannot tell the whole story since the CA experience is still ongoing and eludes a complete account. Future research shedding light on participants' perspective over time would be helpful. Still, the Lipsian school's role has changed through CAE. Open to knowledge about local tradition, the school encourages the experience of change towards sustainability. Learning together affords change for a community on a number of points: a new outlook for endless possibility, social cohesion and empowerment as creators. The collective experience of creation encourages the community to move in a new direction, from the conventional to the unconventional. Known techniques become collective reflections for an unknown future of island sustainability. Instead of being ignored, aesthetics are explored, celebrated, framed and revealed in our analysis through the cultural themes running through the CA: drystone walling, fishnet mending, handicrafts and recycling. Their salience in the CA indicates validation for their continuity and gives them visibility from an alternative perspective.

The three-level analysis also reveals how CAE provides a transformative experience. Reciprocal interaction of participants, meanings and place progressively reshape one another on each level. Alternative meanings of materials and techniques, constructed and communicated collectively through the grammar of visual design, are embodied in the CA experience. Just as an island liberates an artist, a/r/tographic renderings reveal participant empowerment: the ability to change perspective and feel the freedom of endless possibility. "Art can't change the world on its own, but art can contribute to changing the world" (Mouffe, 2016, p. 39). CAE takes participants deeper into notions of continuation and change: even if one project is just a drop in the ocean, like a small, remote Greek island.

## REFERENCES

Baldacchino, G. (Ed.). (2018). *The Routledge international handbook of island studies: A world of islands*. Routledge.

Brinklow, L. (2015). *Artists and the articulation of islandness, sense of place, and story in Newfoundland and Tasmania* [Doctoral dissertation]. The University of Tasmania, Tasmania. https://eprints.utas.edu.au/22748/1/Brinklow_whole_thesis.pdf

Chaita, S., Liarakou, G., & Gavrilakis, C. (2018, March 13–15). Drawing the future today: A collaborative partnership [Paper presentation]. *Fifth conference on arts based research & artistic research provoking research and social intervention*, Liverpool, UK.

Chaita, S., Liarakou, G., & Vasilakakis, V. (2018). A/r/tography: A fluid relationship of theory, time and place. In A. Sinner, R. L. Irwin, & T. Jokela (Eds.), *Visually provoking: Dissertations in art education* (pp. 40–49). Lapland University Press. https://lauda.ulapland.fi/handle/10024/63606

Cresswell, T. (2015). *Place: An introduction*. John Wiley & Sons.

Desai, D. (2020). Educating for social change through art: A personal reckoning. *Studies in Art Education, 61*(1), 10–23. https://doi.org/10.1080/00393541.2019.1699366

Dillon, P. (2015). Education for sustainable development in a cultural ecological frame. In R. Jucker & R. Mathar (Eds.), *Schooling for sustainable development in Europe: Concepts, policies and educational experiences at the end of the UN decade of education for sustainable development* (pp. 109–120). Springer.

Gablik, S. (1992). The ecological imperative. *Art Journal, 51*(2), 49–51. https://doi.org/10.1080/00043249.1992.10791566

Irwin, R. L. (2013). Becoming A/r/tography. *Studies in Art Education, 54*(3), 198–215. https://doi.org/10.1080/00393541.2013.11518894

Irwin, R. L., Beer, R., Springgay, S., Grauer, K., Xiong, G., & Bickel, B. (2006). The rhizomatic relations of A/r/tography. *Studies in Art Education, 48*(1), 70–88. https://doi.org/10.1080/00393541.2006.11650500

Irwin, R. L., & de Cosson, A. (2004). *A/r/tography: Rendering self through arts-based living inquiry*. Pacific Educational Press.

Karnauskaitė, D., Schernewski, G., Støttrup, J. G., & Katarżytė, M. (2019). Indicator-based sustainability assessment tool to support coastal and marine management. *Sustainability, 11*(11), 3175. https://doi.org/10.3390/su11113175

Kress, G. R., & Van Leeuwen, T. (2006). *Reading images: The grammar of visual design*. Routledge.

Liarakou, G., & Flogaitis, E. (2007). *From environmental education to education for sustainable development: Issues, trends and proposals*. Nissos.

Liarakou, G., Gavrilakis, C., & Flogaitis, E. (2014). *Profiles of isolated communities and ways into integration*. ENSI i.n.p.a. https://www.ensi.org/global/downloads/Publications/371/CoDeS-Isolated%20communities.pdf

Liepins, R. (2017). New energies for an old idea: Reworking approaches to "community" in contemporary rural studies. In R. Munton (Ed.), *The rural: Critical essays in human geography*, (pp. 377–389). Routledge. https://doi.org/10.4324/9781315237213-22

Lippard, L. R. (1997). *The lure of the local: Senses of place in a multicentered society*. New Press.

Mouffe, C. (2016). "Art can't change the world on its own": A conversation with Petlin Tan and Florian Malzacher. In F. Malzachre, A. Ogrut, & P. Tan (Eds.), *Silent University* (pp. 34–44). Sternberg Press.

Petzold, J., & Ratter, B. (2019). More than just SIDS: Local solutions for global problems on small islands. *Island Studies Journal, 14*(1), 3–8. https://doi.org/10.24043/isj.77

Schernewski, G., Schönwald, S., & Katarżytė, M. (2014). Application and evaluation of an indicator set to measure and promote sustainable development in coastal areas. *Ocean & Coastal Management, 101*, 2–13. https://doi.org/10.1016/j.ocecoaman.2014.03.028

Springgay, S., Irwin, R. L., & Kind, S. W. (2005). A/r/tography as living inquiry through art and text. *Qualitative Inquiry, 11*(6), 897–912. https://doi.org/10.1177/1077800405280696

# 16

# Finding Possibility in the Liminality of Socially Engaged Arts: Fostering Learning and Wellbeing With Refugee Youth

*Kate Collins*

For resettled refugees, the early days, months and years exist in a liminal space where feelings of home and belonging are complicated, fraught and ambiguous. Forcible displacement to different lands, cultures and languages leaves behind all that is familiar and can be deeply disorienting and traumatizing. "Liminality has been theorized as the transitional moment between spheres of belonging when social actors no longer belong to the group they are leaving behind and do not yet fully belong in their new social sphere" (Suarez-Orozco et al., 2011, p. 444). For teenage refugees whose family roles as child or adult might also fluctuate in confusing ways, the ambiguity of displacement is further compounded. With these profound challenges in mind for young refugees resettling around the world and starting high school in their new home countries, this chapter seeks to examine a different kind of liminality: the liminality of socially engaged arts which can be generative in supporting the learning and wellness of these same young people.

    This chapter introduces a socially engaged arts project called *Youth Artists and Allies Taking Action in Society* (YAAAS), uniquely designed for educators and refugee high-school students to work side by side in a collaborative partnership. After the project overview, I provide a literature review revealing the essential ways in which trauma-informed practice, social-emotional learning and culturally sustaining pedagogy can intersect with socially engaged art to support both the learning and wellness of refugee youth. I then describe the pedagogical and curricular practices of YAAAS to illustrate how the liminality afforded by socially engaged arts has allowed YAAAS to become an exceptionally generative space of learning and wellness.

This chapter addresses the aims of this book by unpacking the ways in which YAAAS creates multi-layered intellectual exchanges and intergenerational dialogues. Furthermore, I offer insights into how socially engaged arts practices can bring together disparate groups to form new communities through collaboration to meaningfully foster spaces of knowledge creation, social change and creative engagement.

## *Socially Engaged Arts, Liminality and the Generative Nature of YAAAS*

YAAAS took place at a Baltimore city high school, an hour north of Washington, D.C. and 10 miles south of Towson University through which the graduate course and project were offered. As the author and project director of YAAAS who identifies as a socially engaged practitioner, I posit that the in-between-ness of socially engaged arts practices enhances the generative potential of this work through the flexible, non-hierarchical process-oriented space we cultivate. Socially engaged arts are based on social interaction, valuing the process of fabrication over the product itself (Helguera, 2011). It is not a traditional art form one would experience in PK–12 art education, yet its experiential nature makes it inherently pedagogical (Schlemmer, 2017). Its location as an out-of-school-time programme disrupts the typical hierarchical student–teacher dynamic. Furthermore, the teaching and learning structures are not beholden to specific learning outcomes, state standards, testing requirements or expectations about art products. For YAAAS, these liminal qualities create a valued space of freedom and opportunity for learning and wellness. Socially engaged arts are also not art therapy. They are not designed to pursue clinical outcomes, yet the practices are highly relational and can be notably transformative. It is the in-between-ness of socially engaged arts and the YAAAS project that gives it such rich potential. Since community artists and community arts centres provide outside-of-school art, socially engaged arts are well positioned to take up these holistic practices in communities of refugee resettlement across the globe.

## *About YAAAS*

This chapter was written after the YAAAS project had run for three years (each fall semester from 2017 through 2019) as part of a community engagement graduate course I designed and teach. The first eight weeks of this sixteen-week course involve only the graduate students, who engage in research and preparations critical for laying a strong theoretical foundation for the next eight weeks: the YAAAS arts residency with refugee youth at their local high school. Baltimore, like many cities throughout the state and nation, is home to a growing number of immigrants and refugees enrolling in public schools. Since I launched this partnership in 2017, refugee students have primarily originated from Eritrea, Sudan and the Democratic Republic of Congo; they speak many languages but predominantly Arabic, Swahili and Tigrinya. Levels of English acquisition for those who join our group range significantly. Some students have studied English for a couple of months, while others have studied two or three years.

When bringing together young people from such linguistically and culturally diverse backgrounds, notions of community are inevitably complicated as relationships with each other and to the place they now find themselves are new in every way. Feelings of displacement and isolation can be significant for our young partners, and communication barriers surely exist, but cultivating a flexible, welcoming atmosphere that prioritizes relational exchanges quickly magnifies the desire to learn and connect. For the YAAAS programme, refugee high-school students partner with graduate students who are adult artists and educators. All of these educators are from different schools and organizations in the metropolitan area, and all possess a range of educational and artistic backgrounds, with anywhere from one to 25 years of teaching experience. Together, the YAAAS graduate students represent the growing number of educators in our region eager to learn how to better support the rapidly growing numbers of newcomer youth enrolling in schools. For these graduate students, working in community means collaborating with young people outside our university walls and outside the schools where they teach. Collectively, the educators and refugee youth in YAAAS come to form their own alternative or contingent community where new knowledge might arise (Richardson, 2010). Community is not assumed, but rather continually worked towards and nurtured.

## *Definitions, Pedagogical Frameworks and Current Research*

### Refugees Internationally and in the United States

According to the United Nations High Commission on Refugees (2020), 26 million people were designated as refugees by the end of 2019.

A refugee is someone who has been forced to flee his or her country because of persecution, war or violence. A refugee has a well-founded fear of persecution for reasons of race, religion, nationality, political opinion or membership in a particular social group (UNHCR, n.d.).

Since the adoption of the Refugee Act in 1980, more than three million refugees have been resettled in the United States (Hooper et al., 2016) with nearly a third of those admitted each year being children (Shafer, 2018). Even though COVID-19 pandemic and government-imposed limitations have slowed refugee resettlement across the globe, these tides may soon shift. In the meantime, when one recognizes that the "psychological and social effects on students of experiencing conflict, forced migration, and long-term residence in refugee camps can linger for decades after resettlement" (Shapiro et al., 2018, p. 4), the need to effectively support refugee youth already resettled in the United States and elsewhere is evident. Multi-cultural education scholars assert that how we prepare educators to work with refugee and immigrant youth must support "genuine cross-cultural relationships over traditional forms of cross-cultural competence in multicultural educational spaces" (Fruja Amthor & Roxas, 2016, p. 156). These points emphasize the value of the relational qualities of socially engaged art, whether in schools, community arts centres or museums.

## Socially Engaged Arts

There is no fully agreed-upon definition of socially engaged arts practice, but its primary characteristic is "its dependence on social intercourse as a factor of its existence" (Helguera, 2011, p. 2). The terms collaboration, participation, dialogue and community are frequently used in describing this work (Helguera, 2011). The outlook of those practising socially engaged arts leads to "a shift in perception moving away from attempting to understand oneself towards developing an understanding of the world" (Schlemmer, 2017, p. 9). The importance of producing art objects is supplanted by communicative exchange as an art form in and of itself.

Art historian Grant Kester (2004) asserts that "starkly different from artists focused on individual self-expression, dialogic artists begin their work, not with the desire to express or articulate an already formed creative vision but rather, to listen" (p. 118). Furthermore, and central to the YAAAS project, "dialogical works can challenge dominant representations of a given community and create a more complex understanding of and empathy for that community among a broader public" (p. 115). While YAAAS is not a project that renounces object-making and authorship entirely (Helguera, 2011), these elements are secondary. Object-making is a vehicle for dialogue and story sharing, and authorship is often blurred between the high-school and graduate student collaborators.

## Trauma-Informed Practice

"Trauma is an exceptional experience in which powerful and dangerous events overwhelm a person's capacity to cope" (Rice & Groves, 2005, p. 3). Recognizing that the widespread nature of trauma in American classrooms is not new, nor is the growing number of English learners, it is important to acknowledge that "the trauma inherent with immigrants and refugees in today's climate brings a new layer of stress to students – one that some teachers may find themselves less prepared to address" (Decious, 2019). Though toxic stress caused by adverse childhood experiences is not exclusive to English learners, its impact is compounded by the fact that refugee children commonly undergo several traumatic events before what is often a stressful acculturation process in their new countries (Schmidt, 2019).

Experts advocate for combatting these responses by building the resilience of learners (Jennings, 2019). The American Psychological Association (2012) defines resiliency as "the process of adapting well in the face of adversity, trauma, tragedy, threats or significant sources of stress" (para. 4). As part of addressing these challenges, researchers advocate for trauma-informed practices, which involve "a safe, calm, and predictable learning environment, with adults and peers who show care and respect toward them" (Jennings, 2019, p. 13). When we provide that environment, we are better able to "recognize and focus on areas of strength and build upon them" (p. 13). For youth in higher grades, strong relationships between teachers and students give students a sense of security and the safety to explore and engage in learning (Jennings, 2019).

## Social-Emotional Learning

For YAAAS, we draw upon the recent social-emotional learning scholarship of Markowitz and Bouffard (2020) who advance seven anchor competencies that include (1) building trusting relationships, (2) fostering self-reflection, (3) fostering a growth mindset, (4) cultivating perseverance, (5) creating community, (6) promoting collaborative learning and (7) responding constructively across differences. Increasingly, scholars who call for holistic approaches to learning (Aspen Institute, 2018) have been pointing out the interconnectedness of cognitive growth and social-emotional learning, asserting that development in one area supports the other. Incorporating social-emotional learning as anchor competencies can help students get ready to learn and keep them intellectually engaged (Markowitz & Bouffard, 2020). Growing numbers of arts educators have been working diligently to reveal the value of the arts in achieving these goals (Eddy et al., 2020; Farrington et al., 2019; Russel & Hutzel, 2007). Eddy et al. (2020)

posit that it is precisely the interactive, creative and experiential learning offered through the arts that make them suited for social-emotional learning.

## Culturally Sustaining Pedagogy

Recent research in culturally responsive teaching has been evolving towards culturally sustaining pedagogy, where the goal is to "support young people in sustaining the cultural and linguistic competence of their communities while simultaneously offering access to dominant cultural competence" (Paris, 2012, p. 95). Calling into question current education policies that centre monolingual, monocultural White middle-class norms, Paris calls for "equally explicit resistances that embrace linguistic plurality" (p. 95). Education scholars specifically concerned with culturally sustaining pedagogies for immigrant youth argue for rejecting assimilationist models. Instead, they assert the importance of recognizing and building on immigrant students' linguistic and cultural flexibility and their unique identities as immigrants, encouraging a critical and inclusive citizenship and preparing them to be change agents in their own lives and communities (Jaffe-Walter & Lee, 2018; Lee & Walsh, 2017).

### *YAAAS – A Generative Space for Learning and Wellness*

Socially engaged arts can be a profound way to embrace social-emotional learning, trauma-informed practice and culturally sustaining pedagogy towards wellness and learning. The YAAAS project, with the liminality that socially engaged arts offers, has been exceptionally generative for bringing all of these practices into a joyful, welcoming creative space for refugee youth and educators.

First, we frame our project as an art learning laboratory where we are all learners. "We" is used here in an attempt to decentre power and acknowledge the highly collaborative nature of this project. Activities are designed by me, but highly responsive and regularly adapted to meet the needs and interests of the group. Our disparate collective of high-school students and educators evolves into a "we" over time. Interdisciplinary from the start, we borrow from all of the major art forms, which allows us to be exceptionally flexible and responsive, tap into different ways of knowing and identify and build upon the many strengths present in our group. Invested in reciprocity, we make sure the high-school students know that while we hope to help them with their English, we also hope to become better educators by learning alongside them.

Working side-by-side as collaborators with me as a facilitator, each week is filled with creative experiments. All participants experience creative risk-taking, problem-solving, failure and success *together*, fostering a growth mindset and allowing for authentic relationships grounded in shared experiences, listening and care. Consistency with these priorities helps resist isolation, fosters resiliency and cultivates a sense of belonging. We remind ourselves that "not only can anxiety distract second language learners from the linguistic input that they encounter, but it can also lead them to withdraw from social interaction, which is critical to learning English as well as academic content" (Lucas et al., 2008, p. 365). Accordingly, we carefully scaffold activities, beginning with fun, highly physical whole-group theatre games that mitigate language barriers and invite laughter. Soon after, we progress to brief, low-risk partner exercises where everyone engages simultaneously. One example involves high-school and graduate student pairs standing across from one another in silence, playfully mirroring each other's movements with increasing levels of complexity (see Figure 16.1). In this manner, we eschew typical student/teacher hierarchies and instead support partnerships grounded in care over control.

We further these relationships by keeping ratios small, employing partner and small-group work as much as possible to allow high-school students to receive much-individualized support with English. Graduate students have creative licence to adapt partner and small-group activities as needed to be inclusive. By working

FIGURE 16.1: Graduate and high-school students play Augusto Boal's theatre game, Columbian Hypnosis, in an early one-on-one partnering activity. Photo by Michael Bussell (2018).

so closely with refugee youth partners, these educators gain a critical window into students' lives, concerns and questions, building relationships that often cannot happen in traditional classrooms.

From day one, we combat deficit perspectives by acknowledging student cultural assets and facilities with multiple languages. Beyond showing that we value them, we work to *sustain* home languages. Our first night involves flipping the traditional student–teacher power dynamic, where high-school students offer language lessons to graduate students. After three years, this has become a treasured tradition that consistently brings joy and humour. The unease that comes with stumbling to remember words and wrapping their lips and tongues around phrases from Arabic, Swahili and Tigrinya is tremendously eye-opening for the graduate students, as is the patience and generosity of their young teacher-partners. It is a brief, but humbling window into the linguistic alienation our young partners encounter every hour of every day at school.

Before long, we integrate short personal exchanges of stories and ideas, which are turned into playful, artful responses. Through this process, we bear witness and respond to each other's humanity and creative capacity in low risk but meaningful ways. Over time, as trust is built, we work towards fostering a brave space where students become more comfortable with vulnerability and criticality: that is, openness to communicating more personal ideas and stories and addressing challenges and inequities. By creating space for verbal and non-verbal interactions, alternating playful with serious, these sessions invite multi-layered intellectual exchanges and intergenerational dialogues that are meaningful for all. "The process of telling and being heard results in self-esteem when we experience that what we have to say is relevant and of value" (Ledwith & Springett, 2009, p. 104). What and how much students share is always determined by them. We never prod for stories of trauma or displacement.

We incorporate various activities that explore identity and invite students to reflect on their past, present and future, expanding English vocabulary in the process. Where English is limited, nuance and complexity are supported through collage. Such symbolic representation affords students the possibility of communicating meaning across languages (Souto-Manning & Martell, 2019). Sifting through and selecting images invites stories and ideas we may never otherwise share. By focusing on the relational element, a seemingly innocuous activity becomes a transformative process through which students find a sense of agency. With support from graduate student partners, the high-school students explore and express their identities through making collages and in the process, create and assert their own counternarratives. They learn to take more risks in communicating their learning *and* communicating across languages, and they enjoy a critical opportunity to be regarded as capable by their peers (Souto-Manning & Martell, 2019).

Designed to further relational exchanges, our culminating events are kept small. We are careful not to overwhelm and to be intentional about inviting guests who will thoughtfully connect with our young partners, and who want to learn about our processes and the work we created. Widening our group circle gives our younger partners a chance to connect and practise English with new people, share their stories and artworks, resist social isolation and practise being part of a larger community.

When the project ends, the high-school students know we will be back to visit in the weeks to follow. They know we can all stay connected through social media and we will see each other again. They know we will be cheering loudly at their graduation or looking for them to join again when we return the next time. And if they don't know it yet, they will soon know that this relationship will continue if they want it to. This is a beginning, not an ending.

## Final Thoughts

When implemented with intentionality, learning and wellness can easily go hand in hand, taking shape in many ways through socially engaged arts. This chapter offers a distillation of the high-impact strategies and beliefs that allowed YAAAS to become a generative space of knowledge creation, social change and creative engagement, effectively supporting refugee youth learning and wellness. While it is my hope that teachers and schools will take up the possibilities described through this chapter, it should not only be schools that do so. I contend that community artists, arts centres and museums working outside of schools are well-positioned to realize the full potential of these practices. Unencumbered by many of the limitations and expectations placed on schools, community artists and arts centres around the world can embrace the liminality that comes with socially engaged arts to support multi-generational, multi-cultural and multi-lingual engagement. Advancing socially engaged arts with intentionality can allow community arts institutions to become anti-racist, culturally sustaining anchors in our resettlement communities and much-needed spaces of sanctuary for young people. In this way, the wellness and learning of newcomer youth can be meaningfully bolstered.

Adults who collaborate with these young people will gain significantly through transformative artistic engagement, authentic connection and expanding global humility that can lead to becoming informed advocates. Furthermore, in this time of crisis – as the world navigates a global pandemic causing widespread isolation and trauma – it is more relevant and necessary than ever for artists and arts organizations to engage in humanizing practices that simultaneously promote wellness and learning. By illustrating the generative space we created through YAAAS and the possibilities of learning and wellness held in socially engaged arts, I hope community artists, arts centres and museums across the globe will step up to meet these challenges, embrace this potential and make wellbeing a strategic and integral part of their artistic work.

## REFERENCES

American Psychological Association. (2012). *Building your resilience*. https://www.apa.org/topics/resilience

Aspen Institute. (2018). *From a nation at risk to a nation at hope: Recommendations from the national commission on social, emotional & academic development*. http://nationathope.org/report-from-the-nation/

Decious, E. (2019, January 4). Trauma presents unique challenges to ELL students. *Storm Lake Pilot Tribune*. https://www.stormlakepilottribune.com/story/2578059.html?fbclid=IwAR0PkEPqZGYiIzWqZLZvbwQE0Gk1Uj3DZJtl3-7rzrBG2zZajNJ2NG9bPag

Eddy, M., Blatt-Gross, C., Edgar S. N., Gohr A., Halverson E., Humphreys K., & Smolin L. (2020, July 7). Local level implementation of social emotional learning in arts education: Moving the heart through the arts. *Arts Education Policy Review*, 122, 193–204. https://doi.org/10.1080/10632913.2020.1788681

Farrington, C. A., Maurer, J., McBride, M. R. A., Nagaoka, J., Puller, J. S., Shewfelt, S., Weiss, E. M., & Wright, L. (2019). *Arts education and social-emotional learning outcomes among K–12 students: Developing a theory of action*. Ingenuity and the University of Chicago Consortium on School Research.

Fruja Amthor, R., & Roxas, K. (2016). Multicultural education and newcomer youth: Re-imagining a more inclusive vision for immigrant and refugee students. *Educational Studies*, 52(2), 155–176. https://doi.org/10.1080/00131946.2016.1142992

Helguera, P. (2011). *Education for socially engaged art: A materials and techniques handbook*. Jorge Pinto Books.

Hooper, K., Zong, J., Capps, R., & Fix, M. (2016). *Young children of refugees in the United States: Integration successes and challenges*. Migration Policy Institute. https://www.migrationpolicy.org/research/young-children-refugees-united-states-integration-successes-and-challenges

Jaffe-Walter, R., & Lee, S. J. (2018). Engaging the transnational lives of immigrant youth in public schooling: Toward a culturally sustaining pedagogy for newcomer immigrant youth. *American Journal of Education*, 124(3), 257–283. https://doi.org/10.1086/697070

Jennings, P. A. (2019). Teaching in a trauma-sensitive classroom: What educators can do to support students. *American Educator*, 43(2), 12–17. https://eric.ed.gov/contentdelivery/servlet/ERICServlet?accno=EJ1218755

Kester, G. H. (2004). *Conversation pieces: Community + communication in modern art*. University of California Press.

Ledwith, M., & Springett, J. (2009). *Participatory practice: Community-based action for transformative change*. Policy Press.

Lee, S. J., & Walsh, D. (2017). Socially just culturally sustaining pedagogy for diverse immigrant youth: Possibilities, challenges and directions. In D. Paris & H. S. Alim (Eds.), *Culturally sustaining pedagogy: Teaching and learning for justice in a changing world* (pp. 191–206). Teachers College Press.

Lucas, T., Villegas, A. M., & Freedson-Gonzalez, M. (2008). Linguistically responsive teacher education: Preparing classroom teachers to teach English language learners. *Journal of Teacher Education, 59*(4), 361–373. http://dx.doi.org/10.1177/0022487108322110

Markowitz, N. L., & Bouffard, S. M. (2020). *Teaching with a social, emotional, and cultural lens: A framework for educators and teacher educators*. Harvard Education Press. https://www.hepg.org/hep-home/books/teaching-with-a-social,-emotional,-and-cultural-le

Paris, D. (2012). Culturally sustaining pedagogies: A needed change in stance, terminology, and practice. *Educational Researcher, 41*(3), 93–97. http://dx.doi.org/10.3102/0013189X12441244

Rice, K. F., & Groves, B. M. (2005). *Hope and healing: A caregiver's guide to helping young children affected by trauma*. Zero to Three.

Richardson, J. (2010). Interventionist art education: Contingent communities, social dialogue, and public collaboration. *Studies in Art Education, 52*(1), 18–33. https://www.jstor.org/stable/25746079

Russel, R. L., & Hutzel, K. (2007). Promoting social and emotional learning through service learning art projects. *Arts Education, 60*(3), 6–11. https://www.jstor.org/stable/27696210

Schlemmer, R. (2017). Socially engaged art education: Defining and defending the practice. In L. N. Hersey & B. Bobick (Eds.), *Handbook of research on the facilitation of civic engagement through community art* (pp. 1–20). Information Science Reference.

Schmidt, L. M. (2019). Trauma in English learners: Examining the influence of previous trauma and PTSD on English learners within the classroom. *TESOL Journal, 10*(1), 1–10. https://doi.org/10.1002/tesj.412

Shafer, L. (2018, March 12). *For refugees in America, an unfillable dream*. Usable Knowledge. https://www.gse.harvard.edu/news/uk/18/02/refugees-us-unfulfilled-dream

Shapiro, S., Farrelly, R., & Curry, M. J. (2018). *Educating refugee-background students: Critical issues and dynamic contexts*. Channel View Publications. https://doi.org/10.21832/SHAPIR9979

Souto-Manning, M., & Martell, J. (2019). Inclusive teaching for bilingual and multilingual learners: Collage as ornithology. In B. R. Berriz, A. C. Wager, & V. Poey (Eds.), *Art as a way of talking for emergent bilingual youth: A foundation for literacy in Pre K-12 schools* (pp. 60–69). Routledge.

Suarez-Orozco, C., Yoshikawa, H., Teranishi, R. T., & Suarez-Orozco, M. M. (2011). Growing up in the shadows: The developmental implications of unauthorized status.

*Harvard Educational Review*, 81(3), 438–473. http://www.metapress.com/content/g23x203763783m75/?p=5d23eecc9e94460c95376c5d27103ade&pi=2

United Nations High Commission on Refugees. (2020, June 18). *Figures at a glance*. https://www.unhcr.org/en-us/figures-at-a-glance.html

United Nations High Commission on Refugees. (n.d.). *What is a refugee?* https://www.unrefugees.org/refugee-facts/what-is-a-refugee/

# 17

## Conversations With Gardens: Artful Spaces in Community Art Education

*Trish Osler*

The educational potential of multimodal digital technologies performed as public pedagogies in a community art context is explored through a heritage garden and museum space in Quebec, Canada. Based on a walking methodologies approach, this chapter chronicles the incubation of an immersive digital technology project which began with an audio walk concept and grew into a collaboration fostered between the PRISME Innovation Lab at the Montreal Museum of Fine Art (MMFA) and *Les Jardins de Métis*/Reford Gardens (http://www.refordJardins.com/discover-the-Jardins). Throughout the development of an interactive digital interface, the multiplicity of human, non-human and more-than-human agents forming the *Jardins* community would become entangled in dynamic thinking-making intra-actions (Barad, 2007) underscoring the complexity of the project.

As the *Jardins* experience combines a historic museum, heritage gardens and an international conceptual landscape design festival, the project's aim was to integrate artist, visitor, curator and digital media in a unique learning environment. This presented an intriguing assemblage of tensions and event encounters reflecting diverse agencies, being and becoming through public art and community exchange. Configured to kindle both affect and effect – aesthetic, ludic, disruptive and instructive – and by dint of its geography, its history, its orientation and the diversity of its curated spaces, the *Jardins* is a fertile and diffractive space for "future-feeling" (Manning, 2015, p. 48). Introducing a digital platform in a remote and principally outdoor environment involved thoughtful intra-action with its shared communities, connecting human and more-than-human narratives through the material agency of the site and through multi-sensory technologies. Moreover, the experimental nature of the project encompassed shifting intergenerational and international demographics of both regular and new visitors, as well as digital designers concerned with reconciling hapticity and accessibility for a more fully immersive visitor experience.

Walking-with this garden initiates a metaphoric conversation – dialogic and relational – among the co-constituents of a place and spaces within that place. Reaching across time, the conversation becomes a running discourse between visitor, artist, the horticultural or conceptual design of the garden and the materiality of its environment – its location, topography and climatic conditions (see Lund & Benediktsson, 2010). Taken together, walking-with introduces a temporary relationality to the space; the visitor, as part of the assemblage, is affected by the event-encounter, resulting in a new narrative. Manning (2015) describes such an encounter as "refractive," for it is "a quality of experience that touches the edgings into form of the material's intuition" (p. 49). The intentionality of this relationship is amplified when the garden is public.

Cole and Bradley (2018) offer a premise which underlies the concept of community and outreach at the *Jardins de Métis*/Reford Gardens:

> A true education, then – one in which we learn about our place in the world, what we know about it, and how to act in it – requires not just cross-cultural communication but understanding of the natural world and its potential and activity beyond human consciousness or practice.
>
> (p. vii)

As such, it is incumbent on the entire *Jardins* community to mindfully bring about true education through its programming. "Community" in this context encompasses the curators, researchers, horticulturalists, gardeners, animators and archivists who make up the *Jardin de Métis* team; the international artists, architects and landscape designers who submit and install conceptual works in the Festival Gardens; a diversity of human visitors both local and foreign; and non-human and more-than-human elements. Community also extends to the various partnering organizations and enterprises that collaborate in realizing the gardens' mission, like the MMFA Innovation Lab team, negotiating both fixed and mutable agencies to develop a collective narrative for its various audiences. Incubated within such a community of stakeholders, important questions were raised around visitor interaction and the strategies (or public pedagogies) that could lead to more fulfilling encounters.

Developing these strategies and dispositions queries intra-actions between humans and the landscape. In this entanglement, the agency of nature is uncovered, co-mingling with human perceptions of landscape in an open, mutable configuration. Through sensorial feedback, humans enact affinities for the natural spaces they encounter, while the landscape's agency resonates with the aesthetic intensities of its human wanderers. Guattari (2008) views art (even, perhaps, botanic and conceptual gardens) as facilitating the conversation: "By means of these transversal tools, subjectivity is able to install itself simultaneously in the realms of the environment [...] and symmetrically in the landscapes and fantasies of the most intimate spheres of the individual" (p. 45).

Arguably, the *Jardins* always embodied a transversal ethos before the proposed inclusion of digital media in their outdoor spaces. From its inception, the gardens' indomitable first designer, Elsie Reford, challenged conventional approaches in the Lower St. Lawrence by boldly introducing exotic plant materials and documenting species and varieties that would adapt surprisingly well to the unique microclimate of the region. Over time and through trial, a privileged fishing retreat metamorphosed into an extraordinarily avant-garde public garden. Honouring Elsie's spirit of innovation, the juried International Festival of Design was introduced in 2000, with multiple conceptual garden spaces adjoining the original botanic site, offering alternative narratives as to what a garden could be (Waugh, 2016). Alexander Reford, Director of the *Jardins* and great-grandson of Elsie, describes the contemporary exhibition as "a different kind of engagement. Conceptual gardens are really offering a *proposal* [emphasis added] and engaging, or trying to elicit a response, and I think it's a whole different response level" (A. Reford, personal communication, 24 June, 2018).

Entry points to visitor encounters extend beyond the conceptual gardens designed by critically acclaimed landscape architects and artists. Throughout the growing season, live performative events are staged progressively within the gardens; contemporary sculptural works are installed amongst colourful peonies, fragrant roses and towering lilies. A gallery featuring the work of local artists and artisans draws visitors into the Villa Estevan while nearby, a prized collection of antique tools presents the workmanship and craft of those who once farmed the land. Here and there, tucked amongst ancient stands of spruce and larch, award-winning eco-sensitive buildings have been designed to house both people and plants: weekend snowshoers, gardeners and dreamers, writers-in-residence, shoots and cultivars. Everywhere, the mindfulness and sustainability of informed practices are in action. Grazing sheep, *moutondeuses*, serve as natural mowers, trimming with abandon the more invasive surrounding grasses, while new and heritage varieties of vegetables grown for the kitchens artfully wend their way through a picket-fenced *potager*. Notoriously delicate Himalayan blue poppies are carefully bedded into sloped and secluded plots under dappled branches, where their precious seeds can be collected for another year's showy display. A wild meadow, with its brief spring tapestry of pink and plum lupines, erect as sceptres, offers a glimpse of the intense growing season to follow; its counterpoint: a stretch of westward facing pines, cool and blue-green in the gloaming, shelters hives in an area devoted to beekeeping. Nearby, a repurposed Montreal Metro tram, set permanently adrift in an alpine sea of pebbles, is underplanted with tufts of lavender. Painted, woven and imaginatively constructed artworks form an ephemeral ribbon of curiosities throughout forested glades, high above the windswept beach. These elements are conjoined with a collective memory of landscape – a *métissage* of lived experience, conjuring the Scottish and French settlers who came, disrupting social histories and the ways of the indigenous Montagnais and later Métis communities who seasonally encamped, fishing the river below: perennially, millennially migrating along the dense woodland trails that follow the *Bas-Saint-Laurent*.

Reflecting both ancient and new art forms, the materiality and memory that combine to such effect in these gardens transcend any fixed temporality or object. Much like the desire to transform rigid, physical and disciplinary architectures at universities into the literal and metaphorical "wild" spaces alluded to by Kochhar-Lindgren and Kochhar-Lindgren (2018), the *Jardins de Métis*/Reford Gardens has already achieved a *dérive* experience: "These interstitial structures enable the movement of transversality, the pragmatic and conceptual practices of modulated cutting-across" (p. 33). The values and aspirations of the *Jardins* are anchored in a desire to engage and provoke the curiosity of visitors aesthetically, physically and environmentally. However, most of the digital content intended for an integrated experience – films, still images and audio narratives – are available only through exhibitions found *inside* the historic Villa Estevan, now a museum. Descriptive signage and guiding brochures in the heritage gardens constitute the main interface between the installations and visitors. Affirming the inclination towards a greater diversity of sensorial content, Gershon (2018) cautions that "privileging the visual can serve to miss important sensory knowledge and sound understandings" (p. 7).

As a possible bridge between media and visitor and to express the nature of conversations with gardens more fully as an artist, I wanted to explore how both curated and natural sounds might influence what Cluett (2014) describes as "the condition of reception for a work of art" (p. 109). My intention is made more explicit in the visual journal entries I kept from that creative endeavour:

> An audio walk provides a way to incorporate and animate voices that may not otherwise be heard within the encounter between audience and visual. In so doing, the agency of the land, its flora, fauna and original inhabitants, whether permanent or transient, can be integrated into the contemporary context. Out of this

multiplicity of interactions, new understandings of expression and response may be elevated.

(4 July, 2017)

## Call and Response

To be meaningful, a sonic walk requires a different level of intra-action with the research. I needed to traverse the pathways multiple times, entangling with the installations to connect in a visceral way, seeking the artful in the conversation, aware of my own narrative insinuating itself within the landscape. This process called upon interwoven arts-based approaches. Dedicated to the "slow scholarship" of *flânerie* (Lasczik Cutcher & Irwin, 2018) and being attentive to the many direct and indirect routes that exist *between* installations, as with *ma* (Sinner et al., 2018), permitted genuine, mindful intra-action. Allowing the recorded segments to evolve both intuitively and responsively engaged immersive, transversal dispositions (Springgay & Truman, 2017, p. 83). The resulting audio walks formed my response to what Gallagher (2015) describes as a "nomadic architecture," "as a way of reconfiguring visitors' movements through the site, using a particular tempo and rhythm to invite imaginative meanderings and shifts in attention" (pp. 471–472).

In the first audio walk, I focused on Elsie Reford's passion and knowledge, cultivated while creating the gardens over the course of three decades. Elsie's relationship with this remote place was intimate and engaging: her journal entries from the 1930s often remarked on the need to respond, year over year, to the vagaries of weather and terrain. Despite such challenges, she countered with determination, curiosity, experimentation and wonder. By bringing her own words and the ambient sounds of the site into the artworks, I sought to sonically trace her imprint on the spaces she revered.

My attention next turned to the International Festival Gardens, intuitively referencing agency within the landscape due to the varied and multiculturally diverse narratives offered by the Festival designers – narratives which become abstractions of the idea of "garden." Whereas the first audio walk followed the route laid out by Elsie alongside the stream known as "Page's Brook" – a pathway governed by an existing topography of embankments, meandering water and hand-carved wooden bridges – the second audio walk was more experimental, departing from any linear or sequential arrangement. The Festival spaces are arrayed over roughly eighteen hectares with an indistinct pattern of progression. For that reason, my attention was focused on a few representative installations that might reflect the theme of "*Playsage*," a fusion of the words "play" and "*paysage*" or playful landscapes (Figure 17.1).

FIGURE 17.1: Veil Garden, *Jardins de Métis*/Reford Gardens. Courtesy of *Les Amis des Jardins de Métis* Collection (2019).

Coinciding with the completion of my audio walks, the *Jardins* was granted an opportunity to collaborate with the MMFA's Innovation Lab. Working with museum digital interface specialists, archival content could be mobilized and selectively integrated into the visitor experience. This transversal detour in design opened up a process of thinking-making or *heterogenesis* (Guattari, 2008), multiplying possible ways and means of integrating desired provocations in a kind of tentacular exploration (Haraway, 2016).

The basic design of the mobile software interface demanded a flexible platform onto which media (such as an interactive index or map) could be populated. This allowed for expansion: optimally, material could be added or updated over time and eventually networked with the *Jardins*' curatorial objectives. Relevant supplementary information connected to location-specific installations would be pushed to the device via proximity sensors within the *Jardins*' spaces, or the visitor would be able to access curated audio walks to accompany – rather than mediate – their visit. Additionally, through the interface, a user might contribute to an installation by incorporating visitor response in real time. In turn, passive and active feedback would be gathered through the interactions between the user and the software to improve curation of the content.

That said, the addition of digital media to installation-based, non-human and more-than-human artefacts alters the metaphoric conversation with a garden. Recognizing the role of material agency in this process is essential: "Foregrounding matter's entanglement with community challenges binary or dualistic notions that emphasize a conception of community as self versus other" (Nicolic & Skinner, 2019, p. 889). Appending digital media provides transversal cuts across time and space, interrupting personal curiosities with new provocations and narratives configured from archival material. For a space that blends the predictable with the extraordinary, weaving together the "wild" (Kochhar-Lindgren & Kochhar-Lindgren, 2018) and conceptual with convention, a more-than-human digital layer opens up new conversations with and about the *Jardins de Métis/ Reford Gardens*, yet potentially interferes with an immersive outdoor experience through its mediation.

Changes of this nature are approached with caution, for "[t]hinking and making are always twists, torques of transversality, and this always creates turbulence" (Kochhar-Lindgren & Kochhar-Lindgren, 2018, p. 40). The coalition of stakeholders on the project endeavoured to develop parameters for the digital interface that respected the essence of the *Jardins* experience. Conceived and oriented around an aesthetically compelling site, the intercession of a small screen or headphones was thought to be counterintuitive to a deeply personal and direct engagement with the surroundings. Nonetheless, a strong interest prevailed in allowing for public access to digital material related to the garden's context, for there are meaningful histories to share. As such, the Innovation Lab design team concluded that interactive stations could be constructed in situ, in locations attuned to the historic, archived content. Fixed placements would also mitigate the technical requirements and potential glitches associated with the addition of a wireless digital network functioning across large outdoor spaces.

In addition to its non-human and more-than-human agencies, the *Jardins* community, through its entanglement with nomadic human visitors, aligns with "immediately transversal processes of collective becoming" (Nicolic & Skinner, 2019, p. 887). The presence, movement and interplay of humans with these sites may amplify or stifle real and metaphoric conversations, recalling Gallagher's (2015) idea that "[w]alkers can also be seen as co-creators of landscapes. Their walking makes and remakes paths rather than merely following them" (p. 472). Therefore, physically locating the stations within the heritage garden without disrupting the flow of human wandering, while ensuring accessibility for all visitors, presented challenges. As the project unfolded, several designs came under consideration, troubling the meeting points between natural, curated and communal environments (Arnott & Alain, 2014).

## *Troubling the Conversation*

These deliberations around form, content and visitor context are illustrative from a public pedagogical perspective. Through its assemblage of installations and displays, the *Jardins* reaches out to dialogically encounter the visitor in liminal spaces, between multiple narratives. Kochhar-Lindgren and Kochhar-Lindgren (2018) observe that "These 'relays' and 'stations' operate through a series of switching points where knowledge, people, places, and systems crossover. [...] It is where translations occur in-between" (p. 42). Still, establishing a balance between curated experience and the desire to empower the visitor in co-creating an event encounter is an uncertain task. Rhetorically, one is confronted with the question of where a conversation, whether real or metaphoric, occurs. As Manning (2015) recounts in her description of an interactive exhibit at the 2010 Venice Biennale, visitors observing the work inattentively contrasted with those who engaged more slowly and purposefully. Given that the Biennale installation needed frequent adjustment and resetting, the variability of community engagement with the work reframed the artist's assumptions and intentions around material agency, audience performativity and place/site (pp. 68–70).

The unforeseeable nature of human and more-than-human intra-action parallels the mobilization of the *Jardins*' digital content: will permanent multisensorial, interactive stations be experienced as intrusive obstacles, temporary distractions or the desired entry point into a co-created narrative? Initially inspired by the future-feeling associated with audio walks operating on familiar territory as complementary and transversal artworks, I sought to facilitate one type of conversation with the *Jardins*, adding another layer of immersion within an already immersive experience. To this end, Nikolic and Skinner (2019) suggest that "[i]n a moment when individual agency is both intensified and dispersed by digital media [...] the question of collective agency becomes all the more crucial and radically transformed" (p. 887). Digital interface technologies are but one kind of response to the multiplicity of non-human and more-than-human agents within the site. While human voices communicate curiosity, wonder, empathy and affect, the non-human articulate order and chaos, growth and decay, difference and indifference. The more-than-human voices of the artworks, installations and digital media traverse time, meaning and narrative. They are at once a refraction of future-feeling and waypoints to the past, becoming in the present. Beighton (2018) summarizes the spirit of these intra-actions: "[I]t is by the development of networks of transversal relations, and especially the interstices they make possible between the individual and the social, that thought takes flight" (p. 51).

As an entity, the *Jardins* seeks to embody this future-feeling by celebrating qualities of remoteness, difference and eclectic provocation that depart from conventional museal interaction. Facilitating and troubling these entanglements underlies the challenge for artists, curators and their audiences, recalling Conrad and Sinner (2015) "inviting voice and positioning community members as agents of change" (p. xviii). While embracing an experimental mindset and striving to offer novel and provocative ways of engaging with its space, its art/design collaborators and its visitors, the *Jardins* voice animates the conversation, mindfully listening for all contributions. According to Manning (2015), art-based provocations transcend subject and object, opening up "a field of expression through which a different quality of experience is crafted" (p. 49). The synthesis of human, non-human and more-than-human content performs simultaneously and intentionally as experiential points of connection and points of departure (Figure 17.2).

For art educators, the *Jardins*' intention to integrate and share its digital content in situ illustrates a refractive but potentially more authentic exploration of pedagogies. Kochhar-Lindgren and Kochhar-Lindgren (2018) assert that learning and discovery are "an *encounter* that constitutes an event out of which precipitates objects of knowledge" (p. 43). Reaching beyond conventional visitor profiles, the *Jardins de Métis*/Reford Gardens challenges itself through programming to share its inspiration, while creating a space for the visitor to, in Haraway's (2016) words, "make with – become-with, [and] compose-with" the environment (p. 102). This

FIGURE 17.2: *Jardins de Métis*/Reford Gardens. Photo credit: Louise Tanguay. Courtesy of *Les Amis des Jardins de Métis* Collection (2019).

collaborative, multimodal exchange of experience becomes a perpetual rededication to learning with and through, co-creating community. For the *Jardins* project, anticipating transversal departures that honour its legacy of possibility is as essential to the process as any data-driven design-thinking strategy. These dispositions of patience, comfort with ambiguity and the confidence to collaborate across disciplinary boundaries will embrace the complexity and nuance of becoming-with its community, furthering both the real and metaphoric conversations within and beyond its sites.

## REFERENCES

Arnott, S. R., & Alain, C. (2014). A brain guide to sound galleries. In S. Lacey, A. Pascual-Leone, & N. S. Levent (Eds.), *The multisensory museum: Cross-disciplinary perspectives on touch, sound, smell, memory, and space* (pp. 85–107). Rowman & Littlefield.

Barad, K. (2007). *Meeting the universe halfway: Quantum physics and the entanglement of matter and meaning.* Duke University Press.

Beighton, C. (2018). A transversal university? Criticality, creativity and catatonia in the globalised pursuit of higher education excellence. In D. R. Cole & J. P. N. Bradley (Eds.), *Principles of transversality in globalization and education* (pp. 47–64). Springer.

Cluett, S. (2014). Ephemeral, immersive, invasive: Sound as a curatorial theme, 1966–2013. In S. Lacey, A. Pascual-Leone, & N. S. Levent (Eds.), *The multisensory museum: Cross-disciplinary perspectives on touch, sound, smell, memory, and space* (pp. 108–118). Rowman & Littlefield.

Cole, D. R., & Bradley, J. P. N. (Eds.). (2018). *Principles of transversality in globalization and education.* Springer.

Conrad, D., & Sinner, A. (Eds.). (2015). *Creating together: Participatory, community-based, and collaborative arts practices and scholarship across Canada.* Wilfrid Laurier University Press.

Gallagher, M. (2015). Sounding ruins: Reflections on the production of an audio drift. *Cultural Geographies, 22*(3), 467–485.

Gershon, W. S. (2018). *Sound curriculum: Sonic studies in education theory, method and practice.* Routledge.

Guattari, F. (2008). *The three ecologies* (I. Pindar & P. Sutton, Trans.). Continuum.

Haraway, D. J. (2016). *Staying with the trouble: Making kin in the Chthulucene.* Duke University Press.

Kochhar-Lindgren, G., & Kochhar-Lindgren, K. (2018). Wild studios: Art, philosophy and the transversal university. In D. R. Cole & J. P. N. Bradley (Eds.), *Principles of transversality in globalization and education* (pp. 31–46). Springer.

Lasczik Cutcher, A., & Irwin, R. L. (2018). A/r/tographic peripatetic inquiry and the Flâneur. In A. Lasczik Cutcher & R. L. Irwin (Eds.), *The Flâneur and education research* (pp. 127–154). Palgrave Pivot.

Lund, K. A., & Benediktsson, K. (2010). *Conversations with landscape.* Routledge.

Manning, E. (2015). Artfulness. In R. Grusin (Ed.), *The nonhuman turn* (pp. 45–79). University of Minnesota Press.

Nicolic, M., & Skinner, S. (2019). Community. *Philosophy Today, 63*(4), 887–901.

Sameshima, P., White, B., & Sinner, A. (2018). Ma: Materiality in teaching and learning. Peter Lang.

Springgay, S., & Truman, S. E. (2017). *Walking methodologies in a more-than-human world.* Routledge.

Waugh, E. (2016). *Experimenting landscapes: Testing the limits of the garden.* Birkhauser-Verlag GimbH.

# 18

# Community Dance as an Approach to Reimagine Place in Aotearoa/New Zealand

*Pauline Hiroti and Rose Martin*

This chapter weaves together themes of arts education, place-based pedagogy and Indigenous Māori philosophies. Reflections on encounters within a community dance project in Aotearoa/New Zealand highlight ideas of how bodily encounters and experiences with the environment provide possibilities for young people to become actively engaged in the learning experience. Such ideas, while situated within a dance context, are considered more broadly in relation to what they might offer arts education and decolonial views of education. We write as two dance educators and researchers engaging with a *kaupapa Māori* approach towards research, writing and art making. *Kaupapa Māori* places people at the centre of life – or in the context of research, at the centre of a study. With such an approach, it is vital to begin by explaining our relationship as authors and how we are situated in relation to the context we are exploring (Tuhiwai Smith, 1999). We have known each other for nearly a decade and are both from Aotearoa/New Zealand, with Pauline from Whanganui and affiliated with the Māori tribe *Ngā Wairiki Ngāti Apa*, and Rose from Auckland and being *pākehā*.

## Te Tīmatanga, *a Place to Start*

As we sat in a circle Hineraumoa's eyes lit up. She was eager to share her first experience of the silent exploration task. I could see the excitement in her smile. She started to talk about all the things she was drawn too, barely giving us time to comprehend what she was saying before moving on to the next thing. She paused, and her eyes began to well up as she said, "This is my home, I love this place, it's my place, I feel connected here." She acknowledged the sky and the earth. She listened to the river, the birds that flew around her, and sat with her hands gripping the earth beneath her. Returning to the dance studio, this embodied experience remained in her heart and mind as she began to re-create her experiences.

(Hiroti, 2020, p. 134)

This narrative highlights a moment observed during a community dance encounter with a group of young people in Aotearoa/New Zealand. The encounter bridged arts education and place-based pedagogy with *kaupapa Māori* philosophies (Tuhiwai Smith, 1999) to provide young people with an opportunity to explore connections with the city of Whanganui, where they live, on the North Island of Aotearoa/New Zealand. In this chapter, we unpack moments of reimaging Whanganui through a conscious and Indigenous perspective of community dance. Community dance places people and process at the centre and has a clear focus on the collective (Amans, 2017). Community dance provides opportunities to foster a collaborative process, offering a platform for equal participation, access and ownership (East, 2016). Within this context, participants are encouraged to bring their identity, life experiences and culture into the learning environment (Wise et al., 2020). When understood in such ways, community dance connects more broadly with contemporary notions of community. While community is an amorphous concept, it involves social connection and can seek to foster a sense of solidarity, worth and security, yet also freedom for those involved (Blokland, 2017).

The researchers for the project engaged in a three-week *wānanga* (conference or seminar) in Whanganui in Aotearoa/New Zealand, where a collective of ten young people participated in workshops, exploration of places and creative practices grounded in the practice of community dance. The group of young people then engaged in interviews as conversation and shared *pūrākau* (stories) through a *hui* (meeting) to unpack the journey experienced. While the research is situated geographically in Aotearoa/New Zealand, it is grounded in community dance as the artistic medium. Though the Indigenous frameworks employed are from a Māori worldview and deeply connect with our own lived experiences, our intention is to offer a discussion that can resonate globally and, arguably, across the arts. We lean on UNESCO's (2010) view of "arts education" as a broad umbrella term encompassing diverse arts practices and note that each art form does not live in a "bubble." Rather, art educators can potentially learn from each other's practices and disciplinary nuances. Visual art educators, for example, can scaffold the tenets of community dance to inform community art education. Through ongoing discussion and inclusion of Indigenous practices and philosophies in other contexts where issues of colonization, marginalization, belonging, place and identity are questioned, this research has the potential to offer new meanings and understandings for those seeking to challenge dominant pedagogical practices, assumptions and discourses, regardless of the artistic discipline they might choose to engage with.

## Te Huarahi, *the Pathway*

Important to note is that the research from which this chapter draws was situated within a much larger research project (see Hiroti, 2020). The methodological approach we have employed is decolonial, Indigenous and specifically embedded in *kaupapa Māori* theory. *Kaupapa Māori* theory places people at the centre of life or (as already noted) at the centre of a study and acts to legitimize Māori cultural philosophies, practices and protocols within academia (Tuhiwai Smith, 1999). A key emphasis of *kaupapa Māori* in the context of research is to serve the needs of Māori as opposed to solely conducting research *on* Māori without culturally responsive theory and practice (Smith, 1997). In employing a *kaupapa Māori* framework, we also use the notion of *whakawhanaungatanga* – building relationships and networks in a culturally relevant way – as a research philosophy. *Whakawhanaungatanga* sits under the wider umbrella of *kaupapa Māori* theory yet is particular in its nuances. *Whakawhanaungatanga* places a strong emphasis on establishing and maintaining relationships and shifting power from the researcher to the research collective (Bishop, 2005, 2012; Tuhiwai Smith, 1999, 2007, 2018). At the same time, the Māori worldviews and methodological approaches resonating throughout this chapter have synergies with more-than-human concepts and understandings (Larsen & Johnson, 2017).

### *Reimagining Whanganui Through a Conscious and Indigenous Perspective of Community Dance*

In the following sections, we unpack some of the moments encountered when the young people engaged in the community dance *wānanga*. Participants' experiences are recounted as they visited locations in the city for the first time, or reimagined locations through learning about the Māori history and significance of the places. In the locations (which included local beaches, rivers and mountains) visited in Whanganui, the group engaged in silent exploration tasks, movement tasks and group discussions with each other and elders within the community. They took their experiences in these locations back into the dance studio space and worked within a collaborative creative process to digest and distil their feelings and encounters. Literature surrounding the teachings of Indigenous history and place-based education is woven with the personal accounts of the *rangatahi* (younger generation) and their *whānau* (family or extended family) throughout this writing.

Throughout the process of visiting and exploring different sites in Whanganui, many of the participants were surprised they had spent their entire lives in Whanganui but had not visited some of these places. This resulted in the *rangatahi* gaining a new view of Whanganui, prompting them to move beyond feelings of complacency about where they live. In a group discussion surrounding the visiting of new places, one participant, Ani, explained

> I never really knew Whanganui as a beautiful place, just like the place I live. But then as we went to these places, like I thought, I didn't even know Whanganui had places like that [...] it was really amazing. I didn't know that kind of stuff existed in Whanganui, and it kind of changed my perspective on Whanganui.

Reflecting on the comments from Ani prompted consideration of the ways we perceive the places we call "home," taking for granted their beauty or value, as we do not tend to pay attention to what we might consider ordinary or "normal" (Penetito, 2009). Because we spend each day in these places, perhaps we tend to stop exploring, connecting and developing a relationship with the *whenua*, the land.

With this in mind, we are drawn to a concept put forward by Geoff Park (1996), who explains "how we inhabit a place can be the most telling expression of how we sense its worth, our intention for it, and our connection with it" (p. 31). If we are complacent about our connection to familiar places and do not seek to deepen or foster our understandings, or to even engage with our surroundings, what might this say about the value we place on where we live? Penetito (2009) feeds into this idea when he discusses how these familiar places are often the most in danger of ruin: "the places where we spend most of our lives are the places most vulnerable to human destruction because we see them every day and find it troublesome to evaluate the changing reality most familiar to us" (p. 11).

As Ani notes above, she was surprised that such places were located just minutes from where she lives, and she seemed to be amazed she had never been to these places. Penetito (2009) touches on the idea of the ordinary and routine being invisible to many of us because it is just that – ordinary and routine. He then reflects on the teachings of Postman and Weingartner (1971), who articulate that in order to bring awareness to the ordinary or to elicit change to the ordinary, the ordinary needs to be made visible to people so that they can think about it. By thinking about it, they can then create change. One method of making the ordinary visible is to interrupt or remove it. By taking our participants to new places within the community they have lived in for years, we were able to interrupt their routine or ordinary interactions with the place where they usually live and spend their time. Another key method to interrupting the ordinary was the combining of physical connection with place, merged with the movement-generation tasks we engaged in as part of our community dance.

Community dance encompasses a physical and embodied experience of processing new understandings and communicating ideas and knowledge. While it could be said that dance in the broader sense allows for this embodied experience and communication, the use of "community" alongside "dance" emphasizes the collective experience of this embodiment and communication that is purposeful, fostered and central to the experience of community dance. The embodied experience of the young people in various locations within their city allowed them to engage in a process of unpacking their visits to these places through movement. Dance scholar Mary-Lynn Smith (2002) explains that "experiences become transformative because they are embodied moments that shift our day-to-day movement patterns into another, an-other way of moving" (p. 137). Through embodying knowledge gained through exploration of place, the *rangatahi* shared within the collective how this new-found knowledge affected them and perhaps changed their perspective in some way. Māori dance scholar Sophie Williams (2015) shares her own experiences of connecting to the environment of her ancestor Hinemoa, and how this connection fostered a deeper understanding of her ancestor's journey: "Through the actual experiencing of this environment first hand, I felt I was able to embody the story, understand my ancestor Hinemoa and her journey further, returning this embodied experience to the studio" (p. 12).

By providing space for the young people to connect with their *whenua* and process this encounter through community dance practices, the research collective embarked on a new and exciting journey. The youth were given the opportunity to embody these experiences and produce work that responded to the journey they took towards a new point of understanding and, perhaps, connection. Barbour (2016a) discusses the ways in which she engages in site-specific dance-making practices:

> Site-specific dance practices utilizing sensory encounters provide methods that support slowing down and paying attention through participatory observation, acclimatization and acculturation, and the development of movement repertoires […]. These methods potentially evoke a sense of belonging, connectedness and responsibility for specific places.
>
> (p. 127)

In addition to focusing on discovering new sites in Whanganui and igniting awareness and appreciation, the participants were prompted to extend their understandings and shift perspectives of certain sites visited as they began to learn about the Māori history and significance of these places. One of the places, *Taumata Karoro*, was the location of a battle in 1829 where over 400 people were killed and whole tribes were trapped within their own *pā* (village), starving to death. Everyone in the group had either walked or driven past this site many times, yet we had little to no knowledge of its history. Tamahau Rowe, a key cultural advisor for the project and a knowledge-holder of Maori culture and local history, told us the stories and history embedded in this place. Learning about our *tupuna* (ancestors), their *pā* sites and a very significant battle that led to the killing of many people right where we were standing had a profound effect on us.

Being in that same space where such events had taken place was also a meaningful experience, as revealed in a dialogue among three participants:

> Ani explained, "We could have talked that hill place we went to – *Taumata Karoro* – like with all those bones there, we could've just talked about it and been like, oh yeah, that happened but then when we went there, you just got this kind of feeling." Shaniqua then said, "You got more of a sense of the place." Kyla also mentioned, "just seeing the place in person is just so different."

Being in that space, standing on top of *Taumata Karoro*, standing where people were once at war and being able to see the view they would have seen, overlooking the river, made the experience meaningful. Place-based education scholar Amy Powers (2004) supports the notion of engaging with the place you are learning about as a means of creating a more meaningful and tangible educational experience: "Students who are engaged in real-world learning are more likely to succeed than are those who learn equivalent material from more abstract textbooks" (p. 18). Powers' study also found that "when the environment is used as an integrating context, student achievement and in-school behaviours improve" (p. 18). This notion of integration is also reflected within site-specific, place-based dance research.

Karen Barbour (2016b) discusses some of the practices she engages with when researching experiences with "place" and enhancing "sense of place" in dance making. This notion of exploring notions of "place" and how it influences and shapes the way we move and create is further discussed by Ali East (2014), who asserts that the experiences of dance artists and their understandings of places and histories of these places influence their movement, creative practice and lives. East shares the experiences of Māori artist and choreographer Louise Potiki Bryant, who acknowledges narratives of ancestors as a source of inspiration for a number of her works. These works inevitably include narratives of land and place. They also record instances of loss of land and its accompanying loss of a people's mana.

(2014, p. 113)

East also shares the thoughts of Māori artist and choreographer Jack Grey: "My dance-making ideas symbolise Te Ao Māori – places of creation and mystery. I think the wairua of the energies that can be perceived and felt, in seen and unseen ways, has always been a huge influence on my choreography" (2014, p. 114).

Grey goes on to discuss the choreographic process of his work as this work stemmed from his personal journey of reconnection to his mother's *tūrangawaewae*. He explains: "There has been a desire within me to feel a land that was part of my essence but not part of my being – to feel it in that space with all its aeons of grief, sorrow and yearning" (p. 114). It is apparent in the comments made by the participants and the literature shared that physically being at the sites made a difference in the way they engaged with, processed and valued the history they were learning.

In addition to the experience of physically engaging with place, another key point of interest was the importance of learning local Māori history and how this had not been fostered in many other educational settings. Visiting *Taumata Karoro* and realizing how significant the history within that place is to local *iwi* – and in fact to many of us from that area and who have family connections to people involved in that battle – led us to question why we might not have had the opportunity to learn this before. From here, we began to trace back through our school years and piece together what we had learned in classes like social studies, history, visual arts and English. In not one of those classes had we ever learned about Māori history specific to our area. We had learned about the 1840 Treaty of Waitangi, Aotearoa/New Zealand's founding document, but that was about it in terms of Māori history. Why was local Māori history not ever discussed? Penetito (2009) highlights the disconnect between school education and curriculum and Indigenous history and knowledge. For all students, learning about the history of their home or the place in which they are living should be a priority. We believe that history should not only be delivered and taught from one worldview and that the integration of Māori history and knowledge is of great importance. We perceive that the community dance experience this project offered was one way to integrate Māori history and knowledge into the curriculum.

## Te mutunga, *a Conclusion*

Throughout the research, a key finding was the link between bodily encounters and experiences with the environment, and young people becoming actively engaged in the learning experience. By escaping the dance studio setting and venturing out into the surrounding natural environment, the students found personal relevance and meaning in the activities we were completing. When they returned to the dance studio space, they had tangible experiences to draw from and memories of the places they visited etched into their bodies and minds. The ten young people in the group became actively engaged in the process of exploration as they were able to engage their senses in the learning experience.

Through exploring places such as beaches, rivers, forests and mountains, the young people had an opportunity to develop agency in their encounters with different environmental settings. The youth shared how they found it easier to relate and to care about what they were learning when they were able to experience it firsthand, as opposed to sitting and learning about places via technology, or through books and discussions. Being *in* the place appeared to make learning more relevant to them. They were able to grasp concepts and ideas through lived experience and connecting to *whenua* through an embodied approach, which allowed them to grow personal roots within these places and foster a sense of belonging.

We believe that while place-based approaches to education are gaining traction globally and locally within educational settings, such approaches could be further encouraged from Indigenous viewpoints. Entering place-based community dance with Indigenous worldviews and incorporating Indigenous history into learning encounters have the potential to open doorways: extending culturally responsive pedagogies and understandings throughout arts education. This in turn can lead towards decolonizing our approaches and understandings of education: specifically, what community dance and more broadly, arts education might mean and look like. Such ideas are not confined to a community dance practice but offer possibilities for the principles of community dance – with people and process at the centre of the pedagogical approach – to be considered in any teaching and learning encounter. Carefully considering the notion of place within our educational experiences opens the potential for developing relevant and meaningful encounters, both locally and globally.

## GLOSSARY

*Kaupapa*: The te reo (or Māori) word which refers to a topic, purpose, issue or matter of discussion.

*Mana*: The Māori term used to describe a person's prestige, authority, control, power, influence, status, spiritual power and charisma.

*Māori*: The Indigenous people and culture of Aotearoa/New Zealand.

*Pākehā*: A Māori term for New Zealanders primarily of European descent.

*Tūrangawaewae*: A Māori concept that is often translated as "a place to stand," but also refers to places where we feel especially empowered and connected.

*Wairua*: The Māori term used to describe a person who, from a Māori worldview, exists beyond death. It is considered to be the non-physical spirit, distinct from the body, but considered by some to reside in the heart or mind of someone, while others believe it is part of the whole person and not located at any particular part of the body.

## REFERENCES

Amans, D. (2017). *An introduction to community dance practice*. Macmillan International Higher Education.

Barbour, K. N. (2016a). Place-responsive choreography and activism. In E. Emerald, R. E. Rinehart, & A. Garcia (Eds.), *Global South ethnographies: Minding the senses* (pp. 127–145). Sense Publishers.

Barbour, K. N. (2016b). Places we call home: Representing place and identity in contemporary dance performance. *International Journal of Social, Political, and Community Agendas in the Arts*, *12*(1), 1–13.

Bishop, R. (2005). Freeing ourselves from the neocolonial domination in research: A *kaupapa Māori* approach in creating knowledge. In N. K. Denzin & Y. L. Lincoln (Eds.), *The handbook of qualitative research* (3rd ed., pp. 109–138). Sage.

Bishop, R. (2012). Pretty difficult: Implementing *kaupapa Māori* theory in English-medium secondary schools. *New Zealand Journal of Educational Studies*, *47*(2), 38–50.

Blokland, T. (2017). *Community as urban practice*. John Wiley & Sons.

East, A. (2014). Dancing Aotearoa: Connections with land identity and ecology. *Dance Research Aotearoa*, *2*(1), 101–124.

East, A. (2016). Dance in/for/with/as/community: Re-defining community dance in 2015–16. *Dance Research Aotearoa*, *4*(1), 57–59.

Hiroti, P. (2020). *Resting our bodies upon* Papatūānuku: *An exploration of how community dance may foster connections to* whenua *for rangatahi* [Unpublished doctoral dissertation]. University of Auckland, Auckland.

Larsen, S. C., & Johnson, J. T. (2017). *Being together in place: Indigenous coexistence in a more than human world*. University of Minnesota Press.

Park, G. (1996). *Ngā Ururoa: The groves of life: Ecology and history in a New Zealand landscape*. Victoria University Press.

Penetito, W. (2009). Place-based education: Catering for curriculum, culture and community. *New Zealand Annual Review of Education*, *18*, 5–29.

Postman, N., & Weingartner, C. (1971). *Teaching as a subversive activity*. Penguin Books.

Powers, A. (2004). An evaluation of four place-based education programs. *The Journal of Environmental Education*, *35*(4), 17–32.

Smith, G. H. (1997). Kaupapa Māori *as transformative praxis* [Unpublished doctoral dissertation]. The University of Auckland, Auckland.

Smith, M. L. (2002). Moving self: The thread which bridges dance and theatre. *Research in Dance Education*, *3*(2), 123–141.

Tuhiwai Smith, L. (1999). *Decolonizing methodologies: Research and Indigenous peoples.* University of Otago Press.

Tuhiwai Smith, L. (2007). On tricky ground. In N. K. Denzin & Y. S. Lincoln (Eds.), *The landscape of qualitative research* (3rd ed., pp. 85–113). Sage.

Tuhiwai Smith, L., Tuck, E., & Yang, K. W. (Eds.). (2018). *Indigenous and decolonizing studies in education: Mapping the long view.* Routledge.

UNESCO. (2010). *Seoul agenda: Goals for the development of arts education.* http://www.unesco.org/new/en/culture/themes/creativity/arts-education/official-texts/development-goals/

Williams, S. (2015). Te Hau Kainga – The breeze of home: Embodying ihi within contemporary dance practice. *Journal of Emerging Dance Scholarship, 3,* 1–18.

Wise, S., Buck, R., Martin, R., & Yu, L. (2020). Community dance as a democratic dialogue. *Policy Futures in Education, 18*(3), 375–390.

# 19

# Pedagogical Implications in *La Austral, S.A. de C.V.*: Collective Storytelling Performances by Pablo Helguera and DREAMers

*Eunji J. Lee*

Over the past two decades, Western European and American artists have created participatory modes of art making informed by progressive education through employing educational strategies, such as lectures, workshops and discussions, as part of the artwork. These participatory modes of art making, combining the activities and goals often found in the field of education, are often categorized as the pedagogical turn in contemporary art (Bishop, 2012; Helguera, 2011; Kalin, 2012; Lázár, 2014; O'Neill & Wilson, 2010; Podesva, 2007). In this article, I discuss *La Austral, S. A. de C. V.* (in short, *La Austral*),[1] a performative storytelling project created by artist Pablo Helguera and a group of DREAMers. These are immigrant individuals who qualify for the Development, Relief, and Education for Alien Minors (DREAM) Act, legislation for undocumented immigrants who arrived in the United States as children to gain a pathway to permanent legal status (America's Voice, 2020). From the position of an art educator, I carried out an empirical study to examine the learning outcomes of this artist-led participatory artwork. I investigated not only the pedagogical intentions and strategies of the artist but also the perceived learning experienced by the project members and public visitors who participated in creating *La Austral*.

Although *La Austral* was first conceived by a renowned artist, the findings from the study refer to various pedagogical implications relevant to community art education (Bastos, 2002; Congdon, 2004; Coutts & Jokela, 2008; Hutzel, 2007; Krensky & Steffen, 2009; Schlemmer, 2016) in which community arts empower people as "catalysts for dialogue about individual and group identity, local and national concerns, and ultimately the pursuit of democracy" (Congdon et al., 2001, p. 3). *La Austral* highlighted how an arts-based community becomes a safe space of knowledge making and identity development among its project members. The project crafted a unique combination of political content and the poetics of storytelling, an aesthetic that prompted imagination and understanding in a time of heightened political division.

## *Background of* La Austral

Pablo Helguera (born in Mexico City, 1971), a New York-based socially engaged artist and educator, often incorporates storytelling as a crucial part of his performative artworks and educational practices. During the Trump/Clinton presidential campaign in the United States, Helguera was commissioned by the International Studio and Curatorial Program to carry out a community-based project in Brooklyn, New York. Trump's presidential campaign had focused attention on immigration issues, and as a Mexican immigrant himself, Helguera wanted to create a work related to the DACA/DREAM Act (personal communication, 4 May 2018). Eventually, Helguera merged his aesthetic and pedagogical interests in storytelling with his political concerns regarding the individuals affected by the proposed elimination of the Deferred Action for Childhood Arrivals (DACA) Program, a policy established during the Obama Administration that had allowed qualified DREAMers to legally work and be protected from deportation. Helguera designed *La Austral* as a space where public visitors could hear live stories delivered by DREAMer-storytellers. Through an open call, eight participants from different areas of New York City joined and remained with the project for the entire ten-month duration (August 2017–May 2018).

## *Structure of* La Austral

*La Austral* was carried out in two phases: first, as a series of private workshop sessions where the project members developed storytelling techniques and confidence with public storytelling; and second, public engagement sessions where the project members directly interacted with visitors by presenting their stories. The public engagement sessions took two forms: as "evening public receptions," where all the project members shared their stories simultaneously across the gallery space; and as "weekend public office hours," where a single project member curated the gallery space with storytelling and interactions with public visitors. The workshops and public engagement sessions all took place at a storefront gallery called *El Museo de Los Sures*, operated by the community organization Los Sures in Williamsburg, Brooklyn.

The eight project members engaged in individual and group performance-based exercises throughout the series of workshops, many of which were based on Augusto Boal's *The Theater of the Oppressed* (1974–2002). Exercises and game-like activities were used to develop the skills of the project members in improvisation, character building and role-playing, shifting between fiction and non-fiction, and in enhancing dramatic effects and persuasiveness in storytelling. They also made two visits to the Theater of the Oppressed NYC during March 2018.

For the public presentations of *La Austral*, which took place during April and May 2018, the bare gallery was transformed into an inviting space resembling a "storytelling restaurant" to make the public visitors feel at home. The white walls were painted burgundy red and displayed intriguing objects and props embedded with personal stories. During the evening receptions and public office hours, these objects served as conversation starters between the visitors and the DREAMer-storytellers.

For the evening public receptions, Helguera curated the gallery's two-room space with multiple DREAMer-storytellers sharing stories simultaneously in various locations and in different styles. In the front room, DREAMer-storytellers relayed what Helguera termed as short "appetizer-like stories" near the entrance. Another DREAMer-storyteller, sitting at a desk, facilitated improvisational storytelling games with the public visitors. In the rear room, with comfortable sofas and a rug for seating, the storytellers told more elaborate stories. The room was dark with dim red lights that prevented visitors from seeing clearly. Audience members were encouraged to close their eyes while listening to stories that were more personal, emotional and autobiographical. These stories described experiences, such as a border crossing, or the first and last visit to their home countries in Central and South America and Mexico, in a setting designed to focus the attention and imagination of the viewers.

## *Responses From Participants*

While many artists claim to work towards educational aims in their participatory work with communities, as an art educator I found the lack of research on the educational philosophies and teaching approaches of these artists problematic. Furthermore, there has been even less scrutiny of the learning outcomes for the project participants and audience members involved in these artworks. Hence, I conducted a case study as part of my multiple case dissertation study that closely observed Helguera's workshops and public engagement sessions to study the artist's pedagogical intentions and methods, and how the project members and visitors perceived "learning" from the experience of participating in an artist-led, community-based project (Lee, 2020; and in press). Through triangulating the experiential responses from different perspectives, I was able to analyse and understand how Helguera's pedagogical intentions and approaches were perceived and processed by the project members and public visitors, and what they had gained as insightful experiences.

### Responses From Project Members

Eight project members contributed to creating *La Austral*. Five were undocumented DACA recipients (three females and two males from Mexico and Central and South America respectively) and two (one female and one male from Mexico) had attained US citizenship after living as undocumented for over fifteen years in the United States. One member from Estonia wanted to migrate to the United States but was confronting difficulty with the immigration process. Their salient responses pertaining to learning involved the following themes: increased confidence from overcoming the challenges of public engagement; performative storytelling techniques and imaginative approaches; social bonding with peers; and a sense of achievement by being part of a "legitimate art project."

Several members discussed the impact the project had on them in their daily performance or at work in relation to communication skills. Alyssa, a DACA recipient originally from Costa Rica, recounted how the project sparked her passion for storytelling, prompting her to keep a journal of stories she hopes to publish. She also became more observant of her surroundings and bolder when approaching people. Carlos, one of the US citizens originally from Mexico who works as an Uber driver, described how the storytelling methods he learned have led to more constructive conversations and discussions of life experiences with his customers. Each member mentioned ways *La Austral* broadened their understanding of people and how it allowed them to express their internal struggles as stories to others.

### Responses From Public Visitors

I also observed and interviewed visitors attending the evening receptions and weekend public office hours. Some said that they first learned of DACA through *La Austral*, while others described their emotional responses by engaging with the DREAMer-storytellers. Alex, Jade and Yessenia, immigrants from Mexico and South

America, stated that they were happy to experience a space that connected to their roots through storytelling. They also compared this interactive project to the traditional art they were accustomed to, expressing surprise that an artwork could be so engaging. The public visitors said they "felt a connection" through the stories told directly by the storytellers. For example, Lola (public visitor from Spain temporarily residing in the United States) and Jade (public visitor, a US citizen who immigrated from Mexico) visited *La Austral* both during evening receptions and weekend office hours, finding each time to be intriguing and the stories relatable even though they knew nothing about the storytellers. Alex explained how, months later, the powerful storytelling experience still vividly resonated with her, evoking nostalgic memories of growing up with stories told by her grandparents in Columbia. Yessenia, a US citizen who immigrated from Peru, also mentioned connecting personally with the stories, which prompted her to reflect upon and record her own experiences.

The unique type of learning evoked by the non-linear and open-ended structure of the project – learning that promoted agency for the public visitors through engagement with the content – was addressed by both Lola and Alex, who are educators. Alex noted the complete contrast of this approach to the top-down, rigid learning she had experienced at school in Colombia. Furthermore, Alex shared her plans to use some of the strategies she experienced through *La Austral* in her own teaching with immigrant adults and highly recommended using projects like *La Austral* for children and after-school programmes. Nearly all the visitors I spoke with described the ambience of space as comfortable and engaging. Several visitors mentioned a surreal quality that provided a unique experience distinct from the outside world, where they could sit and engage with the storytellers and the objects all day. Clearly, the design of the space definitively influenced the visitors' experiences.

## *Educational Implications*

The prominent pedagogical implications in *La Austral* emerged from a cross analysis of interview responses carried out with the project members, the public visitors, and Helguera, who shared his own pedagogical philosophy and intentions in creating the project. Although these outcomes specifically pertain to *La Austral*, the pedagogical implications may also apply to other community art practices.

### Affect and Motivated Learning

Helguera articulated the emotional dimension in his pedagogical practice as an artist–educator and shared memories of teachers who had planted a seed of passion in him:

> The one thing they gave me that I treasure more than anything else was basically a kind of love for something. It's not specific data, it's not that they downloaded any information in my brain, it's that they communicated *a feeling for something* [emphasis added].
>
> (P. Helguera, personal communication, 4 May, 2018)

Helguera's sense of passion was described by the project members as distinctly different from their previous school experiences. As Jose shared, "It's definitely beneficial to have these workshops outside of a school setting. You're working with a hands-on artist who is passionate about something […]. You learn better […] it's freer, less rigid. No grade" (personal communication, 15 April 2018). Camelia expressed how *La Austral* did not "make you feel like a bucket that needs to be filled up in a top-down way. You become a subject as a part of your own process of learning" (personal communication, 20 April 2018).

Such free-choice learning has been emphasized in alternative learning spaces outside of school and as a goal of community-based (art) education. Choice-based education researchers Falk and Dierking (2000, 2018) argue that organic and personally motivated learning involves "considerable choice on the part of the learner as to what to learn, as well as where and when to participate in learning" (2000, p. xii). This was a salient aspect for both the project members and public visitors, which elicited active participation in collaboratively creating *La Austral* as a meaningful experience.

## Community of Practice (CoP): Identity Development

The learning promoted through *La Austral* shared several commonalities with social learning theorist Etienne Wenger's concept of CoP. Wenger (1998) has posited that participation in social communities through a practice is key to learning that elicits identity formation. To Wenger, identity is a layering of participation and reification of events by which our experience and its social interpretation inform each other. He argues that identity exists in the constant work of negotiating the self within a CoP that is formed by three elements: the domain, the community and the practice. In *La Austral*, the domain was the shared identity of the project members as (previously) undocumented and motivated to create the project. The community was formed through the members participating in the workshops, presenting work and engaging with a public audience. The practice was the time and effort put into telling their stories and making *La Austral*. Thus, a base of common interest and the multiple events and activities to create *La Austral* as a collective contributed to furthering the members' identity.

The workshops for *La Austral* were held in the evening after the project members were finished with work and school. Despite the difficulties of making time and matching one another's schedules, the members' self-motivation for storytelling and connecting with one another and the shared goal of creating successful public performances were the driving forces behind *La Austral*. *La Austral* exemplifies Wenger's concept of CoP, where "learning occurs in social contexts that emerge and evolve when people who have common goals interact as they strive towards those goals" (1998, p. 6). Ultimately, *La Austral* promoted a sense of achievement that furthered the members' identity development by collectively creating an artwork that voiced their political concerns.

## Creating Through Relationality: Intersubjectivity, Building a Sense of Community

*La Austral*'s private workshops and public engagement sessions involved continuous interactions and story exchanges among the project members and the visitors as well. This practice of listening and responsive understanding based on reciprocity promoted a sense of community among all the participants. This example of "intersubjectivity," a concept first coined by philosopher Edmund Husserl, refers to the interchange of thoughts and feelings facilitated by empathy (Cooper-White, 2014). Although all the project members had different backgrounds, they shared the commonality of crossing the border to come to the United States and confronting the day-to-day difficulties of living without documentation or as an immigrant. As Alyssa explained, "For me, the most valuable part of this project was that I was part of a group that was open and willing to listen to [my] stories and accept them" (personal communication, 10 May 2018). Carlos said, "We achieved something deep that we might not even be aware of, it was extremely special" (personal communication, 5 May 2018). Sharing stories of their journeys facilitated personal bonds among members of this small group, which has led to ongoing relationships and collaboration in art-making ventures.

## Embodied Approach and Multiple Entries for Engagement

Helguera's unique approach to storytelling was a new experience for the project members. During the workshops, Helguera facilitated a combination of stories to be written out in advance as assignments and developed on the spot in an impromptu manner. Helguera would sometimes ask members to tell stories from the perspective of a pet or an inanimate object, or to build stories from images or words written on cards randomly drawn from a deck, or to start stories with objects. Thus, literary components of storytelling were combined with imagination and the use of sensory modalities. Members mentioned how Helguera's approach pushed them to develop new perspectives in their thinking, with some comparing this experience to the way literature was taught in school. Jose pointed out how performative storytelling was an embodied practice that would not necessarily happen in a school classroom: "Sitting down, not really learning how to use your body [...] English class storytelling [in school], wouldn't make you come up in the front and make you tell a story like here" (personal communication, 15 April 2018). Lola (a public visitor) described her pedagogical experience with *La Austral* as "physically being in the moment, interacting with the bodies of people, the artifacts, and colors in the space," contrasted with learning from a book or lecture. She elaborated on the non-linear quality of the experience, stating that "teaching and learning doesn't follow in one direction but it comes through variance, through different directions and through different means or materials." For Lola, the setting created "a surreal and humorous space where you can talk about serious stuff or say nonsensical things, which are also critical for our development" (personal communication, 26 September 2018).

## Public Engagement Through Cognitive Apprenticeship

In *La Austral*, the project members went through a private working period with Helguera and eventually presented their stories to a public audience in a social context. This type of learning suggests cognitive apprenticeship and situated learning (Brown et al., 1989; Collins et al., 1987; Lave & Wenger, 1991) grounded in constructivism. For learning theorists Collins et al. (1987), cognitive apprenticeship brings "tacit processes into the open, where students can observe, enact, and practice them with help from the teacher" (p. 4). Helguera's design of *La Austral* shared similarities with cognitive apprenticeship by acknowledging the project members' tacit knowledge and applying their learning to real-world contexts via public presentation of their stories. Moreover, the three stages of skill acquisition – the cognitive stage, associative stage and autonomous stage (Fitts & Posner, 1967) – were supported through this approach. The private workshop phase constituted the "associative stage" in which members were allowed to make mistakes; they openly addressed their struggles and received feedback from Helguera and their peers. The public engagement phase, which the members recalled as the most challenging but most rewarding aspect of the project, describes what Fitts and Posner called the "autonomous stage," when the learner's skill becomes honed and perfected. Throughout the public presentations, I observed the members feeling unprepared and unable to fully express their thoughts but learning from their mistakes. Over time, they were able to take full ownership of creating a space to facilitate unique storytelling experiences for the public visitors.

## *Conclusion*

In *La Austral*, a cognitive apprenticeship model enabled project members to engage their imagination through storytelling and gain confidence by presenting personal stories to a public audience. Not only did they advance their communication skills by conveying difficult stories, but they were also able to connect with others empathetically, voicing their social concerns as a marginalized community in the United States.

Creating *La Austral* as a collective artwork, however, deeply resonated with both the project members and public visitors, similar to how artist Rick Lowe explained it: "Art projects tease out a higher value beyond a practical function through somehow telling the story in a way that lingers" (as cited in Cohen-Cruz, 2018, p. 20). The artistic spirit put forth by Helguera was advanced by the project members, providing an outlet for self-expression that eventually sparked what philosopher Maxine Greene called as social imagination, allowing "people to think of things as if they could be otherwise" (Greene, 1995, p. 1). As Jose, one of the project members, stated, "Being an immigrant, having the dilemma of holding everything in. […] Art as a platform definitely helped me. I took a little from each [workshop] and made them my own. I gained the strength to continue too" (personal communication, 20 April 2018). Thus, the reflective and participatory nature of *La Austral* reveals art's capacity to intensify and clarify the human experience – to provide a means of exploring personally meaningful connections between the lives of participants and their communities. In the case of *La Austral*, a sense of camaraderie and bonding contributed to their social identities, allowing the project members to further reflect on their past experiences and discover the depth of who they are and who they can be.

## NOTE

1. In *La Austral, S. A. de C.V.*, "austral" refers to "south" in Spanish but is also a name of a prominent Spanish book publisher, *Austral*. "S. A. de C.V." refers to "sociedad anónima de capital variable," translating as "anonymous society of variable capital," which is typically used to describe independent businesses in Mexico. Helguera intended to transcend the original and economic meaning of the words by creating *La Austral* as a cultural and social place, where visitors could access a range of stories provided by live DREAMer-storytellers (P. Helguera, personal communication, 28 February 2018).

## REFERENCES

America's Voice. (2020). *Immigration 101: What is a DREAMer?* https://www.americasvoice.org/blog/what-is-a-dreamer/

Bastos, F. (2002). Making the familiar strange: A community-based art education framework. In Y. Gaudelius & P. Speirs (Eds.), *Contemporary issues in art education* (pp. 70–83). Prentice Hall.

Bishop, C. (2012). *Artificial hells: Participatory art and the politics of spectatorship*. Verso Books.

Boal, A. (2002). *The theater of the oppressed* (A. Charles, M. L. Mcbride, & E. Fryer, Trans.). Pluto Press. (Original work published 1974)

Brown, J. S., Collins, A., & Duguid, P. (1989). Situated cognition and the culture of learning. *Educational Researcher*, 18(1), 32–42.

Cohen-Cruz, J. (2018). The poetic residue: An interview with Rick Lowe. *A Blade of Grass Magazine*, 1, 16–21.

Collins, A., Brown, J. S., & Newman, S. E. (1987, January). *Cognitive apprenticeship: Teaching the craft of reading, writing and mathematics* (Technical Report No. 403). Centre for the Study of Reading, University of Illinois.

Congdon, K. (2004). *Community art in action*. Davis.

Congdon, K., Blandy, D., & Bolin, P. (2001). *Histories of community-based art education*. National Art Education Association.

Cooper-White, P. (2014). Intersubjectivity. In D. A. Leeming (Ed.), *Encyclopedia of psychology and religion*. Springer. https://doi.org/10.1007/978-1-4614-6086-2_9182

Coutts, G., & Jokela, T. (2008). *Art, community and environment: Educational perspectives*. Intellect.

Falk, J. H., & Dierking, L. D. (2000). *Learning from museums: Visitor experiences and the making of meaning*. Altamira Press.

Falk, J. H., & Dierking, L. D. (2018). *Learning from museums* (2nd ed.). Rowman & Littlefield.

Fitts, P. M., & Posner, M. I. (1967). *Human performance*. Brooks Cole.

Greene, M. (1995). *Releasing the imagination: Essays on education, the arts, and social change*. Jossey-Bass.

Helguera, P. (2011). *Education for socially engaged art: A materials and techniques handbook*. Jorge Pinto Books.

Hutzel, K. (2007). Reconstructing a community, reclaiming a playground: A participatory action research study. *Studies in Art Education*, 48(3), 299–315.

Kalin, N. (2012). (de)Fending art education through the pedagogical turn. *The Journal of Social Theory in Art Education*, 32, 42–55.

Krensky, B., & Steffen, S. L. (2009). *Engaging classrooms and communities through art: A guide to designing and implementing community-based art education*. Altamira Press.

Lave, J., & Wenger, E. (1991). *Situated learning: Legitimate peripheral participation*. Cambridge University Press.

Lázár, E. (2014). Educational turn. *Curatorial Dictionary*. http://tranzit.org/curatorialdictionary/index.php/dictionary/educational-turn

Lee, E. J. (2020). *Art as pedagogical experience: Educational implications of three participatory socially engaged art projects* [Unpublished doctoral dissertation]. Teachers College, Columbia University.

Lee, E. J. (in press). Art as pedagogy: A multiple case study of participatory socially-engaged art. *Visual Arts Research*, 49(1).

Los Sures, Southside United HDFC. (n.d.). *About Los Sures*. http://www.southsideunitedhdfc.org/about-us/mission-history/

O'Neill, P., & Wilson, M. (Eds.). (2010). *Curating and the educational turn*. Open Edition & de Appel.

Podesva, K. L. (2007, Summer). A pedagogical turn: Brief notes on education as art. *Fillip 6*. http://fillip.ca/content/a-pedagogical-turn

Schlemmer, R. H. (2016). Community arts: (Re)contextualizing the narrative of teaching and learning. *Arts Education Policy Review*, 18(1), 1–10.

Wenger, E. (1998). *Community of practice: Learning, meaning, and identity*. Cambridge University Press.

# 20

# Community Arts Education: Experiencing and Creating Our World

*Shelley Hannigan and Merinda Kelly*

The research presented in this chapter unfolded in the regional City of Greater Geelong, Victoria, Australia. As two practitioners creatively active in and across public, institutional and common spaces in Geelong, we became curious about each other's ways of working at the intersection of creative and pedagogic practice in this time of rapid local and global change. Taking up reflective practice as a research method (Bassot, 2015; Schön, 1983), we discuss a series of negotiated tasks, assignments and virtual and embodied encounters through which reflections emerge in and through such practices.

Our chapter offers some background about our research followed by an explanation of our methodology and methods. We include some of our reflective text to provide insights into our multiple approaches to practice work and to share some emergent findings: including how our work has transitioned in this place and how it contributes to the becoming of artful spaces, community art and socially engaged art practices, and public pedagogy opportunities (see Sandlin et al., 2011). Sandlin et al. (2011) define public pedagogy as

- citizenship within and beyond schools
- pedagogical theory on popular culture and everyday life
- informal institutions and public spaces as educative arenas
- dominant cultural discourses
- public intellectualism and social activism (p. 338).

## Context and Background Information

We define community as the public engaging, in different ways, in our community art projects and pedagogical art events and experiences. Public engagement is often the result of the event having been advertised via local council art pages, social media and posters as well as directly through our own contacts. It is our experience that people choose to engage in different ways: as passive viewers, artists, participants or workers. Community members may be part of a central group (as in Merinda's participatory art projects) where the participants have been involved during the evolution of the project and are therefore co-creators of the project itself. Some who engage in our community or socially engaged art practices might be attached to institutions (schools, universities) and therefore have reasons for engaging *because* of these requirements (assessments, etc.). Institutions have also often been involved in our work as the funding bodies that provide financial support, spaces or related opportunities (but expect certain outcomes).

The City of Greater Geelong, Australia, where our research is based, is on First Nations Wadawurrung Country. Since colonization, this regional city has expanded throughout the booming eras of the gold rush and the rise of the wool trade. Geelong has continued to inspire innovation, especially with the invention of iconic designs, including the ute (a word used in New Zealand and Australian for a utility vehicle that has a tonneau behind the passenger compartment. Despite it being truck-like, it can be driven with a regular driver's license). Like so many other industrial cities, Geelong is currently in a state of rapid transition. So too are its citizens as they work to navigate the personal and socio-economic implications of imposed urban change and renewal in the region. Celebrated and contested histories and possible futures unfolding in Geelong inform our responsive approaches to working in and "with" community forms of art in this city.

We have experienced and supported the interplay of art, education and community within the unique regional "art scene" of Geelong with its distinctive identity, infrastructure and institutional art spaces. Working as artist/educators in the same academic institution has led us to connect and engage in different ways with communities, art schools, institutions, galleries and arts events. We have encountered each other in our separate projects and in our work across these spheres; however, we have not actually worked together on the same community art project. We have been "participant" or "spectator" for each other's projects and have engaged in spirited, critical conversations about these over the years.

## Shelley

I am a visual artist working in painting, fibre arts, mixed media and visual arts education. I moved to this region over two decades ago from my home of Aotearoa/New Zealand. As somewhat of an outsider compared to Merinda (not having grown up in Geelong or having family connections to the place), I connected with artists in the region and led community arts projects to help local artists show work publicly. I also helped build art opportunities for artists from a broad range of backgrounds and abilities. My initial work in Geelong was teaching in an art college that offered a range of part-time courses, after-school art programmes and diploma qualifications for post-secondary school students, which meant that my teaching, practice as an artist, and work in the Geelong community were entwined. In these contexts, I shared opportunities with students to undertake their art practices in the region. In addition to my community artwork, I have worked in Geelong as a university-based art educator/researcher since 2007 and maintained my own studio-based practice as research.

## Merinda

I was raised in Geelong and from an early age developed a strong interest in the visual arts. Growing up, I recall a lively but fairly conservative professional arts presence in the region. Also visible were well-established amateur groups and companies with strong community roots and followings. In my late teens and early twenties, I discovered and became involved with some of the more experimental, self-organizing arts collectives and activities rising up in and through the community as Geelong began to evolve as a university city. My enduring creative endeavours in Geelong and beyond encompass object-based creative practice, socially engaged art, experimental pedagogy and arts education in and across a range of institutions, organizations and other spaces in the public sphere.

## *Methodology and Method*

As experienced educators, artists and researchers who are actively engaged in research, teaching and art practices (particularly within artworks, journal writing, art critiques and reviews), we found a reflexive and reflective methodology to be the most natural for our combined research project. Shifting from our usual habits as reflective and reflexive practitioners required us to be able and willing to

> acknowledge and take account of the many ways (researchers) themselves influence research findings and thus what comes to be accepted as knowledge. Reflexivity implies the ability to reflect inward toward oneself as an inquirer; outward to the cultural, historical, linguistic, political, and other forces that shape everything about inquiry; and, in between researcher and participant to the social interaction they share.
> 
> (Sandelowski & Barroso, 2002, p. 222)

Our research method takes up Bassot's (2015) reminder that "reflecting with others enables us to gain insights from them and to question our thoughts and actions in the light of these" (p. 105). We have therefore set tasks as virtual and embodied encounters which have involved discussion and the sharing of reflections, experiences and insights relevant to selected aspects of our pedagogic and creative work. This scholarship in action included a visit to Chengdu, China, where we spent time at a school art department and engaged in art-making processes with artist/educators there. We have also worked on large umbrella projects such as *Mountain to Mouth* (M-to-M) (discussed later) as well as on separate projects. Working together as academics in the same faculty means we regularly engage in writing for publications and teaching materials, drawing on feedback from students and in response to new, emerging art practice events.

By sharing our varied experiences as artist/educators working in and across different communities, we sought to arrive at fresh and nuanced understandings of them. We excavated conversations and responses for emergent patterns, synergies, intersections and dissonances to thicken understandings and insights into our individual and collective practices. As we examined our different and converging practices in the unique place of Geelong, we noted commonalities in the theoretical lenses we had applied to our practices over the years, including critical, transformative, interpretive/constructionist and arts-based inquiry. Revisiting this work brings to light shared insights and challenges that we problematize and navigate to sustain and enrich our intersecting professional practices. Selected reflections and fragments of conversation illuminate notable affinities and themes emerging throughout the research process.

### *Collective Reflections: Practising Art and Art Education in the Geelong Region*

A social turn (Bishop, 2005) has materialized in and through Merinda's practice in response to conditions of uncertainty and rapid change manifesting in Geelong. Informed by her prior experiences as a visual and community artist and arts educator, Merinda returned to work with/in communities through activating a series of social and relational creative experiments and projects in and across unexpected and everyday spaces in the Geelong CBD and its surrounds.

We have both been involved in public pedagogical initiatives, including working with students, local government community workers, academics, researchers and educators in the region to forge community connections and generative spaces for embodied, artful encounters beyond the confines of institutional spaces. These initiatives include the *Knowing Your Place Neighbourhood Walks* (City of Greater

Geelong, 2019) facilitated by Amanda Stirritt and by other public initiatives (see McGill, 2016).

Initially, Merinda's creative practice focused on objects and everyday archives traditionally exhibited within the gallery system. In response to spatial, social and material conditions emerging in Geelong, her creative work has mobilized socially engaged art, a practice that explores the potentialities of using people as a medium and "living as form" (Thompson, 2012). Identifying with artist Jeremy Deller's mantra, Merinda "went from being an artist who makes things, to being an artist who makes things happen" (Thompson, 2012, p. 17). Departing from the "all commodifying" institutionalized "art system" (McKee, 2016, p. 13) afforded her scope for alternative ways of seeing art as "direct action" capable of catalysing a profound re-examination of "how we live" (McKee, 2016, p. 237).

Merinda became involved with a local, creative initiative titled *The New Wilderness Project*, which required working collaboratively with a team of young people, artists and academics to explore and respond creatively to the urgencies of changing social, material and spatial relations associated with de-industrialization in the Geelong community and beyond. The open-ended and transdisciplinary processes of working with young artists inside a gallery space as an experimental lab were generative for all concerned. For a few participants, however, the pressure to present a final exhibition in The Courthouse (a space dedicated to young people to access the arts) appeared to interrupt the flow of ideas and possibilities unfolding in the space. Following the seminal project, four additional variations of *New Wilderness* were activated, with each privileging emerging social relations and processes over the production of refined object-based artworks.

Merinda has come to know adaptability as essential, particularly when working with/in communities amidst potentially ambiguous situations. Her participation in *New Wilderness* catalysed social networks and collective actions that led to a range of performative interventions, responsive to space, time and place. For example, a performative re-enactment of an arts-based collective action during "Melbourne Occupy" worked to temporarily disorient an audience listening to an opening speech in a gallery. The potentiality of the gallery space was temporarily transformed into a site for playful encounter, arts activism and performative action.

## *Geelong's M-to-M*

M-to-M is a bi-annual, community arts-based, environmental/cultural walk across the Geelong region which aims "to bring communities together and immerse them in Geelong's diverse landscape and story, as well as celebrate the region's creatives" (Mountain to Mouth City of Greater Geelong, 2020). The word "communities" is used in this context to recognize the diverse groups of people and individuals who come together and engage in various ways across this geographical region. The *M-to-M* project initially came about when national funding was provided to five regions of Australia undergoing significant social change. Geelong was identified as one of the fastest growing regions of Australia, and their project, *Connecting Identities*, was formed in 2009: this included sub-projects such as *M-to-M*, *Memory Bank* and *Story Vessels* (Mountain to Mouth City of Greater Geelong, 2009). The *Story Vessels* project was facilitated by Shelley and involved community groups sharing stories, which in turn determined the creation of artefacts made by twelve local sculptors (see Hannigan, 2012). This process involved artists' designs for their sculptures being challenged by community members during a series of meetings where community members told stories, and artists interpreted these into sculptural visual form – with some artistic licence but also the community members' approval.

As one of twelve artists in the 2016 *Mountain to Mouth Festival*, Merinda embraced the potential for assembling future artists and local citizens by inviting them to participate in a performative intervention in the industrial precinct. This involved artists, students and citizens in the co-construction of an installation produced by recasting and reimagining plastic materials left behind by humans and industry. *M-to-M* included twelve installations that the public could encounter throughout a two-day, extreme 80-km walk across the region, from the You Yangs to the mouth of the Barwon River.

## *Inviting the Public to Engage With Our Art Practices*

Merinda's involvement in *#Vacant and the Iconic Industries Project* (2017) included working in and with an empty factory as a site for responding to the rapid gentrification of the city and rising inequality emerging through the processes of de-/re-industrialization in Geelong. The mobility and symbolism of the "brick" was explored with an installation that invited participants to ponder possible futures as they playfully tore down, reassembled and reimagined the creative potential of hundreds of transparent bricks. Situated in the Iconic Industries Exhibition at the National Wool Museum in Geelong, this participatory installation interrupted and animated the traditional museum context with its invitation to touch, move and play with the work. The dimensions of these forms mimicked settler-made bricks manufactured from extracted natural clay deposits in the region, which were rapidly depleted.

These projects have included community members and been informed by council funding bodies but have also proven emergent and place-making. We have encountered our secondary or tertiary students in these projects and also shared these projects as forms of local art with our students.

Shelley's more recent work has included environmentally sustainable arts projects as well as exploring arts-science pedagogies (Hannigan et al., 2022). These projects have their roots in the *Story Vessels* project mentioned above, where she engaged with a number of environmental and heritage groups in the region. This in turn informed a series of works in which she tapped into the textile heritage of Geelong and her experiences as a new Australian to capture embodied depictions of Australian women informed by the red dust and copper of this land (see Figure 20.1). For this project, Shelley invited other members of the community to create their own depictions of dress art (Hannigan, 2019) as part of these installations.

Having engaged with urban gardening renewal groups, Shelley's work has become biophilic as she explores the interconnection of humans to the natural environment and works towards a small movement that promotes Geelong as a biophilic city. One of her projects is collaborating with silkworms in sustainable ways involving creating habitats with her textile sculptural forms for the worms to

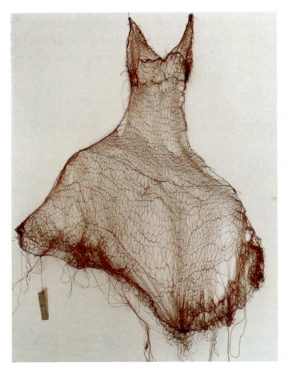

FIGURE 20.1: Shelley Hannigan. Jane, copper thread and wire. Photo by Shelley Hannigan (2019).

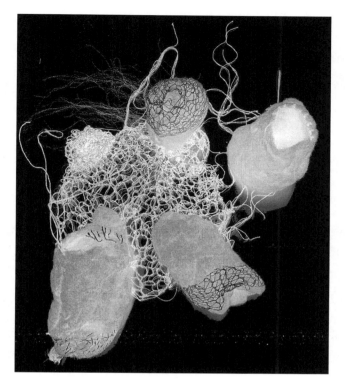

FIGURE 20.2: Shelley Hannigan. Embodied interconnections, wool felt, knitted and stitched threads. Photo by Shelley Hannigan (2019).

live and cocoon in. The moths are allowed to hatch naturally, leaving silk cocoons with unique colouring, openings and formations incorporated into sculptural and textile works. Photographs are also taken of stains made by the worms, mulberry branches and moths in the process. Another of her projects captures community dynamics with fibre art and digital modes (see Figure 20.2), which has resulted in works exhibited with leading women regional artists in the exhibition and conference, *Energetical* (Platform Arts and Deakin University, 2020). Such work links back to Shelley's education and research exploring place (see Bartier et al., 2020) and patterning in education (Hannigan et al., 2018).

## *Agitation and Disruption: Concluding Comments*

Through our work in Geelong, we have come to see ourselves as arts agitators within broader systems that might be seeking to "use" the arts for their own ends and agendas. Our hybrid practices have come to form complex and nuanced ways of adapting to immanent possibilities as these emerge in and through the art spaces we co-construct "with" others. Individually and collectively, we have learned much through our rigorous processes of reflection. In doing so, we have reflectively and reflexively questioned our values, assumptions, community and professional relationships and other elements of critical relevance to our respective practices. The research process has brought into close relief the complex messiness, dynamics of power and potentialities for learning and generative change, emerging with and in the social and political contexts we practise in our region. We have learned from our research together that artists and arts educators in regional and rural places can struggle to locate spaces to install, perform, show, discuss, observe and engage art and funding. However, many artists in Geelong, including ourselves, have transformed places of cultural, historical and environmental significance into artful spaces and sites where public artworks have been installed or performed. Empty shops and mall spaces have housed exhibitions, maker spaces, pop-up galleries and workshops.

An example of the latter is Merinda's socially engaged art intervention *Tread*, which involved the occupation of a vacant shop in the central business district of Geelong. Merinda had negotiated with a local landlord to obtain free tenancy for the high-profile space to experiment with alternative modes of social engagement and exchange during the Christmas rush of 2016. Situated on a highly visible corner, the shop and its occupants worked to disrupt the furious mid-December flow of global capitalism at work. The exchange value of money would be displaced by the currency of generosity, ingenuity and collaborative, social action. Art students, local citizens and drop-in participants engaged in instruction-guided tasks, the first of which was to take no more than ten minutes to find something to sit on within the shop. Each task led to additional provocations and co-constructed proposals to which participants responded in diverse ways, both inside and beyond the shop. These responses manifested as dialogical circles, small acts of conservation, presentations by spontaneous guests and storytellers, and the co-creation of projections featuring dancing statistics moving in response to numerical measurements of unemployment in Geelong. Poetry readings and suddenly unfolding performances also spilled out into the streets. Works, and emerging stories and projects, were documented and co-curated for dissemination in a public gallery. In seeking to reclaim the public sphere as a generative "site" for connection around issues of public concern, social action can work to produce new knowledge of place, time, space and matter and can provide opportunities for public pedagogy to materialize.

We have learned that in community arts, funding organizers want to see that particular aspects of the community have been engaged in some way. At times, we have also found ourselves inevitably complicit in working to generate outcomes desired by funding bodies. As we seek to engage community authentically, we have found that projects are more successful when participants are involved in collaborating and co-creating with others throughout the creative process. Documenting and acknowledging the unique and durational value of community labour, contribution and social engagement have emerged as an essential ethical consideration for our work. This approach generates social, creative and educational opportunities for community participants that extend beyond passive spectatorship. Therefore, we assert the essential value of capturing processes of co-creation, knowledge sharing and collaboration as legitimate ways of responding critically and creatively to space, time and place. Storying the process should be more widely recognized and valued by funding bodies as legitimate quality art practice. Likewise, recording and documenting learning processes in public arts pedagogy should also be recognized in art assessment at schools and universities.

## ACKNOWLEDGEMENTS

We acknowledge the Wadawurrung people of the Kulin nations, the Traditional Owners and Custodians of the land on which we live and practise. We pay our respects to the local people and elders past, present and emerging as much of our work has taken place in Wadawurrung country.

## REFERENCES

Bartier, J., Gardiner, M., Hannigan, S., & Mathison, S. (2020). Embodiment of values. *IDEA Journal, Co-Constructing Body Environments, 17*(2), 180–200. https://doi.org/10.37113/ij.v17i02.389

Bassot, B. (2015). *The reflective practice guide, an interdisciplinary approach to critical reflection*. Routledge.

Bishop, C. (2005). The social turn: Collaboration and its discontents. *Artforum, 44*(6), 178–182. https://www.artforum.com/print/200602/the-social-turn-collaboration-and-its-discontents-10274

City of Greater Geelong. (2019, March 20). *Knowing your place neighbourhood walks*. https://geelongaustralia.com.au/walks/documents/item/8d24fc3b6b65e62.aspx

Hannigan, S. (2012). Turning community stories into community art. *International Journal of Education for the Arts, 8*(2), 135–150. https://doi.org/10.1386/eta.8.2.135_1

Hannigan, S. (2018). A theoretical and practice-informed reflection on the value of failure in art. *Thinking Skills and Creativity, 30*, 171–179. https://doi.org/10.1016/j.tsc.2018.02.012

Hannigan, S. (2019). From the parlour to the forum: How dress-art unsettles place and space. In S. Pinto, S. Hannigan, B. Walker-Gibbs, & E. Charlton (Eds.), *Interdisciplinary unsettlings of place and space* (pp. 45–66). Springer.

Hannigan S., Kilderry A., & Xu L. (2018). Patterning in childhoodnature. In A. Cutter-Mackenzie, L. Malone, & E. Barratt Hacking (Eds.), *Research handbook on childhoodnature* (pp. 1–23). Springer. https://doi.org/10.1007/978-3-319-51949-4_92-1

Hannigan, S., Wickman, P.-O., Ferguson, J. P., Prain, V., & Tytler, R. (2022). The role of aesthetics in learning science in an art-science lesson. *Special Issue: Aesthetics, affect, and making meaning in science education: International Journal of Science Education, 22*(5), 797–814. https://doi.org/10.1080/09500693.2021.1909773

Mountain to Mouth, City of Greater Geelong (2009, June 3). *Story Vessel Artists.* https://www.mountaintomouth.com.au/artistsalumni/tag/Story+Vessel+Artist

Mountain to Mouth, City of Greater Geelong. (2020, February 20). *Mountain to mouth.* https://www.mountaintomouth.com.au/

McGill, B. (2016). Public pedagogy at the Geelong powerhouse: Intercultural understandings through street art within the contact zone. *Journal of Public Pedagogies, 1*, 18–28. http://www.publicpedagogies.org/wp-content/uploads/2016/11MacGillB.pdf

McKee, Y. (2016). *Strike art: contemporary art and the post-occupy condition.* Verso.

Platform Arts and Deakin University. (2020, March 13). *Energetical.* https://platformarts.org.au/events/energetical-symposium

Sandelowski. M., & Barroso, J. (2002). Finding the findings in qualitative studies. *Journal of Nursing Scholarship, 34*(3), 213–220. https://pubmed.ncbi.nlm.nih.gov/12237982/

Sandlin, J. A., O'Malley, M. P., & Burdick, J. (2011). Mapping the complexity of public pedagogy scholarship. *Review of Educational Research 81*(3), 338–375. https://doi.org/10.3102%2F0034654311413395

Schön, D. A. (1983). *The reflective practitioner: How professionals think in action.* Basic Books.

Thompson, N. (2012). *Living as form: Socially engaged art from 1991–2011.* Creative Time Books.

# PART 4

## TRANSVERSAL RELATIONS

# 21

## Colors of Connection:
## Public Art Making as an Activating
## Force for Community Art Education

*Lynn Sanders-Bustle, Christina Mallie and Laurie Reyman*

Located in the commercial district of Mapendo in Goma in the Democratic Republic of the Congo (DRC) is the public art mural titled *The Female Artist* (see Figure 21.1). A vibrant provocation of Colors of Connection's (CC) Tunaweza Portraits, the mural is just one of several public artworks promoting positive

FIGURE 21.1: Participants creating the mural, *The Female Artist*, in the commercial district of Mapendo in Colors of Connection's Tunaweza Portraits Project, Goma, DRC 2019. Photo by Bernadette Vivuya.

roles for women and girls in a community that has seen its share of violence and upheaval (https://colorsofconnection.org/tunaweza-portraits/). As with most public artworks, it is difficult to tell the vast array of energies and interactions that went into the making of a mural by looking at the finished product. Nor is it possible to fully grasp the ever-changing relational constellation that sustains the power of the work long after the final stroke of paint is added. In other words, sometimes art hangs in the air, not on the wall.

In essence, the significance of the work lives in relationships (re)formed through community-based art making in response to a community need: in this case, the need for healing, joy and self-actualization. This outcome is best described by Esther, one of the painters of the 2019 mural, who explained, "I feel as if there is something new that has been born in me because now when I go out to the streets, everyone looks at me. People are surprised to see a woman painter." Since 2011, CC founders Christina Mallie, a visual artist, and Laurie Reyman, a social worker, have facilitated eight public art projects in sub-Saharan Africa, reaching an estimated 200,000 community members. A non-profit arts organization, CC works with youth and communities who have directly or indirectly experienced war and related issues of poverty, displacement, marginalization and trauma. In this chapter, Mallie, Reyman and Sanders-Bustle (a university art educator, CC advisor and former board member) describe how relational qualities associated with social practice inform CC methods, provide an overview of strategies and programming, reflect on the 2019 Tunaweza Portraits Project in the DRC and discuss implications for community art education.

While the community art projects shared in this chapter are specific to sub-Saharan communities, the guiding principles discussed are broad and fluid enough to support work in communities across the globe. As a kind of social practice, we suggest that community art education efforts focused on participation and dialogue are central to developing equitable, accessible and inclusive practices meant to effect social change. We assert that such efforts have the potential to effectuate holistic healing (Huss et al., 2012; Lander & Graham-Pole, 2008; MacNaughton et al., 2005), expression and communication (Johnson, 1990; Weber, 2008; Wheeler, 2012), personal and community agency (Fliegel, 2000), relationship-building (Guetzkow, 2002, p. 3) and deeper thought and reflexivity (Barndt, 2008). Finally, community art education activities support the central premise of critical pedagogy that people can become "transforming agents of their social reality" by developing a critical consciousness of their context (Freire, 1983).

Furthermore, we believe practices that are responsive to community histories, cultures and needs foster relational and emergent qualities of art making that strengthen communities and lead to social change. In contrast to art created solely with a product or object in mind, social practice foregrounds the relational qualities of making as well as social, political and cultural contexts. Like Thompson (2012), who describes the social practice as a living form, we honour the fluid and emergent qualities of community-based art that are only made possible in concert with others.

Transpedagogical (Helguera, 2011), CC capitalizes on a blend of art making, therapeutic and educational processes that take place outside of conventional art academies and are centred around community needs, member assets and qualities of everyday life. While acquiring art-making skills is one aim, skills are not an end in themselves but instead part of a collective vision for public art that supports democratization, relationship-building and collaboration. Consequently, practices emerge from community needs which are transdisciplinary in nature and benefit from "re-conceptualizing particular problems or conditions through artistic practices" (Springgay, 2013, p. 17). With this in mind, social practice strategies activate the unique capabilities and skills that participants bring to a project while imparting new skill sets that increase participants' effectiveness as agents of change in their communities.

At the same time, we recognize that power exercised through discourses (Foucault, 1969) as part of the emergent and complex nature of social practice requires ongoing scrutiny and reflection: especially as practice relates to issues of indigeneity (Bishop, 2014; Kovach, 2014; Smith, 2012), ethics (Bishop, 2006, 2012), quality (Doherty, 2015) and sustainability, which are central to project impact.

## *CC's Guiding Principles of Practice*

CC addresses two primary gaps experienced by conflict-affected individuals and communities: lack of psychosocial support and agency for people who have been denied these rights through violent conflict and systemic marginalization, and post-conflict settings in which many international aid and development organizations perpetuate neo-colonialist systems based on racism and inequalities. Cutting across disciplines including social work, peacebuilding, mental health, gender equality and education, CC strives to fill these gaps by investing directly in arts-based programming that utilizes a collaborative bottom-up approach to promote healing, self-determination, equality and community building.

Based in the Global North and working with communities in the Global South, CC programming seeks to be participatory on all levels to effect positive social change, prevent perpetuating harmful power dynamics and produce culturally relevant, effective and sustainable practices. These values are nurtured through three guiding principles of practice:

- *Engaging community stakeholders in all facets of implementation:* Representing the diversity and interests of the community, community stakeholders form a committee to guide and advise the programme. CC and community stakeholders discuss relevant community issues through dialogue that identifies and expresses new ideas and solutions, which are embodied in creating murals widening the impact of the programme (Colors of Connection, 2017; Lachapelle, 2008). Community members take on assistant and lead roles as facilitators, teaching artists, documentarians and community liaisons tailoring the project, so it is culturally appropriate, enhances participation, and supports skills and knowledge transfer and builds sustained relationships – even when CC foreign-based staff leave (Colors of Connection, 2017). As one community stakeholder explained,

    These murals and messages, they help make sure that girls are listened to when they don't have sufficient voice within society. They make people think twice about what they think they know about girls and what they are capable of doing.

- *Engaging marginalized youth:* With the help of community stakeholders as well as community-mapping tools such as the Girl Roster ™ ( Population Council, 2021), CC learns about existing inequalities and social hierarchies within a community and engages youth who are most excluded from social benefits and protections by using strategies such as situated learning, dialogic discourse, problem-posing and activist learning, as well as involving them in curriculum development (Colors of Connection, 2017; Schlemmer, 2017; Shor, 1992).
- *Providing a range of creative activities:* Activities are designed to nurture holistic healing, expression and communication, personal and community agency, relationship-building, reflexivity and critical social analysis (Adolescent Girl & Creativity Network, 2020; African Centre for Peace and Security Training, 2013; First Aid Arts, 2015; Malchiodi, 2015).

While CC has worked hard to implement these guiding principles, we also recognize that this kind of work is fraught with complexities. With that in mind, the following section describes the Tunaweza Portraits Project as one example of CC's projects and as a point of reflection.

## *The Tunaweza Portraits Project*

Understanding the context of the eastern region of the DRC is essential to understanding the Tunaweza Portraits Project. The region has been affected by war for decades, aggravating traditional socio-cultural norms and beliefs around gender roles, and normalizing and exacerbating sexual and gender-based violence (SGBV) in everyday life (Babaola et al., 2011). As a result, girls are among those most excluded from societal benefits and protections, and many have experienced SGBV (Population Council & UNFPA, 2009). Goma, the city where CC's DRC-based programming takes place, is home to thousands who have been displaced from the endemic conflict.

Equally relevant to our work in Goma is the sustained presence of humanitarian aid and development organizations, at one point the highest concentration in the world (Büscher & Vlassenroot, 2013). Through observation, community dialogue and research, we found that agencies working on the issue of sexual violence in the region tended to focus most of their resources on response as opposed to prevention (Douma & Hilhorst, 2012; IGWG, 2006). In their limited efforts to educate the community around prevention, agencies often presented negative and violent images and stories to convey what should *not* happen. In these representations, survivors, almost always women and girls, are depicted as powerless and without agency to address their own issues. We observed that although women, girls and community members had the abilities to address this issue, they were not engaged by agencies to lead a process of change.

Despite the devastating impact of conflict on the population and the exclusion of those most intimately affected by efforts to address these issues, communities in Goma and the eastern region continuously voice their perspectives, confront problems and even seek to change international public opinion about the "victim" status of their community and country. As an example, in sharp contrast to media images of suffering and sensational violence often shared about the city and region, Kivu Youth Entertainment's video remake of Pharell William's song *Happy* was created as a homage to their city and recognition of its assets such as strength, vitality and creativity (see Batumike, 2014).

The Tunaweza Portraits Project took place in 2019. The overall goal of the project was to shift social norms related to perceptions of girls and their role in society, thus positively impacting individual girls and the community as a whole (36 young women and girls, 130,000 citizens in four communities in Goma over four months). Over the course of the project, community stakeholders and young women and girls formulated positive representations of girls and women through collaboratively created public murals and posters that challenged gender stereotypes contributing to SGBV in these communities. In sum, four murals and 28 posters, conceived by community leaders and designed and painted by the young women and girls themselves, promote different positive roles for women and girls in society. In line with the Tunaweza Portraits' central goal to challenge gender stereotypes, the mural *The Female Artist* (see Figure 21.1) portrays a female artist alongside words in Kiswahili – *Kubali ujuzi wangu* – meaning *consider my talents*. One of several murals created, the centre portrait is based on a photograph of Alice, one of the artists who painted the mural, which is significant because female painters and visual artists are few and far between in Eastern Congo. Other works, as seen on the CC website, include *Women Belong in All Levels of the Justice System*, which portrays a female judge; and *Women Are the Pillars of Education in Society*, which depicts women as creators, nurturers and educators. The impact of this work on the lives of the women who participated is varied, but feelings of belonging, confidence and respect are captured by Rosalie: "There are girls who are underestimated because people haven't seen yet what they are capable of. When someone sees you working on a painting [...] they respect you."

## *Negotiating Power Dynamics Within Community Art*

Regardless of efforts to create spaces for safe expression, facilitate dialogue and enact social change, power hierarchies still exist within community-based art practices. In CC's work, power dynamics are internal, based on existing socio-economic and cultural structural hierarchies within a community, and external due to the positionality of an organization coming from the Global North: offering services and strategies for development to Indigenous spaces in the Global South.

### External Power Dynamics

Goma and the DRC have an extensive history of external power dynamics between Congolese and states, agencies and individual actors from the Global North. This history is rooted in the brutal regime of King Leopold II and Belgian colonial rule; in the present day, the presence of the Global North is sustained by inter- and intra-national actors, including the United Nations, aid agencies, corporations and foreign governments. Without finding ways to balance power dynamics, meaningful participation and collaboration are not possible. Furthermore, CC brings "foreign" or "unknown" skill sets and materials into the community, mirroring the problematic power dynamics of the colonial legacy. For example, painting murals in and of itself is not a familiar form of artistic expression in the Congo. One way CC addresses this is by including activities that utilize Indigenous materials and draw on Indigenous knowledge while allowing for new forms of expression to emerge. For example, in "The Wrapper Activity" participants engage with a piece of cloth (known as wrapper, *lappa*, *pagne* or *kikwembe*) used widely in many cultural and practical ways in Congolese society (and in other contexts across Africa). CC learned this activity from a Kenyan performance scholar, Mshai

Mwangola. In what has proven to be a powerful and rich activity, each participant is invited into the centre of a circle to present something they can do with the wrapper. The only rule is that everyone must present something different, as seen in this video: https://www.youtube.com/watch?v=rOuEUoXL2u0.

Since integrating the wrapper activity into our practice, we noticed that the activity enabled expressive capabilities more so than activities in which the women were unfamiliar with materials (such as block printing). The young women and girls seemed more willing to share their perspectives and experiences freely as spontaneous collaborative storytelling, an interesting and unexpected outcome, emerged without prior intention. Referencing an artistic project in tribal lands in the United States, Kothe (2017) highlights the value of paying attention to particular places and the many stories they contain as part of facilitating the decolonization process and reciprocal pedagogy. In this performance, the women crafted a spontaneous and collaborative performance/story through dance and song that they wanted to tell, as opposed to one already told. In this case, we saw the potential for a safe and generative space through improvisation and spontaneity: supporting a claim by a psychiatrist, educator and founder of psychodrama that "spontaneity is the opposite of anxiety" (Moreno, 1951, p. 235). And last, we noticed the young women and girls seemed to feel confident about what they created and validated in their knowledge-sharing: supporting what Trainor and Bouchard (2013) refer to as institutional legitimization, whereby "participants' knowledge becomes legitimate, valuable, and artistic, and therefore accepted as an official part of program, curriculum, or discipline" (p. 989).

## Internal Power Dynamics

Kester (2011) proposes that socially engaged art projects, which often involve artists as well as NGOs, activists and urban planners, offer new imaginaries for community agency and opportunities for reciprocal creative labour. Of significance, he points out that an important role of collaborative art is not romanticizing Indigenous culture. While an understanding of and respect for Indigenous cultures and traditions is a critical component of Indigenization and ethical practice, from a human rights perspective it is important to also acknowledge the biases and limitations of cultures and traditions and – when appropriate – to challenge these biases through collaborative work. We recognize there is a history of Western liberal thought that casts cultures in the Global South as less enlightened or progressive in human rights. Our intention is to apply a critical lens to culture without assuming that Indigenous cultures will be "less" advanced in human rights than cultures in the Global North (Carby, 1982).

Within the communities we work, CC aims to mitigate unequal power dynamics due to socio-economic and cultural hierarchies, to ensure all voices are being represented. For example, The Tunaweza Portraits Project endeavoured to mitigate unequal power dynamics within Congolese society by working only with girls and young women. Boys are predominantly chosen first by their families to participate in opportunities for education and skill-building, while girls have fewer opportunities to engage in such activities, entrenching gender inequalities in their community and having a detrimental impact on the lives of the girls. In addition, it is more challenging to create spaces within mixed-gender groups where girls feel safe to express themselves, connect with others and relate experiences of gender discrimination. CC also decided to work with only young women as project assistants so that the female-only space would be maintained. In this example, CC sought to challenge, instead of contributing to, harmful power structures that perpetuate gender discrimination.

## Conclusion

In this chapter, we described the possibilities and limitations of implementing a community-based art practice based on participatory and critical methods. While we see much potential for these methods, we recognize that community-based art education projects and the communities in which they live are fluid and emergent; therefore, projects require ongoing reflexivity and a willingness to change course if sustainability, ethical practice and inclusive participation are to be achieved. For example, CC continues to be challenged by how best to mitigate the power dynamics created by our presence as a foreign, Global North-based entity and to avoid participating in neo-colonialist practices that perpetuate racism and inequality. Within this context, how best to work with a community that is always in the making to challenge cultural discriminatory practices, particularly related to gender, becomes even more complicated. To do so relies on a willingness to attend to the unknowns and to recognize what Kwon (1997) refers to as "the productive possibility of uncertainty" (p. 168) when supporting those who are perceived to share experiences such as displacement, trauma and sexual violence. This includes paying attention and reacting to unforeseen methods and strategies revealed by those who are in the best position to name them and letting go of research methodologies which, unlike social practice which attends to the ambiguous and fluid nature of a relational aesthetic (Bourriaud, 1998; Thompson, 2012), can fall short of honouring the ways that the unknown can drive yet-to-be-known actions.

In sum, for community arts-based practices to thrive in a world that continues to pose life-altering challenges for so many, we believe it will take increased involvement in participatory practices and research methodologies that are transversal in nature: that is, practices untethered to disciplinary or social structures that limit possibilities for knowing, being and making. Furthermore, attending to the nebulous qualities of community-based art practice reminds us that "what we think we know and who we think that we are is never straightforward" (Loveless, 2019, p. 41). With this in mind, we suggest a greater willingness to welcome fresh moments of possibility as artists, educators, researchers and community members who can collectively and more effectively attend to the most pressing and complicated challenges of our time.

## REFERENCES

Adolescent Girl & Creativity Network. (2020). Part One: Creative assets. In C. Mallie & S. Soares (Eds.), *Creative assets and program content guide: To build social and emotional learning and promote trauma mitigation and healing* (pp. 8–16). Population Council. https://knowledgecommons.popcouncil.org/departments_sbsr-pgy/1073/

African Centre for Peace and Security Training. (2013, July 8–13). *The artist as peacebuilder: Course from 8–19 July 2013.* https://issafrica.org/amp/events/acpst-course-the-artist-as-peacebuilder

Babalola, S., Neetu, J. A., & Cernigliaro, D. (2011). *Community perspectives on sexual and gender-based violence in Eastern DRC.* Center for Communication Programs.

Barndt, D. (2008). Touching minds and hearts: Community arts as collaborative research. In G. J. Knowles & A. L. Cole (Eds.), *Handbook of the art in qualitative research* (pp. 351–362). Sage Publications.

Batumike, K. (2014, June 7). *Pharrell Williams – Happy we are from Goma DR Congo* [Video]. YouTube. https://www.youtube.com/watch?v=fq1uN2jbPIg

Bishop, C. (2006). The social turn: Collaboration and its discontents. *Art Forum International, 44*(6), 178–183.

Bishop, C. (2012). *Artificial hells: Participatory art and politics of spectatorship.* Verso Books.

Bishop, R. (2014). Freeing ourselves: An Indigenous response to neo-colonial dominance in research, classrooms, schools, and education systems. In N. K. Denzin & M. D. Giardina (Eds.), *Qualitative inquiry outside the academy* (pp. 146–163). Left Coast Press.

Bourriaud, N. (1998). *Relational aesthetics.* Le press du reel.

Büscher, K., & Vlassenroot, K. (2013). *The humanitarian industry and urban change in Goma.* Open Democracy. https://www.opendemocracy.net/en/opensecurity/humanitarian-industry-and-urban-change-in-goma/

Carby, H. V. (1982). White women listen! Black feminism and the boundaries of sisterhood. In L. Back & J. Solomos (Eds.), *Theories of race and racism: A reader* (pp. 110–128). Routledge.

Colors of Connection. (n.d.). *The Colors of Connection mission statement.* https://www.colorsofconnection.org/what-we-believe/

Colors of Connection. (2017). *Creating a community mural: A powerful toolkit about mural making that can be used to transform public spaces, communities and youth.* https://colorsofconnection.org/creating-a-community-mural-toolkit/

Doherty, C. (Ed.). (2015). *Out of time, out of public place: Public art now.* Art Books Publishing.

Douma, N., & Hilhorst, D. (2012). *Fond de commerce? Sexual violence assistance in the Democratic Republic of Congo (Occasional paper 02). Disaster studies* (pp. 3–44). Wageningen University.

First Aid Arts. (2015). *Healing arts toolkit curriculum* (ISSUU version). ISSUU. https://www.firstaidarts.org/

Fliegel, L. S. (2000). An unfound door: Reconceptualizing art therapy. *American Journal of Art Therapy, 38*(3), 81–9.

Foucault, M. (1969). *Archaeology of knowledge and the discourse on language* (S. Smith, Trans.). Tavistock. (Original work published 1972)

Freire, P. (1983). *Education for critical consciousness.* The Continuum Publishing Company.

Guetzkow, J. (2002). How the arts impact communities: An introduction to the literature on arts impact studies. *Working paper series, Princeton University Center for Arts and Cultural Policy Studies* (Vol. 20). Princeton University.

Helguera, P. (2011). *Education for socially engaged art: A materials and technique handbook.* Jorge Pinto Books.

Huss, E., Elhozayel E., & Marcus, E. (2012). Art in group work as an anchor for integrating the micro and macro levels of intervention with incest survivors. *Clinical Social Work Journal, 40,* 401–411. https://doi.org/10.1007/s10615-012-0393-2

IGWG of USAID. (2006). *Addressing gender-based violence through USAID's health programs: A guide for health sector program officers* (2nd ed.). Interagency Gender Working Group. http://www.prb.org/pdf04/AddressGendrBasedViolence.pdf

Johnson, D. R. (1990). Introduction to the special issue on the creative arts therapies with adolescents. *The Arts in Psychotherapy, 17,* 97.

Kester, G. H. (2011). *The one and the many: Contemporary collaborative art in the global context.* Duke University Press.

Kothe, E. L. (2017). Considering reciprocal pedagogy in the borderlands. In C. B. Morris & K. Staikidis (Eds.), *Transforming our practices: Indigenous art, pedagogies, and philosophies* (pp. 84–91). National Art Education Association.

Kovach, M. (2014). Thinking through theory: Contemplating Indigenous situated research and policy. In N. K. Denzin & M. D. Giardina (Eds.), *Qualitative inquiry outside the academy* (pp. 92–106). Left Coast Press.

Kwon, M. (1997). *One place after another: Notes on site specificity.* The MIT Press.

Lander, D. A., & Graham-Pole, J. R. (2008). *Art as a determinant of health.* National Collaborating Centre, Determinants of Health.

Lachapelle, P. (2008). A sense of ownership in community development: Understanding the potential for participation in community planning efforts. *Community Development, 39*(2), 52–59.

Loveless, N. (2019). *How to make art at the end of the world*. Duke University Press.

MacNaughton, J., White, M., & Stacy, R. (2005). Researching the benefits of arts in health. *Health Education, 105*(5), 332–339.

Malchiodi, C. A. (Ed.). (2015). *Creative interventions with traumatized children* (2nd ed.). The Guilford Press.

Moreno, J. L. (1951). *Who shall survive? Sociometry, experimental method and the science of society*. Beacon House.

Population Council. (2021). *The Girl Roster™: A practical tool for strengthening girl centered programming*. https://www.popcouncil.org/research/girl-roster

Population Council & UNFPA. (2009). Democratic Republic of Congo 2007. *The Adolescent experience in-depth: Using data to identify and reach the most vulnerable young people*. https://www.popcouncil.org/uploads/pdfs/PGY_AdolDataGuides/CongoDemRep2007.pdf

Schlemmer, R. H. (2017). Socially engaged art education: Defining and defending the practice. In L. N. Hersey & B. Bobick (Eds.), *Handbook of research on the facilitation of civic engagement through community art* (pp. 1–20). IGI Global.

Shor, I. (1992). *Empowering education: Critical teaching for social change*. University of Chicago Press.

Smith, L. T. (2012). *Decolonizing methodologies: Research and Indigenous peoples* (2nd ed.). Zed Books.

Springgay, S. (2013, Autumn). The pedagogical impulse: Aberrant residencies and classroom ecologies. *C Magazine for Art and Culture, 119*, 17–23.

Thompson, N. (2012). Living as form. In N. Thompson (Ed.), *Living as form: Socially engaged art from 1991–2011* (pp. 16–24). Creative Time Books.

Trainor A., & Bouchard, K. A. (2013). Exploring and developing reciprocity in research design. *International Journal of Qualitative Studies in Education, 26*(8), 986–1003. https://doi.org/10.1080/09518398.2012.724467

Weber, S. (2008). Visual images in research. In G. J. Knowles & A. L. Cole (Eds.), *Handbook of the arts in qualitative research* (pp. 41–54). Sage.

Wheeler, J. (2012). Using participatory video to engage in policy processes: Representation, power, and knowledge in public screenings. In E. J. Milne, C. Mitchell, & N. De Lange (Eds.), *Handbook of participatory video* (pp. 350–382). AltaMira Press.

# 22

# Residing in Pedagogical Spaces Through Community Cultural Production

*Jing Li*

As a recognized field of practice, the potential of community arts in connecting the philosophies of art and education with "the lives and stories of the community" (Schlemmer, 2017, p. 28) and generating new ways of community engagement and participation has drawn increased attention in recent years. Specifically, Cleveland (2002) summarizes the generative force of community arts in four aspects – that is, "to educate and inform us about ourselves and the world; to inspire and mobilize individuals and groups; to nurture and heal people and/or communities; to build and improve community capacity" (p. 17, as cited in Barndt, 2011). In the realms of arts and education, studies have shown that community cultural and art resources have been and can be mobilized as effective pedagogical tools to facilitate the production of knowledge, political participation and social change (Clennon et al., 2015; Li, 2020; Schlemmer, 2017). In Canadian contexts, for example, scholars have explored the use of community art and cultural production to engage disadvantaged individuals and groups in intercultural learning (Li & Moore, 2020) and intergenerational Indigenous learning (Hanson, 2018; Hanson & Griffith, 2016), as well as community development and civic participation (Barndt, 2011; Li, 2020).

In this chapter, I present findings from a selection of data from a four-year ethnographic study on how residents and artists in a community festival setting generated intercultural collaboration and civic education through multi-modal art and cultural production in the Downtown Eastside (DTES) neighbourhood in Vancouver, Canada. Drawing upon the perspectives of cultural production as political participation (Gaztambide-Fernández & Matute, 2015) and connected civic learning (Ito et al., 2013, 2015), I present an example of a cultural event called *Terrain of Thought*, featured at the yearly Downtown Eastside Heart of the City Festival, to illustrate how cultural production practices and processes created pedagogical possibilities for connecting community art with civic engagement, critical meaning-making and personal transformation. I aim to show that social actors' engagement with socially and community-engaged cultural production contributes to the construction of a shared civic interest-driven community. The festival event discussed here also spotlights community cultural production as a space for intercultural education and community building.

The term "community" used throughout the chapter has multiple connotations. In this study, community refers not only to a shared sense of place in a given geographical region, as in the case of the DTES community, but also refers to the ephemeral communities emergent "in the ongoing present, forming relations and connections" (Leander & Boldt, 2012, p. 22) at various phases of cultural production for the *Terrain of Thought* project. As is shown below, these communities – real or imagined – are seen during the forming of shared practices and experiences of community artists and festival participants collaboratively engaging with participatory art making, contributing meanings to socially engaged cultural production and navigating the relationships among art, community, reconciliation and (de)colonization. In a literal and symbolic manner, these communities reflect the notion of community that this chapter attempts to explore and unravel: community that is in the making.

## *Cultural Production, Political Participation and Civic Pedagogy*

Following Albers and Harste (2007) and Gaztambide-Fernández (2013), cultural production here refers to cultural and artistic practices, processes and products that involve "the creation and organization of the representation, the actual product or text (song, artwork, dance, play, photograph, webpage, and so on), as well as the technical skills ... used when working with media in creating the text" (Albers & Harste, 2007, p. 14). Following Kuttner (2015), I see the art as "a sub-set of cultural production" (p. 71) – that is, a social process of meaning-making in relation to a cultural product. Gaztambide-Fernández and Matute (2015) argue that cultural production should be seen as "forms of political participation in their own right" (p. 2) in that it plays an important role in the construction of individuals' political identities when they "express, create, and recreate ideas, feelings, and various aspects of cultural life" (p. 3). This socially and politically oriented view sees cultural production as an essential means that social actors use to take concerted action to "reinforce and challenge existing social systems" (Kuttner, 2015, p. 70).

In addition to its participatory nature, cultural production also holds pedagogical potential. Gaztambide-Fernández (2013) maintains that culture can be mobilized in the process of (re)making available materials through cultural production and exchanges to create spaces for teaching and learning. In this chapter, I specifically draw upon the conception of "connected civic learning" put forward by Ito et al. (2012, 2015), which proposes that common interests and purposes, shared social and cultural relationships, shared contexts and shared civic practices can facilitate "deep and consequential forms of civic and political involvement" (p. 16). Though initially used to study youth and online learning environments, the connected approach to civic learning, rooted in progressive education and research on informal learning, is particularly relevant to the case described below. As will be shown, participating residents and artists collectively engaged in socially engaged cultural and art practices and processes to influence and (re)shape the social structures they resided in, which in turn generated connected learning and new modes of meaning-making and place-making.

## *The Terrain of Thought Project*

### The Context

Vancouver's Downtown Eastside (DTES) neighbourhood, often described as the "historic heart of the city," is one of the city's oldest neighbourhoods around which Vancouver has grown and developed. Although the DTES is characterized by considerable cultural and ethnic diversity and thriving community arts, it has a long history of being on the socio-economic margins of the city. Inadequate social housing, homelessness, drug addictions, poverty and a lack of services for people suffering mental illness, together with continued experiences of colonialism, have led to social and spatial conflicts as well as a culture of community activism.

The *Terrain of Thought Workshop & Interactive Exhibit* was featured at the yearly Downtown Eastside Heart of the City Festival in 2015. The two-week festival has taken place in the DTES every year since 2004 during the last week of October and the first week of November. Using a multiplicity of communication modes and media – including dance, music, visual arts, theatre, art/history walks and talks, gallery exhibits, and other cultural and art activities – this community event brings together community residents, local artists and arts organizations to celebrate the history, culture, stories and people of the DTES.

The *Terrain of Thought* project was created and presented at the Heart of the City Festival in the fall of 2015. This intercultural production was inspired by, and the legacy of, a west-to-east coast arts journey called *Train of Thought*, which had taken place in spring 2015. The main purpose of that tour, as described in the Heart of the City Festival program guide, was to seek "reconciliation and collaboration through participatory art-making between First Nations and settler-immigrant artists and communities" (Vancouver Moving Theatre, 2015, p. 16). Ontario-based Jumblies Theatre took the lead, with Vancouver Moving Theatre – a DTES-based arts organization – among the main collaborative partners. Over 75 Indigenous and non-Indigenous artists embarked on the cross-country train journey from Vancouver to Prince Edward Island between 12 May and 10 June 2015. The artists visited over 25 Canadian cities, towns and First Nations communities along the way. At each stop, local arts organizations hosted interactive events including ceremonies of arrival and departure, presentations, panels and site visits to local community arts venues, sharing knowledge and community arts practices.

To carry on the legacy of this community art initiative, some participating artists returned to the DTES and collaborated with community members and festival visitors to create the *Terrain of Thought* exhibition. To mount the exhibition, community artists first worked with DTES residents and festival visitors to build a mini-landscape for the community centre gallery during a series of four-day, drop-in workshops (30 October–2 November). The exhibition was intended to reflect a real and imaginative terrain "woven from thoughts on how we can live together on shared territory" (Vancouver Moving Theatre, 2015, p. 16). Then an open discussion was held on 2 November to celebrate the exhibition and invite public conversation, where participating artists shared their stories, images and video about the *Train of Thought* journey. The mini-landscape was displayed in three window cases in the community centre gallery throughout the month.

## The Intercultural Exhibition and Open Discussion

After four days of participatory art making, the mini-landscape exhibition was completed and displayed in the three window cases in the community centre gallery. Each of the three cabinets featured a theme – *Where We Started*, *Where We Went*, and *Where We Are Now*. For the theme *Where We Started*, a display window was adorned with paper-made lands, waters, roads and houses. A road extended from west to east, with the houses representing the community feasts held at each host venue during the train tour. The biggest house represented the departure point of the journey: The Big House community gathering and cultural feast (8–10 May 2015) at the Ukrainian Hall in Vancouver's DTES, honouring the pedagogical and governance traditions of the Coast Salish and urban Indigenous peoples. The four seasons of the year scripted in conspicuous Chinese characters on the landscape enriched the exhibit with intercultural elements. The use of four seasons signified the community cultural practices nested in Indigenous meanings and natural cycles.

In another display window, speech bubbles scattered across the landscape showed the travelling artists' reflections on the train journey. Here are some examples:

> *Engage in community arts to get connected.*
> *The reclaiming my dignity as an Aboriginal has been the hardest journey of my life.*
> *This opportunity opened me up to the visions of others, and relationships we need to nurture and the need to re-write our imperfect history.*
> *The people we've met, stories we've been told, where they've been from, how they've been passed on. ...*

These personal thoughts articulated by travelling artists were effective conversations about reconciliation, collaboration and socially engaged art practices, provoking exhibition viewers to think and empathize. It can be inferred that travellers engaged themselves in exploring what the journey meant to them, at the same time, navigating responsibilities and relationships emerging out of the journey.

An open discussion evening was held to celebrate the mounting of the exhibition and showcase community artists' attempt of incorporating traditional protocols in community artwork and intercultural settings. The discussion, which included community artists and residents from the DTES, centred on engaging with collective practices, advancing a civic and political agenda and creating profound impacts in a sustainable way. Participating audiences asked: How do we carry on the legacy of this community art project? How can community art be used to build cross-cultural connections? What would a future look like that takes into account community history, the country's history of colonization and social justice?

One artist shared her understanding of participating in the journey and exhibition production: "It was very clear that we were using arts practices to build community between, through, and among us." To continue the legacy created through these practices, she argued about the importance of "taking the opportunity and making the opportunity to have a conversation and allow that thinking to get to a physical space and creative things." As well, she emphasized, "The more you will do, the more help you will get. And the more people will have these conversations and it will create a ripple effect."

Furthermore, participants in the discussion exchanged opinions and explored how to live together on shared territory in the here-and-now narrative of decolonization and reconciliation, with a projection into a common future they desired and needed. The process re-contextualized the narratives of (de)colonization and (re)conciliation in ways that drew out civic dimensions. One example is from a participant who described the civic responsibility she would like to take on because of her involvement in this cultural production:

> I came to realize that my task was to witness the journey: to watch and listen and carry in my heart the work taking place around me. My responsibility is to carry the messages back to my home community, and to be prepared – for the rest of my life – to recall and share what I've heard and seen.
> (Walling, as cited in Walling et al., 2016, p. 20)

## *Evolving Communities and Connected Learning Through Cultural Production*

In the *Terrain of Thought* case, it seems clear that when a multitude of art organizations and individuals participated in the cross-country train journey and then mounted the festival exhibition, they were connected through shared art practices and civic interest, exploring reconciliation and connection-building between Indigenous and non-Indigenous communities/cultures. According to Fine (2012), a local group or community is in formation when "aggregations of persons" engage in "interpersonal collaboration, collective focus, ongoing interaction, and a shared history" (p. 21). The *Terrain of Thought* project brings out the very conception of the community that Fine (2012) has described. As joint art practices progressed across social-cultural contexts, these social actors built on "deeply felt interests, bonds, passions, and affinities" (Ito et al., 2015, p. 14), and invented a shared local community that was crucial in supporting "meaningful learning and development as products of participation in civic, political, and public life" (p. 12). As a result, what formed was not just a community – "an aggregation of persons," but also those "evolving transient communities – real or imagined – that took shape during the production of critical multiliteracies" (Li, 2020, p. 127). As described by one traveller artist, Sam Egan (2016),

> [the] artistic merit [of *Train of Thought*] might be thought of as the way the tour provided travellers with an experience that extended beyond professional development or a networking opportunity: that is, how the shared experiences of travel and exploration build an ephemeral community.
> (p. 23)

Such an "evolving transient community" took shape at different stages throughout the cultural production – whether it was travelling across the country, or doing culture sharing in communities, or collectively creating the festival mini-landscape exhibition or carrying out an open discussion. In the process, participants became connected with each other through relationships and experiences that were unlikely to be generated in the absence of such engagement.

Moreover, learning possibilities arose when participants engaged themselves in constant reflections, sense-making and confrontation of difficult issues and topics, as indicated in the speech bubbles. Those reflections revealed that, along the way, the participants navigated a series of emerging themes and relationships between themselves and others (local hosts/visitors, peer travellers, Indigenous/non-Indigenous artists and more); between themselves and the world; and between their multiple and shifting selves as a traveller/host/(non-)Indigenous artist/community member/citizen. As these social actors moved across boundaries of relationality while exploring these relations across time and space, they engaged in the process of inventing and reinventing available materials and symbolic resources for active meaning-making. In the midst of making sense of and conveying meanings through art, these social actors "move along a pathway towards learning connected civics" (Ito et al., 2015, p. 17).

## *Conclusion*

The social, political and educative power of community arts lies in its engagement in the community and its ability to respond to the community's burning issues and concerns in a participatory and responsive way. As Wherry (2011) puts it, "arts and culture provide nourishment for the community" (p. 70); in turn, the community cultivates artistic and cultural creativity. As the theme of this book, *transversalities*, implies, the creation of artful spaces helps create pedagogical possibilities in ways that provoke new understandings of community art practice and sustained social change and innovation. The *Terrain of Thought* project and annual Heart of the City Festival discussed in this chapter offer an example of this sort, wherein we see community cultural production act as a performative arena for civic engagement and change making, as well as a "situated and local site of learning where people are linked by a sense of belonging, meaning, identity and practice" (Hanson & Griffith, 2016, p. 227).

Though the community art and cultural production project discussed here takes place in a local Canadian context, this example contributes to our broader understanding of the role of community and community arts in nurturing "creative processes of knowledge production" and empowering people to "act collectively to challenge inequalities and to create more sustainable and just communities" (Barndt, 2011, p. 19). This project displays the intersecting, reciprocal relationships among community art practices, intercultural collaboration, civic engagement, public pedagogy and community building. In this sense, such an initiative provides insight into and inspiration for how we can re-envision and reimagine the value, function and impact of community and community arts practice in a broader, international context of community art education.

## REFERENCES

Albers, P., & Harste, J. (2007). The arts, new literacies, and multimodality. *English Education*, 40(1), 6–20.

Barndt, D. (Ed.). (2011). *VIVA! Community arts and popular education in the Americas*. SUNY Press.

Cleveland, W. (2002). Mapping the field: Arts-based community development. *Art in the Public Interest*. http://www.communityarts.net/readingroom/archive/intro-develop.php

Egan, S. (2016). What is a "community arts tour?" *Alt. Theatre*, 12(4), 21–24.

Fine, G. A. (2012). *Tiny publics: A theory of group action and culture*. Russell Sage Foundation.

Gaztambide-Fernández, R. A. (2013). Why the arts don't do anything: Toward a new vision for cultural production in education. *Harvard Education Review*, 83(1), 211–236.

Gaztambide-Fernández, R. A., & Matute, A. A. (2015). Creation as participation/participation as creation: Cultural production, participatory politics, and the intersecting lines of identification and activism. *Curriculum Inquiry*, 45(1), 1–9. https://doi.org/10.1080/03626784.2014.997535

Hanson, C. (2018). Stitching together an arts-based inquiry with Indigenous communities in Canada and Chile. *Canadian Journal of Studies for Adult Education*, 30(2), 11–22.

Hanson, G., & Griffith, H. F. (2016). Tanning, spinning, and gathering together: Intergenerational Indigenous learning in textile arts. *Engaging with Indigenous Communities*, 2(1), 225–243.

Ito, M., Guitiérrez, K., Livingstone, S., Penuel, B., Rhodes, J., Salen, K., Schor, J., Sefton-Green, J., & Watkins, C. S. (2012). *Connected learning: An agenda for research and design*. DML Research Hub. https://dmlhub.net/publications/connected-learning-agenda-for-research-and-design/index.html

Ito, M., Soep, E., Kligler-Vilenchik, N., Shresthova, S., Gamber-Thompson, L., & Zimmerman, A. (2015). Learning connected civics: Narratives, practices, infrastructures. *Curriculum Inquiry*, 45(1), 10–29. https://doi.org/10.1080/03626784.2014.995063

Kuttner, P. (2015). Educating for cultural citizenship: Reframing the goals of arts education. *Curriculum Inquiry*, 45(1), 69–92. https://doi.org/10.1080/03626784.2014.980940

Li, J. (2020). *Community in the making: Weaving places of learning, cultural production, and community building within a community festival space in Vancouver's Downtown Eastside* [Unpublished doctoral dissertation]. Simon Fraser University.

Li, J., & Moore, D. (2020). (Inter)cultural production as public pedagogy: Weaving art, interculturality and civic learning in a community festival context. *Language and Intercultural Communication*, 20(4), 375–387. https://doi.org/10.1080/14708477.2019.1674866

Li, J., Moore, D., & Smythe, S. (2018). Voices from the "Heart": Understanding a community-engaged festival in Vancouver's Downtown Eastside. *Journal of Contemporary Ethnography*, 47(4), 399–425. https://doi.org/10.1177/0891241617696808

Ornette, D. C., Kagan, C., Lawthom, R., & Swindells, R. (2016). Participation in community arts: Lessons from the inner-city. *International Journal of Inclusive Education*, 20(3), 331–346. https://doi.org/10.1080/13603116.2015.1047660

Schlemmer, R. (2017). Community arts: (Re)contextualizing the narrative of teaching and learning. *Arts Education Policy Review*, 118(1), 27–36. https://doi/pdf/10.1080/10632913.2015.1051255

Smythe, S., Hill, C., Dagenais, D., Sinclair, N., & Toohey, K. (2017). *Disrupting boundaries in education*. Cambridge University Press.

Vancouver Moving Theatre. (2015). *Downtown Eastside Heart of the City Festival. Program Guide*. [Brochure]. Vancouver Moving Theatre.

Walling, S., Bobb, S., Bobb, C., Couchie, P., Maracle, L., & Jacob-Morris, D. (2016). Unpacking our understanding of "conduct." *Alt. Theatre*. 12(4), 14–20.

Wherry, F. (2011). *The Philadelphia Barrio: The arts, branding, and neighborhood transformation*. University of Chicago Press.

# 23

# Intercultural Eye for Art: Becoming a Member of a Global Community Through Arts-Based Exchange

*Kazuyo Nakamura, Hye-Seung (Theresa) Kang,
Wataru Inoue, Leah H. Morgan, Hisae Aoyama,
Hannah Shuler, Atsuo Nakashima, Cheryl J. Maxwell,
Takunori Okamoto and Mari Sankyo*

Preparing children to live in the globalized world is urgently needed (UNESCO, 2014). Contemporary globalization has affected traditional patterns of life. The intercultural social space in which people meet and interact with others from foreign countries has drastically expanded. To manage this rapidly changing environment, schoolwork methods and materials should be altered to help children adapt to these changes (Trilling & Fadel, 2012).

Traditional schools engage primarily with the local community and in local organizations, specifically, those closed by geographic boundaries. This study aimed to transcend geographic boundaries to develop a global community by interconnecting schools across borders using new information technology. This creates a virtual community in which teachers and children interact in cyberspace and build interconnectedness with those living in foreign countries. This community is designed to grow out of and evolve relative to each school's local community. The essential functions of traditional community-based education are revitalized to create such a community. These functions include training the individual to adjust to a changing environment, relating schoolwork to broader community life, empowering the individual to become an active member of the working community and introducing mutual understanding and deeper sympathy to create a harmonious relationship among different groups (e.g. Clark & Zimmerman, 2000; Dewey, 2003a).

To become effective members of the global community and contribute to local and global cultural development, children should develop "an intercultural eye for art" in school. We define this as an active interest in and ability to perceive and empathize with an encultured worldview expressed through artwork from one's own viewpoint. We expect such an intercultural eye to transfer to daily life, cultivating relationships with culturally different others and developing individuality. Any artistic expression serves as a means of acquiring this eye. According to anthropologist Clifford Geertz, elements of artistic expression are the materialization of "a way of experiencing, [bringing] a particular cast of mind out into the world of objects, where men can look at it" (Geertz, 1983, p. 99). John Dewey believed that artistic expression can transform crude relationships into humane ones when it serves to share life's meaning and values with others (Dewey, 2003b).

In this chapter, we introduce the *Indiana-Hiroshima Intercultural Eye for Art Project* and demonstrate how children cooperatively develop a transborder community by engaging in intercultural communication in schools.

## *Indiana-Hiroshima Intercultural Eye for Art Project*

This project was initiated in 2015 by Indiana University's East Asian Studies Center in the United States, involving local schools in Indiana and in Hiroshima, Japan. It comprises research and curriculum development to promote educational theory and practice that facilitate children becoming global citizens, focusing on connections with local communities through arts-based exchange across borders. Sixteen schools from the two communities have participated as of 2021.

We adopt three approaches to introduce a transborder learning environment in schools:

1. American and Japanese teachers meet with each other face-to-face (online) to develop trust and enhance cultural awareness of each other's local community. They exchange ideas about effective intercultural teaching and learning and discuss successes and challenges based on case studies of particular children.
2. Teachers consider children active global citizens who can explore the local community's aesthetic value and participate in creating a new transborder community with culturally different others in a foreign country. Children interact with foreign art through the lens of an "anthropologist's eyes" (Chalmers, 2019). This allows them to explore meaning in art regarding daily

life in a foreign society and facilitates their acquisition of an intercultural eye for art.
3. The research team undertakes collaborative action research, the key features of which lie in an experimental process involving a self-reflective spiral to improve intercultural curriculum and instruction (Kemmis & McTaggart, 1988). Through this approach, we transform our action into praxis: more informed, self-reflective and self-consciously moral.

## *International Collaborative Action Research Design*

During the project's first two years, we determined the appropriate path forward. Exchanging art units on local art and life, we focused on learning about each other's community and developing a network of Indiana and Hiroshima schoolteachers. In 2017, we designed action research to systematically understand the nature of children's intercultural learning. Overall, 534 children from three American and four Japanese schools participated. Our focal research question was – "How do children develop viewpoints to form intercultural communication through art with culturally different others living in a foreign country?" Additionally, we addressed another question that emerged during our research: "What types of interests do children develop through intercultural art learning?" We conducted arts-informed case studies on children's intercultural learning and administered a survey to 534 children. Children's classroom artwork and related documents and their descriptive survey responses were used as data. During the case studies, we focused on mind activity represented as feelings, which are best revealed through artistic expression (Eisner, 2008). We attempted to identify meaningful patterns and general tendencies in survey responses through qualitative content analysis. The survey asked two questions: "What have you become newly aware of during this art exchange lesson?" and "Is there anything you are curious about and want to do following this art exchange lesson?" By employing these approaches interactively, we expected to achieve a deeper and more valid understanding of the nature of children's intercultural learning.

The research team comprised schoolteachers, curriculum specialists and a psychologist, and multiple data and theoretical sources were used to enhance research validity (Eisner, 2006; Stake, 1995). We were also mindful of what Eisner calls "referential adequacy" (Eisner, 2006, p. 15). We attempted to empathize with the context in which children's mind activities emerge, which is helpful in refining sensitivity to significant aspects of classroom learning.

*Arts-Informed Case Studies*

We present three cases to demonstrate the nature of children's intercultural learning through arts-based exchange. The cases are from schools that have developed intercultural art curricula through the project for over two years.

### The Case of Childs Elementary School and Kuba Elementary School

Kuba Elementary School is located in the Kamo community and serves 52 students. Its ethnic composition is 98% Japanese and 2% Chinese. Childs Elementary School, in Monroe County, Indiana, serves 549 students, of whom 77% are Caucasian, 11% Asian, 7% multi-racial, 3% Hispanic and 2% African American. For both schools and their students, this was the first experience with arts-based exchange with foreign students. Both regions have rich natural environments, in which various wild animals live. Nakashima (Kuba) and Shuler (Childs) took advantage of these regional characteristics and cultural resources available in daily life for their curriculum design.

One unit Shuler and Nakashima developed for sixth graders was "Let's express my hometown." This unit involved studying Grant Wood's landscapes and philosophy of regionalism, which opposes the centralization and standardization of art and culture and claims the importance of local soil for growing true art expression (Kroiz, 2018). The students painted landscapes to express their ideas and feelings about their hometown. Originally developed by Shuler, the unit was taught by Nakashima with some revisions. The unit focused on fostering students' interest in intercultural communication with their counterparts by exchanging paintings that expressed their ideas and feelings about their hometown.

This learning consisted of four stages. First, students were introduced to the partner school and their natural and cultural environments. Kuba's students viewed Childs' landscape paintings and discussed key questions, such as what Indiana friends were proud of regarding their hometown and from which parts of the painting this pride resonated. Second, students searched for things they valued and wanted to represent in their works. Third, students invented patterns based on their chosen subjects, prompting them to notice geometric shapes in nature. They created depth in their artwork using curved lines and then coloured their pieces with watercolours and pastels. Finally, students wrote statements about their pieces to send to the partner school with their artwork.

Figure 23.1 shows Kuba sixth-grader Meina's landscape painting. Living in a small town, she did not have a realistic sense of foreign life; however, through art exchange, she developed affective feelings towards other cultures, especially when she recognized her Indiana friends' love of their community and how their tastes

FIGURE 23.1: A photo of Meina Okubo's Hometown Landscape. Photo by Atsuo Nakashima (2020). Copyright © 2020 Meina Okubo.

were similar to hers in their selection of favourite subjects from their hometown. Sympathizing with her Indiana friends' expressed feelings, Meina selected subjects from her hometown's natural environment and, through her work, conveyed to her Indiana friends a hopeful image of and affection for her hometown.

Following the learning, Meina reflected that "knowing and feeling my Indiana friends' sense of pride toward their hometown helped me think more deeply about my hometown and led me to care more about it." Her newly formed interest was also noted; she expressed that, in a future art class, she wants to paint Monroe County's landscape, ask Indiana friends to create a landscape of her hometown and then exchange the artwork. This case implies that children are likely to develop a sense of interconnectedness with foreign friends when recognizing feelings similar to theirs and the value of their own growth. This recognition prompts them to respect and accept differences.

## The Case of Grandview Elementary School and Kasugano Elementary School

Grandview Elementary is in suburban/rural southern Indiana. More than half of the school's 488 students are considered at risk and in need of special assistance and support. Its ethnic composition is 80% Caucasian, 9% Hispanic, 6% multi-racial, 4% African American and 1% Hawaiian or Pacific Islander. Kasugano Elementary School in Hiroshima City serves 1,098 students: 99% Japanese and 1% Chinese. In fall 2019, students at Grandview and Kasugano began a collaboration – the first time that both schools engaged in a global learning project involving art.

The project was designed to foster friendship between students at the schools. It exceeded expectations, resulting in the development of compassionate feelings towards other students half a world away, although the two schools' students never met.

Maxwell at Grandview and Okamoto at Kasugano collaboratively developed a unit titled "Rhapsody Across the Blue: An Artistic Exchange of Musical Interpretations." *Rhapsody in Blue* by American composer George Gershwin was chosen as a subject because these students were acquainted with it through their education.

Each teacher exchanged three simple music pieces from their country and introduced them to students as a form of cultural expression. Children selected one piece and completed an introductory assignment to express feelings it evoked. They used watercolour paper, highly pigmented watercolour paint and Conte crayons. Next, students listened without prompts to *Rhapsody in Blue* three times and then created their works while listening for the fourth time. The song has a range of instruments and tempo, leading students on an artistic adventure; thus, students used art elements and design principles in their own way to create paintings based on feelings the music evoked.

As part of their global learning, students at both schools were exposed to different civilizations' art and culture by visiting nearby art museums. Grandview students visited the Indiana University Musical Art Center and the Eskanazi Art Museum, while Kasugano students visited the Hiroshima Museum of Art.

Figure 23.2 shows the artwork of Madison at Grandview. In this work, she represented the emotional quality she captured through her senses while listening. The image effectively conveys the joy of creative expression and the melody, rhythm and tempo of her emotions.

In the project's final stage, students exchanged their paintings with their partner-school counterparts and discussed what they felt and imagined from each painting, focusing on the qualities of colours and lines. Students at Kasugano created art message cards for their Indiana friends, which included a drawing of what each student imagined from the received painting. Kota, a Kasugano student, expressed his message to Madison: "Your picture is mild and peaceful. I feel this because your picture is watery. I see many round lines, the edges of those lines are moving towards the centre, and many things are crossing together." Other comments were made in the classroom, such as "I wish I could ask what that person was thinking about when they made this image" or "I want to know more about the uniqueness of the individual's feelings by exchanging the way of feeling using different music." Shortly thereafter, students began to request pen-pal connections. Following this activity, Kota became more curious about what American friends imagined when they painted; Madison became more attentive to how Japanese students create artwork.

FIGURE 23.2: Photo of Madison Porter's Painting. Photo by Cheryl J. Maxwell. Copyright © 2020 Madison Porter.

This case demonstrates that when students successfully perceive artwork's emotional quality through intercultural communication, they are likely to make personal connections, which may be facilitated by grouping students of similar ages and having them share subject matter, such as music and art materials for artistic expression.

### The Case of Orleans Junior–Senior High School and Samba Elementary School

Orleans Jr–Sr High School is in Orange County, Indiana. Founded in 1815, Orleans has many historic buildings, including a town square built in the 1800s. Samba Elementary School is also in an old city, Onomichi, which originated more than 800 years ago. Orleans serves 359 students in Grades 7–12, and its ethnic composition is 99% Caucasian and 1% Black and Hispanic. Samba serves 247 students, all Japanese. To develop their collaborative art unit, Morgan at Orleans and Aoyama at Samba utilized the *Hyakki Yagyozu* (the *Book of the Night Parade of One Hundred Creatures*, created in the 1880s) housed in the Kousanji Museum. Various imaginative creatures are on parade in the *Hyakki Yagyozu*. They are creatively deformed, some invented by combining animals and inanimate objects. Inspired by such inventive features, the Samba fourth graders and Orleans seventh graders created original mythical creatures for their art exchange and made a picture book incorporating them, with a story about Indiana creatures visiting

Onomichi. On each page, a pair of creatures from the two schools serve as main characters and are superimposed onto pictures of Onomichi's sightseeing areas that Samba students selected as their favourites.

Figure 23.3 shows two students' collaborative artwork. The scenery was chosen from Jodo-ji Temple. Orleans' Maycee made her creature by combining a bird, snail, frog and baseball cap and called it "Stew" because a stew is a mixture of things. Samba's Takuto created a monster pigeon by enlarging its legs and adding a crown. Their creatures have wings to show that they belong to a flock of pigeons, messengers of peace.

Viewing and discussing each picture, Samba students created an imaginative story to complete the book. Himari described the scene in Figure 23.3:

*This place is the precincts of the Jodo-ji Temple. A snail creature and a pigeon creature first met in the woods. The snail wished to visit the temple, but it was unrealistic because the temple was far away for the snail to move up to. A pigeon creature perched above and said, "I can take you to the Jodo-ji Temple. Please take my hand." The snail hesitated to fly because its feathers are too short to fly, but finally the snail made up his mind, and they flew together. When they reached the temple, the pigeon, who lives around this area, showed the temple to the snail, and together, they travelled around Hiroshima.*

FIGURE 23.3: Photo of Maycee Taylor and Takuto Hatano's Collaborative Work. Photo by Hisae Aoyama. Copyright © 2021 Maycee Taylor, Copyright © 2021 Takuto Hatano.

While creating this description, Himari observed details of the Stew creature's form and felt the pigeon's adventurous quality, integrating her observations and feelings aesthetically into one imaginative story. Through engaging in this intercultural learning, Himari found that "Americans and Japanese are common in a way that they want to create a work to convey meaning to others." At the end of this experience, she expressed her wishes to meet with her Indiana friends and ask what thoughts they had when making their creatures. This case demonstrates that sharing a space of artistic creation and expression, such as a picture book in which each country's students interact, is effective in building their affective bonds.

## *Children's Viewpoints to Frame Intercultural Communication*

We examined meaningful patterns in the children's viewpoints that could frame their ways of intercultural communication in depth. Through two lenses, micro and macro, we attempted to gain a deeper understanding of children's intercultural learning. Overall, 449 children from Japanese schools and 85 children from American schools participated in the survey. To analyse their descriptive answers, we used a framework of patterns of children's viewpoints from a previous study (Nakamura et al., 2022). These patterns include (1) positive view, forming a positive attitude towards other countries' art and culture; (2) cultural otherness, being aware of the otherness of other countries' lifestyles and art; (3) emotional qualities, being aware of differences and/or similarities in emotional qualities in art; (4) means of expression, being aware of differences and/or similarities in ideas and means of expression in art; (5) worldview, being aware of the worldview expressed in art from other countries in relation to one's own; and (6) cultural and historical (ideas and means of expression), being aware of the relationships of other countries' ideas and means of artistic expression along with social, cultural and historical contexts.

Figure 23.4 shows the ratio of these viewpoint patterns exhibited in the children's awareness based on student grade level and country. The concordance rate of categorizing the descriptive answers was 92.9% for one-quarter of the data.

Figure 23.4 shows that 77.3% of first and second graders gained a positive viewpoint about perceiving cultural differences through intercultural art learning, especially when subjects of the artwork were drawn from the region's natural environment or cultural products. Additionally, more than 40% of the other three groups – third and fourth, fifth and sixth, and eighth graders – broadened their perception of ideas and means of expression, suggesting that the children were ready to learn art as a language for intercultural communication. All three cases described above demonstrate this readiness for intercultural learning,

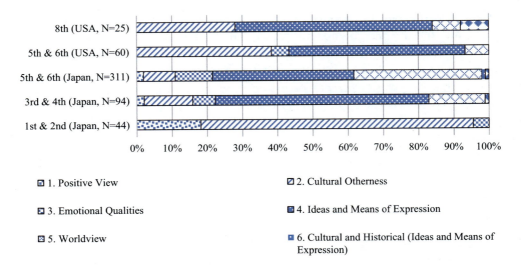

FIGURE 23.4: Ratio of six viewpoints of children's awareness at each grade level.

in which intercommunication happens between American and Japanese children through deciphering meanings based on artistic expression.

Comparing the ratios between fifth and sixth-grade American and Japanese children demonstrates that American children gained increased attention to cultural differences in visual symbols, while Japanese children gained a heightened awareness of an encultured worldview. We speculate that this difference may arise because Western ways of thinking are more analytic and Oriental ones are more holistic (Oliveira & Nisbett, 2017). Although the case studies demonstrated that both American and Japanese children successfully perceived an emotional quality in foreign artwork, a notable difference arose in instructional approaches: American teachers tended to have children attend to elements of art and principles of design, the outer aspects of artistic expression, while Japanese teachers tended to encourage children to empathize with the inner aspects.

## Children's New Interests Following Intercultural Learning

Children's newly formed interests following intercultural learning were identified through qualitative content analysis of textual data obtained from a survey, which was administered to 240 children who participated in our study after 2018. Overall, 68.5% of American children and 88.7% of Japanese children gained new interests. Four types of new interests emerged: (1) Intercultural communication;

(2) different ways of making art; (3) art appreciation of foreign artwork; and (4) lifestyles of foreign countries. The concordance rate of this categorization was 90.0% for one-quarter of the data.

More than 30% of both groups gained an interest in intercultural communication with an appreciation of sharing ideas and feelings with foreign friends and learning from different perspectives. Approximately 30% of both groups developed an interest in trying out different techniques and means of expression encountered through art exchange. The Japanese group noticed the quality of diversity and freedom in the American students' expression, appreciated the spirit and expressed their desire to integrate that quality into their expression, while the American group's interest was mostly in Japanese subjects such as Chinese characters, and some showed their interest by incorporating these in their works. Approximately 30% of both groups became interested in the lifestyles of foreign countries. Notably, the ratio of the Japanese group's interest in appreciating foreign artwork was three times greater than that of the American group. As the development of these interests shows, intercultural learning through art was effective in developing children's mindsets towards becoming members of a global community.

## *Conclusion*

As our study demonstrates, intercultural learning can foster children's interest in art and develop their mindset towards becoming members of a global community. The arts-informed case studies revealed that arts-based exchange facilitates intercultural communication, in which children build affective ties with those living in a foreign country. This study also suggests younger children's readiness to learn visual arts as a means of intercultural communication; from the third to fourth grades, children become more attentive to elements of art and principles of design and can perceive artistic expression as a visual language. Additionally, the study indicated that arts-based intercultural learning fosters children's interest in learning more about foreign art and culture in relation to their lives.

To the best of our knowledge, this type of intercultural project across borders is a new enterprise. From local communities in Indiana and Hiroshima, we built within schools a third communal space where children are empowered as active global citizens and can interrelate with those living in foreign countries. It is our challenge to foster children to become global citizens who can continue to develop their own individuality through art while deepening their relationships with culturally different others living in foreign countries.

## ACKNOWLEDGEMENTS

We extend our appreciation to Enid Zimmerman, Norihisa Nakase and Gilbert Clark. We are also grateful to Yuya Fujita and Yuki Nishimoto for their research assistance.

## REFERENCES

Chalmers, F. G. (2019). Art education as ethnology. In D. Garnet & A. Sinner (Eds.), *Art, culture, and pedagogy: Revisiting the work of F. Graeme Chalmers* (pp. 131–142). Brill Sense. (Original work published 1981)

Clark, G., & Zimmerman, E. (2000). Greater understanding of the local community: A community-based art education program for rural schools. *Art Education, 53*(2), 33–39. https://doi.org/10.2307/3193848

Dewey, J. (2003a). The school as social centre. In L. Hickman (Ed.), *The collected works of John Dewey, 1882–1953; The middle works of John Dewey, 1899–1924* (Vol. 2). InteLex. (Original work published 1902)

Dewey, J. (2003b). Art as experience. In L. Hickman (Ed.), *The collected works of John Dewey, 1882–1953; The later works of John Dewey, 1925 1953* (Vol. 10). InteLex. (Original work published 1934)

Eisner, E. (2006). Does arts-based research have a future? *Studies in Art Education, 48*(1), 9–18.

Eisner, E. (2008). Art and knowledge. In J. G. Knowles & A. L. Cole (Eds.), *Handbook of the arts in qualitative research* (pp. 3–12). Sage Publications.

Geertz, C. (1983). *Local knowledge*. Basic Books.

Kemmis, S., & McTaggart, R. (1988). *The action research planner*. Deakin University.

Kroiz, L. (2018). *Cultivating citizens: The regional work of art in the new deal era*. University of California Press.

Nakamura, K., Inoue, W., Alicea, G., Morinaga, S., Beaulieu, A., & Matsuzaki, S. (2022). Transnational progressive vision of educating children through art: Revisiting Dewey's sojourn in Japan in 1919 for global citizenship education. In A. Sinner & D. Garnet (Eds.), *Living histories: Global conversations in art education*. Intellect.

Oliveira, S., & Nisbett, R. (2017). Culture changes how we think about thinking: From "Human Influence" to "Geography of Thought." *Perspectives on Psychological Science, 12*(5), 783–790.

Stake, R. (1995). *The art of case study research*. Sage Publications.

Trilling, B., & Fadel, C. (2012). *21st century skills: Learning for life in our time*. John Wiley and Sons Inc.

UNESCO. (2014). *Global citizenship education: Preparing learners for the challenges of the 21st century*. UNESCO.

# 24

# The Creation of a Community Teaching Artist Certificate Programme: Professionalization in the Gig Economy

*Dustin Garnet*

Community-based art education (CBAE) has become a well-established source of informal learning across the United States and around the world. Research studies have solidified its importance as a vehicle for inclusivity, positive physical and mental health, and as an outlet for social justice actions (Catterall, 2009; National Endowment for the Arts, 2019). Luo and Lau (2020) note that "CBAE is concerned to a great extent with students' social life and culture, and emphasizes a cognitive and aesthetic understanding of the meaning of art in a particular context" (pp. 45–46). Contributing to this definition, Krensky and Steffen (2009) describe CBAE as "community art used as both a creative practice and a teaching method to fulfil educational objectives ranging from creative self-expression to competency with discipline-specific standards" (p. 12). Adding context to these definitions, this chapter describes an ongoing teaching-artist professional development programme that I developed and still teach in Los Angeles, California. After first discussing the political context and the philosophical perspectives surrounding the professionalization of teaching artists, I outline the development of the Community Teaching Artist (CTA) certificate programme at California State University, Los Angeles (CSULA), then conclude by focusing on the goals and future directions of the CTA certificate as the field of CBAE matures across the United States and around the world.

The locations of CBAE programmes vary, so in this chapter CBAE will refer to programmes *on-site* at K–12 schools as part of artist-in-the-school programmes, *extended day learning* after school, or *off-site* at community organizations that may involve multi-generational participants.

## Mapping the Territory

As we enter the 2020s, the field of CBAE – along with its purposes and participants – is becoming more diverse and complex (Crehan, 2020; Harris et al., 2019; Haviland, 2017; Snepvangers et al., 2018). As communities change with immigration, gentrification and improved education, the content and quality of community art education must adapt to cultural change. The sophistication and expectations of CBAE students are increasing, which means dynamic professional development opportunities for teaching artists should also grow. As well, over the past decade, Los Angeles has seen an unprecedented expansion and investment in community arts spaces and offerings. This has increased the demand for professionally trained artists who also possess teaching skill sets akin to those of certified schoolteachers: a demand amplified by the loss of veteran teaching artists who are retiring at a steady pace. The DCA has recognized this complex challenge and in conjunction with CSULA, set out in spring 2019 to develop an intensive professional certificate for CTAs.

The Association of Teaching Artists "defines a teaching artist as a practicing professional artist with the complementary skills and sensibilities of an educator, who engages people in learning experiences in, though, and about the arts" (Levy, 2019, p. 2). Artists who practise CBAE are part of a hybrid profession. The Berklee Career Communities webpage notes that "[a] teaching artist fuses the skills, practices, and sensibilities of an artist with the expertise of an educator; a foot in two fields is required of a successful teaching artist" (https://www.berklee.edu/careers/roles/teaching-artist). However, credentialed art teachers are different from teaching artists because they earn a Bachelor of Education degree (B.Ed.) that certifies their abilities and dispositions to teach K–12 students in schools. The teaching profession is also linked to a set of professional standards that may differ between states. CTAs will often be self-taught or have a Bachelor of Fine Arts (BFA) or a Master of Fine Arts (MFA) degree. Most fine-arts master's programmes in the United States and Canada have a teaching component where a student can receive mentorship and learn the basics of teaching at a university/college level. As well, specialized programmes offer a joint MFA and B.Ed., resulting in certification to teach in K–12 schools.

On the other hand, a self-taught artist or an artist with an art degree can find contract positions in classrooms, after-school programmes during the school year or summer programmes. Some could instruct courses at an art centre or summer camp or be involved in a community grant application that requires specific artistic expertise. Thus, while teaching artists are professionals, they can be classified as "gig workers" who develop methods of earning income outside of traditional, long-term employer–employee relationships (Abraham et al., 2018; Koustas, 2019).

## Teaching Artists and the Gig Economy

Though California Bill AB5, recently codified into law, seeks to curb the purposeful misclassification of workers in major corporations as "gig workers" (Lin, 2019), the law did not carefully consider artists and the various ways they supplement their incomes. The bill was not written with careful consideration of artists and the various ways they supplement their incomes. As mentioned above, the work available to teaching artists is often part-time, project-based or contract-based (Rabkin et al., 2011). Jean Johnstone (n.d.), Executive Director of the Teaching Artists Guild, notes on the Guild's website that

> As any gig worker knows, without a long term, regular, or otherwise stable employment situation, a teaching artist pieces together work at a variety of organizations in order to make a sustainable living, often wearing different hats: teaching artist, artist, educator, arts administrator, and other related and unrelated work.

The protections offered by Bill AB5 require employers to recognize teaching artists as employees rather than independent contractors. Yet, while Bill AB5 is a push in the right direction towards treating professional artists and technicians in a more responsible manner, the impact associated with the transition has raised operation costs for an already resource-tight arts and culture community – with severe financial consequences for both teaching artists and their employers. The requirement to pay artists as employees with benefits, like pensions and health insurance, has resulted in layoffs and closures of arts programmes across California (Easter, 2020). The Los Angeles Department of Cultural Affairs (DCA) has also felt the effects of Bill AB5 through rising costs, including ensuring their new artist-employees have access to appropriate professional development.

## Prioritizing Professional Development

Professional development for teaching artists is both inconsistent and riddled with philosophical concerns (Levy, 2019; Rabkin et al., 2011; Winkler & Denmead, 2016). Many teaching artists draw the line between their independence, freedom and artistic license and the perceived confines of institutional expectations and requirements in the teaching profession. As Reeder (2009) explains,

> We are afraid that we will lose the thing that differentiates a teaching artist from an arts teacher. We are protective of the time that we maintain to pursue our art – this is

perceived as a selfish endeavour. We are defensive of our value to society – cautious that we will sell out artistic integrity for social activism.

(p. 15)

A two-year study (Rabkin et al., 2011) exploring the teaching artist's way of life and professional concerns on a national scale focused on teaching artists at the centre of dynamic arts education programmes. Collecting demographic, economic, artistic and educational data about teaching artists, Rabkin et al. noted that they

did not find that all teaching artists are equally inclined or capable of consistently delivering that kind of teaching and learning, or that every programme for which they work is designed to support it. There is significant diversity among teaching artists. [...] TAs are not, by themselves, a solution to the persistent failure of too many schools to meet so many students' needs. But they are a vital resource in plain sight that has been consistently overlooked.

(2011, pp. 28–29)

This report deepened our "understanding of the supports, conditions, professional standards, and development that teaching artists need to do their very best work" (Reeder, 2009, p. 21). It also offered "practical policy suggestions designed to support teaching artists and advance their practice" (p. 21), addressing questions like – How could professional development in CBAE be deepened, refined and made more engaging? What kind of programme would effectively incorporate teaching artistry, scholarship, training and local involvement? And what kind of support system is required to help teaching artists who want to innovate and create new educational programmes in the communities they serve? Indeed, this report helped me position and inform my creation of a new professional development programme.

A decade after Rabkin et al.'s (2011) report, California's demand for arts education *has* grown. In Los Angeles, demand and funding for community arts programming through the DCA have risen significantly since 2015 (City of Los Angeles, 2018, 2019). Additionally, non-profit organizations offering maker spaces, art classes and community hubs have popped up throughout LA and surrounding areas, providing niche offerings to ever more discerning participants.

## *Collaboration and Community Insights*

Discussions about developing a professional certificate and programme began between Dr Linda Essig, Dean of Arts and Letters at California State University, and Danielle Brazell, General Manager of the Los Angeles DCA. As Essig explains,

Our initial discussion was unscripted and without an agenda. Having newly relocated to LA, I reached out to several public sector arts leaders. My conversation with Danielle Brazelle led to the question, "What can we do together? The city owns and manages 23 community arts centers, all of which hire teaching artists. The director was looking for a way to credential those teaching artists and the city wanted to work with a public institution located within the city itself."

(Personal communication, 26 May 2020)

Formed in 1925, the DCA promotes arts and culture as a way to ignite a powerful dialogue, engage LA's residents and visitors and ensure LA's varied cultures are recognized, acknowledged and experienced. The DCA's mission is to strengthen the quality of life in Los Angeles by stimulating and supporting arts and cultural activities, ensuring public access to the arts for residents and visitors alike (City of Los Angeles, 2019). This mandate includes providing arts and cultural programming through its Community Arts Division, which serves 36 neighbourhood arts and cultural centres, theatres and historic sites serving young people and adults.

Leslie Thomas, Community Arts Division Director at DCA, and Elizabeth Morin, Arts Manager and Coordinator of Special Projects at the DCA, were soon brought into the conversation to contribute their expertise. A teaching artist professional certificate programme at CSULA began to coalesce when several faculty members were also asked to consult on this project. I was invited to lead and was tasked with coordinating the programme, writing the curriculum and facilitating the course of study. Initial meetings focused on developing a vision for the certificate.

Recognizing the need to bring community voices to the project, the development team invited groups of teaching artists, arts administrators, art centre directors and arts association representatives to two focus group meetings. The focus groups began with introductions and an overview of the proposed CTA certificate. Several questions were developed ahead of time to guide the groups' discussions, which in turn led to more significant questions, insights and perspectives.

One central topic in the focus groups was the quality of teaching artistry. Most participants agreed that professional development is directly related to preparing more qualified and competitive teaching artists for employment. Several group members explicitly argued that many teaching artists could benefit from learning skills essential to success in the classroom. One veteran teaching artist noted that there are successful and unsuccessful teaching artists, and a few unskilled teaching artists give a bad name to everyone else.

There was some agreement that a university-level training programme would make professional development seem too academic or even intimidating to some teacher-artists. Some participants feared this kind of training might affect the field's artistry and spirit by promoting pedagogy based on research, not actual practice.

Some contributors were sceptical about creating a single curriculum for teaching artists with so much diversity in the field. Overall, however, focus groups were encouraged by this initiative; they believed it would build confidence in teaching artists' abilities and generate interest by assuring teaching artists of attaining greater success at their community sites.

## Building a Professional Certificate

The goal of creating the CTA certificate was to provide a solid grounding in the essential tools and skills of community arts teaching and to develop healthy mindsets and realistic expectations for teaching artists. The programme's curriculum is both practical and aspirational and provides both seasoned and young career teaching artists with the knowledge to shape their own professional pathways in alignment with their artistic passions. In developing learning objectives and content for the CTA certificate, I considered literature that focused on professional development for teaching artists (Booth, n.d.; Harris et al., 2019; McCaslin et al., 2004; Reeder, 2008; Saraniero, 2009) and insights from the focus groups to establish seven teaching principles:

### Instructor Positionality

The designers and instructors of a professional development course do not need to know and be able to execute all the skills that teaching artists need to master. But they should be knowledgeable, up-to-date and involved in broad issues of teaching artistry to confidently lead, adapt and evolve the program.

### Student-Centred Learning

The teaching artists must have confidence that the issues, theories and skills addressed will align with their own aspirations and the mission of the teaching artist training. A student-centred model will require the teaching artist to provide individualized guidance and resources to each student.

### Personal Relevance

The teaching artists must see the professional development goals as relevant to their own practice and personal goals. Opportunities must be provided to discuss and work with new ideas. Experimentation in groups will allow reflection and openings for teaching artists to internalize new material through deliberation with colleagues.

## *Multiple Tracks*

A "one certificate fits all" model will not effectively meet the challenges and needs of teacher-artists as they progress through stages of professional learning. A major concern around professional development is that the curriculum is not flexible or diverse enough to engage with a wide range of developmental stages, needs and interests of teaching artists. Experienced teaching artists need to be challenged with new kinds of work such as research for curriculum development, developing best practices in assessment and evaluation, learning through mentorship and leading professional development.

## *Pedagogy*

Culturally responsive pedagogy consists of leadership policies, practices and philosophies that build diverse, inclusive community sites for participants (Chung & Li, 2019; Gay, 2002; Ladson-Billings, 1995; Villegas & Lucas, 2002). Culturally responsive pedagogical practices often include emphasizing excellence for participants' success. These practices incorporate the cultural histories, values and knowledge of participants' local communities to create frameworks and structures within local arts programmes, with hopes of empowering participants from diverse backgrounds. A culturally sensitive and relevant pedagogical approach creates a safe space in a community arts education setting. Safe space does not necessarily refer to physical safety but a psychological, atmospheric and emotional space which allows us to create and express ourselves to our optimal abilities. Safe space is considered in terms of comfort and trust amongst the collective of students and between the students and teaching artist.

## *Atmosphere*

A teaching artist's professional development must seek to create an atmosphere of serious play, of inquiry and of personal desire in order to tap into the intrinsic motivation essential for deep understanding. Teaching-artist work is often isolating; professional development should seek to build a collegial atmosphere that supports the growth of distributed knowledge and should encourage creative inquiry among those who are exploring ways to achieve best practices (Booth, n.d.).

## *Goals*

Goals should always be clearly communicated for each class, and the goals of each class should include showing how the material is scaffolded and connected with the larger programmatic mission. These goals should be crafted meaningfully and should link to the creative and personal aspirations of the teaching artists.

These seven teaching principles were vital in shaping the three core competencies of this professional certificate. The core competencies are umbrella themes informing the development of the CTA course curriculum learning objectives:

**Cross-cultural communication**
Cross-cultural communication is a process of creating and sharing meaning among people from different cultural backgrounds using a variety of means. This form of communication enables teaching artist to succeed in varied socio-cultural settings, to understand teaching and learning in multicultural contexts, as well as to work with classes that consist of multi-ethnic students from diverse cultural backgrounds.

**Classroom management**
Classroom management in the context of community arts teaching is the process by which teaching artists and community organizations create and maintain an environment that encourages positive behaviours and interactions. The purpose of implementing classroom management strategies is to enhance prosocial behaviour and increase student engagement. Good classroom management implies more than eliciting student cooperation and maintaining order. It also implies that worthwhile learning activities that are engaging to students are taking place continuously, that a welcoming physical environment suitable for the desired learning is provided, that developed rules of conduct are observed and that continuous monitoring of progress toward the desired learning outcomes is achieved.

**Trauma-informed pedagogy**
Trauma-informed pedagogy is a way of teaching that ensures the physical and emotional safety of students in all traditional, virtual and field settings. Policies and practices in trauma-informed pedagogy are responsive to issues of diversity and oppression, allowing students to feel safe in individual and group interpersonal interactions and to feel safe to make and learn from mistakes. Trust and transparency in the classroom are enhanced by making expectations clear, ensuring consistency

in practice, maintaining appropriate boundaries and offering accommodations and adaptations to minimize potential disappointment. Teaching artists are able to act as allies toward student success rather than as perceived adversaries. Teaching artists and students recognize each other's strengths and resilience, and they provide feedback to help each other grow and change.

## *Teaching Artistry and Professionalization*

Teaching artists have become a common fixture in California schools, as boards attempt to cut costs by favouring short-term contracts with teaching artists over hiring a credentialed art educator. Politics are at play in this discussion. One certainty is that teaching artists keep arts education alive when boards are faced with budget cuts, and they bring the arts to areas where they might not have existed. The overall goal of the CTA professionalization certificate is for teaching artists to increase the quality of their educational practice and the strength of the programmes in which they work. Teaching artists are dedicated to their practice because it gives significant intrinsic satisfaction, but they must balance that against the struggle this work often involves. Many believe teaching makes them better artists and has a positive effect on their art making. Interest in improving teaching capacities is growing within teaching artists' ranks. What we already know is this:

> There are a few elements that seem to be fairly widespread across the many [professional development] programs […] across the country. TAs need to learn how to write curriculum, lessons, and units that have an arc that starts at the beginning, moves students through the middle and toward an end point. They need to develop their capacity to be attentive to all of the students in the classroom, notice when some are losing their way and get them back on the pathway to learning.
>
> (Rabkin et al., 2011, p. 153)

Rabkin et al. (2011) also noted that veteran teaching artists had additional concerns about training curricula too often directed at novices and failing to stimulate or challenge them. In contrast, teaching artists described professional development as sporadic and confined to brief workshops that could take from one to three days (Rabkin et al., 2011). The CTA certificate incorporates an introduction to ground teaching artists' work in history and current practice. The course also moves beyond introductions and overviews to more nuanced instruction like arts integration with different school subjects and working with students of various abilities, as well as school politics and dynamics. The CTA programme was originally conceptualized as a stackable group of courses that teaching artists could add to their CTA certificate. It is hoped that funding and interest allow the development of future modules that offer mentorship with veteran teaching artists for on-the-job experience.

One of the unique qualities of the CTA certificate is that it does not familiarize teaching artists with a universal curriculum. Instead, students are offered multiple choices and focus materials, allowing for customizable learning relevant to the multivalent educational purposes of community arts organizations. While formalized training is useful for making a successful and smooth programme, such training can often create too rigid a structure for teaching artists' practice and constrict effective partnerships, leaving little space for teaching artists to bring their own teaching artistry into their classrooms. Instead, the CTA certificate broadens the scope of arts curriculum to reflect California's "great variety and complexity" of arts learning (Seidel et al., 2009, p. 48). The CTA certificate will enhance the marketability of dynamic cultural leaders by focusing on broad areas of curriculum, pedagogy and professionalism in applied community arts education. Teaching artists will build on their cultural capital and gain insights into adapting to and orienting themselves within diverse twenty-first-century community settings.

## REFERENCES

Abraham, K. G., Haltiwanger, J. C., Sandusky, K., & Spletzer, J. R. (2018). Measuring the gig economy: Current knowledge and open issues. [Working paper]. *National Bureau of Economic Research*. No. w24950.

Booth, E. (n.d.). *Basic elements of strong professional development for teaching artists*. http://ericbooth.net/basic-elements-of-strong-professional-development-for-teaching-artists/

Catterall, J. S. (2009). *Doing well and doing good by doing art: A 12-year national study of education in the visual and performing arts*. I-Group Books.

Chung, S. K., & Li, D. (2019). Culturally responsive art education. National Art Education Association Advisory. https://arteducators-prod.s3.amazonaws.com/documents/1363/e95e043b-bdf3-4a4d-a43c-a2057714da71.pdf?1555333824

City of Los Angeles. (2018). *Department of Cultural Affairs*. [Brochure]. Department of Cultural Affairs.

City of Los Angeles. (2019). *Department of Cultural Affairs*. [Brochure]. Department of Cultural Affairs.

Crehan, K. A. F. (2020). *Community art: An anthropological perspective*. Routledge.

Easter, M. (2020, February 12) The AB5 backlash: Singers, actors, dancers, theatres sound off on freelance law. *Los Angeles Times*. https://www.latimes.com/entertainment-arts/story/2020-02-12/how-ab5-is-impacting-california-readers-in-the-performing-arts

Gay, G. (2002). Preparing for culturally responsive teaching. *Journal of Teacher Education, 53*(2), 106–116. https://doi.org/10.1177/0022487102053002003

Harris, L. P., Walker, M., & Green, M. (2019). *Community-based art education across the lifespan: Finding common ground.* Teachers College Press.

Haviland, M. (2017). *Side by side? Community art and the challenge of co-creativity.* Routledge.

Johnstone, J. (n.d.). *Making teaching artists employees.* Teaching Artists Guild. https://teachingartists.com/blog_posts/making-teaching-artists-employees/

Krensky, B., & Steffen, S. L. (2009). *Engaging classrooms and communities through art: A guide to designing and implementing community-based art education.* Altamira Press.

Ladson-Billings, G. (1995). But that's just good teaching! The case for culturally relevant pedagogy. *Theory into Practice, 34*(3), 159–165.

Levy, D. (2019). *A teaching artist's companion: How to define and develop your practice.* Oxford University Press.

Lin, J. (2019, July 6). California debates law requiring 2 million independent contractors to become employees. *Times of San Diego.* https://timesofsandiego.com/politics/2019/07/06/california-debates-law-requiring-2-million-independent-contractors-to-become-employees/

Luo, N., & Lau, C. (2020). Community-based art education in China: Practices, issues and challenges. *International Journal of Art & Design Education, 39*(2), 445–460.

McCaslin, G., Rhodes, A., & Lind, T. (2004). Professional development for teaching artists: A sampling. *Teaching Artist Journal, 2*(3), 140–152.

National Endowment for the Arts. (2019). *Artists and other cultural workers: A statistical portrait.* National Endowment for the Arts Office of Research & Analysis. https://www.arts.gov/impact/research/publications/artists-and-other-cultural-workers-statistical-portrait

Rabkin, N., Reynolds, M., Hedberg, E. C., & Shelby, J. (2011). *Teaching artists and the future of education: A report on the teaching artist research project.* NORC: University of Chicago. https://www.norc.org/PDFs/TARP%20Findings/Teaching_Artists_Research_Project_Final_Report_%209-14-11.pdf

Reeder, L. (2008). Hurry up and wait: A national scan of teaching artist research and professional development. *Teaching Artist Journal, 7*(1), 14–22.

Saraniero, P. (2009). Training and preparation of teaching artists. *Teaching Artist Journal, 7*(4), 236–43.

Seidel, S., Tishman, S., Winner, E., Hetland, L., & Palmer, P. (2009). A study of excellence in arts education. *Principal Leadership, 10*(3), 46–51.

Snepvangers, K., Thomson, P., & Harris, A. M. (2018). *Creativity policy, partnerships and practice in education.* Palgrave Macmillan.

Villegas, A. M., & Lucas, T. (2002). Preparing culturally responsive teachers rethinking the curriculum. *Journal of Teacher Education, 53*(1), 20–32.

Winkler, H., & Denmead, T. (2016). The future of homegrown teaching artists? Negotiating contradictions of professionalisation in the youth arts and humanities field. *International Journal of Education & the Arts, 17*(10), 1–16.

# 25

# Creative for Life: Planning and Delivering Intergenerational Art Programmes

*Jodie Davidson and Miles Openshaw*

Community intergenerational arts projects, particularly those involving participants from a common location such as a town or suburb, can bridge ever-decreasing opportunities for young and older people to interact. Projects are often characterized as interactive or in dialogue with the community through "collaborative activities which can act as a way to challenge the gerontophobia" (Rubin et al., 2015, p. 1), bringing "often-separated groups of young and old together and foster relationships and understanding between the generations" (Bales et al., 2000, p. 1). Such projects nurture good contact and positive exchanges between old and young that lead to opportunities to discover the person behind the generational stereotypes: enhancing wellbeing and shaping individuals who value quality human relationships (MacCallum et al., 2010). The arts approach is an essential ingredient where the focus of the groups' meeting is to enable thinking, feeling, doing and reflecting – not only for participants but all those taking part, including partner organizations, their staff and the teaching artists facilitating the projects or events. Our intent is always to construct well-designed arts activities exploring materials and methods that fit the needs, abilities and confidence levels of diverse groups of older and younger people so that no one feels left out. This enables the arts' focus to become a channel for the emotional bonds, the sense of understanding, acceptance and compassion that develop through a project. "Intergenerational projects like these are essential for generations to develop a mutual understanding and appreciation of each other" (Emily Lees, Manager Enrichment and Volunteer Services, Amana Living).

Our 2019 project – based in Perth, Western Australia – worked with a not-for-profit provider of care services for people as they age, as well as with a metropolitan nursing home and a local independent primary school. Using applied arts approaches over an eight-week period, our project brought together a group of twelve older people with twelve year 5 and 6 students. They met once a week for 90 minutes to explore the development of mutually rewarding relationships through creative activities.

## *Importance of Partnerships*

The initial groundwork had to be done with partner organizations to ensure building strong associations, understanding of working practices and identifying and agreeing on project practicalities. We attach a great deal of importance to these relationships and stress qualities of thoughtful, detailed, careful hard work alongside committed partners to move from an original idea to the reality of a project. The more we understand the complexities of full timetables, academic pressures or the workings of multi-use community spaces, the better we can create the right amount of scaffolding to allow magical things to happen. Several months before a planned start date, conversations began with senior staff at John Wollaston Anglican Community School (JWAPS) and age-care provider Amana Living, to work through practical and logistical implications, discuss group and individual needs, uncover any areas of resistance and agree on the practical necessities.

Our meetings with staff members who would be involved in the project were particularly enlightening for discovering tensions and forthright opinions around the feasibility of the project. Overlooking a seemingly small detail, such as factoring in time for the older participants to enjoy their usual morning cup of tea, can potentially derail a project if not addressed at the outset. The need and ability to have open and honest discussions with partner organizations were crucial to the success of the project. Working within a residential care home setting means we are effectively working in the participants' home. Rearranging routines as well as furniture can cause initial consternation and resistance, and we needed to be ready to resolve any number of these potential pitfalls before and during the project.

> As we started the project, the care home staff were protective of the residents; quick to step in with advice, to "solve" problems even take-over. As artists bringing in musical instruments, paints, noise and disarray, we were, naturally, viewed with a certain amount of suspicion. We were determined to gain the trust of staff, so the setup and clean down of the utilised dining room space became our tightly choreographed routine of building and un-building a space; tables, chairs, cutlery, place names and salt and pepper shakers removed and precisely replaced at the start and end of the session. By week three, the staff were sitting with the residents

and children, pencil or paintbrush in hand, chatting away, totally immersed in the activity. They had allowed themselves to let go of the timetables and schedules and enjoy being creative.

(Jodie Davidson, teaching artist, *Creative for Life* project)

Finding the right mix of participants is as crucial to the success of a project as establishing strong, collaborative working relationships. Too large a group requires additional management and resources; too small a group may lead to uniformity in the project. The purpose of an intergenerational project is to bring two diverse generational groups together to generate an enthusiasm that is contagious.

We acknowledge that the organizations are best placed to pick the participants, but we offer guidance based on knowledge and experience gained from previous community projects:

- Twelve young and twelve older participants work well for a community intergenerational arts project, offering a wide range of experience and skills without the group size feeling overwhelming.
- For young participants, an age range of 10–12 requires less management; as well, they possess natural energy, creativity and fresh enthusiasm. Programmes can work just as easily with younger children, but they require additional supervision.
- Consider how the group will work together in addition to the needs and contributions of individuals.
- Participants do not have to be "good" at art.
- Do not be afraid to take a risk by inviting more reticent people; the less confident ones may blossom with the attention of an interested older or younger partner.

The experiences of the participants are fundamentally related to programme leadership and how that promotes an environment of spontaneity and social connection rather than task completion (Mayo et al., 2012, p. 25).

The choice of teaching artist (a teaching artist is a professional artist who also facilitates community art) is the third key ingredient needed for a project to really succeed. The artists enable participants to fully engage with the project aims in the most creative and challenging way possible. Our two multi-disciplinary teaching artists have the talent, confidence and enthusiasm in their chosen art forms and the skills to inspire, guide, excite and challenge participants to go beyond the ordinary.

(Miles Openshaw, artistic director, *Globe Town Project*)

One aspect we are unable to fully explore and expand on before the start of an intergenerational arts project is the content. With minimal knowledge of the participants' interests, skills and restrictions in health or mobility, it is hard to plan activities or determine what approaches will or will not work with a particular group. For partner organizations, it is a leap of faith to work without a plan, but preparations made months before help establish a level of trust that ignites excitement about an impending journey of discovery.

## *Everyone Has a Story to Share*

Before a group comes together, they need time to prepare. A week before the first session in 2019, project facilitators and staff from the aged care organization ran a preparatory workshop at the school with the selected students and staff to present information on the project. This provided an opportunity through open-group discussion for the children to ask questions and voice concerns in anticipation of working with older partners, along with strategies for how they might like to connect. Because the conversation was not mediated but instead facilitated, participants were given time to explore, reflect and come up with their own ideas for dealing with potential scenarios.

> The students drew a large composite picture of what they thought the residents might look like; glasses, grey hair, cardigans, floral dresses, stripy socks, knitting and to complete the outfit – rocket launchers on the soles of their shoes! Inside the picture, students wrote words and phrases to describe the way the residents might be feeling meeting the children and any health difficulties they may experience. We were able to discuss strategies of how to connect with an older person in the group who couldn't see very well, was hard of hearing or was clouded by dementia.
>
> (Jodie Davidson)

A similar session took place with the twelve older participants from the aged care hostel, with members of school staff invited to answer any of the elders' questions about the school and its pupils. Due to lack of mobility, dementia and limited vision for some residents, afternoon tea provided a familiar environment and process, enabling them to discuss their concerns. As a provocation to assist with finding commonalities at the two groups' first meeting, participants had their photos taken during each group's preliminary session, and they were asked about themselves:

- What is your hidden talent?
- What is your family's tradition?
- What's your favourite TV show, movie or book?

The images and answers to the questions became individual Friendship Passports, which helped open conversations. Vivienne, an older resident, had some initial hesitations, but partnering with Oscar and his hidden talent of "making people happy" helped overcome her reservations. "We made quick connections and became friends easily. We did art together, shared memories, sang songs and discovered lots about each other. After the first session, we felt invigorated and looked forward to the next one" (Vivienne, aged 81).

In the preparatory session with the senior participants, we had discovered that they were keen for the children to greet them with a handshake and proper introduction: something they thought had been lost to the younger generation, replaced by high-fives and fist bumps. The children played their part enthusiastically; firm handshakes and confident introductions upon entering the room made a lasting impression on the older people and swept away some of their apprehension. A classic theatre game, Name and Action, allowed everyone to introduce themselves in a playful way, with each participant announcing their name and demonstrating an action for everyone to repeat and copy. With their Friendship Passports around their necks, the group quickly found commonalities and differences, sharing stories as friends. Breaking down barriers continued as the group worked to form lyrics to form a communal song:

> We've all come together,
> leaving from this port,
> we're off on new adventures,
> travelling on our friendship passport.
>
> (*Creative for Life* song chorus)

Intentionally establishing these rituals of meeting and ways of starting the sessions played an important part in building authentic connections, helping create a sense of identity and establishing trust. Each week the scheduled session passed quickly, and the atmosphere in the room appeared more relaxed. After the session ended, residents chatted amongst themselves as the children made their way towards the bus, their heads full of stories to share with their classmates. "We love these young ones and would have liked more time talking to them and hearing more of their stories" (Marion, aged 73).

No matter the art approach for a project, for us the starting point will always be sharing real-life experiences. These non-fictional narratives can be developed through word and storytelling games which quickly establish commonalities: school, pets and food among the favourites. Other activities take more of a fictional, imaginative and fantastical turn; in our case, we found ourselves in a world of *burglar bears, grocery shopping giraffes* and *llamas in helicopters* as tales became intertwined. Stories were woven together into a collective narrative represented through a variety of arts approaches: song, visual art and spoken word. The different art forms created a singular dynamic and added layers of richness to what the group produced.

A successful visual arts approach for this group was integrating stories into loosely coloured drawn pictures (Figure 25.1). This way of working was suited to visually impaired older participants who were able to relate a story whilst their younger partner drew it. The nature of the ink medium used and the collaged result removed any pressure to stay within the lines, and mixing the colours encouraged experimentation with colour and form. "I've enjoyed sharing memories with the older people, it's been so much fun" (Ben, aged 10).

Over the weeks we developed a group song, adding a new verse to the familiar chorus each week. The chorus was sung at the start and end of each session, with Mark's guitar as accompaniment. This was important as a focal point for building community and as continuity for each session since the art activity itself changed each week. As the project unfolded, some of the children began playing pieces on the piano in the corner of the dining hall as residents clapped along or accompanied them on percussion instruments. These musical moments and the act of singing as

FIGURE 25.1: Intergenerational visual storytelling during a creative session. Photo by Jodie Davidson (2019).

a group were galvanizing; an improvised icebreaker activity requiring very little facilitation had become a focal point of the project, rapidly building closeness and connection. In those moments, it felt like the hearts of the group beat in unison. (In our experience, we have found that singing improves a sense of happiness and wellbeing; indeed, Pearce and Launay [2015] suggest that the improved mood in part comes directly from the release of positive neurochemicals and is also likely to be influenced by changes in our sense of social closeness with others.) Upon completing the project, the school and care home formed a community choir: continuing the connection between the two groups and fostering the health and wellbeing benefits this activity offered. "It's really fun because you get to learn what they used to do when they were young" (Amy, aged 10).

Brad, a student in the group, was a gifted young pianist. He and his elderly project partner Betty would sit quietly discussing elements of their lives, inspired by Brad's piano playing and their shared love of drawing. Betty commented that she had always stood in the background, never encouraged or comfortable to step forward, but her smile during the sessions said maybe now was her time to shine. Brad flourished in this friendship, growing in confidence and encouraging Betty. At the end of a painting session, Betty would use a sponge to wipe marks from Brad's arm, just as a mother would her child.

> The culmination of the project, when the Thomas Scott residents visited our school, was a moving example of empathy, joint affection and the love of humanity. When both students and residents described their experiences, it was clearly evident that the project has made a significant impact on the wellbeing and sense of belonging of all concerned.
>
> (Wayne Revitt, head of Primary, John Wollaston Anglican Community School)

As soon as Sophie, a student and Patricia, a resident, sat down next to each other in the first session, they immediately bonded. They were fascinated to hear each other's stories, each starting to see and experience the world through a different lens. Patricia, who had infrequent visitors and seldom socialized with others at the care home, flourished through this weekly association. At the end of the project, Sophie gave Patricia a gift of silk flowers to go in her hair to accompany the pink and purple ones she wore each week. At the celebration event, held at the school at the culmination of the eight-week project, the two friends sat together as they prepared to tell the assembled audience (about 200 additional students, school and care home staff, family and community members) about their friendship, following a shared morning tea with Sophie's family.

The project has significantly helped build social capital within this community, increasing a sense of belonging for participants and their families and strengthening the ties between the school and the aged care hostel. Some of the students and their families made their own arrangements to continue visiting residents after the completion of the project.

> You never know what's next,
> What's up around the bend,
> One thing's for sure,
> I'll always call you a friend.
>
> (*Creative for Life* song verse)

## *Keeping It Flexible*

> Our job is to facilitate the creative process, deal with curveballs and changes to proceedings by mixing it up when something's not working or sticking with something that is. It's creative thinking and problem-solving in the moment. Finding activities that develop relationships in meaningful ways and give people time and space to share their stories. It's about the project evolving based on the needs of the participants. It is making people feel special and bringing smiles and experiences that are sometimes completely new and finding enjoyment in every one of them.
>
> (Mark Storen, teaching artist, *Creative for Life*)

A deeper level of acceptance, cooperation and understanding developed as the project unfolded and a caring space opened for everyone to play and to experiment, to be creative and to make fools of themselves without fear of judgement. For some, this was drawing with impaired vision, trusting that a partner will guide them. For others, it was singing a song when they have forgotten the words. For students, it was playing the piano when their playing wasn't perfect or acting foolish in games to help older people to feel more at ease and comfortable in their participation. The activities became the vehicle for conversations; this dialogue, during the making process, strengthened the bonds between generations. The exchange of experience, skills and knowledge, ways of being and behaving, increased connectedness and improved wellbeing. The project's adaptive, responsive approach also appeared to influence participants' thinking. For example, Kiera swims competitively and has dreams of going to the Olympic Games. She is disciplined and a natural planner but hesitant about moving out of her comfort zone. At the end of the project, she added a note to her reflection book: "I have learnt that it is ok to let go of control because there are always possible solutions to anything that might happen."

In working with JWAPS and Amana Living, we found that the activities naturally lent themselves to a process-orientated collaboration as opposed to a predetermined final outcome. As creative practitioners, we found that participants' reflections were vital and supported the organic evolution of the project, allowing for a variety of methods and mediums to be tried each week. Intergenerational projects have also been found to benefit children's development and ability to self-regulate (Radford et al., 2018). "We have really enjoyed being part of this project; getting to know the kids has been the best part. We were all impressed by how helpful and well-spoken the children were and how confident!" (Shirley, aged 76).

For both organizations, the project provided a space to observe a range of ideas, experimentation, reflection, imagination, discipline and the meaning made from images, practice and participation.

> *Creative for Life* was able to celebrate the skills and strengths of older and younger people and build a lasting beneficial relationship between them. Activities were designed to stimulate conversation and facilitate an exchange of ideas. Our students grew in confidence, improved their social skills and increased their motivation levels in the classroom.
>
> (Wayne Revitt)

As facilitators, this collaboration has added to our toolbox of ideas and methods through the use of cross-disciplinary arts practices and building relational interactions among students, the aged, partner organizations and each other. These interactions enabled us to harness the appropriate creative elements: pulling pieces together to transition from ideas to activities, switch from creative to targeted and develop opportunities for continuity beyond the length of the project. Observing friendships grow through dialogue between participants more than 70 years apart in age indicated that even through generational cultural changes, commonalities can still be discovered. Feelings, experiences, stories, skills, family, memories and friends wrap themselves like a blanket into the sensory world of sound, colour, movement and touch through creative expression. Continuously working alongside carers, staff, teachers and participants throughout the project, and being reflective about understanding their diverse needs, leads us to discover and design ways to tackle activities that may normally pose barriers for participants and facilitators, resulting in avoidance. This reflective, collaborative approach opens the potential for possibilities that lie beyond whatever may be imagined at the beginning of a project with a predetermined outcome. Facilitating projects with an unknown outcome and generating momentum by reflecting on the results of the collaborative process as it progresses do not place restrictions on possibilities before giving them a chance to grow exponentially. Instead, we are providing space for participants, observers and facilitators to discover the broad potential of human interaction through the physicality of the arts.

## REFERENCES

Bales, S. S., Eklund, S. J., & Siffin, C. F. (2000). Children's perceptions of elders before and after a school-based intergenerational program. *Educational Gerontology, 26*(7), 677–689. https://doi.org/10.1080/03601270050200662

MacCallum, J., Palmer, D., Wright, P., Cumming-Potvin, W., Brooker, M., & Tero, C. (2010). Australian perspectives: Community building through intergenerational exchange programs. *Journal of Intergenerational Relationships, 8*(2), 113–127. https://doi.org/10.1080/15350771003741899

Mayo, S., McAvinchey, C., & O'Dair, C. (2012). *Detail and daring research into the art and the craft of intergenerational work*. Magicme.co.uk. https://magicme.co.uk/wp-content/uploads/2018/03/Magic-Mes-Detail-and-Daring-Report_lores.pdf

Pearce, E., & Launay, J. (2015). Choir singing improves health, happiness – And is the perfect icebreaker. *The Conversation*. https://theconversation.com/choir-singing-improves-health-happiness-and-is-the-perfect-icebreaker-47619

Radford, K., Gould, R., Vecchio, N., & Fitzgerald, A. (2018). Unpacking intergenerational (IG) programs for policy implications: A systematic review of the literature. *Journal of Intergenerational Relationships, 16*(3), 302–329. https://doi.org/10.1080/15350770.2018.1477650

Rubin, S., Gendron, T., Wren, C., Ogbonna, K., Gonzales, E., & Peron, E. (2015). Challenging gerontophobia and ageism through a collaborative intergenerational art program. *Journal of Intergenerational Relationships, 13*(3), 241–254. https://doi.org/10.1080/15350770.2015.1058213

# 26

## Croatian Naïve Art as an Incentive for Multimodal Research With Children

*Helena Burić and Nikolina Fišer Sedinić*

Naïve art represents a special segment of modern artistic creation that arose as a consequence of democratization. Its aspiration is that every person has the right to artistic expression and that arts education is not a guarantee of artistic value. Naïve art is recognized, and often imitated, for its childlike simplicity and frankness (Walker, 1992, p. 433). The affirmation of naïve art began in the late nineteenth century when the avant-garde movement took it as an argument for overthrowing the classical manner of shaping and seeking new expressive possibilities. This initiative succeeded the Surrealist movement, extending to the latest trends that follow the anatomy of reality and the valuation of the ordinary (l'art brut, pop art and their echoes). The adopted term "naïve art" was preceded by a number of other terms: painters of the sacred heart, Sunday painters, folk masters of reality, folk art, painters of instinct, primitive art, marginal art and self-taught or original art. The French post-impressionist Henri Rousseau, whom the French avant-garde had discovered, established what is now considered naïve art (Croatian Encyclopedia, 2020).

In Croatia, representatives of naïve art are self-taught folk and local artists with a recognizable personal style characterized by artistic excellence. Movements derived from Croatian naïve art (Earth Group and Hlebine School), in addition to the artistic, also emphasize a social dimension and appear as a kind of answer to community questions. The Earth Group (*Grupa Zemlja*) – Croatian artists, architects and intellectuals active in Zagreb (Croatia) from 1929 to 1935 – searched for answers to social issues and felt that art should reflect the reality of life and the needs of the modern community. The Hlebine School is a term applied to Croatian naïve painters working in or around the village of Hlebine, a small municipality in the North of Croatia. In the 1920s, it became a setting against which a group of self-taught peasants began to develop a unique and somewhat revolutionary style of painting. This was instigated by leading intellectuals of the time, such as the poet Antun Gustav Matoš and the biggest name in Croatian literature, Miroslav Krleža, who called for an individual national artistic style that would be independent of Western influences. A celebrated artist from Hlebine, Krsto Hegedušić, picked up these ideas and later founded the Hlebine School of Art in 1930 to search for a national "rural artistic expression." From the perspective of defining the directions of naïve art, a parallel can be clearly drawn with community art (also called "dialogical art," "community-engaged art" or "community-based art") as a kind of interaction and dialogue with the environment.

The link between the stylistic features of Croatian naïve artists and the manner of children's original artistic expression inspired by naïve art provides the impetus for our research. This chapter focuses on selected works of Croatian naïve art, primarily the works of Ivan Lacković Croata, through different modalities of a child's artistic expression.

## Folk and Naïve Art as an Incentive for Children's Exploration

In the Kindergarten Špansko in Zagreb, the music and folklore programme "tamburica" is part of the regular educational programme (tamburica is a stringed musical instrument played with a pick and the most widespread traditional instrument in Croatia). The coordinators of the "tamburica" programme are preschool teachers who are certified to nurture cultural heritage and tradition through art during their non-formal professional development. The programme is framed within the humanistic-oriented, developmentally appropriate curriculum, with the basic assumption that play is the main determinant of children's learning. Parents have the option of choosing this programme when enrolling their children in the kindergarten. The programme explores areas of folk and naïve art in the context of contemporary children's lives.

Folk art (*Narodna umjetnost*) is an expression of community that originated in the tradition of artistic heritage, in which folk artists repeat the forms, eventually changing the details while meeting the real needs and aesthetic standards of their environment. In today's environment, children become motivated to change details based on their artistic heritage and thus meet their environment's needs and aesthetic standards in their own way. Traditional heritage enriches early and preschool-aged children's everyday cultural experience and represents inspiration and encouragement for application in work (see Figure 26.1).

Naïve art (*Naivna umjetnost*) refers to the cultural identity of a community by which its common values and aesthetics are transmitted. It is a creative

FIGURE 26.1: Children's art inspired by folk motifs. Photos by Nikolina Fišer Sedinić (2019).

FIGURE 26.2: Ivan Lacković Croata, Late Autumn, 1964. © HMNU/CMNA (left). Late Autumn/aesthetic transfer, combined technique (felt-tip pen, graph paper, watercolours). Lota, R., 5, 10 years (right). Photos by Nikolina Fišer Sedinić (2020).

expression of the human struggle towards civilization within a particular environment through producing useful and aesthetically appealing objects. The fluctuating combination of retained and inventive elements has been of significant interest with regard to preschool-aged children. From our experience of working in the programme, traditional heritage is a great inspiration in work and encourages new creativity, enabling the enrichment of early and preschool-aged children's everyday cultural experience (see Figure 26.2). In this chapter, we are guided by the idea that "[i]n an early childhood setting, educators must acknowledge that arts education is a site for creativity, where children can explore their identities and understandings of the world while continuously advancing their holistic development" (Grierson, 2011, as cited in Jenson, 2018, p. 75).

## The Artistic Production of Ivan Lacković Croata

The appearance of folklore elements in naïve art is a consequence of the so-called collective artistic experience: in other words, a positive attitude towards folk art heritage. These elements appear on the motif, iconographic and morphological levels, such as on the key artistic and poetic features of works of art (Fišer, 1997). Folklore motifs and iconography are also unavoidable in the vast drawing and painting oeuvre of the Croatian naïve artist Ivan Lacković Croata, whose work we have chosen as a point of research. Ivan Lacković Croata is a self-taught Croatian painter, a classic representative of the Hlebine School and Croatian naïve art, and one of the most eminent drawers of naïve art (Crnković, 2005). He is often called the greatest drawer of naïve art and a contemporary of figurative drawing.

Croata gained this status by "introducing drawing as an independent discipline into naïve art" (Depolo, as cited in Biškupić, 1985, p. 93), while other naïve artists use drawing only as a sketch for further creativity. Like a child, he treats it as a wholesome work of art. He nurtured and realized drawing as the final product of his art; as such, it represents an inexhaustible treasure trove for further research and a new aesthetic experience for preschool-aged children. Particularly interesting are the folklore motifs and iconography that are so prevalent in his drawing and painting oeuvre.

Croata's artworks represent a "pure atmosphere" because he artistically creates his experience of the observed. He provides his answer to the stimuli from nature and life in it. His naïve world represents the lost childhood paradise in his native Batinska, a Podravina village in northern Croatia. Namely, the artist began to create intensively upon leaving his home and arriving in Zagreb. Based on his memories and emotionally driven, he draws and paints a world of children's fantasy: his initial guiding principle is the memory image seen through the eyes of a gifted boy (Crnković, 2005). His artworks emphasize a sense of cyclicality, both in nature and human life. The frame and content of his paintings are the four seasons and nature that represents the fifth season. The basic means of expression in his drawing, in addition to the paper, is the line. The line he creates is rich and indented to the extreme; it is musical, clear and simple. He draws a complete clean line, using a single continuous stroke; he models space and opens and closes forms, thus achieving volume (Biškupić, 1985).

## Exploring Croata's Oeuvre

Our work was preceded by preschool teachers' research related to learning about the totality of the artist's work:

As the purpose of arts education is to encourage motivation and interest in the arts, educators must provide selections of the most accessible works that faithfully present the characteristics of artists. Furthermore, in arts education, educators should research children's interests to help them expand on their explorations with guided support, furthering their potential in their art journey.

(Helm & Benke, 2003, as cited in Jenson, 2018, p. 3)

Guided by the principles of the method of aesthetic transfer, our research of Ivan Lacković Croata's oeuvre began at the end of 2018 by examining preschool children's work. As our initial research stimulus, we visited the Old Town of Đurđevac, the most famous cultural and historical monument of Podravina. This is also the only registered monument of Croatian cultural heritage dating back to the fifteenth century. During this visit, the children had the opportunity to experience the idyllic landscape of Podravina, which has been an inexhaustible inspiration for Croata. The artworks donated by Croata are in the Old Town attic: a 1,000 m$^2$ gallery space containing more than a thousand paintings and works by over 200 authors from twenty different countries around the world. In this environment, children had the opportunity to become familiar with the artist's selected original works and thus discover his inner personality and vision of the world, as well as his appearance. They also had the opportunity to compare the features of Lacković's style with that of other naïve artists.

The intense experience of original works served later as starting points for new artistic creations stimulated by children's experiences. It is apparent to us how significant it is to give children the freedom to independently discover, explore, imagine and experiment when learning within the arts (Jenson, 2018). During our observation, in conversation with the children, we tried to evoke their previous experiences to stimulate their emotional reaction to the works of art they had seen. The purpose of arts education is to capture and maintain interest in learning. Therefore, a child's pool of knowledge – relevant prior knowledge – must be considered when planning appropriate art activities so that these activities relate to a child's culture and experiences. Such artistic play allows children to use their imagination in exploring their culture and identity (Jenson, 2018, p. 22).

## *Method of Aesthetic Transfer*

In contact with art, children enrich their artistic and aesthetic development and establish a positive attitude towards art, which at the same time encourages their own artistic research. The main emphasis of the programme is on the method of transmitting aesthetic messages that works of art contain, and on how the children in our case participate in and accept the pedagogical process (Duh & Župančić,

2011). By observing a work of art, children can react emotionally, associatively and intellectually. The sensory stimulus that arises is connected to memories, past experiences, feelings and associations, which can lead to an artistic reaction representing each child's individual expressive response and resulting in a new aesthetic experience. To make this possible, children need encouragement to notice and observe a work of art.

The method of aesthetic transfer comprises three phases (Duh & Župančić, 2011):

- perception of the work of art with all senses, with an emphasis on stimulating an emotional reaction
- reception – an internal reaction to a work of art
- reaction – a productive reaction to a work of art.

We adapted this aesthetic transfer method to preschool-age children, building upon their previous experiences and knowledge and their level of artistic competencies and skills. Children were immersed in the experience with the use of various resources and media. In this way, we strove to influence the shaping of each child's artistic and aesthetic taste.

## A Multimodal Approach to Research

In addition to aesthetic transfer, we applied a multimodal approach allowing children to use different semiotic sources (visual aids, music, activities and traditional objects) in activities aimed at encouraging creative expression. We have adopted Knežević-Florić's (2011) definition of multimodal as "the expression of reflective thinking through a combination of words and symbols, images, sounds, and a wide range of associations and activities" (as cited in Gazibara, 2016, p. 324). It emphasizes "the importance of the social context and available resources for meaning creation, with an emphasis on people who choose resources" (Jewitt, 2013, as cited in Gazibara, 2016, p. 324). In our context, the multimodal approach refers to communication and interpretation through different channels commonly referred to as modes (Kress & van Leeuwen, 2001): that is, interweaving different communication channels of children's expression. In the first phase of getting to know the artist and his works, the children came across motifs related to the landscape of Podravina in the fall, as well as regional architecture and scenes from people's everyday lives. The classroom environment was created as "a kind of aquarium that reflects the ideas, values, abilities, and culture of those who live in it" (Malaguzzi, 1998, as cited in Silić, 2007, p. 80). Guided by the features of the artist's creative work and children's current developmental possibilities, we offered the children means and techniques by which they could express their vision of the artist and his works. In turn, they offered their artistic solutions:

> [A]rt experiences play a vital role in the development of a child, with artistic thinking providing a particular way of conceiving reality and, therefore, similar to how children construct knowledge during play, their artistic learning and activities need to make sense to them and be embedded in their own experiences.
>
> (Jenson, 2018, p. 77)

This was preceded by an introduction to Croata's graphics and works in combined techniques, and then the children interpreted their experiences using a pencil and later, ink and watercolours. The graphics also served as templates that the children painted on tracing paper according to their own vision.

In the drawing technique on transparency papers, the children were directly exposed to Croata's oils on canvas with the theme "Fall," "Great Fall" and "Late Fall." By searching for and playing with the lines they found in Croata's works of art and drawing with a felt-tip pen on transparency paper, the children became familiar with and aware of the features of the line itself and its richness. Through analytical observation, in addition to the line, the children also learned about the richness of colours in Croata's works. The next step was to play with paint on paper using the watercolour technique. In this process, the children had the opportunity to become familiar with naïve artists' creativity of painting on glass through a combined technique.

Motivated by visual means and local music from the Podravina area, in an environment full of local objects that we acquired in collaboration with children's family members, the children created various associations, which they then verbally expressed. Based on verbal associations, a new "Fall" story was created, resonating with the sounds of children's traditional instruments and Orff's instruments. With the preschool teachers' support, the story was enriched with appropriate children's traditional songs and children's sing-along games. In this way, an improvised musical-scenic performance was created, exemplifying the principle that "the arts are meaningful not just in the doing, making, or unfolding of a work, but also in how a culture, ways of being together, and a sense of belonging are created through the arts" (Kind, 2018, p. 6).

## *Synthesis of Experiences*

In researching and becoming familiar with the artist's work, the children's depictions of folk customs related to Christmas and the Carnival period also proved interesting. To present the traditional elements of the holidays present in the artist's work, the children had the opportunity during Christmas to visit a retrospective exhibition of Sister Samuela at the Ethnographic Museum in Zagreb. Especially interesting was Croata's oeuvre related to motifs depicting musicians with bagpipes, violins and other instruments that were and are played in the Podravina region. In that period, we completed our artistic research with the collaboration of Stjepan Večković, a soloist on traditional instruments in the ensemble of folk dances and songs of the Croatian Lado, the National Folk Dance Ensemble of Croatia. In this part of the process, we emphasized active cooperation with the parents because a quality partnership between preschool teachers and parents/caregivers is achieved when parents/caregivers are allowed to spend time with their children in the educational group and monitor and actively participate in children's immediate educational process (Ministry of Science, Education and Sport, 2014). During the workshops, the children – in collaboration with their parents and the soloist – had the opportunity to learn how traditional instruments were created and how they were played in the past, to hear how they sound and to participate in the production of instruments.

## *Cooperation With Cultural Institutions in the Community*

In the next step of the research, cooperation was established with the Croatian Museum of Naïve Art. In collaboration with museum educators, a timeline of activities was designed that included introductory observation of selected works of art with appropriate guidance for children, and a workshop for preschoolers. The research resulted in a musical-scenic presentation of children's traditional games with songs from Podravina called "Peacock grazes, grass grows," performed in front of an audience at the local cultural community centre.

## *Conclusion*

The experience of working on this project has led us to several conclusions. We see special importance in bringing art closer to children through the inclusion of various cultural institutions and associations in the community as well as original places and products, and these strong community associations contribute positively to children's overall experience. The development, encouragement and realization of artistic activities within the local community are made possible only through constant interaction and dialogue with the environment. Art as social practice emphasizes art as relational, as a "set of artistic practices which take as their theoretical and practical point of departure the whole of human relations and their social context, rather than as an independent and private space" (Bourriaud, 2002, as cited in Kind, 2018, p. 8). To achieve these goals, it is extremely important for preschool teachers to carefully participate in the design of each visit together with museum educators and/or community artists to prevent a developmentally inappropriate or "drop-off approach" to culture (a superficial approach to art culture). In this way, spreading the idea of art as a tool for social development is the basic idea of community art. For a complete experience, it is necessary for children to get to know the original works of art (the source) because this approach contributes to a stronger experience as well as to psychosocial growth and development. It is therefore important to devise ways for children to express their own reactions to works of art and stimuli on an emotional, associative, intellectual and artistic level, making the preschool teacher's flexibility extremely important. Through the method of aesthetic transfer and by placing an emphasis on stimulating an emotional reaction, the child can experience a work of art through all senses and communication channels (a multimodal approach). These experiences lead to an artistic reaction that represents a new aesthetic experience and a kind of artistic dialogue.

It should always be kept in mind that "[p]lay is crucial for the child's understanding and use of symbols, signs, and representations" (Eisner & Day, 2008, p. 284). Arts education should ultimately promote the growth of infants', toddlers' and young children's holistic development: to encourage their learning and aesthetic appreciation in a free-play artistic environment with guided support if necessary, using culturally appropriate activities that capture and maintain their interest (Jenson, 2018).

## REFERENCES

Biškupić, B. (1985). *Ivan Lacković Croata: crteži*. [Ivan Lacković Croata: Drawings]. Graphic Institute of Croatia.

Crnković, V. (2005). *Umjetnost Hlebinske škole*. [Hlebine School art]. Croatian Museum of Naïve Art.

Duh M., & Zupančič T. (2011). The method of aesthetic transfer: An outline of a specific method of visual arts didactics. *Croatian Journal of Education*, 13(1), 42–75. https://hrcak.srce.hr/index.php?show=clanak&id_clanak_jezik=113045

Eisner, W. E., & Day, M. D. (Eds.). (2008). *Handbook of research and policy in art education*. Taylor and Francis. https://www.amazon.com/Handbook-Research-Policy-Art-Education/dp/0805849726

Fišer, E. (1997). Folklorni (narodnoumjetnički) elementi u hrvatskoj naivnoj umjetnosti. [Folklore (folk art) elements in Croatian naïve art]. *Radovi hrvatskog društva folklorista*, 5(6), 77–86.

Gazibara, S. (2016). Aktivno učenje u multimodalnom okruženju. [Active learning in a multimodal environment]. *Školski vjesnik: časopis za pedagogijsku teoriju i praksu, 65* (special edition), 323–334. https://hrcak.srce.hr/160224

Jenson, K. (2018). Early childhood: Learning through visual art. *He Kupu, 5*(3), 75–82. https://www.hekupu.ac.nz/article/early-childhood-learning-through-visual-art

Kind, S. (2018). Collective improvisations: The emergence of the early childhood studio as an event-full place. In C. M. Schulte & T. C. Marmé (Eds.), *Communities of practice: Art, play, and aesthetics in early childhood* (pp. 5–23). Springer.

Kress, G. R., & van Leeuwen, T. (2001). *Multimodal discourse: The modes and media of contemporary communication.* Edward Arnold.

Ministry of Science, Education and Sport. (2014). *Nacionalni kurikulum za predškolski odgoj i obrazovanje.* [National curriculum for early childhood and preschool education]. https://www.azoo.hr/images/strucni2015/Nacionalni-kurikulum-za-rani-i-predskolski-odgoj-i-obrazovanje.pdf

Silić, A. (2007). Stvaranje poticajnoga okruženja u dječjemu vrtiću za komunikaciju na stranome jeziku. [Creating a stimulating preschool environment for communication in a foreign language]. *Odgojne znanosti, 9*(2), 67–84.

Walker, J. A. (1992). *Glossary of art, architecture, and design since 1945.* Library Association Publishing.

# 27

Visual Ecologies:
Artistic Research Transversing Stable,
Dynamic and Interstitial Relations in an
Australian Settler Colonial Context

*Kim Snepvangers*

*Contemporary Art Education and Community*

My artworks are located in exhibition sites and alternative educational and curatorial spaces beyond the archive. Therefore, community art education in this context focuses on a space of creative practice and pedagogical knowledge creation. Locating myself in alternative spaces entails traversing archives for interstitial ancestral stories with the artistic collective of Indigenous and non-Indigenous women: "SISTAS Holding Space" (SHS). Members note "[t]here are few stories in archives; instead, scientific dehumanized records dominate. Record keepers' clinical interpretations track, categorise and surveil" (Bunda et al., 2019, p. 156). For me, there is a kind of personal identity crisis without a strong sense of my own ancestry, my own archive. My First Nation (preferred term) paternal family history was hidden, not spoken about, with no Western documentation in genealogies or family trees. Traversing the pedagogical dimensions of my artwork challenges dominant social progress narratives to "reclaim, disrupt and humanise the archives" (Bunda et al., 2019, p. 156). Working with SHS prompted me to search for my ancestral records in the public domain, nested within a broader conception of historical race relations. Whilst many chance "discoveries" were made along the path, mine was a latent history, already there. I prioritize working with First Nation Mentors as collaborators (Bunda et al., 2019; Chapman in Snepvangers, 2016; Snepvangers & Allas, 2015; Snepvangers & Bulger, 2016; Snepvangers & Ingrey-Arndell, 2017) as well as with research students in universities. These groups constitute an ever-changing, non-fixed community of mentors and learners with potentiality as social change agents.

In the broader sense of adult community education, Connolly (2010) positions community as a caring "process" rather than place-based, with a large emphasis on relationships and personal connection. Building the capacity for learners to literally live, feel and see themselves in storying through artworks (Bunda et al., 2019; Phillips & Bunda, 2018) is a response to educational and structural disadvantage. A visual ecological lens (Snepvangers & Mathewson-Mitchell, 2018) is used to traverse ongoing debates about how to negotiate belonging and shared, yet contested, histories in the context of settler colonialism in contemporary Australia. Sharing stories invites pedagogical prompts through affective connection with a listening audience to create personal resonance with histories of colonization in Australia. A timeline exemplar has been included for international readers (https://ccca.com.au/Frontend/Content/Ccca/CCCA_Factsheet_Timeline.pdf) alongside a key question: How does a person come to belong in contemporary Australia within the diverse identities and available community transversalities?

## Settler Colonialism

On this continent, settler colonialism is a specific form of colonialism where a typically imperial non-native metropole, in this case the United Kingdom, invaded Indigenous lands and established settlements with the intention of being permanent. Moreton-Robinson (2015), Wolfe (2006) and Veracini (2015) have described the ongoing effects of settler colonialism on intergenerational trauma, ownership of conquered lands, extraction of natural resources in the mining industry and exploitation of conquered workforces. Here, social ordering, classifying and establishing hierarchies are essential processes for maintaining power. What this chapter argues is that the establishment of social hierarchies, which are frequently invisible yet fixed, tends to preserve stable patterns of relationships. Of interest here is disruption, the troubling of this stability through the creation of artworks as new self-organizational pattern morphologies in an archivally poor environment. Using an a/r/tographic (Irwin, 2013) creative practice methodology signals attentiveness to how "[t]hese in-between spaces of becoming prompt disruption of duelling binaries, conceptions of identities, and the rush to certainty. Instead, invention becomes integral to social, cultural, economic, and political processes that are reimagined as concepts situated within events" (pp. 199–200). I offer some serendipitous concepts as a research process, based on events in a personal research journey of "discovery" where new pattern morphologies are constantly becoming. This is an in-between space that values unfolding, unexpectedness and uncertainty (Sinner, 2013), a counterpoint to pre-determined social progress narratives.

## *Social Progress*

Pedagogically, making artworks as a creative practice in 2018 in Sydney, Australia, uncovers previously invisible social hierarchies and investigates processes involved in questions of belonging. My collection of familial textual snippets, available as morsels of family information in the public domain, slices transversally into how language has been used in artworks. Combinations of text and image are not new in contemporary art, such as in the work of Jenny Holzer (https://projects.jennyholzer.com/) and many others. In the Australian context, Vernon Ah Kee's artworks and T-shirts (an everyday item of clothing) are sold under the name "Dark + Disturbing" (https://www.darkanddisturbing.com.au/shop/aboriginal-all-the-time/) provide a rich starting point for my research. Ah Kee's curatorial project uses text to "reference the place 'aborigine' holds in this country" (Ah Kee, 2016, About section). In prioritizing First Nation voices and challenging conventional punctuation/typeface by selecting snippets of text such as "notawillingparticipant," Ah Kee foregrounds identity, visibility and social change. Rather than sourcing forms of conventional written text or following the artwork of a particular artist, my research is based on the purposeful selection of ideas within continuing educational contexts.

In thinking about inclusion, Brookfield (2002) suggests that Marcuse "challenged the self-evident truth, that a tolerant embrace of diverse view is inherently humanistic and democratic and confronted us with the uncomfortable proposition that an apparent engagement with diversity can be manipulated to reinforce dominant ideology" (p. 279). This problem highlights the re-thinking required in presenting/representing a marginalized view alongside a more powerful view. I am interested in how Brookfield issues a challenge to adult education to argue for true tolerance and aesthetic immersion by providing "a completely different perspective that is not widely accessible" (p. 279). The necessarily serendipitous collection of my personal ancestry (as written records do not exist) and prioritizing First Nation authors and artists address this diverse perspective directly.

My paternal ancestry is set against the contested historical politics of the nation-state, as for example, in this contemporary blog post: "The ignorance of our shared history is shocking. Morrison's denial shows us time for truth-telling is NOW"

(Hogarth, 2020). As Convenor of the Aboriginal and Torres Strait Islander Special Interest Group within the Australian Association for Research in Education, Hogarth states: "Never has the cultural gap been so evident." The cultural gap, particularly the denial of modern slavery, identifies the Prime Minister's "failure to recall such histories as blackbirding or the forced indentured labour of Aboriginal peoples as domestic help or station hands after removal from family up until the 1960s" (Hogarth, 2020). Here, Hogarth is making the point that while slavery may feel like a thing of the past, it still exists today. The transversalities apparent in opening a previously closed, invisible familial history mirror how sentiments such as Hogarth's rethink colonial verisimilitudes: ordering, sorting and classifying people using a racialized lens. This research offers a high degree of openness in removing the circumscribed past relations that hamper what Guattari called the "'coefficient of transversality' […] transversality is the tool used to open hitherto closed logics and hierarchies" (Genosko, 2002, p. 78). Readers of this chapter have the opportunity to engage with two artistic encounters. Flipping the traditional notion of an encounter as a historical-discovery narrative, my work relocates a kind of counter-encounter as a research protocol. The premise is that actively planning for interstitial and alternative educational space, with minimal stability, forces a rethinking of micronarratives of discovery and progress in creative situations. Opening spaces of conceptual sensemaking through transversal tools is the subject of the next section.

## *Encounter*

Encounter is a well-honed term in artistic practice. As it relates to First Nation/settler relations though, the term is a key point of tension in colonial timelines. For example, Australia was purportedly "discovered" by Captain James Cook. Tension surrounds the passive acceptance of this event in the historical record, described merely as an "encounter" between First Nation peoples and British invaders. To countermand such ingrained novelty, in serendipitous historical moments of written and received history, I propose a pedagogical "counter-encounter" to highlight previously hidden histories through a transversal contemporary lens of re-encountering. As a pedagogical tool, the encounter has been deployed by several art educational theorists: MacDougall et al. (2017), Justice (2015), Garoian (2014) and in the broader educational context, Connell (2013). Like Brookfield, Connell writes about neoliberal "human capital" agendas, noting how managerial concerns extend to social reproduction as an explanatory structure for educational progress. Connell argues for alternative educational spaces, the deployment of "encounters" and recognition of social labour as care, to countermand the non-critical privilege of dominant social groups. Criteria for establishing an encounter have been articulated in arts-based community engagement as "practice encounters" (Snepvangers & Mathewson-Mitchell, 2018, p. 2). The problem of historical encounter becoming historical truth is investigated through "discovery."

## *Discovery*

Progress and pioneering narratives of the metropole are part of a process that Furniss (2001) describes as being about "condensed symbols." These reduce and mask complexity, typically by focusing on series, singularity, heroes and events such as the so-called discovery of Australia by Captain Cook. According to Furniss, "discovery narratives erase any prior indigenous history, suggesting instead that the land and its inhabitants somehow did not exist, or their existence was unimportant, until they were 'found' and incorporated into Western systems of knowledge" (p. 283). Such erasure through processes of "condensing" provides a visual lens to reconsider complexity in my artwork: personal ancestry is condensed – both in the sense that there is not much to find and that setting up counter–encounters involves selecting condensed text in a similar way to settler colonial processes of singular reportage. The use of textual social media by First Nation people, especially to question promised futures through disruption in the Twittersphere (Carlson, 2019), provides another salient example. Carlson notes how the use of small bites of condensed text can be used to question national mythologies and counter ignorance of First Nation histories. One clear challenge is to resist chronologies with clear dates and markers of "discovery": for example, timeline histories of white settlement (Furniss, 2001). Marking events with a particular time and place allows linear social progress narratives to dominate (Smith, 2012) and unhelpful comparisons to emerge.

To countermand these tendencies, my artwork involves clear dates and markers of "discovery," yet my family history is possible to describe only iteratively, as a "discovery" of a history that was always there. My discoveries are all serendipitous, based on fragments of history that have only recently started to emerge. Only interstitial possibilities exist in paternal ancestry, as stable and even dynamic elements of scene setting are not available. Making my intangible history visible links my artwork to storying as belonging methodology (Bunda et al., 2018). I do so by illuminating, through lightboxes, previously unknown ancestry using deliberately clipped and condensed text: one from a historical newspaper article (Figure 27.1) and one from contemporary packaging (Figure 27.2). My family did not talk about Aboriginality, as it was always denied and neatly marked off as "We are Spanish." "Discovery" is positioned here as two artistic scenarios with implications for challenging existent ways of belonging in Australia through creation of artful spaces to generate new critical interfaces in community engagement.

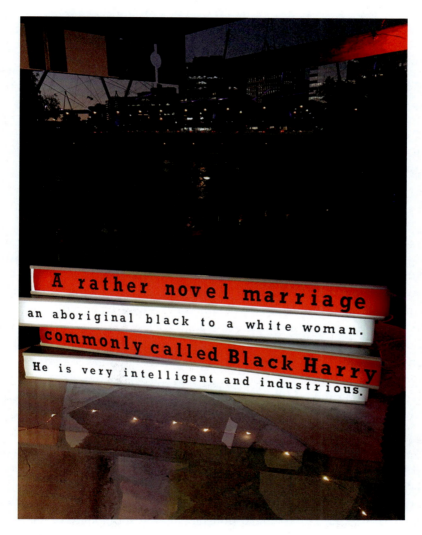

FIGURE 27.1: Kim Snepvangers (2018). "A rather novel marriage" in *Stories of Belonging*. Brisbane Anywhere Festival performance. Lightboxes, digital print on coloured film. Photo by Kim Snepvangers (2018).

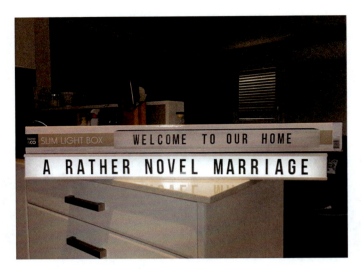

FIGURE 27.2: Kim Snepvangers (2018). "Welcome to Our Home" – A4 Ilford Gallery Print using Ultra Chrome Ink (21.0 × 29.7 cm). Photo by Kim Snepvangers (2018).

## *Ecologies*

Scientific/ethnographic approaches to human affairs have a vexed history in Australia (Moreton-Robinson, 2018) as biological accounts have been damaging. As Snepvangers and Allas (2015) note, Vic Chapman – the first Indigenous principal of a public school in New South Wales – was not considered to be part of the teaching service nor part of Australian society until 1967. These authors question fixed ethnographic ways of being as a counter–encounter, allowing access to non-confirmational material as a matter where outcomes are not predicated on a positive experience. For Coole and Frost (2010), matter is "indeterminate, constantly forming and reforming in unexpected ways [...] 'matter becomes' rather than that 'matter is'" (p. 10). Providing access to dilemmas, diversities and unexpected experiences opens other possibilities than the passive reception of content. Counter–encounter provides a structure to investigate critical research frameworks with a serendipitous quality that suits artistic human-centred projects where creative, sensitive outcomes are of utmost importance.

Ecological perspectives are closely allied to a number of established system theories (Barad, 2003), particularly holistic thinking about kinds of relationships in physical materialities. Within the desert ecology of remote Western Australia are recently "discovered" "Desert Circles" (https://www.abc.net.au/news/science/2016-03-15/fairy-circles-discovered-in-australian-outback/7245736), relying on a discrete set of ecological circumstances for sustenance and reproducibility. The emergent circular patterns are driven by the nature and quality of "instabilities" in resource-poor environments (Getzin et al., 2016, p. 3554). Responding to environmental extremes by redispersing growth according to a self-organizational ecology prioritizes the survival of the group as a holistic network. Scientific thinking posits how previously unexplored ecologies in extreme resource-poor desert environments can inspire creative research: specifically, a lack of archival family resources. Prioritizing interstitial relationships anticipates sustainable and self-organizing concepts of artistic research to re-establish and sustain new networks of familial race relations. Two visual ecologies exemplifying "counter–encounter" as a pedagogical device are now explored.

### *Artistic Encounter: Scenario One*

The artwork "A rather novel marriage" is one of six stories exhibited and performed by SHS at the 2018 Anywhere Festival in Brisbane. The performance (Bunda et al., 2018) was titled "Stories of Belonging." Artworks were created by six artist/researchers to trouble the notion of belonging in the colonial nation of Australia through performed storying. Each textual component of the artwork was uncovered recently through chance encounters in a family history investigation. During a relative's genealogy search, they came upon a marriage certificate and a brief newspaper text about one of my ancestors, Black Harry from an 1848 newspaper article (*The Sydney Morning Herald* [SMH], 1848). What an exciting "discovery" this was, as the *SMH* is the largest circulation newspaper in Australia and the report was about a vexed subject: interracial marriage – a black man marrying a white woman. This popularist text was the earliest 2017 "discovery" regarding my paternal ancestry as it was the first time we had "found" a trace to stories and living relatives. The tone of the article exemplified the way that Aboriginal people typically received conditional acceptance in 1848: through novelty, appeals to intelligence and industriousness.

The following text from the newspaper article was distilled from the full text, as advised by First Nation Cultural Mentors Tess Allas and Tracey Bunda, as follows:

> A rather novel marriage
> an aboriginal black to a white woman.
> commonly called Black Harry
> He is very intelligent and industrious

The lightboxes interrogate my ontological positionality as a researcher: in particular what belonging means in Australia, a colonized nation populated through waves of migration (http://www.globalwords.edu.au/units/Refugees_UPY6_html/documents/Timeline.pdf).

A range of historical typefaces was researched and rendered through digital printing on an array of coloured films. The strip illuminations, although designed to fit neatly into the lightboxes, also establish instability as they are replaceable. Additionally, they replace the commercially available individually lettered text provided with the lightboxes. The artwork celebrates colour, interchangeability and replaceability in an a/r/tographic work that is deliberately never finished, remaining unstable. Condensing the text proffers a counter–encounter with historical materiality – to make visible personages, events and familial histories and bring invisible histories into the light. Rendering the lightboxes as a stackable series alludes to re-sorting, re-ordering and re-categorization at the hands of the artist-researcher, rather than received histories written from the perspective of historical victors.

The next step in terms of interstitial relations will be to research the witnesses named on the marriage certificate – to create new pattern morphologies. Through my work with SHS, scars of colonization, migration and shame are held and heard in relation to, with and through Black and White Australian women creating and interrogating personal ancestry. Belonging alongside each other becomes an interstitial space of generative possibilities of reclamation in a resource-poor environment with few records in Western archives. "Resource" signals the lack of "resources" relating to my personal ancestry. Humans as resources also resonate with the broader project of historical extraction of First Nation people from the archive: specifically, how individuals are not named and ancestries were deliberately hidden to escape scrutiny by government departments, especially around the removal of children. For more information, see Track the History Timeline: The Stolen Generations: (https://humanrights.gov.au/our-work/education/track-history-timeline-stolen-generations).

## *Artistic Encounter: Scenario Two*

Shrouded in whiteness, the artwork "Welcome to Our Home" juxtaposes a slim light box purchased from BigW, a large chain store well-known for everyday domestic items, with some illuminated words: "A rather novel marriage." The lightbox cardboard packaging, emblazoned with the words "Welcome to Our Home," is stacked on top of the lightbox itself which sits atop my kitchen benchtop. The everyday casualness of the lightbox in a contemporary kitchen environment calls into question the commercial and serendipitous aspects of the artwork; placing the lightbox and the packaging in a kitchen belies the commercial intent of the welcome message utilizing a lightbox format, as perhaps the interchangeable letters and media are more typically suited for a celebration – to light up one's domestic life. The illuminated text "A rather novel marriage," thus interferes with the mock historical acceptance of "novelty" in this intermarriage and seeks new narratives of domesticity and celebration in a contemporary well-lit space of illumination. Questioning the collective use of the word "Our" in the packaging text as commercial aspiration and as a chronicle of quasi-inclusion sheds new light on contemporary narratives of home. My home is at once our home and yet, in this commercialized space, not our home. This artwork directly highlights slippages in language and habitual ways of thinking about a typically sentimentalized environment – home. Engaging an illusion of homeliness and stability with a hothouse of dynamic familial relations situates notions of "Our" within a destabilizing narrative. Destabilization is necessary for commercialized placements of "Our" as such collective and presumptive usage supposes a type of all-seeing inclusiveness, a metropole, a civility aligned within a pattern morphology that welcomes equality. In challenging the authority of this civility, the claim being made in this chapter is about the significance of disrupting habituated patterns that seem like natural kinds of talk ("our home," for example), and in this case, creating deliberate juxtapositions. Conscious tension is created between the box (packaging) and the lightbox (product) within the sentimentality of a purported celebration – a serendipitous welcome. The artwork is also colour-coded and temporal, where racialized historical relations are presented in a "novel" contemporary way. Just as my ancestor's marriage was considered "novel," such considered novelty sets up a kind of forced counter–encounter in the everyday spacialization of domestic space.

This research protocol, similar to that of the collaboration with Snepvangers and Ingrey-Arndell (2017), consisted of focusing on the collection of fragments of speech to illuminate previously hidden and habituated social talk. As described in our 2017 co-authored chapter, Ingrey-Arndell collected fragments of speech on an iPhone whilst working with customers, friends and co-workers who were unaware of First Nation ancestry. Selected snippets of speech were then enmeshed in a series of double-coded pencil drawings alongside early Australian children's book imagery. The chance, serendipitous encountering of everyday racist talk pinpoints the ugliness of throw-away speech acts to reveal poorly conceived, yet persistent stereotypes of First Nation peoples. Interstitial and in-between talk perpetrated by friends, acquaintances, co-workers and customers was combined in skilfully executed, subtle pencil drawings, referring to history and contemporaneity in a kind of counter-encounter. The way the text is incorporated into the image invites the viewer to review the "half-said" implications of colonization from a First Nation perspective.

## *Conclusion*

Combining text with image in these two artworks illuminates previously invisible histories and creates new networked ecologies as exhibition and performative practice where none existed before. Making mechanics visible through everyday newspaper talk and fleeting oral commentary illuminates previously overlooked conversations. This text moves beyond inclusion narratives by reimagining scenarios that are self-organizing, sustainable and reproducible. They induce a sense of belonging through storying as research when there is no text in the Western sense of documentation: for example, in family tree research/genealogy. The layout and collation of text/image in each scenario indicate ambiguous interchangeability, a suite of slippages using the language of condensed exchange, to challenge linearity. Swapping everyday textual conversations (from a daily newspaper report and everyday life) into the realm of research data allows new relationships among seemingly chance and inconsequential encounters to be valued, then collated iteratively for redeployment and display.

Elements of stasis, dynamism and co-occurrence can therefore be accommodated in creative encountering to actively encourage contingent, interstitial and chance elements. Such intellectual histories of condensed artistic research are imperative when there is no written history and/or when historical records are contested and archived from single points of view. Prioritizing the unforeseen and improbability of experience is a counterpoint to socially static, passive ways of working with First Nation colleagues and contested histories. Re-imagining new visual ecologies in interstitial relation offers fresh intellectual insights into ongoing dilemmas through arts-based research. The serendipitous qualities of each encounter reveal hidden histories that lead to the next encounter. Significantly, it is possible to have a series of encounters only iteratively as no linear evolution through causal effect is possible. Here, the value of the interstitial as a self-organizational system offers new, yet unfinished artforms of "discovery" and "progress" in contemporary Australia.

## REFERENCES

Ah Kee, V. (2016). *Dark + Disturbing*. https://www.darkanddisturbing.com.au/about/

Barad, K. (2003). Posthuman performativity: Toward an understanding of how matter comes to matter. *Signs: Journal of Women in Culture and Society*, 28(3), 801–831. https://doi.org.10.1086/345321

Bunda, T., Heckenberg, R., Snepvangers, K., Phillips, L., Lasczik, A., & Black, A. (2019). Storymaking belonging. *Art/Research International: A Transdisciplinary Journal*, 4(1), 153–179. https://doi.org/10.18432/ari29429

Carlson, B. (2019). Disrupting the master narrative: Indigenous people and tweeting colonial history. *Griffith Review*, 64, 224–234. https://www.griffithreview.com/wp-content/uploads/woocommerce_uploads/GR64_The-New-Disruptors.pdf

Coole, D., & Frost, S. (2010). *New materialisms: Ontology, agency and politics*. Duke University Press.

Connell, R. (2013). The neoliberal cascade and education: An essay on the market agenda and its consequences. *Critical Studies in Education*, 54(2), 99–112. https://doi.org/10.1080/17508487.2013.776990

Connolly, B. (2010). Community based education. In P. Peterson, E. Baker, & B. McGaw (Eds.), *International encyclopaedia of education* (3rd ed., pp. 120–126). Elsevier.

Furniss, E. (2001). Timeline history and the Anzac myth: Settler narratives of local history in a north Australian town. *Oceania*, 71(4), 279–297. https://doi.org/10.1002/j.1834-4461.2001.tb02754.x

Garoian, C. R. (2014). In the event that art and teaching encounter. *Studies in Art Education*, 56(1), 384–396. https://doi.org/10.1080/00393541.2014.11518947

Genosko, G. (2002). *Félix Guattari: An aberrant introduction*. Continuum.

Getzin, S., Yizhaq, H., Bell, B., Erickson, T., Postleg, A., Katrah, I., Tzuki, O., Zelnikb, Y., Wiegandj, K., Wieganda, T., & Meron, E. (2016). Discovery of fairy circles in Australia supports self-organization theory. *Proceedings of the National Academy of Science*, 13(13), 3551–2556. https://doi.org/10.1073/pnas.1522130113

Hogarth, M. (2020, June 22). The ignorance of our shared history is shocking. Morrison's denial shows us time for truth-telling is NOW. *EduResearch Matters, Australian Association for Research in Education (AARE)*. https://www.aare.edu.au/blog/?p=6858

Irwin, R. L. (2013). Becoming A/r/tography. *Studies in Art Education*, 54(3), 198–215.

Justice, S. (2015). Learning to teach in the digital age: Enacted encounters with materiality. *Marilyn Zermuehlen Working Papers in Art Education, Teachers College, Columbia University*, 2015(1), 1–25. http://doi.org/10.17077/2326-7070.1487

MacDougall, D., Irwin, R. L., Boulton, A., LeBlanc, N., & May, H. (2017). Encountering research as creative practice: Participants giving voice to the research. In L. Knight & A. Cutcher (Eds.), *Arts, research, education: Connections and directions* (pp. 31–60). Springer.

Moreton-Robinson, A. (2015). *The white possessive: Property, power, and Indigenous sovereignty*. University of Minnesota Press.

Moreton-Robinson, A. (2018, April). Bodies that matter on the beach. *e-Flux Journal*, 90, 1–13.

Phillips, L., & Bunda, T. (2018). *Research through, with and as storying*. Routledge.

Sinner, A. (2013). *Unfolding the unexpectedness of uncertainty: Creative nonfiction and the lives of becoming teachers*. Sense Publishers.

Smith, L. T. (2012). *Decolonizing methodologies: Research and Indigenous peoples* (2nd ed.). Zed Books.

Snepvangers, K. (2016). Bending the twig: Indigenous perspectives in tertiary art and design. *Art Education Australia*, 37(2), 165–183.

Snepvangers, K. (2018a). "A rather novel marriage" in *Stories of Belonging*: SISTAS Holding Space. [Curated Exhibition and Performance]. Brisbane Anywhere Festival in Kuril Dhagun Indigenous Talking Circle Space, State Library of Queensland, Brisbane.

Snepvangers, K. (2018b). "Welcome to Our Home" in *At Home*. [Curated Exhibition]. 21 May–1 June, Academy Gallery, Inveresk Campus, University of Tasmania.

Snepvangers, K., & Allas, T. (2015). Developing expertise and engagement with Indigenous perspectives in tertiary art and design. In A. Rourke & V. Rees (Eds.), *Moving from novice to expert: Developing expertise in the visual domain* (pp. 255–286). Common Ground Publishing.

Snepvangers, K., & Bulger, J. (2016). Learning in liminal spaces: Encountering Indigenous Knowledge and artworks in professional education. *fusion [Special issue]. Professional education in the e-learning world: Scholarship, practice and digital technologies*, 8. https://fusion-journal.com/learning-in-liminal-spaces-encountering-indigenous-knowledge-and-artworks-in-professional-education/

Snepvangers, K., & Ingrey-Arndell, J. (2017). Spaces of speaking: Liminality and case-based knowledge in arts research and practice. In L. Knight & A. Cutcher (Eds.), *Arts, research, education: Connections and directions* (pp. 61–87). Springer.

Snepvangers, K., & Mathewson-Mitchell, D. (2018). Transforming dialogues through ecologies of practice in art, education and the cultural sphere. In K. Snepvangers & D. Mathewson-Mitchell (Eds.), *Beyond community engagement: Transforming dialogues in art, education and the cultural sphere* (pp. 1–22). Common Ground Publishing.

*The Sydney Morning Herald*. (1848, December 12). News from the interior (p. 2). TROVE, National Library of Australia.

Veracini, L. (2015). *The settler colonial present*. Palgrave McMillan.

Wolfe, P. (2006). Settler colonialism and the elimination of the native. *Journal of Genocide Research*, 8(4), 387–409. https://doi.org/10.1080/14623520601056240

# Contributors

HISAE AOYAMA is an elementary school teacher at Shigei Elementary School in Hiroshima, Japan. Her interests include community-based and international art education.

\* \* \* \* \*

JUDITH BROWNE was the *atelierista* at Mimosa School in Johannesburg while involved in the project discussed here. After helping establish an outdoor nature programme for 3–4-year-olds in Pennsylvania, she is taking some time to be a full-time mom.

\* \* \* \* \*

HELENA BURIĆ works as a pedagogue (professional consultant) at the Kindergarten "Špansko" in Zagreb, Croatia. Her area of interest is exploring children's art and fostering children's original creativity. She is a long-time associate at the Faculty of Teacher Education, University of Zagreb, and an active member of numerous professional associations.

\* \* \* \* \*

GERALDINE BURKE lectures on visual and creative art education at the Faculty of Education at Monash University. A practising artist/researcher/teacher–educator passionate about art-based educational research, her interests are connecting the visual arts to local knowledge, place and community across generations.

\* \* \* \* \*

SOPHIA CHAITA is the visual arts education coordinator for primary and secondary education in the Southern Aegean and Crete. A PhD candidate at the University of the Aegean, Greece, her interests include community art education, a/r/tography, sustainability, remote islands, visual arts curriculum and visual literacy.

* * * * *

KATHRYN COLEMAN is an arts-based researcher, teacher and senior lecturer at the Melbourne Graduate School of Education. Interested in the intersection of art, design, digital spaces, practice and culture, Kate researches digital and creative practices, practices of identity and knowledge as practice.

* * * * *

KATE COLLINS is the graduate director for the MA in Interdisciplinary Arts Infusion at Towson University, Maryland. She focuses on innovative arts-based pedagogies to forge new communities among multigenerational and multilingual groups, where collaborative interdisciplinary artmaking becomes a vehicle for learning, well-being and humanization.

* * * * *

STEPHANIE H. DANKER creates integrated learning experiences with students and colleagues and expands awareness, critical thinking and empathy through art experiences. She is an associate professor of art education and coordinator of the pre-art therapy program at Miami University, Ohio.

* * * * *

JODIE DAVIDSON is a creative consultant and visual arts practitioner in Perth, Western Australia. Her interests include sustainability, the environment, community arts and education.

* * * * *

DUSTIN GARNET, an assistant professor of art education at CSULA, is president-elect of the California Art Education Association. He presents and publishes nationally and internationally on various topics: curriculum studies, archives, qualitative methodologies, social justice-related issues, art education and oral histories. www.dustingarnet.com

* * * * *

CONTRIBUTORS

Sue Girak is a visual arts specialist teacher at a metropolitan primary school and visual arts education lecturer at Edith Cowan University, Western Australia. She encourages collaborative and environmentally sustainable art practices through the creative reuse of salvageable materials. Sue fosters a culture of a/r/tography by encouraging greater autonomy in students' artmaking.

\* \* \* \* \*

Alex Halligey was a postdoctoral fellow with the South African Research Chair in Spatial Analysis and City Planning, Wits School of Architecture and Planning, Johannesburg while involved in the project discussed in this book. She is currently a research fellow with the University of Johannesburg's Johannesburg Institute for Advanced Study.

\* \* \* \* \*

Shelley Hannigan is a senior lecturer in art education as well as a visual artist and researcher. Her interests involve artistic practice and thinking, visual literacies, materiality, embodiment and the usefulness of art in interdisciplinary education and wellbeing. Her work can be viewed at https://www.hanniganshelley.com/

\* \* \* \* \*

Mirja Hiltunen is a professor of Art Education in the Faculty of Art and Design, University of Lapland in Finland. Community-based art education, place-specificity, performativity and socially engaged art are particular interests for her.

\* \* \* \* \*

Pauline Hiroti is a researcher at Te Rūnanga O Ngā Wairiki Ngāti Apa, Aotearoa/New Zealand. Her research interests include dance education, community dance, *Kaupapa Māori* research and decolonizing arts practices.

\* \* \* \* \*

Maria Huhmarniemi is an artist-researcher-teacher at the University of Lapland engaged with community art and education for sustainability. She has researched socially and environmentally engaged contemporary art and art education, as well as art-based environmental education. She has published various research articles and edited books.

\* \* \* \* \*

JESSICA CASTILLO INOSTROZA holds a PhD in Arts and Education and is an academic researcher at Universidad de las Américas, Chile. Her interests are printmaking, arts-based research methods, a/r/tographic perspective and teacher training in art education.

\* \* \* \* \*

WATARU INOUE is a professor emeritus at Hiroshima University in Japan. His interests include educational assessment in schools, teachers' professional development and adequateness of the teaching profession.

\* \* \* \* \*

RITA L. IRWIN is a Distinguished University Scholar and professor of Art Education at the University of British Columbia, Canada. While her research interests include arts teacher education, artist-in-schools programmes and sociocultural issues, she is best known for her work in expanding how we might enact arts practice-based research methodologies through collaborative collectives.

\* \* \* \* \*

TIMO JOKELA is a professor of Art Education in the Faculty of Art and Design, University of Lapland, Finland. Place-specificity, Arctic art and design and education for sustainability are his particular interests.

\* \* \* \* \*

KATJA JUHOLA is a curator, artist and founder of the International Socially Engaged Art Symposium. Active as an artist for over twenty years, she studies socially engaged art symposiums, including activist and educational aims. She has held over a hundred exhibitions abroad and in Finland.

\* \* \* \* \*

## CONTRIBUTORS

ELINA JULIN is a teaching artist and Art Education MA student at Aalto University. She is interested in questions of class through the perspectives of generational and societal structures.

\* \* \* \* \*

HYE-SEUNG (THERESA) KANG is an associate director of the Indiana University East Asian Studies Center in the United States. Her interests include in-service teacher education and global education.

\* \* \* \* \*

MERINDA KELLY is an artist, researcher and lecturer in arts education at Deakin University, Australia. Her interests include socially engaged art, art activism and experimental pedagogy. Individually and collectively, she activates inclusive, participatory arts-based projects in public and institutional spaces.

\* \* \* \* \*

JULIAN LAWRENCE is a senior lecturer in Comics and Graphic Novels at Teesside University in Middlesbrough, United Kingdom. His comics-based research interests include narrative drawing, identity, community art education, authorship and semiotics.

\* \* \* \* \*

EUNJI J. LEE is an assistant professor in the Fine Arts Education Program at Kyungnam University, Korea. Her interests lie in meaning-making experiences facilitated at the intersection of artistic practices, public engagement and education.

\* \* \* \* \*

JING LI is a lecturer in the School of Engineering at the University of British Columbia – Okanagan, Canada. Her interests include community research in culture, art and education. She draws on a range of interdisciplinary theories and approaches to explore critical pedagogies: their sites, formation and roles in generating transformative education and sustained social change.

\* \* \* \* \*

CHING-CHIU LIN is an assistant professor in the Faculty of Education at Simon Fraser University, British Columbia, Canada. Her research interests lie in community arts education, digital media and learning through the arts, K–12 arts education and arts-based methodologies.

\* \* \* \* \*

GEORGIA LIARAKOU is an associate professor of Environmental and Sustainability Education at the Department of Early Childhood Education at the National and Kapodistrian University of Athens. Her research focuses on which processes of teaching contribute to sustainability education at individual and institutional levels.

\* \* \* \* \*

ELIZABETH J. LOKON has combined her work as an educator, gerontologist and artist to found Opening Minds through Art, a program for people living with dementia. She is a research associate at Scripps Gerontology Center at Miami University, Ohio, and a fibre artist.

\* \* \* \* \*

CHRISTINA MALLIE is the co-founder and executive director of Colors of Connection, a US-based non-profit with programs in sub-Saharan Africa. Her interests include arts and creativity for trauma healing, socially engaged art and gender.

\* \* \* \* \*

ROSE MARTIN is a professor of Arts Education, with a focus on Dance and Multiculturalism, at the Norwegian University of Science and Technology. Her research interests include dance education, contemporary ethnography, arts and politics.

\* \* \* \* \*

MIRIAN CELESTE MARTINS is a professor in the postgraduate programme in Education, Art, and History of Culture at Presbyterian University Mackenzie, Brazil. She leads research groups in Art in Pedagogy and Cultural Mediation and is a world councillor for Latin America at the International Society of Education through Art.

\* \* \* \* \*

## CONTRIBUTORS

CHERYL J. MAXWELL is an art specialist at Grandview Elementary School in Bloomington, Indiana, United States. Her interests include STEAM education as well as community-based and international art education.

* * * * *

MERNA MEYER is a lecturer and subject head for Creative Arts in the Faculty of Education at North-West University, South Africa. Her interests include socially engaged leadership, community-based educational research, arts-based research methods and curriculum studies in art education.

* * * * *

LEAH H. MORGAN is a grade 7–12 art teacher at Orleans Community Schools in Indiana, United States. Her interests include community and international art education.

* * * * *

KAZUYO NAKAMURA is a professor in the Faculty of Education at Hiroshima University in Japan. Her interests include philosophy of art education and international art education.

* * * * *

ATSUO NAKASHIMA is a supervisor of the Education Board of Hiroshima Prefecture in Japan. His interests include moral education as well as community-based and international art education.

* * * * *

TAKUNORI OKAMOTO is an elementary school teacher at Kasugano Elementary School in Hiroshima, Japan. His interests include peace education as well as community-based and international art education.

* * * * *

MILES OPENSHAW is a multi-disciplinary creative practitioner. He is artistic director of the *Globe Town Project* in Fremantle, Western Australia and associate director of Green Shoes Arts in London, United Kingdom.

* * * * *

TRISH OSLER is a PhD candidate (Art Education) and Public Scholar with Concordia University, Montreal. Her transdisciplinary practice uses arts-based approaches to critical thinking, drawing upon the neuroscience of creativity, art-as-research, museum education and the posthuman turn to reimagine the discrete and integrated persona of the a/r/tographer.

\* \* \* \* \*

CASEY PAX is a licensed professional counsellor and art therapist who earned her master's degree from The School of the Art Institute of Chicago. Using an intersectional and person-centred approach, she works with older adults and their families, striving to reduce aging and memory loss stigmas.

\* \* \* \* \*

TIINA PUSA, head of the Art Education Degree Programme at Aalto University in Finland, teaches, develops curricula and conducts research. Her interests are queer issues in the context of art education and the societal and political role of a teacher.

\* \* \* \* \*

LAURIE REYMAN, MSW, is co-founder of Colors of Connections and works in social services in Washington state, United States, supporting children and families. Her interests are child welfare, trauma, and arts-based and nature-based interventions. She currently serves on the Board of Directors of Colors of Connections.

\* \* \* \* \*

LYNN SANDERS-BUSTLE is an associate professor of Art Education at the University of Georgia, United States. Her interests include socially engaged art, community-based art education, service-learning and teacher preparation. She currently serves on the advisory board of Colors of Connections.

\* \* \* \* \*

MARI SANKYO is the principal of Tomohigashi Elementary School in Hiroshima, Japan. Her interests include peace education and community-based art education.

\* \* \* \* \*

CONTRIBUTORS

Leísa Sasso is a professor at the State Department of Education of the Federal District, Brasília, Brazil. As a researcher at the University of Brasília, her interests include art education, everyday visuals, innovative schools and art-based education and research. https://saosebastiao.se.df.gov.br/escolaartografica/

\* \* \* \* \*

Nikolina Fišer Sedinić works as a preschool teacher at the Kindergarten "Špansko" in Zagreb, Croatia. Her focus is traditional children's music and art expression, aiming to make the educational process more diverse by stimulating a child's freedom, creative imagination and emotional experience.

\* \* \* \* \*

Sara Carrasco Segovia is an adjunct professor in the Faculty of Fine Arts and a postdoctoral researcher at the University of Barcelona. She is a member of the research group ESBRINA – Contemporary, Subjectivities, Visualities and Educational Environments (2017 SGR 1248) http://esbrina.eu. Her interests include artistic research, ABR, body/corporeality, post-qualitative research, posthumanism, new materialism, art education and performativity. She has participated in research and teaching innovation projects.

\* \* \* \* \*

Hannah Shuler is an art specialist at Childs Elementary School in Bloomington, Indiana, United States. Her interests include community-based and international art education.

\* \* \* \* \*

Anita Sinner is a professor, art education, The University of British Columbia. Her interests include arts research methods, life writing, teacher education, international art education and community art education.

\* \* \* \* \*

Kim Snepvangers is the Principal Fellow (HEA) and adjunct professor in the Faculty of Education, Southern Cross University, Queensland, Australia and an adjunct associate professor at UNSW, Australia. Her interests include arts-based educational research and creative ecologies. She works with Cultural Mentors in

Aboriginal and Torres Strait Islander research and pedagogies in settler colonial contexts.

\* \* \* \* \*

ANNIINA SUOMINEN is a professor of Art Pedagogy with experience in two different academic systems and cultures (Finland and the United States). Her perspective influences her scholarship and assessment of the state of democracy and solidarity in contemporary Finnish arts education at different levels.

\* \* \* \* \*

MINNA SUONIEMI, lecturer in Art Education at Aalto University, Finland, is an artist with lens-based practices. Focused on gender roles, motherhood, family and micro histories, she is interested in how disruption and failure can make societal structures visible.

\* \* \* \* \*

ELJAS SUVANTO is currently a master's student of Art History at the University of Helsinki and a museum guide with experience in public programmes. He has studied adult education, communication and museology, with a growing interest in feminist theories and intersectional approaches.

\* \* \* \* \*

RAPHAEL VELLA is an associate professor in the Faculty of Education at the University of Malta. His interests include art education, curating, contemporary and socially engaged art.

\* \* \* \* \*

MARNEE WATKINS is a senior lecturer in Visual Arts Education at the University of Melbourne. Working in the Melbourne Graduate School of Education as a mid-career researcher and teaching academic, she contributes to subject coordination and development across undergraduate, postgraduate and university-wide breadth subjects.

\* \* \* \* \*

CONTRIBUTORS

GERALYN (GIGI) YU is an assistant professor in Art Education at the University of New Mexico, United States, and the editor of *Innovations in Early Education: The International Reggio Emilia Exchange*. Her interests include ecologies of creative practices and aesthetics and their educational applications.